Supreme Court
Watch—1993

SUPREME COURT WATCH—1993

Highlights of the 1990–1993 Terms
Preview of the 1993–1994 Term

DAVID M. O'BRIEN

UNIVERSITY OF VIRGINIA

W. W. NORTON & COMPANY
New York • *London*

Printed in the United States of America

The text of this book is composed in Baskerville
Composition by ComCom
Manufacturing by Haddon Craftsmen

ISBN 0-393-03552-2 (cl)
ISBN 0-393-96453-1 (pa)

W. W. Norton & Company, Inc., 500 Fifth Avenue, New York, N.Y. 10110
W. W. Norton & Company Ltd., 10 Coptic Street, London WC1A 1PU

1 2 3 4 5 6 7 8 9 0

CONTENTS

Cases in italics only are excerpted; cases within brackets are discussed and extensively quoted in the topic introductions.

Volume Two

PREFACE

Changes in the composition of the Supreme Court often bring changes
in constitutional law as well. The dynamics of the Court, of course,
change with each new appointee. Major changes in constitutional law
and politics, moreover, are not uncommon when there are several
changes on the high bench in a brief period of time. With the retirements
of Justices William J. Brennan and Thurgood Marshall at the end of the
1989 and 1990 terms, respectively, and the seating of their successors
Justices David H. Souter and Clarence Thomas came a number of
important changes in constitutional law. Then, during the 1992 term,
Justice Byron White, the only remaining appointee of a Democratic
president on the high bench, announced that he would resign at the end
of the term and give President Bill Clinton the opportunity to become the
first Democratic president in over twenty-five years to name a member
of the Court.

Supreme Court Watch—1993 is intended to examine the changes and
decisions made during the Supreme Court's 1990–1991, 1991–1992,
and 1992–1993 terms. Besides highlighting the major rulings in excerpts
from leading cases, I discuss in section-by-section introductions other
important decisions as well as analyze recent developments in various
areas of constitutional law. I preview here some of the important cases
that the Court has granted review and will decide in its 1993–1994 term.
To offer even more information in an efficient format, I have included
special boxes titled "Constitutional History," "The Development of
Law," and "Inside the Court." This 1993 edition incorporates material
from the 1991 and 1992 editions.

The favorable reception of and comments received on previous editions of the *Watch* have been gratifying, and I hope this 1993 edition will further contribute to students' understanding of constitutional law, politics, and history, as well as to their appreciation for how the politics of constitutional interpretation turn on differing interpretations of constitutional politics. Finally, I am grateful for the assistance of Kent C. Olson and Stephen Bragaw, for the timely and careful copy-editing of Joan Benham, as well as for the support of Donald Fusting, a friend and faithful editor.

D.M.O.
July 1, 1993

VOLUME ONE

2

LAW AND POLITICS IN THE SUPREME COURT: JURISDICTION AND DECISION-MAKING PROCESS

M AJOR CHANGES IN THE Court's directions have historically occurred when there is a turnover in its composition in a short period
of time. In 1986, Republican President Ronald Reagan elevated Justice
William H. Rehnquist to chief justice and named Antonin Scalia to his
seat as associate justice; then, in 1988, after unsuccessfully nominating
Judges Robert H. Bork and Douglas Ginsburg, Reagan appointed Justice Anthony Kennedy. With these new appointees came changes in
constitutional law and politics. And then, after thirty-four years on the
Court, Justice William J. Brennan, Jr., retired on July 20, 1990. Appointed by Republican President Dwight D. Eisenhower in 1956, Justice
Brennan is widely considered one of the most liberal and influential
justices of the twentieth century. Within three days of Justice Brennan's
announced retirement, Republican President George Bush nominated
Judge David Hackett Souter, whom less than a year earlier Bush had
appointed to the Court of Appeals for the First Circuit.

At age fifty, Justice Souter was the same age as Brennan when he was
named to the high bench. A bachelor, Souter was a Rhodes scholar at
Oxford University and received his law degree from Harvard Law
School. In the late 1970s, he served as New Hampshire's attorney general and was appointed in 1983 to that state's supreme court by then-
governor (and later Bush's White House chief of staff) John Sununu.
Souter testified for three days before the Senate Judiciary Committee,
which also heard two days of testimony from witnesses for and against
him. Throughout his testimony, Souter endeavored to reassure senators

3

that he had no agenda or commitment to a rigid philosophy of "original intent." The "magestic clauses" of the Constitution were broad, he declared, and required attention to history and precedent as well as the text. By a vote of thirteen to one (with only Massachusetts Democratic Senator Edward Kennedy dissenting), the Senate Judiciary Committee recommended confirmation of Souter. Subsequently, Souter was confirmed by a vote of ninety to nine (with only liberal Democratic senators voting against him) on October 2, 1990, and sworn into office as the 105th Supreme Court justice on October 8, 1990.

Then, on the last day of the 1990 term, Justice Thurgood Marshall retired after twenty-four years on the bench. The first black to sit on the Court and the last appointee of a Democratic president, Marshall was appointed by Lyndon B. Johnson in 1967. His appointment was politically symbolic of the times. LBJ and a democratically controlled Congress pushed through the first major civil rights legislation in more than a century. They reached out to strike down barriers and expand opportunities for blacks, women, and other minorities. Marshall was a kind of larger-than-life metaphor for that controversial period in American politics.

Four days after Justice Marshall announced that he would step down, on July 1, 1991, President George Bush nominated his successor, Judge Clarence Thomas, whom fifteen months earlier Bush had named to fill the seat of Judge Robert H. Bork on the Court of Appeals for the District of Columbia Circuit. Despite the president's disclaiming that his nominee—the second black to sit on the high bench—was "a quota" and defending him as "the best man for the job on the merits," his qualifications were immediately called into question. At age forty-three, Judge Thomas was one of the youngest ever to join the Court; the average age of the preceding 105 justices was a full decade older, and only 9 were Thomas's age, or younger, at the time of their appointments. Thomas also had little prior judicial experience; in his brief time on the appellate bench he wrote only twenty-two opinions. Before that, he spent almost eight years as chairman of the Equal Employment Opportunities Commission (EEOC). Still, he earned his law degree at Yale Law School and pulled himself up from an impoverished childhood in Pin Point, Georgia, where he was raised by his grandparents and attended a Catholic school. More than his qualifications and legal experience sparked controversy, however. During the 1980s, Thomas had established a reputation as a rising young black within the Republican party and champion of a conservative "natural law" approach to constitutional interpretation. In speeches and articles, he attacked affirmative action, lamented the welfare state, and sharply criticized the judiciary's efforts to integrate public schools. His nomination was thus not unexpected but bound to invite controversy: Thomas and Justice Marshall stood for and symbolized very different legal policies and eras in American politics.

During his testimony before the Senate Judiciary Committee, Thomas repeatedly emphasized his up-by-the-bootstraps philosophy and personal struggle in overcoming the poverty of his youth. When asked about his judicial philosophy and prior writings, though, he followed Souter in offering only circumspect, closely guarded answers. Thomas distanced himself from previous statements advocating a "natural law" approach to constitutional interpretation, claiming that he now "did not see a role for the application of natural rights to constitutional adjudication." Although conceding that the Fourteenth Amendment embraced a "right of privacy," Thomas steadfastly and surprisingly maintained, when responding to more than seventy questions about the constitutionality of *Roe v. Wade,* that he had never seriously thought about or debated the legitimacy of that watershed ruling on a woman's right to choose an abortion. As with Bork in 1987 and Souter in 1990, Thomas's dismissal of his earlier positions left some senators wondering whether he was undergoing a "confirmation conversion."

After almost two weeks of hearings in late September, the judiciary committee was deadlocked. Split seven to seven over whether to recommend Thomas's confirmation, it voted thirteen to one to send his nomination without a recommendation to the full Senate. Then several new allegations surfaced, including one that Thomas sexually harassed an assistant a decade earlier when he chaired the EEOC. It was also revealed that Senator Biden had known of the allegations and, although telling several Democratic senators about them, failed to conduct a full investigation. An FBI report on the allegations was later leaked to the press and law school professor Anita F. Hill was pressed into holding a press conference to explain her allegations and why she had sought confidentiality.

Amid growing public anger over the accusations and countercharges, the judiciary committee held hearings that pitted Hill against Thomas. Hill coolly and confidently claimed that in the early 1980s Thomas sexually harassed her, repeatedly asked for dates, frequently talked about pornographic movies, and created a hostile work environment. Thomas in turn categorically denied the accusations and angrily protested that the confirmation process had become a "high-tech lynching for uppity blacks." The nasty drama of "she said, he said" raised larger issues of racism and sexism, but failed to resolve the immediate questions about the integrity and credibility of both Hill and Thomas. The confrontation also intensified the personal attacks waged by Thomas's supporters and opponents, and heightened public disgust over the Senate's conduct of the confirmation process. At the end of another week of bitter fighting, the Senate voted fifty-two to forty-eight to confirm Thomas as the 106th justice to serve on the Supreme Court.

With the retirements of Justices Brennan and Marshall, and the arrival of Justices Souter and Thomas, the conservative majority on the Rehnquist Court further solidified and the Court has been less often split five to four: Only 16 percent of the decisions handed down in the 1990 term,

Rehnquist Court Terms	Five-to-Four Decisions	Total Number Decided
1986	45 (29.6%)	152
1987	12 (8.5%)	142
1988	33 (23.1%)	143
1989	39 (28.1%)	139
1990	21 (16.2%)	129
1991	17 (12.8%)	132
1992	18 (15.3%)	117

as compared with 28 percent in Brennan's last term on the Court, were by bare majority vote. In the 1990 and 1991 terms, the Rehnquist Court was more frequently split six to three. In the 1991–1992 term, for example, the justices split six to three in 22 percent of the cases, whereas only 12 percent of the decisions were decided by bare majorities. Notably, in dealing with the controversial issues of abortion and freedom of speech and religion, Justices Kennedy, Souter, and O'Connor broke rank with the chief justice and Justices Scalia and Thomas. The shift of Justices O'Connor and Souter away from the chief justice and Justices Scalia and Thomas continued during the Court's 1992–1993 term, which also produced slightly more five-to-four decisions (15.3 percent) than in the prior term.

Midway through the 1992 term, Justice Bryon White announced his decision to resign at the end of the term. After ten consecutive appointments to the Court by Republican presidents, Justice White remained the last appointee of a Democratic president. Appointed by John F. Kennedy in 1962 at age forty-four, Justice White served thirty-one years on the bench. In that time he established a staunch, though by no means uniformly, conservative track record. On some of the most controversial social–civil rights issues, he voted with conservatives. Justice White dissented from the landmark decision in *Roe v. Wade,* 410 U.S. 113 (1973) (see Vol. 2, Ch. 11),[1] and all subsequent rulings affirming a woman's right to have an abortion, as well as authored the opinion for a bare majority rejecting an extension of the right of privacy to protect private consensual sexual relations, in *Bowers v. Hardwick,* 478 U.S. 186 (1986) (see Vol. 2, Ch. 11). Except for upholding Congress's power to enact affirmative action programs, Justice White opposed such state and local programs, unless adopted to remedy specific policies of past discrimination (see Vol. 2, Ch. 12). With respect to the rights of the accused and criminal justice matters, he also generally sided with conservatives, dissenting from the watershed ruling in *Miranda v. Arizona,* 384 U.S. 436 (1966) (in Vol. 2, Ch. 8), for instance, and writing the majority's opinion upholding a "good faith exception" to the Fourth Amendment's exclusionary rule in *United States v. Leon,* 468 U.S. 902 (1984) (in Vol. 2, Ch. 7). Although supportive of First Amendment free speech claims in many

---

[1]References to Vol. 1 or 2 are to the author's two-volume *Constitutional Law and Politics* (Norton, 1991).

cases, Justice White often dissented from the Court's decisions enforcing a "separation of church and state" under the First Amendment's (dis)establishment clause (see Vol. 2, Ch. 6).

In announcing his decision to retire almost four months in advance of the end of the Court's 1992 term, Justice White gave President Clinton not only a chance to fill his seat, but ample time to select his successor. Among others on the Court, Justice White reportedly lamented how the televised coverage of the Senate confirmation hearings for controversial nominees—in particular, the ill-fated 1987 nomination of Robert H. Bork and the bitter 1991 struggle over Justice Thomas's confirmation—denigrated the Court. Besides emphasizing the Court's institutional prestige, Justice White may have wanted to ensure that Clinton had time to pick a suitable successor, given both the spat over the withdrawal of Clinton's first two nominees for attorney general and the extraordinary controversy that doomed the last Democratic president's nominee to the Court; in 1968 President Lyndon Johnson's proposed elevation of Justice Abe Fortas to the seat of chief justice was defeated by Republicans and conservative southern Democrats in the Senate. In any event, Justice White's announcement gave Clinton the first of several possible opportunities during his time in the Oval Office to fill seats on the high bench and to shift the Court's direction on abortion and the right of privacy, and affirmative action, among other matters.

For his part, President Clinton immediately announced that he would search for a nominee who possessed "a fine mind, good judgment, wide experience in the law and the problems of real people . . . and who has a big heart." Yet more than three months passed before Clinton finally settled on Judge Ruth Bader Ginsburg as the 107th justice of the Supreme Court. Clinton had wanted a politician—a "consensus builder" for the Court. But several prominent and potential nominees withdrew from consideration: New York's governor Mario M. Cuomo and that state's chief judge, Judith Kaye, as well as the secretary of the Department of Education, Richard Riley. From a list of over forty potential nominees (including federal judges Jose Cabranes, Jon O. Newman, Amalya Kearse, and Patrica Wald, along with Tennessee's supreme court justice, Gilbert Merritt), the president narrowed the contenders to a handful. In the week before he announced his nominee, Clinton vacillated between elevating his secretary of the Department of Interior, Bruce Babbitt—a friend and former Arizona governor—and naming federal appellate court judge Stephen G. Breyer. Environmentalists wanted Babbitt to stay at Interior, however, and he faced strong opposition from Utah's Republican senator and senior minority member on the Senate Judiciary Committee, Orrin Hatch. Praised by both Hatch and Senator Edward Kennedy (D.-Mass.) as a moderate and able jurist, Judge Breyer met with the president for lunch on the Friday before the final selection. Both Babbitt and Breyer were "superbly qualified" and might be appointed in the future, Clinton said when announcing his nominee on June 14, 1993. Judge Ginsburg, Clinton proclaimed, was "the Thurgood Marshall of the women's movement" and a moderate, "neither liberal or conservative." Clinton explained further that Ginsburg was selected for three reasons: she was one of the "best judges," who also had "a historic record of achievement" in pushing women's rights, and she held out the promise of becoming a "force of consensus building" in the Court.

A sixty-year-old jurist on the Court of Appeals for the District of Columbia Circuit, Ginsburg would become the second woman and sixth Jewish justice in the Court's history. Although no Jewish justice has sat on the high bench in almost a quarter of a century (since Justice Abe Fortas resigned in 1969), Jewish groups welcomed her nomination while also rejecting the mythology of a "Jewish seat" and emphasizing her selection as based on merit. Women's groups were also generally pleased, though some voiced concerns about Ginsburg's criticisms of *Roe v. Wade.* In a 1993 speech at New York University Law School, Ginsburg expressed reservations about the scope, though not the result, of that controversial ruling on abortion. In her words:

[W]ithout taking giant strides and thereby risking a backlash too forceful to contain, the Court, through constitutional adjudication, can reinforce or signal a green light for a social change. In most of the post-1970 gender classification cases, unlike *Roe,* the Court functioned in just that way. It approved the direction of change through a temperate brand of decision-making, one that was not extravagant or divisive.

Roe v. Wade, on the other hand, halted a political process that was moving in a reform direction and thereby, I believe, prolonged divisiveness and deterred stable settlement of the issue. The most recent *Planned Parenthood [of Southeastern Pennsylvania v. Casey* (1992) (see page 240)] decision, although a retreat from *Roe,* appears to have prompted a renewed dialogue, a revival of the political movement in progress in the early 1970s. That renewed dialogue, one may hope, will, within a relatively short span, yield an enduring resolution of this vital matter.

At the forefront of the woman's movement in law in the 1970s, Ginsburg taught at Columbia and Rutgers schools of law, before Democratic President Jimmy Carter appointed her to the appellate bench in 1980. On the bench, Ginsburg established a reputation as a careful, moderate, and collegial judge (who in spite of disagreements developed a warm relationship with then-Judge Antonin Scalia). In selecting Ginsburg, Clinton bet that she would add to the Court's centrists—Justices O'Connor, Kennedy, and Souter—and possibly nudge them in slightly more liberal directions on social–civil rights issues.

A. JURISDICTION AND JUSTICIABLE CONTROVERSIES

Besides sharply cutting back on *habeas corpus* appeals from state courts (see, e.g., *Coleman v. Thompson* (1991) (page 70), the Rehnquist Court has sounded retrenchment in access to federal courts in other ways as well. Almost two decades after the Burger Court liberalized the law of standing so as to allow citizens suits for environmental damages (see Vol. 1 or 2, Ch. 2), a majority of the Court tightened standing requirements by raising new obstacles for citizens bringing environmental lawsuits. Writing for the majority in *Lujan v. Defenders of Wildlife*, 112 S.Ct. 2130 (1992) (see page 00), Justice Scalia denied two environmentalists standing because they failed to show "imminent injury," or that they were in immediate danger of suffering a concrete harm that supported their filing a suit under the Endangered Species Act of 1973. Although Justice Stevens concurred, he would have granted standing, as would have the two dissenters, Justices Blackmun and O'Connor.

In *Nixon v. United States*, 113 S.Ct. 732 (1993) (see page 46), the Court reexamined the "political question" doctrine in holding that a former federal judge's challenge to the Senate's expedited impeachment procedure was nonjusticiable. While also upholding the constitutionality of the Senate's procedure in his opinion for the Court, Chief Justice Rehnquist appeared to go out of his way to justify the application of the doctrine and ostensible exercise of judicial sel-restraint. Concurring, Justice White repudiated the majority's apparent refusal to exercise judicial review, while agreeing that the Senate's procedure was constitutional.

The Rehnquist Court also signaled a change in its posture toward granting standing in cases challenging the "overbreadth" of state and federal laws for impinging on First Amendment freedoms, in *Renne v. Geary*, 111 S.Ct. 2331 (1991). Writing for the majority, Justice Kennedy held that a challenge to a section of Article II of California's state constitution, which prohibits political parties from endorsing candidates in nonpartisan elections for judgeships and local government offices, was nonjusticiable, because members of the San Francisco County Republican and Democratic central committees did not have standing and failed to present a ripe case in challenging the restrictions as violation of their First Amendment freedoms. Dissenting Justices Blackmun and Marshall sharply criticized the majority's "novel" theory of justiciability.

In *Wyoming v. Oklahoma*, 112 S.Ct. 789 (1992), however, a majority expanded standing for states to challenge the constitutionality of other states' regulations under the commerce clause on the grounds that those regulations diminished the state's tax revenues. To promote local jobs and to increase tax revenues, in 1986 Oklahoma enacted a law requiring its public utilities to purchase at least 10 percent of the coal they used from mines within the state. As a result, Oklahoma's public utilities purchased less Wyoming-mined coal and Wyoming lost revenues from severance taxes on coal that would have otherwise been sold to Oklahoma's public utilities. Writing for the Court, Justice White struck down Oklahoma's statute as a violation of the commerce clause, which "prohibits economic protectionism—that is, regulatory measures designed to benefit in-state economic interests by burdening out-of-state competitors." In doing so, he held that states could invoke the Court's original jurisdiction, granted in Article III, and rejected Oklahoma's argument that Wyoming was neither engaged in interstate commerce nor had asserted an injury or interest covered by the commerce clause. "It is beyond peradventure," Justice White claimed, "that Wyoming has raised a claim of 'sufficient seriousness and dignity.' Oklahoma, acting in its sovereign capacity, passed the Act, which directly affects Wyoming's ability to collect severance tax revenues, an action undertaken in its sovereign capacity." Having granted Wyoming standing to sue on the basis of its loss of revenue, Justice White struck down Oklahoma's law, observing that "when a state statute clearly discriminates against inter-state commerce, it will be struck down, unless the discrimination is demonstrably justified by a valid factor unrelated to economic protec-tionism, see, e.g., *Maine v. Taylor*, 477 U.S. 131 (1986)" (see Vol. 1, Ch. 7). By contrast, in a dissenting opinion joined by Chief Justice Rehnquist and Justice Thomas, Justice Scalia took strong exception to the major-ity's exercise of its original jurisdiction, granting of standing to Wyoming and holding that a state's loss of revenue was within the "zone of interests" covered by the commerce clause. Wyoming, in his view, failed to assert a direct injury or an interest within the zone of interests em-braced by the commerce clause; a state's interests in collecting taxes, as he put it, was "only marginally related to the national market/free trade foundation of our jurisprudence" of applying the commerce clause in the absence of congressional legislation to strike state regulations deemed to burden interstate commerce. And Justice Scalia warned that the Court's expansion of standing would invite a flood of litigation from the states. In a separate opinion, Justice Thomas also dissented.

In another important ruling on standing, in *Northeastern Florida Chapter of the Associated General Contractors of America v. City of Jacksonville, Florida*, 113 S.Ct. 2297 (1993) (see page 18), the Rehnquist Court made it easier for whites to gain standing to challenge affirmative action and minority set-aside programs. With Justices O'Connor and Blackmun dissenting, the Court held that a building association could challenge a city's set-aside program, even though during the course of the litigation the city had repealed it's program. Writing for the majority, Justice Thomas held that in asserting standing to sue a building association did not have to show that any of its members, in the absence of the program, would have received building contracts set aside for women and minorities. While the ruling makes it easier to bring suits attacking set-aside and affirmative action programs, the decision more generally invites lawsuits against governments over the administration of benefit programs by individuals who need not show they were actually denied or would have obtained benefits.

The Rehnquist Court's deference to *stare decisis* has been a matter of controversy on and off the bench for several years (see Vol. 1, Ch. 2 and Vol. 2, Ch. 2). The justices have debated the value of adhering to the doctrine of *stare decisis* in several cases, most notably in their abortion ruling in *Webster v. Reproductive Health Services,* 492 U.S. 490 (1989) (see Vol. 2, Ch. 11). Indeed, Justice Scalia's sharp attack on a number of prior rulings prompted a response from retired Justice Lewis F. Powell, Jr., in his 1989 Leslie H. Arps Lecture, delivered to the Association of the Bar of the City of New York, titled *"Stare Decisis* and Judicial Restraint." In Justice Powell's words:

> Those who would eliminate *stare decisis* in constitutional cases argue that the doctrine is simply one of convenience. . . . But elimination of constitutional *stare decisis* would represent explicit endorsement of the idea that the Constitution is nothing more than what five Justices say it is. This would undermine the rule of law. . . .

> It is evident that I consider *stare decisis* essential to the rule of law. . . . After two centuries of vast change, the original intent of the Founders is difficult to discern or is irrelevant. Indeed, there may be no evidence of intent. The Framers of the Constitution were wise enough to write broadly, using language that must be construed in light of changing conditions that could not be foreseen. Yet the doctrine of *stare decisis* has remained a constant thread in preserving continuity and stability.

In the span of seven terms, the Rehnquist Court has overturned twenty-one prior rulings. But the debate over *stare decisis* was especially sharp when by a six-to-three vote the Rehnquist Court overturned two of its own earlier decisions, striking down the use of victim-impact statements in death penalty cases in *Payne v. Tennessee* (see page 226). Justices O'Connor, Kennedy, and Souter, however, balked at applying *Payne's* analysis of *stare decisis* in *Planned Parenthood of Southeastern Pennsylvania v. Casey* (1992) (see page 240). There, they gave the doctrine of *stare decisis* a new twist in justifying their refusal to overrule *Roe v. Wade* (1973) (see Vol. 2, Ch. 11), the controversial watershed ruling on abortion. Their analysis was in turn sharply rejected by Chief Justice Rehnquist and Justices Scalia, Thomas, and White.

INSIDE THE COURT

The Supreme Court's Reversal of Precedent in Historical Perspective

The Supreme Court's reversal of prior rulings registers the politics of the changing composition of the high bench. Between 1791 and 1991, the Court reversed itself on average about once each term. Last century, though, reversals were more infrequent, if only because there were fewer decisions to overturn. There were just 32 reversals in the nineteenth century, whereas the Court has reversed itself 174 times in this century, and 157 of those reversals have been since 1937.

The year 1937, of course, was a turning point for the Court and the country.

An economically conservative Court had struck down much of the early New Deal program and, after his landslide reelection, Democratic President Franklin D. Roosevelt proposed that the number of justices be changed from nine to fifteen, thereby enabling him to pack the Court. In the spring of 1937, however, the Court abruptly reversed itself, upholding major pieces of New Deal legislation, and the Senate defeated FDR's "Court-packing plan." Conservative Justice Willis Van Devanter then retired and FDR had the first of eight opportunities during the next six years to fill vacancies on the Court, as well as the opportunity to elevate Justice Harlan F. Stone to the chief justiceship. Between 1937 and 1946, the Roosevelt Court overturned some thirty precedents.

When the Court's composition changes dramatically in a short period of time, or a pivotal justice leaves the bench, the Court tends to overturn prior rulings. The Warren Court (1953–1969) was even more activist than the Roosevelt Court in reversing forty-five precedents. Yet its record shows how crucial the timing of one or two changes on the bench may prove for the direction of the Court. From the landmark school desegregation ruling in *Brown v. Board of Education*, 347 U.S. 483 (1954) (see Vol. 2, Ch. 12), to the appointment of Justice Potter Stewart in 1959, the Warren Court reversed only six precedents. With Justice Stewart's arrival, six more precedents were overturned in the following four years. In 1962, the Court's composition changed again with Democratic President John F. Kennedy's appointments of Justices Byron White and Arthur Goldberg. Over the following three years fourteen prior rulings were discarded, and in the remaining four years of the Warren Court another twenty were reversed, as constitutional law was pushed in even more liberal and egalitarian directions.

During Chief Justice Warren E. Burger's tenure (1969–1986), the Court gradually became more conservative, particularly in the area of criminal procedure. As its composition changed, the Burger Court also continued reconsidering precedents, although typically liberal ones, reversing a total of fifty-two prior rulings. After Republican President Richard M. Nixon made the last two of his four appointments, Justices Harry Blackmun and William Rehnquist, ten decisions were reversed between 1972 and 1975. A critical conservative mass comparable to the liberal bloc on the Warren Court, however, failed to emerge. Then, liberal Justice William O. Douglas retired and his seat was filled by Republican President Gerald R. Ford's sole appointee, Justice John Paul Stevens. Between 1975 and 1981 the Burger Court then reversed no less than twenty-two decisions. Following the arrival of Republican President Ronald Reagan's first appointee, Justice Sandra Day O'Connor, another twelve precedents were overturned in the last five terms of the Burger Court.

The Rehnquist Court has reversed twenty-three decisions in the past seven years. Notably, with each successive change in its composition the Rehnquist Court has also more actively reconsidered precedents laid down by its predecessors. In the year following Reagan's elevation of Justice Rehnquist to the chief justiceship and appointment of Justice Antonin Scalia, three precedents were reversed. After Reagan's fourth appointee, Justice Anthony Kennedy, joined the Court in 1987, another eight reversals came down in the 1987 to 1989 terms. Republican President George Bush's first appointee, Justice David H. Souter, then replaced the retired liberal Justice William J. Brennan. In the 1990 term, the Rehnquist Court overturned seven prior decisions. At the end of that term, Justice Thurgood Marshall announced his retirement and predicted, in *Payne v. Tennessee*, 111 S.Ct. 2597 (1991) (see page 226) that the Rehnquist Court would reverse many earlier liberal rulings. With Bush's second appointee, Justice Clarence Thomas, on the bench, the Rehnquist Court reversed, in whole or in part, five decisions during the 1991 term. But compare the treatments of the doctrine of *stare decisis* in the opinions in *Payne* with those in *Planned Parenthood of Southeastern Pennsylvania v. Casey*, 112 S.Ct. 2791 (1992) (see page 240).

The following table places the Rehnquist Court's reversals of precedents in historical perspective: [a]

Court	Number of Precedents Overturned
Marshall Court (1801–1836)	3
Taney Court (1836–1864)	4
Chase Court (1864–1873)	4
Waite Court (1874–1888)	13
Fuller Court (1888–1910)	4
White Court (1910–1921)	5
Taft Court (1921–1930)	6
Hughes Court (1930–1941)	21
Stone Court (1941–1945)	15
Vinson Court (1946–1953)	13
Warren Court (1953–1969)	45
Burger Court (1969–1986)	52
Rehnquist Court (1986–)	23
Total	208

[a]This table updates data collected and analyzed by the author's graduate student Christopher Banks. For a further discussion of the Supreme Court's reversal of precedents, see, Christopher Banks, "The Supreme Court and Precedent: An Analysis of Natural Courts and Reversal Trends," 75 *Judicature* 262 (Feb./Mar. 1992).

Lujan v. Defenders of Wildlife

112 S.Ct. 2130 (1992)

Under the Endangered Species Act (ESA) of 1973, federal agencies are required to consult with the Department of Interior (DOI) to make sure that their policies and actions will not jeopardize endangered or threatened species or their habitats. For more than a decade DOI interpreted that act to apply to federally funded projects at home and abroad. But in 1986 the Reagan administration reversed course, announcing that the law no longer applied to projects overseas. Immediately, Defenders of Wildlife, other environmental groups, and their members challenged that reinterpretation of the law.

To gain standing to file a lawsuit, members of Defenders of Wildlife—its president, Joyce Kelly, and another member, Amy Skilbred—filed affidavits alleging that they would suffer injuries due to the failure of the Agency for International Development (AID) and other agencies to consult with DOI about a federally funded irrigation project on the Mahaweli River in Sri Lanka and a redevelopment project on the Nile River in Egypt. Those projects, they claimed, threatened endangered elephants and leopards in Sri Lanka and the crocodile and other species in Egypt. And when asserting their standing to sue and personal injuries, Kelly and Skilbred testified that they were environmentalists and had traveled to each site, although neither indicated specifically when she would again visit those sites. A federal district court dismissed the suit for lacking standing, but the Court of Appeals for the Eighth Circuit reversed.

The Bush administration appealed the appellate court's holding that Kelly and Skilbred had standing to sue under the ESA's provision conveying on citizens the right to sue the secretary of DOI for failure to consult with other federal agencies on projects potentially threatening to endangered species and their habitats, even though they failed to allege concrete injuries. Relying on *dicta* in several recent cases (see Justice Scalia's concurring opinion in *Gwaltney of Smithfield, Ltd. v. Chesapeake Bay Foundation*, 484 U.S. 49 [1987], and *Lujan v. National Wildlife Federation*, 110 S.Ct. 3177 [1989]), the Bush administration asked the Court to sharply limit standing in such citizen suits.

The Court's decision was seven to two; the opinion was announced by Justice Scalia. Concurring opinions were delivered by Justice Kennedy, whom Justice Souter joined, and by Justice Stevens. Justice Blackmun's dissent was joined by Justice O'Connor.

Justice SCALIA delivers the opinion of the Court with respect to Parts I, II, III-A, and IV, and an opinion with respect to Part III-B in which Chief Justice REHNQUIST and Justices WHITE, KENNEDY, SOUTER, and THOMAS join, and an opinion with respect to Part III-B, in which Chief Justice REHNQUIST and Justices WHITE and THOMAS join.

. . .

II

Over the years, our cases have established that the irreducible constitutional minimum of standing contains three elements: First, the plaintiff must have suffered an "injury in fact"—an invasion of a legally-protected interest which is (a) concrete and particularized, *Warth v. Seldin*, 422 U.S. 490 (1975); *Sierra Club v. Morton*, 405 U.S. 727 (1972); and (b) "actual or imminent, not 'conjectural' or 'hypothetical.' " Second, there must be a causal connection between the injury and the conduct complained of— the injury has to be "fairly . . . traceable to the challenged action of the defendant, and not . . . the result [of] the independent action of some third party not before the court." *Simon v. Eastern Kentucky Welfare Rights Org.*, 426 U.S. 26 (1976). Third, it must be "likely," as opposed to merely "speculative," that the injury will be "redressed by a favorable decision." . . .

When the suit is one challenging the legality of government action or inaction, the nature and extent of facts that must be averred (at the summary judgment stage) or proved (at the trial stage) in order to establish standing depends considerably upon whether the plaintiff is himself an object of the action (or foregone action) at issue. If he is, there is ordinarily little question that the action or inaction has caused him injury, and that a judgment preventing or requiring the action will redress it. When, however, as in this case, a plaintiff's asserted injury arises from the government's allegedly unlawful regulation (or lack of regulation) of someone else, much more is needed. In that circumstance, causation and redressability ordinarily hinge on the response of the regulated (or regulable) third party to the government action or inaction—and perhaps on the response of others as well. The existence of one or more of the essential elements of standing "depends on the unfettered choices made by independent actors not before the courts and whose exercise of broad and legitimate discretion the courts cannot presume either to control or to predict," *ASARCO Inc. v. Kadish*, 490 U.S. 605 (1989); and it becomes the burden of the plaintiff to adduce facts showing that those choices have been or will be made in such manner as to produce causation and permit redressability of injury. Thus, when the plaintiff is not himself the object of the government action or inaction he challenges, standing is not precluded, but it is ordinarily "substantially more difficult" to establish.

III

We think the Court of Appeals failed to apply the foregoing principles. . . . Respondents had not made the requisite demonstration of (at least) injury and redressability.

A Respondents' claim to injury is that the lack of consultation with respect to certain funded activities abroad "increases the rate of extinction of endangered and threatened species." Of course, the desire to use or observe an animal species, even for purely aesthetic purposes, is undeniably a cognizable interest for purpose of standing. "But the 'injury in fact' test requires more than an injury to a cognizable interest. It requires that the party seeking review be himself among the injured." . . . [R]espondents had to submit affidavits or other evidence showing, through specific facts, not only that listed species were in fact being threatened by funded activities abroad, but also that one or more of respondents' members would thereby be "directly" affected apart from their " 'special interest' in the subject." . . .

We shall assume for the sake of argument that these affidavits contain facts showing that certain agency-funded projects threaten listed species—though that is questionable. They plainly contain no facts, however, showing how damage to the species will produce "imminent" injury to Mss. Kelly and Skilbred. That the women "had visited" the areas of the projects before the projects commenced proves nothing. . . .

Besides relying upon the Kelly and Skilbred affidavits, respondents propose a series of novel standing theories. The first, inelegantly styled "ecosystem nexus," proposes that any person who uses any part of a "contiguous ecosystem" adversely affected by a funded activity has standing even if the activity is located a great distance away. . . . [But to] say that the Act protects ecosystems is not to say that the Act creates (if it were possible) rights of action in persons who have not been injured in fact, that is, persons who use portions of an ecosystem not perceptibly affected by the unlawful action in question.

Respondents' other theories are called, alas, the "animal nexus" approach, whereby anyone who has an interest in studying or seeing the endangered animals anywhere on the globe has standing; and the "vocational nexus" approach, under which anyone with a professional interest in such animals can sue. Under these theories, anyone who goes to see Asian elephants in the Bronx Zoo, and anyone who is a keeper of Asian elephants in the Bronx Zoo, has standing to sue because the Director of AID did not consult with the Secretary regarding the AID-funded project in Sri Lanka. This is beyond all reason. . . .

B   The most obvious problem in the present case is redressability. Since the agencies funding the projects were not parties to the case, the District Court could accord relief only against the Secretary: He could be ordered to revise his regulation to require consultation for foreign projects. But this would not remedy respondents' alleged injury unless the funding agencies were bound by the Secretary's regulation, which is very much an open question. Whereas in other contexts the ESA is quite explicit as to the Secretary's controlling authority, with respect to consultation, the initiative, and hence arguably the initial responsibility for determining statutory necessity, lies with the agencies. When the Secretary promulgated the regulation at issue here, he thought it was binding on the agencies. The Solicitor General, however, has repudiated that position here, and the agencies themselves apparently deny the Secretary's authority. . . .

A further impediment to redressability is the fact that the agencies generally supply only a fraction of the funding for a foreign project. AID, for example, has provided less than 10% of the funding for the Mahaweli Project. Respondents have produced nothing to indicate that the projects they have named will either be suspended, or do less harm to listed species, if that fraction is eliminated. . . .

We hold that respondents lack standing to bring this action.

. . .

Justice KENNEDY, joined by Justice SOUTER, concurred in a separate opinion.

Justice STEVENS concurred in the judgment, but disagreed with the decision to deny standing.

Justice BLACKMUN, with whom Justice O'CONNOR joins, dissenting.

I part company with the Court in this case in two respects. First, I believe that respondents have raised genuine issues of fact—sufficient to survive summary judgment—both as to injury and as to redressability. Second, I question the Court's breadth of language in rejecting standing for "procedural" injuries. I fear the Court seeks to impose fresh limitations on the constitutional authority of Congress to allow citizen-suits in the federal courts for injuries deemed "procedural" in nature. I dissent. . . .

To survive petitioner's motion for summary judgment on standing, respondents need not prove that they are actually or imminently harmed. They need show only a "genuine issue" of material fact as to standing. Federal Rules of Civil Procedure 56(c). This is not a heavy burden. A "genuine issue" exists so long as "the evidence is such that a reasonable jury could return a verdict for the nonmoving party respondents." *Anderson v. Liberty Lobby, Inc.,* 477 U.S. 242 (1986). This Court's "function is not itself to weigh the evidence and determine the truth of the matter but to determine whether there is a genuine issue for trial."

The Court never mentions the "genuine issue" standard. Rather, the Court refers to the type of evidence it feels respondents failed to produce, namely, "affidavits or other evidence showing, through specific facts" the existence of injury. The Court thereby confuses respondents' evidentiary burden (i.e., affidavits asserting "specific facts") in withstanding a summary judgment motion under Rule 56(e) with the standard of proof (i.e., the existence of a "genuine issue" of "material fact") under Rule 56(c). . . .

I think a reasonable finder of fact could conclude from the information in the affidavits and deposition testimony that either Kelly or Skilbred will soon return to the project sites, thereby satisfying the "actual or imminent" injury standard. . . .

By requiring a "description of concrete plans" or "specification of when the some day [for a return visit] will be," the Court, in my view, demands what is likely an empty formality. No substantial barriers prevent Kelly or Skilbred from simply purchasing plane tickets to return to the Aswan and Mahaweli projects. . . .

In conclusion, I cannot join the Court on what amounts to a slash-and-burn expedition through the law of environmental standing. In my view, "the very essence of civil liberty certainly consists in the right of every individual to claim the protection of the laws, whenever he receives an injury." *Marbury v. Madison,* 1 Cranch 137 (1803).

Northeastern Florida Chapter of the Associated General Contractors of America v. City of Jacksonville, Florida

113 S.Ct. 2297 (1993)

In 1984 Jacksonville, Florida, adopted a "Minority Business Enterprise Participation" program, under which 10 percent of the city's construction contracts were set aside for "minority business enterprises" (MBEs). An MBE was defined as a business whose ownership was at least 51 percent female or "minority"—minority was in turn defined as black, Spanish-speaking, Oriental, Indian, Eskimo, Aleut, or handicapped. The program was modeled after a federal minority set-aside program, which was upheld by the Burger Court in *Fullilove v. Klutznick,* 448 U.S. 448 (1980) (in Vol. 2, Ch. 12).

Five years later, the Northeastern Florida Chapter of the Associated General Contractors of America (AGC), an association of construction companies whose members do business in Jacksonville and do not qualify as MBEs, challenged the constitutionality of the program as a violation of the Fourteenth Amendment's equal protection clause. The AGC claimed that its members "would have . . . bid on . . . designated set aside contracts but for the restrictions imposed" by the city's ordinance. That lawsuit resulted in a federal district court's issuing an injunction restraining the city from further using its set-aside program. But a federal appellate court reversed upon concluding that the AGC failed to show an irreparable injury. Then, on remand in 1990, the district court found that the city's program was inconsistent with the Rehnquist Court's ruling in *City of Richmond v. J. A. Croson,* 488 U.S. 469 (1989) (in Vol. 2, Ch. 2), which struck down a minority set-aside program and makes affirmative action programs extremely difficult to defend and enforce. Once again Jacksonville appealed, and the Court of Appeals for the Eleventh Circuit held that the AGC lacked standing to sue because it had failed to show that, in the absence of the set-aside program, any of its members would have bid successfully for any of the construction contracts.

The AGC appealed that decision to the Supreme Court, which granted *certiorari.* Subsequently, the city repealed its set-aside ordinance and replaced it with another entitled "African-American and Women's Business Enterprise Participation," which was more narrowly tailored in light of the guidelines laid down in *J. A. Croson.* Unlike its 1984 ordinance, Jacksonville's 1992 ordinance (1) benefited only women and blacks; (2) eliminated the 10 percent set-aside and substituted "participation goals," ranging from 5 to 16 percent, depending on the type of contract; and (3) provided five alternative methods for companies to meet its "participation goals" for women and blacks. The city also filed at the Supreme Court a motion asking that the case be dismissed as moot, since it had abandoned the original set-aside program, but that motion was denied.

The Court's decision was seven to two, with Justice Thomas announcing the majority's opinion. Justice O'Connor's dissent was joined by Justice Blackmun.

Justice THOMAS delivers the opinion of the Court.

In their brief on the merits, respondents reassert their claim that the repeal of the challenged ordinance renders the case moot. We decline to disturb our earlier ruling, however; now, as then, the mootness question is controlled by City of *Mesquite v. Aladdin's Castle, Inc.*, 455 U.S. 283 (1982), where we applied the "well settled" rule that "a defendant's voluntary cessation of a challenged practice does not deprive a federal court of its power to determine the legality of the practice." . . .

We hold that the case is not moot, and we now turn to the question on which we granted *certiorari:* whether petitioner has standing to challenge Jacksonville's ordinance.

The doctrine of standing is "an essential and unchanging part of the case-or-controversy requirement of Article III," *Lujan v. Defenders of Wildlife,* [112 S.Ct. 2130] (1992), which itself "defines with respect to the Judicial Branch the idea of separation of powers on which the Federal Government is founded," *Allen v. Wright,* 468 U.S. 737 (1984). It has been established by a long line of cases that a party seeking to invoke a federal court's jurisdiction must demonstrate three things: (1) "injury in fact," by which we mean an invasion of a legally protected interest that is "(a) concrete and particularized, and (b) actual or imminent, not conjectural or hypothetical;" (2) a causal relationship between the injury and the challenged conduct, by which we mean that the injury "fairly can be traced to the challenged action of the defendant," and has not resulted "from the independent action of some third party not before the court," *Simon v. Eastern Kentucky Welfare Rights Org.,* 426 U.S. 26 (1976); and (3) a likelihood that the injury will be redressed by a favorable decision, by which we mean that the "prospect of obtaining relief from the injury as a result of a favorable ruling" is not "too speculative." These elements are the "irreducible minimum," *Valley Forge Christian College v. Americans United for Separation of Church and State, Inc.,* 454 U.S. 464 (1982), required by the Constitution. . . .

The decision that is most closely analogous to this case, however, is *Regents of University of California v. Bakke,* 438 U.S. 265 (1978), where a twice-rejected white male applicant claimed that a medical school's admissions program, which reserved 16 of the 100 places in the entering class for minority applicants, was inconsistent with the Equal Protection Clause. Addressing the argument that the applicant lacked standing to challenge the program, Justice Powell concluded that the "constitutional requirements of Art. III" had been satisfied, because the requisite "injury" was the medical school's "decision not to permit Bakke to compete for all 100 places in the class, simply because of his race." Thus, "even if Bakke had been unable to prove that he would have been admitted in the absence of the special program, it would not follow that he lacked standing." This portion of Justice Powell's opinion was joined by four other Justices.

When the government erects a barrier that makes it more difficult for members of one group to obtain a benefit than it is for members of another group, a member of the former group seeking to challenge the barrier need not allege that he would have obtained the benefit but for the barrier in order to establish standing. The "injury in fact" in an equal protection case of this variety is the denial of equal treatment resulting from the imposition of the barrier, not the ultimate inability to obtain the benefit. And in the context of a challenge to a set-aside program, the "injury in fact" is the inability to compete on an equal footing in the bidding process, not the loss of a contract. See [*City of Richmond v. J.A.*] *Croson*, 488 U. S. [469 (1989)]. To establish standing, therefore, a party challenging a set-aside program like Jacksonville's need only demonstrate that it is able and ready to bid on contracts and that a discriminatory policy prevents it from doing so on an equal basis.

In urging affirmance, respondents rely primarily upon *Warth v. Seldin*, 422 U.S. 490 (1975). There the plaintiffs claimed that a town's zoning ordinance, both by its terms and as enforced, violated the Fourteenth Amendment insofar as it had the effect of preventing people of low and moderate income from living in the town. Seeking to intervene in the suit, an association of construction firms alleged that the zoning restrictions had deprived some of its members of business opportunities and profits. We held that the association lacked standing, [because in that case the plaintiffs] . . . "failed to show the existence of any injury to its members of sufficient immediacy and ripeness to warrant judicial intervention."

We think *Warth* is distinguishable. Unlike the other cases that we have discussed, *Warth* did not involve an allegation that some discriminatory classification prevented the plaintiff from competing on an equal footing in its quest for a benefit. In both *Bakke* and this case, the allegation was that the plaintiff (or the plaintiff's membership) was excluded from consideration for a certain portion of benefits—in Bakke, places in a medical school class; here, municipal contracts. In *Warth*, by contrast, there was no claim that the construction association's members could not apply for variances and building permits on the same basis as other firms; what the association objected to were the "refusals by the town officials to grant variances and permits." The firms' complaint, in other words, was not that they could not compete equally; it was that they did not win. Thus, while there is undoubtedly some tension between Warth and the aforementioned line of cases, this case is governed by the latter. . . .

In its complaint petitioner alleged that its members regularly bid on construction contracts in Jacksonville, and that they would have bid on contracts set aside pursuant to the city's ordinance were they so able. Because those allegations have not been challenged (by way of a motion for summary judgment, for example), we must assume that they are true. Given that assumption, and given the legal standard we have reaffirmed today, it was inappropriate for the Court of Appeals to order that petitioner's complaint be dismissed for lack of standing. The judgment of the Court of Appeals is therefore reversed, and the case is remanded for further proceedings consistent with this opinion.

Justice O'CONNOR, with whom Justice BLACKMUN joined, dissented in an opinion expressing the view that the case was moot and that the majority should not have addressed the standing issue.

B. THE COURT'S DOCKET AND SCREENING CASES

While its docket continued to grow, the Rehnquist Court pressed ahead with granting fewer cases review and plenary consideration. In its 1990 term, for the first time in the Court's history, its docket rose above 6,000 cases. There were 6,770 cases on the 1991 docket, whereas there were 6,316 on the 1990 docket, up from 5,746 in 1989, and 5,657 in 1988. The justices, however, granted just over 100 cases plenary consideration, down from 125 in 1990, 144 in 1989, and 170 cases in 1988. In its 1992 term, the Court gave plenary consideration to only 107 cases. Despite the increasing number of cases on its docket, the Court has not granted as few cases review since the 1970 term. Several explanations have been advanced for the Rehnquist Court's refusal to grant more cases review. For almost two decades members of the Burger and Rehnquist Courts complained that they considered too many cases. But in 1988 the Act for the Improvement of the Administration of Justice eliminated virtually all of the Court's nondiscretionary appellate jurisdiction. With that elimination of mandatory appeals, the Rehnquist Court has simply granted 20 to 30 fewer cases each term. Another factor may be that as the lower federal courts have become more conservative in the last decade, due to the appointments of Republican presidents Ronald Reagan and George Bush, the Rehnquist Court has become less inclined to grant cases in order to reverse decisions of federal appellate courts. In addition, the Bush administration lost fewer cases in the lower federal courts and the solicitor general thus appealed fewer cases in the last couple of years. The Rehnquist Court's practice of granting review to fewer cases than during the Burger Court years (1986) has prompted some justices to file dissents from the denial of *certiorari* and to argue that more cases ought to be granted in order to resolve confusion in lower federal and state courts over following the Court's rulings. Notably, Justice White frequently files dissents from the denial of *certiorari*, as illustrated in the discussion on *Mueller v. Virginia*, 113 S.CT. 1880 (1993), at page 190.

A majority of the Rehnquist Court also continued sending signals that it will no longer abide "frivolous" petitions filed by indigents.[1] In historical perspective, the number of unpaid filings has fluctuated with changes in the Court's composition, as well as with changes in the criminal justice system and the country. Prior to the Court's "switch-in-time-that-saved-nine" in 1937, the number of unpaid filings was negligible, less than 80 a year. But as the Court became more solicitous in reviewing cases involving the rights of the accused and civil liberties, unpaid filings increased incrementally during the 1940s and 1950s. By Chief Justice Earl Warren's first year on the bench (1953) the number of unpaid and paid cases was about the same (618 unpaid and 884 paid cases). When the Warren Court (1953–1968) then forged its "revolution in criminal procedure" the number of unpaid cases swelled to 1,947 (while paid cases grew to only 1,324) in 1968. The rising tide of unpaid filings went unabated in the 1970s, but so did that of paid filings. By 1979 paid cases outnumbered unpaid cases by 2,084 to 1,899. That remained so until the mid-1980s when prison populations dramatically expanded, due to the "war on drugs." Since 1985 the number of "jailhouse lawyers" filing petitions has steadily grown; in 1990 there were 3,951 unpaid filings, compared with 2,351 paid filings.

Finally, the justices amended the Court's rules governing appeals to provide for the denial of motions to proceed *in forma pauperis* if the majority deems them frivolous or malicious. In the unsigned order, *In re Amendment to Rule 39*, 111 S.Ct. 1572 (1991), the Court's majority explained that "[i]t is vital that the right to file *in forma pauperis* not be incumbered by those who would abuse the integrity of our process by frivolous filings, particularly those few persons whose filings are repetitive with the obvious effect of burdening the office of the Clerk and other members of the Court staff." Rule 39 was amended as follows: "39.8 If satisfied that a petition for a writ of certiorari, jurisdictional statement, or petition for an extraordinary writ, as the case may be, is frivolous or malicious, the Court may deny a motion for leave to proceed *in forma pauperis.*"

Dissenting Justices Blackmun, Marshall, and Stevens, however, lamented the political symbolism of the Court's action. In Marshall's words, "This Court once had a great tradition [echoed in the oath taken by the justices when sworn into office]: All men and women are entitled to their day in Court.' That guarantee has now been conditioned on monetary worth. It now will read: All men and women are entitled to their day in Court only if they have the *means* and the *money*' " (emphasis in the original).

[1] See *In re Jesse McDonald*, 489 U.S. 180 (1989); *In re Sindram*, 111 S.Ct. 596 (1991); and *In re John Robert Demos*, 111 S.Ct. 1579 (1991).

INSIDE THE COURT

The Business of the Supreme Court in the 1992–1993 Term

Subject of Court Opinions[a]	Summary	Plenary
Admiralty		
Antitrust		4
Bankruptcy	1	3
Bill of Rights (clauses, except rights of accused)		8
Commerce clause		
1. Constitutionality and construction of federal regulation and administrative action		6
2. Constitutionality of state regulation		
Common law		
Miscellaneous statutory interpretation		18
Due process		
1. Economic interests		4
2. Procedure and rights of accused	7	16
3. Substantive (noneconomic)		1
Impairment of contract and just compensation		
Native Americans		3
International law, war, and peace		
Jurisdiction, procedure, and practice	2	18
Land legislation		
Patents, copyright, and trademarks		1
Other suits against the government and officials		10
Suits by states		6
Taxation (federal and state)		9
Totals	10	107

[a]*Note:* The categorizations here are adapted from Felix Frankfurter and James Landis, *The Business of the Supreme Court* (New York: Macmillan, 1927). The classification of cases is that of the author and necessarily invites differences of opinion as to the dominant issue in some cases. For further discussion see David M. O'Brien, *Storm Center: The Supreme Court in American Politics,* 3d ed. (New York: W. W. Norton, 1993). Note that opinions disposing of two or more companion cases are counted, respectively, twice or more. Also, as noted, the table includes opinions and cases whether rendered summarily or given plenary consideration, but not cases summarily disposed of by simple orders.

H. OPINION DAYS AND COMMUNICATING DECISIONS

INSIDE THE COURT

Opinion Writing in the 1992–1993 Term*

Opinions (Summary and Plenary)	Majority	Concurring	Dissenting	Separate	Totals
Per curiam	7				7
Rehnquist	15	2	2	3	22
Rehnquist	15	2	2	3	22
White	13	4	4	2	23
White	13	4	4	2	23
Blackmun	10	7	13	2	32
Blackmun	10	7	13	2	32
Stevens	13	10	19		42
Stevens	13	10	19		42
Scalia	14	13	2	2	31
Scalia	14	13	2	2	31
O'Connor	13	6	9	2	30
O'Connor	13	6	9	2	30
Kennedy	10	7	4	2	23
Kennedy	10	7	4	2	23
Souter	10	4	8	3	25
Souter	10	4	8	3	25
Thomas	11	6	4	1	22
Thomas	11	6	4	1	22
Totals	116	59	65	17	257

*Court opinions disposing of two companion cases are counted only once here, whereas the cases are counted separately in the table in "Inside the Court: The Business of the Supreme Court in the 1992–1993 term." In addition, this table includes cases disposed of either summarily or upon plenary consideration, but does not include concurring or dissenting opinions from the denial of *certiorari*. Note that in *Republic National Bank of Miami v. United States*, 113 S.Ct. 554 (1992), Chief Justice Rehnquist and Justice Blackmun each delivered opinions announcing in part the decision of the Court; each of their opinions in that case is counted here as an opinion for the Court. So too, in *Hartford Fire Insurance Co. v. California*, 113 S.Ct. 2891 (1993), the Court's opinion was delivered in part by two justices—Justices Souter and Scalia—and both of their opinions are counted as opinions for the Court, and Justice Scalia's opinion as a separate opinion as well. Separate opinions are those that both concur and dissent in part.

I. THE IMPACT OF SUPREME COURT DECISIONS: COMPLIANCE AND IMPLEMENTATION

As the Court has moved in more conservative directions in areas of civil rights and liberties, state supreme courts increasingly have refused to follow its construction of federal law and have recognized new rights or extended protection on the basis of state constitutions to claims that the Supreme Court has declined to embrace (see Vol. 1, Ch. 7). In *Bowers v. Hardwick,* 478 U.S. 186 (1986) (in Vol. 2, Ch. 11), for instance, a bare majority of the Court refused to extend the constitutional right of privacy in a challenge to Georgia's law punishing sodomy. But in *Commonwealth of Kentucky v. Wasson,* 842 S.W.2d 487 (1992), Kentucky's supreme court expressly declined to follow *Bowers* when striking down its state law against homosexual sodomy.

Commonwealth of Kentucky v. Jeffrey Wasson

Supreme Court of Kentucky, 842 S.W.2d 487 (1992)

Jeffrey Wasson was arrested in a public parking lot and charged with soliciting an undercover police officer to engage in "deviate sexual intercourse." Under a Kentucky statute (KRS 510.100), "deviate sexual intercourse with another person of the same sex" is a criminal offense; the statute also provides that "consent of the other person shall not be a defense." At Wasson's trial, however, a district judge dismissed the charge and held that the statute violated provisions in the Kentucky Constitution that guarantee a "right of privacy" and the equal protection of the laws. A state appellate court affirmed and the Commonwealth of Kentucky appealed that ruling to its supreme court.

OPINION OF THE COURT BY JUSTICE Leibson

The Commonwealth maintains that the United States Supreme Court's decision in *Bowers v. Hardwick,* [478 U.S. 186 (1986)], is dispositive of the right to privacy issue; that the "Kentucky Constitution did not intend to confer any greater right to privacy than was afforded by the U.S. Constitution." Turning to the equal protection argument raised by a statute which criminalizes oral or anal intercourse between persons of the same sex, but not between persons of different sexes, which was not addressed in the *Bowers* case, the Commonwealth argues there is "a rational basis for making such a distinction." . . . The thrust of the argument advanced by the Commonwealth as a rational basis for criminalizing consensual intercourse between persons of the same sex, when the same acts between persons of the opposite sex are not punished, is that the level of moral indignation felt by the majority of society against the sexual preference of homosexuals justifies having their legislative representatives criminalize these sexual activities. The Commonwealth believes that homosexual intercourse is immoral, and that what is beyond the pale of majoritarian morality is beyond the limits of constitutional protection. . . .

The grounds stated by the District Court for striking down the statute as unconstitutional are: "KRS 510.100 clearly seeks to regulate the most profoundly private conduct and in so doing impermissibly invades the privacy of the citizens of this state." . . . The Fayette Circuit Court "agreed with that conclusion," and further held the statute "unjustifiably discriminates, and thus is unconstitutional under Sections 2 and 3 of our Kentucky Constitution." These Sections are:

"Section 2. Absolute and arbitrary power over the lives, liberty and property of freemen exists nowhere in a republic, not even in the largest majority.
Section 3. All men, when they form a social compact, are equal. . . ."

These Sections [together with other provisions of the Kentucky Constitution] express the guarantee of equal treatment provided by the law in our Kentucky Constitution. The lower courts' judgments limit their finding of unconstitutionality to state constitutional grounds. *Bowers v. Hardwick* speaks neither to rights of privacy under the state constitution nor to equal protection rights under either federal or state constitutions. *Bowers* addressed the constitutionality of a Georgia statute prohibiting acts of consensual sodomy between persons of the same sex or the opposite sex. Because the Georgia statute embraced both heterosexual and homosexual conduct, the *Bowers* opinion did not involve the Equal Protection Clause of the Fourteenth Amendment.

For reasons that follow, we hold the guarantees of individual liberty provided in our 1891 Kentucky Constitution offer greater protection of the right of privacy than provided by the Federal constitution as interpreted by the United States Supreme Court, and that the statute in question is a violation of such rights; and, further, we hold that the statute in question violates rights of equal protection guaranteed by our Kentucky Constitution.

I. Rights of Privacy

No language specifying "rights of privacy," as such, appears in either the federal or State Constitution. The Commonwealth recognizes such rights exist, but takes the position that, since they are implicit rather than explicit, our Court should march in lock step with the United States Supreme Court in declaring when such rights exist. Such is not the formulation of federalism. On the contrary, under our system of dual sovereignty, it is our responsibility to interpret and apply our state constitution independently. We are not bound by decisions of the United States Supreme Court when deciding whether a state statute impermissibly infringes upon individual rights guaranteed in the State Constitution so long as state constitutional protection does not fall below the federal floor, meaning the minimum guarantee of individual rights under the United States Constitution as interpreted by the United States Supreme Court. . . .

Kentucky cases recognized a legally protected right of privacy based on our own constitution and common law tradition long before the United States Supreme Court first took notice of whether there were any rights of privacy inherent in the Federal Bill of Rights. . . .

[Moreover,] the United States Supreme Court is extremely reticent in extending the reach of the Due Process Clauses in substantive matters [pertaining to privacy]. . . . *Bowers v. Hardwick* decides that rights protected by the Due Process Clauses in the Fifth and Fourteenth Amendments to the United States Constitution do not "extend a fundamental right to homosexuals to engage in acts of consensual sodomy."

Bowers decides nothing beyond this. But state constitutional jurisprudence in this area is not limited by the constraints inherent in federal due process analysis. Deviate sexual intercourse conducted in private by consenting adults is not beyond the protections of the guarantees of individual liberty in our Kentucky Constitution simply because "proscriptions against that conduct have ancient roots." Kentucky constitutional guarantees against government intrusion address substantive rights. . . . [T]he Kentucky Constitution of 1891 . . . amplifies [its guarantee of individual liberty] with a Bill of Rights in 26 sections, the first of which states:

"Section 1. All men are, by nature, free and equal, and have certain inherent and inalienable rights, among which may be reckoned:
First: The right of enjoying and defending their lives and liberties. . . . .
Third: The right of seeking and pursuing their safety and happiness. . . . .
Section 2. Absolute and arbitrary power over the lives, liberty and property of freemen exists nowhere in a republic, not even in the largest majority." . . .

The leading case on this subject is *Commonwealth v. Campbell*, [133 Ky. 50 (1909)]. At issue was an ordinance that criminalized possession of intoxicating liquor, even for "private use." Our Court held that the Bill of Rights in the 1891 Constitution prohibited state action thus intruding upon the "inalienable rights possessed by the citizens" of Kentucky. Our Court interpreted the Kentucky Bill of Rights as defining a right of privacy, even though the constitution did not say so in that terminology. . . .

In the *Campbell* case our Court quoted at length from the "great work" *On Liberty* of the 19th century English philosopher and economist, John Stuart Mill. . . . Mill's premise is that "physical force in the form of legal penalties," i.e., criminal sanctions, should not be used as a means to improve the citizen. The majority has no moral right to dictate how everyone else should live. Public indignation, while given due weight, should be subject to the overriding test of rational and critical analysis, drawing the line at harmful consequences to others. Modern legal philosophers who follow Mill temper this test with an enlightened paternalism, permitting the law to intervene to stop self-inflicted harm such as the result of drug taking, or failure to use seat belts or crash helmets, not to enforce majoritarian or conventional morality, but because the victim of such self-inflicted harm becomes a burden on society.

Based on the *Campbell* opinion, and on the Comments of the 1891 Convention Delegates, there is little doubt but that the views of John Stuart Mill, which were then held in high esteem, provided the philosophical underpinnings for the reworking and broadening of protection of individual rights that occurs throughout the 1891 Constitution.

We have recognized protection of individual rights greater than the federal floor in a number of cases, most recently: *Ingram v. Commonwealth, Ky.*, 801 S.W.2d 321 (1990), involving protection against double jeopardy and *Dean v. Commonwealth, Ky.*, 777 S.W.2d 900 (1989), involving the right of confrontation. Perhaps the most dramatic recent example of protection of individual rights under the state Constitution where the United States Supreme Court had refused to afford protection under the Federal Constitution, is *Rose v. Council for Better Educ., Inc., Ky.*, 790 S.W.2d 186 (1989). In *Rose*, our Court recognized our Kentucky Constitution afforded individual school children from property poor districts a fundamental right to an adequate education such as provided in wealthier school districts, even though 16 years earlier the United States Supreme Court held the Federal Constitution provided no such protection in *San Antonio Independent School District v. Rodriguez*, 411 U.S. 1 (1973). . . .

We view the United States Supreme Court decision in *Bowers v. Hardwick* as a misdirected application of the theory of original intent. To illustrate: as a theory of majoritarian morality, miscegenation was an offense with ancient roots. It is highly unlikely that protecting the rights of persons of different races to copulate was one of the considerations behind the Fourteenth Amendment. Nevertheless, in *Loving v. Virginia*, 388 U.S. 1 (1967), the United States Supreme Court recognized that a contemporary, enlightened interpretation of the liberty interest involved in the sexual act made its punishment constitutionally impermissible.

According to *Bowers v. Hardwick*, "until 1961, all 50 States outlawed sodomy, and today, 25 States and District of Colombia continue to provide criminal penalties for sodomy performed in private and between consenting adults." In the space of three decades half the states decriminalized this conduct. . . . Two states [New York and Pennsylvania] by court decisions hold homosexual sodomy statutes of this nature unconstitutional for reasons similar to those stated here. . . . Thus our decision, rather than being the leading edge of change, is but a part of the moving stream. . . .

II. Equal Protection

As stated earlier, in *Bowers v. Hardwick*, the Equal Protection Clause was not implicated because the Georgia statute criminalized both heterosexual and homosexual sodomy. Unlike the Due Process Clause analysis provided in *Bowers v. Hardwick*, equal protection analysis does not turn on whether the law (KRS 510.100), transgresses "liberties that are 'deeply rooted in this Nation's history and tradition.' " *Bowers v. Hardwick*. . . .

Certainly, the practice of deviate sexual intercourse violates traditional morality. But so does the same act between heterosexuals, which activity is decriminalized. Going one step further, all sexual activity between consenting adults outside of marriage violates our traditional morality. The issue here is not whether sexual activity traditionally viewed as immoral can be punished by society, but whether it can be punished solely on the basis of sexual preference. . . .

We need not speculate as to whether male and/or female homosexuals will be allowed status as a protected class if and when the United States Supreme Court confronts this issue. They are a separate and identifiable class for Kentucky constitutional law analysis because no class of persons can be discriminated against under the Kentucky Constitution. All are entitled to equal treatment, unless there is a substantial governmental interest, a rational basis, for different treatment.

In the final analysis we can attribute no legislative purpose to this statute except to single out homosexuals for different treatment for indulging their sexual preference by engaging in the same activity heterosexuals are now at liberty to perform. By 1974 there had already been a sea change in societal values insofar as attaching criminal penalties to extramarital sex. The question is whether a society that no longer criminalizes adultery, fornication, or deviate sexual intercourse between heterosexuals, has a rational basis to single out homosexual acts for different treatment. Is there a rational basis for declaring this one type of sexual immorality so destructive of family values as to merit criminal punishment whereas other acts of sexual immorality which were likewise forbidden by the same religious and traditional heritage of Western civilization are now decriminalized? If there is a rational basis for different treatment it has yet to be demonstrated in this case.

The purpose of the present statute is not to protect the marital relationship against sexual activity outside of marriage, but only to punish one aspect of it while other activities similarly destructive of the marital relationship, if not more so, go unpunished. Sexual preference, and not the act committed, determines criminality, and is being punished. Simply because the majority, speaking through the General Assembly, finds one type of extramarital intercourse more offensive than another, does not provide a rational basis for criminalizing the sexual preference of homosexuals.

For the reasons stated, we affirm the decision of the Fayette Circuit Court, and the judgment on appeal from the Fayette District Court.

Justices LAMBERT, WINTERSHEIMBER, and REYNOLDS dissented.

Congress Reverses the Supreme Court—
The Civil Rights Act of 1991

Congress cannot overturn the Supreme Court's constitutional rulings, except by a constitutional amendment ratified by three-fourths of the states (see Vol. 1, Constitutional History, on pages 445–446). But Congress may enact legislation overriding the Court's interpretation of congressional statutes. After a two-year battle, for example, Congress passed and President George Bush signed into law the Civil Rights Act of 1991, overturning 12 rulings of the Court. Congress, moreover, has tended recently to reconsider and reverse more statutory decisions of the Court. Between 1967 and 1990, Congress overrode 121 of the Court's statutory decisions;[a] by contrast, between 1945 and 1957 only 21 rulings were overridden.[b]

The major provisions of the Civil Rights Act of 1991 returned the burden to employers, who are sued for discrimination, of proving that their hiring practices are "job-related to the position in question and consistent with business necessity." Congress thereby overturned *Wards Cove Packing, Inc. v. Atonio*, 490 U.S. 642 (1989), which had reversed an earlier ruling, in *Griggs v. Duke Power Company*, 401 U.S. 424 (1971) (see Vol. 2, n. 19, pages 1269–1270) and had shifted the burden to employees of proving that an employer's hiring practices were discriminatory. Congress also expanded the coverage of the 1866 Civil Rights Act to bar discrimination in all phases of employment and not just in hiring practices, as the Rehnquist Court had held in *Patterson v. McLean Credit Union*, 485 U.S. 617 (1988). The Civil Rights Act also extended protection against discrimination based on race, religion, gender, and national origin to employees of U.S. companies that are stationed abroad.[c] In addition, Congress overturned eight other rulings that had made it more difficult for African-Americans and women to prove discrimination in employment[d] and had made it easier for whites to challenge court-ordered affirmative action programs.[e] Finally, a 1986 ruling was overridden so as to permit winning parties in cases against the federal government to recover interest payments as compensation for delays in obtaining awards for past discrimination.[f]

Congress's reversal of the Court's rulings in the Civil Rights Act of 1991 was by no means exceptional, as indicated in the following table:[g]

Congress	Number of Statutes	Supreme Court Decisions Overridden	Lower Federal Court Decisions Overridden	Total Reversals
90th (1967–1968)	14	6	10	16
91st (1969–1970)	8	2	13	15
92nd (1971–1972)	7	8	4	12

Congress	Number of Statutes	Supreme Court Decisions Overridden	Lower Federal Court Decisions Overridden	Total Reversals
93rd (1973–1974)	10	7	7	14
94th (1975–1976)	17	12	22	34
95th (1977–1978)	14	19	24	43
96th (1979–1980)	20	8	23	31
97th (1981–1982)	17	8	16	24
98th (1983–1984)	16	15	29	44
99th (1985–1986)	25	18	27	45
100th (1987–1988)	24	12	27	39
101st (1989–1990)	15	9	18	27
Totals	187	124	220	344

The 124 Supreme Court rulings overridden between 1967 and 1990 include 3 that more than one Congress overrode; thus only 121 different rulings of the Court were actually reversed. Notably, Professor William N. Eskridge found that 73 percent (89) of the 121 decisions overturned were handed by the Court less than ten years earlier.[h] Eskridge also found that 38 percent of the statutes reversed conservative rulings, whereas 20 percent reversed liberal holdings: in 42 percent there was no clean liberal-conservative split on the Court. The leading subject matter of the Court's decisions reversed by Congress involved civil rights, if the 12 rulings reversed by the Civil Rights Act of 1991 are added to those overturned between 1967 and 1990. Following civil rights, Congress most often overrode rulings in the areas of criminal law (overriding 18 decisions), antitrust (11), bankruptcy (10), jurisdiction and procedure (9), and environmental law (9).

A number of factors have contributed to Congress's reversal of the federal judiciary's statutory rulings. The federal bench became more conservative in the 1980s due to the appointments of Republican Presidents Ronald Reagan and George Bush, while Democrats retained control of both houses of Congress, except for the early part of the 1980s when a Republican majority controlled the Senate. Besides the persistence of divided government and an increasingly conservative federal bench, in the 1970s and 1980s Congress also passed more omnibus legislation and increased the number of federal judgeships. As a result, there are both more federal laws for courts to construe and more lower federal court decisions to which Congress may respond. In addition, Eskridge points out that organized interest groups proliferated in the 1970s, along with the size of the staffs of congressional committees. Both interest groups and larger congressional staffs contributed to greater monitoring of judicial rulings and to congressional over-rides of decisions not only of the Supreme Court but also of the lower federal judiciary.

*a*See William N. Eskridge, Jr., "Overriding Supreme Court Statutory Interpretation Decisions," 101 *Yale Law Journal* 331, 338 (1991).
*b*See Note, "Congressional Reversals of Supreme Court Decisions," 71 *Harvard Law Review* 1324 (1958). For further discussions of Congress's reversal of the Court's statutory rulings, see Thomas Marshall, "Policymaking and the Modern Court: When Do Supreme Court Rulings Prevail?" 42 *Western Political Quarterly* 493 (1989): Beth Henschen, "Statutory Interpretations of the Supreme Court: Congressional Response," 11 *American Political Quarterly* 441 (1983); and Abner Mikva and Jeff Bleich, "When Congress Overrides the Court," 79 *California Law Review* 729 (1991).
*c*Overturning *Equal Employment Opportunity Commission v. Arabian American Oil,* 111 S.Ct. 1227 (1991).
*d*Overturning *Crawford Fitting Co. v. J. T. Gibbons, Inc.,* 482 U.S. 437 (1987); *Price Waterhouse v. Hopkins,* 490 U.S. 228 (1989); *West Virginia University Hospitals v. Casey,* 111 S.Ct. 1138 (1991); *Independent Federation of Flight Attendants v. Zipes,* 491 U.S. 754 (1989); *Evans v. Jeff D.,* 475 U.S. 717 (1986); and *Marek v. Chesney,* 473 U.S. 1 (1985).
*e*Overturning *Lorance v. AT&T,* 490 U.S. 900 (1989), and *Martin v. Wilks,* 490 U.S. 755 (1989).
*f*Overturning *Library of Congress v. Shaw,* 478 U.S. 310 (1986).
*g*These data come from Table 1 in Eskridge, "Overriding Supreme Court Statutory Interpretation Decisions," 338. An appendix in Eskridge's article lists the statutes overturning judicial decisions.
*h*Eskridge, "Overriding Supreme Court Statutory Interpretation Decisions."

3

PRESIDENTIAL POWER, THE RULE OF LAW, AND FOREIGN AFFAIRS

B. AS COMMANDER IN CHIEF AND IN FOREIGN AFFAIRS

In its 1992–1993 term the Court reviewed a challenge to the controversial federal legal policy of intercepting Haitian boat people at sea and returning them to their homeland. That policy was adopted by President George Bush after the military overthrew Haitian President Jean-Bertrand Aristide and thousands of Haitians began trying to escape to Florida and elsewhere. Although as a Democratic presidential candidate Bill Clinton denounced the policy, he reversed course after his inauguration and defended the policy of interception and immediate return of, without holding of asylum hearings for, Haitian "boat people." By an eight-to-one vote in *Sale v. Haitian Centers Council, Inc.,* 113 S.Ct. 2549 (1993) (see excerpt below), the Court upheld the policy, with only Justice Blackmun dissenting.

Sale v. Haitian Centers Council, Inc.,

113 S.Ct. 2549 (1993)

In 1981, the United States and Haiti entered into an agreement authorizing the U.S. Coast Guard to intercept vessels illegally transporting undocumented aliens. That agreement included provisions guaranteeing that repatriated citizens would not be prosecuted in Haiti and that the U.S. would not return any aliens whom it "determined to qualify for refugee status." Along with that agreement the Reagan administration's

Department of Justice interpreted the United Nations Protocol Relating to the Status of Refugees to require asylum hearings for intercepted Haitians. The Immigration and Naturalization Act also provides that the government "shall not deport or return any alien . . . to a country if the Attorney General determines that such alien's life or freedom would be threatened." For a decade, the government's legal policy was to provide asylum hearings for intercepted Haitians prior to their deportation.

But the government's policy on the interception and return of Haitian boat people changed following the overthrow of Haiti's President Jean-Bertrand Aristide and the dramatic increase in the number of Haitians risking the perilous 700-mile sail to reach Florida. In 1992, in order to discourage Haitians from attempting to flee to Florida President George Bush announced an abrupt change in policy: Haitians would henceforth be intercepted at sea and immediately returned to their homeland. The Bush administration contended that neither the U.N. protocol nor the Immigration and Naturalization Act applied to aliens who had not already arrived on U.S. shores, and that the courts were precluded from reviewing the president's order. When the Court of Appeals for the Second Circuit overruled that change in legal policy, Democratic presidential candidate Bill Clinton applauded the court's ruling. Yet after his inauguration Clinton reversed course and had his Department of Justice defend the policy of intercepting and immediately returning Haitian refugees. The acting commissioner of the INS, Chris Sales, appealed the appellate court's decision and the Supreme Court granted *certiorari*.

The Court's decision was eight to one. The majority's opinion was announced by Justice John Paul Stevens. Justice Harry Blackmun dissented.

Justice STEVENS delivers the opinion of the Court.

Both parties argue that the plain language of Section 243(h)(1) [of the Immigration and Naturalization Act] is dispositive. It reads as follows:

"The Attorney General shall not deport or return any alien (other than an alien described in Section 1251(a)(4)(D) of this title) to a country if the Attorney General determines that such alien's life or freedom would be threatened in such country on account of race, religion, nationality, membership in a particular social group, or political opinion."

Respondents emphasize the words "any alien" and "return"; neither term is limited to aliens within the United States. Respondents also contend that the 1980 amendment deleting the words "within the United States" from the prior text of Section 243(h) obviously gave the statute an extraterritorial effect. This change, they further argue, was required in order to conform the statute to the text of Article 33.1 of the Convention [Relating to the Status of Refugees], which they find as unambiguous as the present statutory text. . . .

Respondents' expansive interpretation of the word "return" raises [a] problem: it would make the word "deport" redundant. If "return" referred solely to the destination to which the alien is to be removed, it alone would have been sufficient to encompass aliens involved in both deportation and exclusion proceedings. And if Congress had meant to refer to all aliens who might be sent back to potential oppressors, regardless of their location, the word "deport" would have been unnecessary. By using both words, the statute implies an exclusively territorial application, in the context of both kinds of domestic immigration proceedings. . . .

As enacted in 1952, Section 243(h) authorized the Attorney General to withhold deportation of aliens "within the United States." Six years later we considered the question whether it applied to an alien who had been paroled into the country while her admissibility was being determined. We held that even though she was physically present within our borders, she was not "within the United States" as those words were used in Section 243(h). *Leng May Ma v. Barber,* 357 U.S. 185 (1958). . . .

The 1980 amendment erased the long-maintained distinction between deportable and excludable aliens for purposes of Section 243(h). By adding the word "return" and removing the words "within the United States" from Section 243(h), Congress extended the statute's protection to both types of aliens, but it did nothing to change the presumption that both types of aliens would continue to be found only within United States territory. The removal of the phrase "within the United States" cured the most obvious drawback of Section 243(h): as interpreted in *Leng May Ma,* its protection was available only to aliens subject to deportation proceedings.

Of course, in addition to this most obvious purpose, it is possible that the 1980 amendment also removed any territorial limitation of the statute, and Congress might have intended a double-barreled result. That possibility, however, is not a substitute for the affirmative evidence of intended extraterritorial application that our cases require. Moreover, in our review of the history of the amendment, we have found no support whatsoever for that latter, alternative, purpose. . . .

Like the text and the history of Section 243(h), the text and negotiating history of Article 33 of the United Nations Convention are both completely silent with respect to the Article's possible application to actions taken by a country outside its own borders. Respondents argue that the Protocol's broad remedial goals require that a nation be prevented from repatriating refugees to their potential oppressors whether or not the refugees are within that nation's borders. In spite of the moral weight of that argument, both the text and negotiating history of Article 33 affirmatively indicate that it was not intended to have extraterritorial effect. . . .

As we have already noted, Acts of Congress normally do not have extraterritorial application unless such an intent is clearly manifested. That presumption has special force when we are construing treaty and statutory provisions that may involve foreign and military affairs for which the President has unique responsibility. Cf. *United States v. Curtiss-Wright Export Corp.,* 299 U.S. 304 (1936). . . . The judgment of the Court of Appeals is reversed.

Justice BLACKMUN dissenting.

I believe that the duty of nonreturn expressed in both the Protocol and the statute is clear. . . . Comparison with the pre-1980 version of Section 243(h) confirms that the statute means what it says. Before 1980, Section 243(h) provided:

> "The Attorney General is authorized to withhold deportation of any alien . . . within the United States to any country in which in his opinion the alien would be subject to persecution on account of race, religion, or political opinion and for such period of time as he deems to be necessary for such reason."

The Refugee Act of 1980 explicitly amended this provision in three critical respects. Congress (1) deleted the words "within the United States"; (2) barred the Government from "returning," as well as "deporting," alien refugees; and (3) made the prohibition against return mandatory, thereby eliminating the discretion of the Attorney General over such decisions.

The import of these changes is clear. Whether "within the United States" or not, a refugee may not be returned to his persecutors. To read into Section 243(h)'s mandate a territorial restriction is to restore the very language that Congress removed. "Few principles of statutory construction are more compelling than the proposition that Congress does not intend sub silentio to enact statutory language that it has earlier discarded in favor of other language." *INS v. Cardoza-Fonseca,* 480 U. S. [421 (1987)]. Moreover, as all parties to this case acknowledge, the 1980 changes were made in order to conform our law to the United Nations Protocol. . . .

That the clarity of the text and the implausibility of its theories do not give the majority more pause is due, I think, to the majority's heavy reliance on the presumption against extraterritoriality. The presumption runs throughout the majority's opinion, and it stacks the deck by requiring the Haitians to produce "affirmative evidence" that when Congress prohibited the return of "any" alien, it indeed meant to prohibit the interception and return of aliens at sea. . . .

In this regard, the majority's dictum that the presumption has "special force" when we construe "statutory provisions that may involve foreign and military affairs for which the President has unique responsibility" is completely wrong. The presumption that Congress did not intend to legislate extraterritorially has less force—perhaps, indeed, no force at all—when a statute on its face relates to foreign affairs. What the majority appears to be getting at, as its citation to *United States v. Curtiss-Wright Export Corp.,* 299 U.S. 304 (1936), suggests is that in some areas, the President, and not Congress, has sole constitutional authority. Immigration is decidedly not one of those areas. And the suggestion that the President somehow is acting in his capacity as Commander-in-Chief is thwarted by the fact that nowhere among Executive Order No. 12,807's numerous references to the immigration laws is that authority even once invoked. . . .

The refugees attempting to escape from Haiti do not claim a right of admission to this country. They do not even argue that the Government has no right to intercept their boats. They demand only that the United States, land of refugees and guardian of freedom, cease forcibly driving them back to detention, abuse, and death. That is a modest plea, vindicated by the Treaty and the statute. We should not close our ears to it.

I dissent.

C. THE TREATY-MAKING POWER AND EXECUTIVE INDEPENDENCE

During the presidencies of Ronald Reagan and George Bush, the executive branch staunchly asserted its power to reinterpret what it deemed ambiguous congressional statutes and treaties with foreign governments. In *Rust v. Sullivan*, 111 S.Ct. 1759 (1991) (see page 103), the Court upheld the administration's reinterpretation of a congressional statute to forbid organizations receiving federal funding from providing counseling on abortion. The Court has not squarely confronted the related issue of the president's reinterpretation of a treaty that contravenes the understanding of the Senate when it consented to the treaty (see Vol. 1, Ch. 3). However, in *United States v. Alvarez-Machain*, 112 S.Ct. 2188 (1992) (see below), the Court upheld the Bush administration's reinterpretation of an extradition treaty to permit it to order the kidnapping and bringing of a foreign national to the United States for trial. Subsequently, Mexico filed a formal protest with the federal government and requested a renegotiation of its treaty with the United States.

United States v. Alvarez-Machain

112 S.Ct. 2188 (1992)

Humberto Alvarez-Machain, a citizen and resident of Mexico, was indicted for participating in the kidnapping and murder of a U.S. Drug Enforcement Administration (DEA) special agent. The DEA believed that Alvarez-Machain, a medical doctor, participated in the murder by prolonging the agent's life so that others could torture and interrogate him. In 1990, Alvarez-Machain was forcibly kidnapped from his medical office and flown by private plane to Texas, where he was arrested by DEA officials. Alvarez-Machain moved to dismiss the indictment on the grounds that his abduction constituted outrageous governmental conduct and that federal courts lacked jurisdiction to try him because he was abducted in violation of a treaty between the United States and Mexico. A federal district court ruled that it lacked jurisdiction to try Alvarez-Machain because his abduction violated the Extradition

Treaty. The Court of Appeals for the Ninth Circuit affirmed that decision, relying on its own ruling in *United States v. Verdugo-Urquidez*, 939 F. 2d 1341 (CA9 1991). In that case, the court of appeals held that the forcible abduction of a Mexican national with the authorization or participation of the United States violates the Extradition Treaty between the United States and Mexico. The Bush administration appealed that ruling to the Supreme Court of the United States, which granted review. Following the Rehnquist Court's ruling upholding the unusual bounty-hunting operation in apprehending Dr. Alvarez-Machain, the federal government's prosecution was dismissed by a federal district court judge for lack of evidence that he had participated in torture and murder of a DEA agent. And Dr. Alvarez-Machain was permitted to return to Mexico.

The Court's decision was six to three; the opinion was announced by Cheif Justice Rehnquist. Justice Stevens's dissent was joined by Justice Blackmun and O'Connor.

Chief Justice REHNQUIST delivers the opinion of the Court.

The issue in this case is whether a criminal defendant, abducted to the United States from a nation with which it has an extradition treaty, thereby acquires a defense to the jurisdiction of this country's courts. We hold that he does not, and that he may be tried in federal district court for violations of the criminal law of the United States. . . .

Although we have never before addressed the precise issue raised in the present case, we have previously considered proceedings in claimed violation of an extradition treaty, and proceedings against a defendant brought before a court by means of a forcible abduction. We addressed the former issue in *United States v. Rauscher*, 119 U.S. 407 (1886); more precisely, the issue of whether the Webster-Ashburton Treaty of 1842, which governed extraditions between England and the United States, prohibited the prosecution of defendant Rauscher for a crime other than the crime for which he had been extradited. Whether this prohibition, known as the doctrine of specialty, was an intended part of the treaty had been disputed between the two nations for some time. Justice MILLER delivered the opinion of the Court, which reached the following conclusion:

[A] person who has been brought within the jurisdiction of the court by virtue of proceedings under an extradition treaty, can only be tried for one of the offences described in that treaty, and for the offence with which he is charged in the proceedings for his extradition, until a reasonable time and opportunity have been given him, after his release or trial upon such charge, to return to the country from whose asylum he had been forcibly taken under those proceedings. . . .

In *Ker v. Illinois*, 119 U.S. 436 (1886), also written by Justice MILLER and decided the same day as *Rauscher*, we addressed the issue of a defendant brought before the court by way of a forcible abduction. Frederick Ker had been tried and convicted in an Illinois court for larceny;

his presence before the court was procured by means of forcible abduction from Peru. A messenger was sent to Lima with the proper warrant to demand Ker by virtue of the extradition treaty between Peru and the United States. The messenger, however, disdained reliance on the treaty processes, and instead forcibly kidnapped Ker and brought him to the United States. We distinguished Ker's case from *Rauscher,* on the basis that Ker was not brought into the United States by virtue of the extradition treaty between the United States and Peru, and rejected Ker's argument that he had a right under the extradition treaty to be returned to this country only in accordance with its terms. We rejected Ker's due process argument more broadly, holding in line with "the highest authorities" that "such forcible abduction is no sufficient reason why the party should not answer when brought within the jurisdiction of the court which has the right to try him for such an offence, and presents no valid objection to his trial in such court." . . .

The only differences between *Ker* and the present case are that *Ker* was decided on the premise that there was no governmental involvement in the abduction, and Peru, from which Ker was abducted, did not object to his prosecution. Respondent finds these differences to be dispositive, as did the Court of Appeals in *Verdugo,* contending that they show that respondent's prosecution, like the prosecution of Rauscher, violates the implied terms of a valid extradition treaty. The Government, on the other hand, argues that *Rauscher* stands as an "exception" to the rule in *Ker* only when an extradition treaty is invoked, and the terms of the treaty provide that its breach will limit the jurisdiction of a court. . . .

According to respondent, [provisions of the treaty embody a] bargain which the United States struck: if the United States wishes to prosecute a Mexican national, it may request that individual's extradition. . . .

We do not read the Treaty in such a fashion. [It] does not purport to specify the only way in which one country may gain custody of a national of the other country for the purposes of prosecution. In the absence of an extradition treaty, nations are under no obligation to surrender those in their country to foreign authorities for prosecution. Extradition treaties exist so as to impose mutual obligations to surrender individuals in certain defined sets of circumstances, following established procedures. The Treaty thus provides a mechanism which would not otherwise exist, requiring, under certain circumstances, the United States and Mexico to extradite individuals to the other country, and establishing the procedures to be followed when the Treaty is invoked. . . .

Thus, the language of the Treaty, in the context of its history, does not support the proposition that the Treaty prohibits abductions outside of its terms. . . .

The judgment of the Court of Appeals is therefore reversed, and the case is remanded for further proceedings consistent with this opinion.

Justice STEVENS, with whom Justices BLACKMUN and O'CONNOR join, dissenting.

A critical flaw pervades the Court's entire opinion. It fails to differentiate between the conduct of private citizens, which does not violate any treaty obligation, and conduct expressly authorized by the Executive Branch of the Government, which unquestionably constitutes a flagrant violation of international law, and in my opinion, also constitutes a breach of our treaty obligations. Thus, at the outset of its opinion, the Court states the issue as "whether a criminal defendant, abducted to the United States from a nation with which it has an extradition treaty, thereby acquires a defense to the jurisdiction of this country's courts." That, of course, is the question decided in *Ker v. Illinois,* 119 U.S. 436 (1886); it is not, however, the question presented for decision today.

The importance of the distinction between a court's exercise of jurisdiction over either a person or property that has been wrongfully seized by a private citizen, or even by a state law enforcement agent, on the one hand, and the attempted exercise of jurisdiction predicated on a seizure by federal officers acting beyond the authority conferred by treaty, on the other hand, is explained by Justice BRANDEIS in his opinion for the Court in *Cook v. United States,* 288 U.S. 102 (1933). That case involved a construction of a prohibition era treaty with Great Britain that authorized American agents to board certain British vessels to ascertain whether they were engaged in importing alcoholic beverages. A British vessel was boarded 11½ miles off the coast of Massachusetts, found to be carrying unmanifested alcoholic beverages, and taken into port. The Collector of Customs assessed a penalty which he attempted to collect by means of libels against both the cargo and the seized vessel.

The Court held that the seizure was not authorized by the treaty because it occurred more than 10 miles off shore. The Government argued that the illegality of the seizure was immaterial because, as in *Ker,* the Court's jurisdiction was supported by possession even if the seizure was wrongful. Justice BRANDEIS acknowledged that the argument would succeed if the seizure had been made by a private party without authority to act for the Government, but that a different rule prevails when the Government itself lacks the power to seize. . . .

The same reasoning was employed by Justice MILLER to explain why the holding in *Rauscher* did not apply to the *Ker* case. The arresting officer in *Ker* did not pretend to be acting in any official capacity when he kidnaped Ker. . . . The exact opposite is true in this case, as it was in *Cook.* . . .

As the Court observes at the outset of its opinion, there is reason to believe that respondent participated in an especially brutal murder of an American law enforcement agent. That fact, if true, may explain the Executive's intense interest in punishing respondent in our courts. Such an explanation, however, provides no justification for disregarding the Rule of Law that this Court has a duty to uphold. That the Executive may wish to reinterpret the Treaty to allow for an action that the Treaty in no way authorizes should not influence this Court's interpretation. . . .

4

THE PRESIDENT AS CHIEF EXECUTIVE IN DOMESTIC AFFAIRS

B. APPOINTMENT AND REMOVAL POWERS

In *Freytag v. Commissioner of Internal Revenue*, 111 S.Ct. 2631 (1991), the Rehnquist Court considered a complicated challenge to constitutionality of a section of the Tax Reform Act of 1986. In the Tax Reform Act of 1969, Congress established, under Article I of the Constitution, the U.S. Tax Court, which resolves taxpayer disputes and other such matters and whose functions had been previously exercised by a tribunal in the executive branch. The U.S. Tax Court presently consists of nineteen judges appointed to fifteen-year terms by the president, with the advice and consent of the Senate. Congress subsequently amended that act in 1984 and 1986 and in the process changed the title "commissioner" to "special trial judge," as well as authorized the chief judge of the Tax Court to appoint these special trial judges to hear certain specifically described proceedings and "any other proceeding which the chief judge may designate." Under provisions of the Tax Reform Act, the special trial judges may hear cases involving disputes with the Internal Revenue Service and prepare proposed findings and an opinion, but the actual decision is rendered by a Tax Court judge.

In 1982 Thomas Freytag and several others sought a review in the Tax Court of an Internal Revenue Service determination that their businesses owed approximately $1.5 billion in federal income tax. Their cases were assigned to a Tax Court judge but were later reassigned to a special trial judge. That judge's unfavorable opinion was later adopted as the opinion of the Tax Court. Freytag then appealed that decision to the Court of Appeals for the Fifth Circuit. Freytag argued that the assignment of complex tax cases to special trial judges was not authorized by Congress and, in any event, such assignment violated the appointments clause of the Constitution. The appointments clause, Freytag contended, limits congressional discretion to vest the appointment of "inferior Officers" to the president, the heads of departments of the federal government, and "courts of law."

Writing for the Court in *Freytag*, Justice Blackmun affirmed the lower court's ruling and found no constitutional violation of the appointments clause or the principle of separation of powers. Justice Blackmun rejected the claim of the Commissioner of the Internal Revenue and the Bush administration that the U.S. Tax Court should be considered part of the executive branch, as well as Freytag's argument that the tax court is neither a department of the executive branch nor a court of law for the purposes of the appointments clause and separation of powers. After finding that the special trial judges are inferior officers, Blackmun turned to the principal constitutional question presented: Can the chief judge of the Tax Court constitutionally be vested by Congress with the power to appoint? In answering that question, Blackmun first rejected the government's position that the Tax Court should be considered as "a department with the chief judge as its head," as well as rejected Freytag's argument that the Tax Court is neither a department nor a court of law and, therefore, the power of appointing special trial judges could not be constitutionally vested in the chief judge of the Tax Court. The appointments clause, reasoned Blackmun, does not limit courts of law to only those courts established under Article III of the Constitution. He conceded that the Constitution "nowhere makes reference to 'legislative courts.' " But he pointed out that "the Constitution [gives] Congress wide discretion to assign the task of adjudication in cases arising under federal law to legislative tribunals."

C. LEGISLATIVE POWERS IN THE ADMINISTRATIVE STATE

Despite Chief Justice Rehnquist's occasional call to reinvigorate the nondelegation doctrine (see his concurring opinion in *Industrial Union Department, AFL-CIO v. American Petroleum Institute*, 448 U.S. 607 [1980] [Vol. 1, Ch. 4]), the Court was in no mood to invoke the nondelegation doctrine in *Touby v. United States*, 111 S.Ct. 1752 (1991). Daniel Touby, after being convicted and imprisoned for manufacturing a "designer drug" known as "Euphoria," argued that Congress unconstitutionally delegated its legislative powers to the attorney general in giving him the authority to list a drug as a controlled substance under the Controlled Substances Act of 1970.

The Controlled Substances Act authorizes the attorney general, in accord with specified procedures, to add new drugs to five "schedules" of controlled substances, the manufacture, possession, and distribution of which the act regulates or prohibits. But because compliance with the act's procedures resulted in lengthy delays, drug traffickers were able to develop and market new designer drugs, which had pharmacological effects similar to, but chemical compositions slightly different from, scheduled substances, long before the government was able to schedule them and initiate prosecutions. To combat this problem in 1984, Congress amended the law and added Section 201(h), creating an expedited procedure for the attorney general to schedule a designer drug on a temporary basis as a "controlled substance." The amendment delegated him that power based on his finding that a designer drug was a controlled substance that presented an "imminent hazard to the public safety." The attorney general, in turn, promulgated regulations delegating his temporary scheduling power to the Drug Enforcement Administration (DEA).

Writing for a unanimous Court, Justice O'Connor held that the 1984 amendments do not unconstitutionally delegate legislative power to the attorney general. In doing so, Justice O'Connor noted that the nondelegation doctrine does not prevent Congress from seeking assistance from the executive branch so long as it lays down an "intelligible principle" for the exercise of delegated powers. On that basis, the Court ruled that the amendment's "imminent hazard to public safety" standard was a constitutionally permissible principle. Moreover, O'Connor rebutted Touby's argument that the amendments violated the principle of separation of powers by concentrating too much power in the hands of the attorney general. Citing the Court's ruling in *Mistretta v. United States,* 488 U.S. 361 (1989), which upheld Congress's delegation of power to set sentencing guidelines to the U.S. Sentencing Commission, O'Connor observed that the separation-of-powers principle focuses on the distribution of powers among the three coequal branches of government and does not speak to the manner in which Congress delegates power to agencies within the executive branch.

Another separation of powers question arose in *Metropolitan Washington Airports Authority v. Citizens for the Abatement of Aircraft Noise, Inc.,* 111 S.Ct. 2298 (1991). This case involved an appeal of a ruling by the Court of Appeals for the District of Columbia that held that Congress in 1986, when establishing an agency to operate Dulles Airport and the Washington, D.C., National Airport, had unconstitutionally usurped executive branch powers. By a six-to-three vote, the Court affirmed the lower court's ruling that Congress had usurped the power of the executive branch, in an opinion by Justice Stevens; Chief Justice Rehnquist and Justice Marshall joined Justice White's dissenting opinion that sharply criticizes the majority's understanding of separation of powers and prior rulings in the area.

Finally, in *Rust v. Sullivan,* 111 S.Ct. 1759 (1991) (see page 103), the Court upheld regulations adopted by the Reagan administration that forbid federal funding of family planning organizations that provide abortion counseling or other abortion-related services. In doing so, Chief Justice Rehnquist reiterated that when statutory language is ambiguous, courts should defer to the executive branch's construction of the legislative mandates, and thus reaffirmed the holding in *Chevron v. Natural Resources Defense Council,* 467 U.S. 837 (1984), that if a statute is "silent or ambiguous with respect to the specific issue, the question for the court is whether the agency's answer is based on a permissible construction of the statute." But compare *Presley v. Etowah County Commission,* 112 S.Ct. 820 (1992) (see page 77).

5

CONGRESS: MEMBERSHIP, IMMUNITIES, AND INVESTIGATORY POWERS

IN AN UNUSUAL MOVE the Rehnquist Court expedited an appeal of a three-judge district court ruling that the 1991 apportionment of seats in the House of Representatives violated the principle of "one person, one vote." In the Court's words, "The goal of Article I, section 2 [which requires the representatives be apportioned 'according to their respective Numbers'] is equal representation, not relatively equal representation." Montana sued over the loss of one of its two representatives, arguing that its population of 803,000 would make it the most populous congressional district in the country; under the 1991 reapportionment scheme the average district includes 570,000 people. The size of the House of Representatives was frozen at 435 in 1911 and in 1941 Congress adopted a method of reapportionment that aims at the smallest relative, rather than absolute, differences in representation (see Vol. 1, Ch. 5). The district court, however, held that equal representation required a reduction in the state's absolute, instead of relative, difference from the theoretically ideal congressional district. Under this method of apportioning the 435 House seats, Montana would retain two seats, while Washington would forfeit one of its seats. The disparity in terms of raw numbers would be smaller, though Washington's average congressional district would be 52 percent bigger than Montana's two smaller districts.

Still, in its earlier reapportionment ruling the Court had never addressed the question of extending the principle of one person, one vote from redistricting within a state to the allocation of congrssional districts among the states. Moreover, the principle of one person, one vote appeared impossible to enforce in this area because the Constitution mandates both that each state have at least one representative and that no congressional district cut across state lines.

When reversing the lower court's ruling in *United States Department of Commerce v. Montana*, 112 S.Ct. 1415 (1992), the Court unanimously rejected both the federal government's claim that the political question doctrine applied and Montana's claim that it was unconstitutionally denied equal respresentation. In dismissing the argument that the case presented a nonjusticiable political question, Justice Stevens reaffirmed that federal courts have jurisdiction over reapportionment controversies (see *Baker v. Carr*, 369 U.S. 186 (1992), in Vol. 1, Ch. 1; and Vol. 2, Ch. 1). When turning then to the mertis of the case, Stevens observed that

[t]he constitutional guarantee of a minimum of one Representative for each State inexorably compels a significant departure from the ideal [of equal representation]. In Alaska, Vermont, and Wyoming, where the statewide districts are less populous than the ideal district, every vote is more valuable than the national average. Moreover, the need to allocate a fixed number of indivisible Representatives among 50 States of varying populations makes it virtually impossible to have the same size district in any pair of States, let alone in all 50. Accordingly, although "common sense" supports a test requiring "a good-faith effort to achieve precise mathematical equality" within each State, the constraints imposed by Article I, Section 2, itself make that goal illusionary for the Nation as a whole.

In its 1992 term the Rehnquist Court heard a challenge to the Senate's procedure for impeaching federal judges in *Nixon v. United States*, 113 S.Ct. 732 (1993) (see page 47). The Constitution gives the Senate the sole power to "try all impeachments," and throughout the nineteenth century the full Senate in effect functioned like a jury in hearing the evidence presented in impeachment trials conducted on the floor of the Senate. In 1935 the Senate adopted a new procedure, although not used until the mid-1980s, under which a committee of twelve senators conduct an impeachment hearing and then present a report to the full Senate, which votes on each article of impeachment. Former federal judge Walter Nixon challenged the constitutionality of the Senate's committee procedure, but in his opinion for the Court Chief Justice Rehnquist held that Nixon presented a nonjusticiable political question and that the Senate's procedure was constitutional. By contrast, concurring Justices White and Blackmun found no barrier to judicial review, while also agreeing that the impeachment committee procedure did not violate the Constitution.

Walter L. Nixon v. United States
113 S.Ct. 732 (1993)

Walter Nixon, a former chief judge of the federal district court for southern Mississippi, was tried and convicted by a jury of two counts of making false statements before a federal grand jury and sentenced to prison. The grand jury had investigated reports that Nixon accepted money from a friend in exchange for seeking to halt the federal prosecution of his friend's son. Subsequently, because Nixon refused to resign from his judgeship and continued to receive his judicial salary while in prison, the House of Representatives adopted three articles of impeachment; two articles charged Nixon with giving false testimony to the grand jury and the third with bringing the judiciary into disrepute. The Senate then voted to invoke its own Impeachment Rule XI, under which the presiding officer appoints a committee of Senators to "receive evidence and take testimony." That committee held four days of hearings, during which ten witnesses, including Nixon, testified. The committee subsequently presented a transcript and a report to the full Senate, which debated the articles of impeachment for three hours and allowed Nixon to make a personal appeal. Following Nixon's conviction by a vote of eighty-nine to eight in the Senate, he filed a suit claiming that the Senate's expedited impeachment procedure was unconstitutional. After a federal district and appellate court rejected his claim as nonjusticiable, Nixon appealed to the Supreme Court.

The Court's decision was unanimous. Chief Justice Rehnquist announced the opinion. Justices Stevens, White, and Souter concurred.

Chief Justice REHNQUIST delivers the opinion of the Court.

A controversy is nonjusticiable—i.e., involves a political question—where there is "a textually demonstrable constitutional commitment of the issue to a coordinate political department; or a lack of judicially discoverable and manageable standards for resolving it" *Baker v. Carr*, 369 U.S. 186 (1962). But the courts must, in the first instance, interpret the text in question and determine whether and to what extent the issue is textually committed. As the discussion that follows makes clear, the concept of a textual commitment to a coordinate political department is not completely separate from the concept of a lack of judicially discoverable and manageable standards for resolving it; the lack of judicially manageable standards may strengthen the conclusion that there is a textually demonstrable commitment to a coordinate branch.

In this case, we must examine Article I, section 3, clause 6, to determine the scope of authority conferred upon the Senate by the Framers regarding impeachment. It provides:

"The Senate shall have the sole Power to try all Impeachments. When sitting for that Purpose, they shall be on Oath or Affirmation. When the President of the United States is tried, the Chief Justice shall preside: And no Person shall be convicted without the Concurrence of two thirds of the Members present."

The language and structure of this Clause are revealing. The first sentence is a grant of authority to the Senate, and the word "sole" indicates that this authority is reposed in the Senate and nowhere else. . . .

Petitioner argues that the word "try" in the first sentence imposes by implication an additional requirement on the Senate in that the proceedings must be in the nature of a judicial trial. From there petitioner goes on to argue that this limitation precludes the Senate from delegating to a select committee the task of hearing the testimony of witnesses, as was done pursuant to Senate Rule XI. . . .

There are several difficulties with this position which lead us ultimately to reject it. The word "try," both in 1787 and later, has considerably broader meanings than those to which petitioner would limit it. . . .

The Framers labored over the question of where the impeachment power should lie. Significantly, in at least two considered scenarios the power was placed with the Federal Judiciary. . . . According to Alexander Hamilton, the Senate was the "most fit depositary of this important trust" because its members are representatives of the people. See *The Federalist* No. 65. The Supreme Court was not the proper body because the Framers "doubted whether the members of that tribunal would, at all times, be endowed with so eminent a portion of fortitude as would be called for in the execution of so difficult a task" or whether the Court "would possess the degree of credit and authority" to carry out its judgment if it conflicted with the accusation brought by the Legislature—the people's representative. . . .

There are two additional reasons why the Judiciary, and the Supreme Court in particular, were not chosen to have any role in impeachments. First, the Framers recognized that most likely there would be two sets of proceedings for individuals who commit impeachable offenses—the impeachment trial and a separate criminal trial. . . . The Framers deliberately separated the two forums to avoid raising the specter of bias and to ensure independent judgments. . . .

Second, judicial review would be inconsistent with the Framers' insistence that our system be one of checks and balances. In our constitutional system, impeachment was designed to be the only check on the Judicial Branch by the Legislature. . . .

In addition to the textual commitment argument, we are persuaded that the lack of finality and the difficulty of fashioning relief counsel against justiciability. See *Baker v. Carr*. We agree with the Court of Appeals that opening the door of judicial review to the procedures used by the Senate in trying impeachments would "expose the political life of the country to months, or perhaps years, of chaos." This lack of finality would manifest itself most dramatically if the President were impeached. The legitimacy of any successor, and hence his effectiveness, would be impaired severely, not merely while the judicial process was running its course, but during any retrial that a differently constituted Senate might conduct if its first judgment of conviction were invalidated. Equally uncertain is the question of what relief a court may give other than simply setting aside the judgment of conviction. Could it order the reinstatement of a convicted federal judge, or order Congress to create an additional judgeship if the seat had been filled in the interim?

Petitioner finally contends that a holding of nonjusticiability cannot be reconciled with our opinion in *Powell v. McCormack*, 395 U.S. 486 (1969). The relevant issue in *Powell* was whether courts could review the House of Representatives' conclusion that Powell was "unqualified" to sit as a Member because he had been accused of misappropriating public funds and abusing the process of the New York courts. We stated that the question of justiciability turned on whether the Constitution committed authority to the House to judge its members' qualifications, and if so, the extent of that commitment. Article I, section 5 provides that "Each House shall be the Judge of the Elections, Returns and Qualifications of its own Members." In turn, Article I, section 2 specifies three requirements for membership in the House: The candidate must be at least 25 years of age, a citizen of the United States for no less than seven years, and an inhabitant of the State he is chosen to represent. We held that, in light of the three requirements specified in the Constitution, the word "qualifications"—of which the House was to be the Judge—was of a precise, limited nature.

Our conclusion in *Powell* was based on the fixed meaning of "qualifications" set forth in Article I, section 2. . . . In the case before us, there is no separate provision of the Constitution which could be defeated by allowing the Senate final authority to determine the meaning of the word "try" in the Impeachment Trial Clause. We agree with Nixon that courts possess power to review either legislative or executive action that transgresses identifiable textual limits. . . . But we conclude, after exercising that delicate responsibility, that the word "try" in the Impeachment Clause does not provide an identifiable textual limit on the authority which is committed to the Senate.

Justice STEVENS concurred in a separate opinion.

Justice WHITE, with whom Justice BLACKMUN joins, concurring in the judgment.

The Court is of the view that the Constitution forbids us even to consider [Nixon's] contention. I find no such prohibition and would therefore reach the merits of the claim. I concur in the judgment because the Senate fulfilled its constitutional obligation to "try" petitioner. . . .

Of course the issue in the political question doctrine is not whether the Constitutional text commits exclusive responsibility for a particular governmental function to one of the political branches. There are numerous instances of this sort of textual commitment, e. g., Article I, section 8, and it is not thought that disputes implicating these provisions are nonjusticiable. Rather, the issue is whether the Constitution has given one of the political branches final responsibility for interpreting the scope and nature of such a power.

Although *Baker* directs the Court to search for "a textually demonstrable constitutional commitment" of such responsibility, there are few, if any, explicit and unequivocal instances in the Constitution of this sort of textual commitment. Conferral on Congress of the power to "Judge" qualifications of its members by Article I, section 5 may, for example, preclude judicial review of whether a prospective member in fact meets those qualifications. The courts therefore are usually left to infer the presence of a political question from the text and structure of the Constitution. In drawing the inference that the Constitution has committed final interpretive authority to one of the political branches, courts are sometimes aided by textual evidence that the judiciary was not meant to exercise judicial review—a coordinate inquiry expressed in *Baker*'s "lack of judicially discoverable and manageable standards" criterion. See, e.g., *Coleman v. Miller,* 307 U.S. 433 (1939), where the Court refused to determine the life span of a proposed constitutional amendment given Article V's placement of the amendment process with Congress and the lack of any judicial standard for resolving the question. . . .

[T]he Court's willingness to abandon its obligation to review the constitutionality of legislative acts merely on the strength of the word "sole" is perplexing. Consider, by comparison, the treatment of Article I, section 1, which grants "All legislative powers" to the House and Senate. As used in that context "all" is nearly synonymous with "sole"—both connote entire and exclusive authority. Yet the Court has never thought it would unduly interfere with the operation of the Legislative Branch to entertain difficult and important questions as to the extent of the legislative power. Quite the opposite, we have stated that the proper interpretation of the Clause falls within the province of the judiciary. . . .

The majority's review of the historical record thus explains why the power to try impeachments properly resides with the Senate. It does not explain, however, the sweeping statement that the judiciary was "not chosen to have any role in impeachments." Not a single word in the historical materials cited by the majority addresses judicial review of the Impeachment Trial Clause. And a glance at the arguments surrounding the Impeachment Clauses negates the majority's attempt to infer nonjusticiability from the Framers' arguments in support of the Senate's power to try impeachments.

[T]he question of impeachment vexed the Framers. The pages of the Convention debates reveal diverse plans for resolving this exceedingly difficult issue. Both before and during the convention, Madison maintained that the judiciary ought to try impeachments. Shortly thereafter, however, he devised a quite complicated scheme that involved the participation of each branch. . . . Even Hamilton's eloquent defense of the scheme adopted by the Constitution was based on a pragmatic decision to further the cause of ratification rather than a strong belief in the superiority of a scheme vesting the Senate with the sole power to try impeachments. While at the Convention, Hamilton advocated that impeachment trials be conducted by a court made up of state court judges. Four months after publishing the *Federalist* Nos. 65 and 66, however, he urged the New York Ratifying Convention to amend the Clause he had so ably defended to have the Senate, the Supreme Court, and judges from each state jointly try impeachments. . . .

Viewed against this history, the discord between the majority's position and the basic principles of checks and balances underlying the Constitution's separation of powers is clear. In essence, the majority suggests that the Framers' conferred upon Congress a potential tool of legislative dominance yet at the same time rendered Congress' exercise of that power one of the very few areas of legislative authority immune from any judicial review. While the majority rejects petitioner's justiciability argument as espousing a view "inconsistent with the Framers' insistence that our system be one of checks and balances," it is the Court's finding of nonjusticiability that truly upsets the Framers' careful design. In a truly balanced system, impeachments tried by the Senate would serve as a means of controlling the largely unaccountable judiciary, even as judicial review would ensure that the Senate adhered to a minimal set of procedural standards in conducting impeachment trials. . . .

The majority's conclusion that "try" is incapable of meaningful judicial construction is not without irony. One might think that if any class of concepts would fall within the definitional abilities of the judiciary, it would be that class having to do with procedural justice. Examination of the remaining question—whether proceedings in accordance with Senate Rule XI are compatible with the Impeachment Trial Clause—confirms this intuition. . . .

The fact that Article III, section 2, clause 3 specifically exempts impeachment trials from the jury requirement provides some evidence that the Framers were anxious not to have additional specific procedural requirements read into the term "try." Contemporaneous commentary further supports this view. Hamilton, for example, stressed that a trial by so large a body as the Senate (which at the time promised to boast 26 members) necessitated that the proceedings not "be tied down to . . . strict rules, either in the delineation of the offence by the prosecutors, or in the construction of it by the Judges . . . ." *The Federalist* No. 65. . . .

In short, textual and historical evidence reveals that the Impeachment Trial Clause was not meant to bind the hands of the Senate beyond establishing a set of minimal procedures. . . . Petitioner's challenge to his conviction must therefore fail.

Justice SOUTER concurred in separate opinion in which, unlike Justice WHITE, he argued that the issue was nonjusticiable, though for different reasons than given by Chief Justice REHNQUIST.

6

CONGRESS: LEGISLATIVE, TAXING, AND SPENDING POWERS

an "emperor, king, prince, or foreign power." In 1861 Congress passed an amendment allowing slavery to continue. And in 1924 Congress approved another allowing it to regulate child labor and overturning rulings of the Supreme Court to the contrary.

In addition, thirty-two states—two short of the necessary two-thirds—have petitioned Congress to pass a balanced budget amendment, and nineteen have asked for an amendment banning abortion. Two other amendments—the Equal Rights Amendment (Vol. 2, "Constitutional History", on pages 1422–1423) and a proposal giving the District of Columbia representation in Congress—were defeated.

The first Congress did not set a deadline for ratification of its amendments. Nor did Congress do so until 1917, when it required ratification of the prohibition amendment within seven years. When that requirement was challenged in *Dillion v. Gloss,* 256 U.S. 368 (1921), the Court held that "ratification must be within some reasonable time after [an amendment's] proposal" and Congress's power to set a deadline was "an incident of its power to designate the mode of ratification." Subsequently, the question of whether the proposed child labor amendment could be ratified thirteen years after its proposal arose in *Coleman v. Miller,* 307 U.S. 433 (1939). In that case, the Court ruled that that was a political question for Congress, not the judiciary, to decide.

States ratifying the amendment:

1789	Maryland	1986	New Mexico		Minnesota
	North Carolina		Indiana		Texas
1790	South Carolina		Utah	1990	Kansas
	Delaware	1987	Arkansas		Florida
1791	Vermont		Montana	1991	North Dakota
	Virginia		Connecticut	1992	Missouri
1873	Ohio		Wisconsin		Alabama
1978	Wyoming	1988	Georgia		Illinois
1983	Maine		West Virginia		Michigan
1984	Colorado		Louisiana		New Jersey
1985	South Dakota	1989	Iowa		
	New Hampshire		Idaho		
	Arizona		Nevada		
	Tennessee		Alaska		
	Oklahoma		Oregon		

7

THE STATES AND AMERICAN FEDERALISM

A. STATES' POWER OVER COMMERCE AND REGULATION

As usual, the Court handed down a number of rulings involving state regulations and laws that allegedly conflict with federal law or Congress's power to regulate interstate commerce. The major rulings of the Court are summarized in "The Development of Law" sections here.

One of the most important cases involved two Missouri state judges who attacked the constitutionality of the state's seventy-year-old mandatory retirement for judges and other public officials. They contended that Missouri's retirement law violated the Fourteenth Amendment equal protection clause and the federal Age Discrimination in Employment Act (ADEA) of 1967. But attorneys for the state defended the retirement law on federalist grounds.

Writing for the Court in *Gregory v. Ashcroft*, 111 S.Ct. 2395 (1991), Justice O'Connor upheld Missouri's mandatory retirement law as applied to state judges on recognizing the "dual sovereignty" of the national and state governments. In her words,

> As every schoolchild learns, our Constitution establishes a system of dual sovereignty between the States and the Federal Government. This Court also has recognized this fundamental principle [in *Texas v. White*, 7 Wall. 700, 725 (1869), and *Lane County v. Oregon*, 7 Wall. 71, 76 (1869)]. . . . The Constitution created a Federal Government of limited powers. "The powers not delegated to the United States by the Constitution, nor prohibited by it to the States, are reserved to the States respectively, or to the people." U.S. Const., Amdt. 10. The States thus retain substantial sovereign authority under our constitutional system.

Upon that constitutional analysis, Justice O'Connor reasoned that when important principles of federalism are at stake, Congress must make a "plain statement" of whether in exercising its powers under the commerce clause it "intends to pre-empt the historic powers of the States." "This plain statement rule," according to O'Connor, "is nothing more than an acknowledgement that the States retain substantial sovereign powers under our constitutional scheme, powers with which Congress does not readily interfere." O'Connor also noted with regard to Congress's powers under Section 5 of the Fourteenth Amendment, and the Court's application of the Fourteenth Amendment equal protection clause, that prior cases had upheld state regulations—pertaining to the denial of public employment to aliens (see Vol. 2, Ch. 12)—on a "political function" exception theory. On that basis, the Court had held that states may exclude individuals from positions "intimately related to the process of democratic self-government." "These cases," O'Connor claimed, also "stand in recognition of the authority of the people of the States to determine the qualifications of their most important government officials. . . . It is a power reserved to the States under the Tenth Amendment and guaranteed them by that provision of the Constitution under which the United States 'guarantee[s] to every State in this Union a Republican Form of Government.' U.S. Const., Art. IV, Sec. 4."

Conceding that the Court was "constrained in our ability to consider the limits that the state-federal balance places on Congress' powers under the Commerce Clause,[1] O'Connor nonetheless emphasized that "the plain statement rule" would permit the Court to strike down the application of federal requirement to the states, and uphold state regulations, unless Congress expressly stated that it intended to preempt the states. As she put it, "[I]nasmuch as this Court in *Garcia* has left primarily to the political process the protection of the States against intrusive exercises of Congress' Commerce Clause powers, we must be absolutely certain that Congress intended such an exercise."

Turning to the statutory question of whether the ADEA applies to state judges, O'Connor noted that Congress amended the act in 1974 to "exclude all elected and most high-ranking government officials," and that Missouri claimed that state judges fell under this exception for a number of reasons, including the facts that they are appointed by the governor and are subject to retention elections and because "they make policy" and "on the policymaking level" of state government. But O'-Connor observed that the statutory language of excluding an "appointee at the policymaking level," particularly in the context of the other exceptions that surround it, is an odd way for Congress to exclude judges; "a plain statement that judges are not 'employees' would seem the most efficient phrasing. . . . In the context of a statute that plainly excludes most important state public officials, 'appointee on the policymaking

---

[1] See *Garcia v. San Antonio Metropolitan Trust Authority*, 469 U.S. 528 (1985) in Vol. 1, Ch. 7.

level' is sufficiently broad that we cannot conclude that the statute plainly covers appointed state judges. Therefore," O'Connor concluded, "it does not" apply to state judges.

In a separate opinion, in part concurring and dissenting and in which Justice Stevens joined, Justice White agreed that "neither the ADEA nor the Equal Protection Clause prohibits Missouri's mandatory retirement provision as applied" there. Justices White and Stevens had no problems with the majority's statutory analysis, but took strong exception to its broad application of the plain statement rule in determining whether Congress has preempted state laws and regulations. As Justice White explained,

The majority's plain statement rule is not only unprecedented, it directly contravenes our decisions in *Garcia v. San Antonio Metropolitan Transit Authority,* 469 U.S. 528 (1985), and *South Carolina v. Baker,* 485 U.S. 505 (1988). In those cases we made it clear "that States must find their protection from congressional regulation through the national political process, not through judicially defined spheres of unregulable state activity." We also rejected as "unsound in principle and unworkable in practice" any test for state immunity that requires a judicial determination of which state activities are "traditional," "integral," or "necessary." The majority disregards those decisions in its attempt to carve out areas of state activity that will receive special protection from federal legislation.

The majority's approach is also unsound because it will serve only to confuse the law. First, the majority fails to explain the scope of its rule. Is the rule limited to federal regulation of the qualifications of state officials? Or does it apply more broadly to the regulation of any "state governmental functions"? Second, the majority does not explain its requirement that Congress' intent to regulate a particular state activity be "plain to anyone reading [the federal statute]." Does that mean that it is now improper to look to the purpose or history of a federal statute in determining the scope of the statute's limitations on state activities? If so, the majority's rule is completely inconsistent with our pre-emption jurisprudence. See, e.g., *Hillsborough County v. Automated Medical Laboratories, Inc.,* 471 U.S. 707, 715 (1985) (pre-emption will be found where there is a "clear and manifest purpose" to displace state law). The vagueness of the majority's rule undoubtedly will lead States to assert that various federal statutes no longer apply to a wide variety of State activities if Congress has not expressly referred to those activities in the statute. Congress, in turn, will be forced to draft long and detailed lists of which particular state functions it meant to regulate.

My disagreement with the majority does not end with its unwarranted announcement of the plain statement rule. Even more disturbing is its treatment of Congress' power under Sec. 5 of the Fourteenth Amendment. Section 5 provides that "[t]he Congress shall have power to enforce, by appropriate legislation, the provisions of this article." Despite that sweeping constitutional delegation of authority to Congress, the majority holds that its plain statement rule will apply with full force to legislation enacted to enforce the Fourteenth Amendment.

Dissenting Justices Blackmun and Marshall agreed with Justice White's criticisms of the majority's invitation for courts to limit the application of federal laws to the states where Congress has not expressly preempted the states, but parted company on whether state judges were statutorily excluded from the ADEA's ban against age discrimination. In their view, state judges should not be excluded from Congress's barring age-discrimination in employment.

In its 1993 term the Court will take up an interstate commerce challenge that is the mirror image of recent cases involving state restrictions on the importation and disposal of garbage and waste (see "The Development of Law" boxes in this section). *C&A Carbone Inc. v. Clarkstown* (No. 92–1402) involves a challenge to a New York ordinance requiring the disposal of trash at designated local facilities and prohibiting companies from exporting trash to other states.

THE DEVELOPMENT OF LAW

Rulings on State Regulations of Commerce in the Absence of Federal Legislation

Case	Ruling
Trinova Corporation v. Michigan Department of Treasury 111 S.Ct. 818 (1991)	Upheld Michigan's "single business tax," a value added tax (VAT), levied against a multistate business. With Justice Souter not partipating, Justice Kennedy held for the majority that Michigan's tax did not discriminate against out-of-state businesses or run afoul of either the commerce clause or the due

process clause. State taxes, when challenged by multistate businesses for violating the commerce clause, are permissible, observed Justice Kennedy, so long as they meet a four-pronged test: "the tax is applied to an activity with a substantial nexus with the taxing State, is fairly apportioned, does not discriminate against interstate commerce, and is fairly related to the services provided by the State."[a] Under this test, state tax schemes also satisfy the due process requirement that (1) there be a "minimum connection" between the taxes and interstate business activities and (2) there is "a rational relationship between the income attributed to the State and the interstate values of the enterprise." Justice Scalia concurred, while Justice Stevens, joined by Justice Blackmun, dissented on the grounds that due process principles were violated by the state's value added taxes.

Wyoming v. Oklahoma 112 S.Ct. 789 (1992)	To promote local jobs and to increase tax revenues, in 1986 Oklahoma enacted a law requiring its public utilities to purchase a certain percentage of Oklahoma-mined coal. As a result, its public utilities

purchased less Wyoming-mined coal, and Wyoming lost revenues that it would have received from severance taxes on coal that would have otherwise

THE DEVELOPMENT OF LAW *(Continued)*

Case	Ruling

been sold to Oklahoma's public utilities. Writing for the Court, Justice White struck down Oklahoma's statute as violating the commerce clause, which "prohibits economic protectionism—that is, regulatory measures designed to benefit in-state economic interests by burdening out-of-state competitors." In a dissenting opinion, Justice Scalia, joined by Chief Justice Rehnquist and Justice Thomas, argued that Wyoming did not have standing to bring the suit and objected to the majority's finding that the state's loss of revenue was within the "zone of interests" covered by the commerce clause. Justice Thomas wrote a dissenting opinion as well.

Chemical Waste
Management v. Hunt
112 S.Ct. 2009
(1992)

States may not impose a fee on hazardous waste generated in another state and dumped at a commercial facility in its jurisdiction, while not imposing the same fee on waste generated and dumped within its borders. The Alabama State Supreme Court held that, although the fee posed a burden on interstate commerce, the fee was permissible because it aimed at protecting health and safety and not economic protectionism for in-state businesses. But by an eight-to-one vote the Court reversed on the basis of its prior ruling in *Philadelphia v. New Jersey,* 437 U.S. 617 (1978), that state prohibitions of solid waste imported from other states amount to economic protectionism in violation of the commerce clause. In Justice White's words for the majority, "No State may attempt to isolate itself from a problem common to the several States by raising barriers to the free flow of interstate trade." Chief Justice Rehnquist dissented.

Fort Gratiot Sanitary
Landfill v. Michigan
Department of Natural
Resources
112 S.Ct. 2019
(1992)

Held that a county's refusal, authorized by state law, to allow the disposal within the county of any solid waste generated outside the county unconstitutionally discriminates against interstate commerce. A federal appellate court had upheld the law on the grounds that the county's policy treated both out-of-county and out-of-state solid waste equally. But by a seven-to-one vote the Court struck down Michigan's waste import restrictions as protectionist and discriminatory in violation of the interstate commerce clause. Chief Justice Rehnquist and Justice Blackmun dissented.

Quill Corporation v.
North Dakota
112 S.Ct. 1904
(1992)

Quill Corporation, an office supply company, challenged a state law that required companies located in other states to collect a state sales tax on mail order sales as a violation of the due process clause and Congress's power to regulate interstate

THE DEVELOPMENT OF LAW *(Continued)*

Case	Ruling

commerce. Writing for the majority, Justice Stevens overturned in part a ruling in *National Bellas Hess v. Department of Revenue of Illinois,* 386 U.S. 753 (1967), that had upheld a due process challenge to such state sales taxes. Although now reversing that holding, Stevens reaffirmed *National Bellas Hess's* ruling that such taxes pose an undue burden on interstate commerce in the absence of congressional legislation. He underscored, however, that Congress could authorize states to levy such taxes, observing that "Congress is now free to decide whether, when, and to what extent the states may burden interstate mail order concerns with a duty to collect use taxes." The sole dissenter, Justice White, argued that even in the absence of congressional legislation, states should have the power to collect such taxes and *National Bellas Hess* should be given "the complete burial it justly deserves."

Case	Ruling
Kraft General Foods v. Iowa Dept. of Revenue 112 S.Ct. 2365 (1992)	Struck down Iowa's provision disallowing tax credits for business taxes paid to foreign countries. Writing for the Court, Justice Stevens held that that provision discriminates against foreign commerce in violation of the commerce clause. Chief Justice Rehnquist and

Justice Blackmun dissented.

Case	Ruling
Itel Containers International Corporation v. Huddleston 113 S.Ct. 1095 (1993)	Writing for the Court, Justice Kennedy upheld a state tax on international transport containers and rejected a commerce clause challenge upon concluding that Congress had not intended to preempt such taxation in approving an international Container Convention. Justice Scalia concurred but reiterated his objections to dormant or negative

commerce clause jurisprudence. Only Justice Blackmun dissented.

[a]*Complete Auto Transit, Inc. v. Brady,* 430 U.S. 274 (1977).

Rulings on State Regulatory Powers in Alleged Conflict with Federal Legislation

Case	Ruling
Gregory v. Ashcroft 111 S.Ct. 2395 (1991)	Upheld Missouri's law requiring mandatory retirement of state judges at the age of seventy over objections that the law violated the Fourteenth Amendment equal protection clause and the federal

Age Discrimination in Employment Act. Justices White and Stevens concurred and dissented in part; Justices Blackmun and Marshall dissented.

Wisconsin Public *Intervenor v. Mortier* 111 S.Ct. 2476 (1991)	The Court held that local and state governments may regulate pesticide uses because such regulations were not preempted by the federal Fungicide and Rodenticide Act of 1972.

Dennis v. Higgins 111 S.Ct. 865 (1991)	The Court held that government officials could be held liable under Section 1983 of the U.S. Code when they are found to have violated the commerce clause. Writing for the majority, Justice White

construed the commerce clause to confer "rights, privileges, or immunities" within the meaning of Section 1983. Justice Kennedy, joined by Chief Justice Rehnquist, dissented from the Court's expansive reading of the commerce clause, pointing out that the majority's ruling would increase "the burden that a state or local government will face in defending its economic regulation and taxation."

Ingersoll-Rand v. *McClendon* 111 S.Ct. 478 (1991)	The Rehnquist Court unanimously held that employees who claim they were fired so their employers would not have to pay pension benefits may not bring suits in state courts for punitive damages. Writing for the Court, Justice O'Connor

held that the Employee Retirement Income Security Act of 1974 preempts such action in state courts by barring such firing and providing for reinstatement of employees and payment of lost wages and benefits.

County of Yakima v. *Confederated Tribes and* *Bands of the Yakima* *Indian Nation* 112 S.Ct. 683 (1992)	Held that the Indiana General Allotment Act of 1887 permits states and localities to impose *ad valorem* taxes on land owned by Native Americans but does not allow excise taxes on the sale of Indian lands.

Case	Ruling
Gade v. National Solid Wastes Management Association 112 S.Ct. 2374 (1992)	The Court affirmed a federal appellate court decision that struck Illinois's licensing and training requirements for workers in hazardous waste sites on the grounds that the Occupational Safety and Health Act (OSHA) preempted states from adopting standards stricter than mandated by OSHA, even

though the state asserted its requirements were adopted for environmental, and not occupational, reasons. Justices Souter, Blackmun, Stevens, and Thomas dissented.

Morales v. Trans World Airlines 112 S.Ct. 2031 (1992)	Held that states ban deceptive advertising by airplane companies. A federal appellate court held that state regulations of how airlines advertise their fares were preempted by the Federal Aviation Act, which gives the federal government sole regulatory

authority over airline "rates, routes, or services." With Justice Souter not participating, a bare majority affirmed the lower court's decision that states were preempted by federal law from regulating airlines' advertising. In a dissenting opinion joined by Chief Justice Rehnquist and Justice Blackmun, Justice Stevens took exception to the majority's interpretation of Congress's intent and language in the Airline Deregulation Act of 1978.

Arkansas v. Oklahoma and Environmental Protection Agency v. Oklahoma 112 S.Ct. 1046 (1992)	Upheld the Environmental Protection Agency's (EPA) action permitting discharges from a new disposal site in Arkansas, located thirty-eight miles above the Oklahoma state line, over the objections that the discharges would violate Oklahoma's environmental standards, and ruled that the EPA's regulatory decisions under the Clean Water Act

preempt state common law and the federal common law of nuisance.

Cipollone v. Liggett Group, Inc., 112 S.Ct. 2608 (1992)	Held that the Federal Cigarette Labeling and Advertising Act of 1965, as amended by the Public Health Cigarette Smoking Act of 1969, preempts some lawsuits but not those based on breach of warranty, intentionally fraudulent misrepresentation,

and concealment of health risks as well as conspiracy to misrepresent the health consequences of smoking. Justices Scalia and Thomas, dissenting in part, would have held that all suits were preempted.

THE DEVELOPMENT OF LAW *(Continued)*

Case	Ruling
The District of Columbia v. The Greater Washington Board of Trade 113 S.Ct. 580 (1992)	Held that the Employee Retirement Income Security Act (ERISA) does not preempt a District of Columbia statute requiring employers who provide health-insurance coverage to continue to provide coverage to employees who are receiving workers' compensation.
CSX Transportation v. Easterwood 113 S.Ct. 1732 (1993)	Held that the Federal Railroad Saftey Act of 1970 preempts a wrongful-death suit against a railroad for the death of a truck driver who collided with a train, allegedly due to inadequate warnings at a crossing and the train's excessive speed. Justice Thomas and Souter dissented and concurred in part.

B. THE TENTH AMENDMENT AND THE STATES

The Rehnquist Court moved in decidedly more conservative directions during its 1990–1991 terms and renewed its deference to the states and the Tenth Amendment with rulings handed down in *Gregory v. Ashcroft*, 111 S.Ct. 2395 (1991) (see page 54), for example, and *Coleman v. Thompson*, 111 S.Ct. 2546 (1991) (see page 70). In his last opinion, dissenting in *Payne v. Tennessee*, 111 S.Ct. 2597 (1991) (see page 226), Justice Marshall warned that the Court was posed to overturn *Garcia v. San Antonio Metropolitan Transit Authority*, 469 U.S. 528 (1985) (see Vol. 1, Ch. 7). In *Garcia* a bare majority of the Court rejected the theory that the Tenth Amendment provides immunity to states from some kinds of federal regulation and overturned an earlier decision that held contrawise and was authored by Justice Rehnquist, in *National League of Cities v. Usery*, 426 U.S. 833 (1976) (see Vol. 1, Ch. 7).

In its 1991 term, *New York v. United States*, 112 S.Ct. 2408 (1992), invited the Rehnquist Court to reconsider *Garcia's* holding that the national political process, not the federal courts under the Tenth Amendment as *Usery* held, should protect states' interests against overbearing congressional legislation. Writing for the majority in *New York v. United States* (see page 63), Justice O'Connor nevertheless declined to overrule *Garcia* and tried to put that controversy aside. O'Connor did offer a strong defense of "state sovereignty" in striking down one section of Congress's 1985 statute that required states that failed to comply with their obligation to provide disposal sites for radioactive waste by 1996 to take title of and assume liability for all undisposed waste. However dissenting Justices White, Blackmun, and Stevens took strong exception to her analysis and conclusion.

New York v. United States
112 S.Ct. 2408 (1992)

In the late 1970s, federal policymakers began confronting the prospect that the country would soon run out of disposal sites for low-level radioactive waste. Federal authorities began targeting three states—Nevada, South Carolina, and Washington—as possible disposal sites but encountered widespread criticism from those and other states. Finally, based largely on recommendations made by the National Governors' Association, Congress enacted the Low-Level Radioactive Waste Policy Act of 1980, which established a federal policy of holding each state "responsible for providing for the availability of capacity either within or outside the State for the disposal of low-level radioactive waste generated within its borders," upon finding that such waste could be disposed of "most safely and efficiently . . . on a regional basis." The act authorized the states to enter into regional compacts that, after ratification by Congress, would have authority in 1986 to restrict the use of disposal facilities to waste generated by states within each region.

By 1985, however, only three regional compacts had been formed, all around the three targeted states. As a result, the following year the authorities for three regional compacts would have the authority to exclude the disposal of radioactive waste generated in states not belonging to one of the compacts, and thirty-one states would thus be left with no ensured site for the disposal of their radioactive wastes. Congress therefore amended its earlier legislation with the Low-Level Radioactive Waste Policy Amendments Act of 1985.

The 1985 act, which was also based on proposals submitted by the National Governors' Association, achieved a kind of political compromise between the targeted and untargeted states. The targeted states agreed to continue, for seven years, to dispose of radioactive waste generated in other states, while the nontargeted states agreed to provide disposal sites for their own waste by 1992. The law also provides three kinds of incentives for states to comply with their obligation to dispose of waste generated within their own borders by 1992. (1) Monetary incentives: States or compacts disposing of all radioactive waste generated within their borders by January 1, 1993, may receive special funding from surcharges collected by the targeted states and held in escrow by the Department of Energy. (2) Access incentives: States or compacts that failed to meet specified deadlines for disposing of their waste would be charged double surcharges and be denied access to disposal sites in targeted states thereafter, and those states failing to operate disposal facilities by January 1, 1992, could be charged triple surcharges. (3) A "take-title provision" provides that states or compacts that failed to provide disposal sites for all wastes generated within the state or compact by January 1, 1996, would be obligated to take title of all undisposed waste and assume liability for all damages incurred by the waste's generator, which could not dispose of it because of the state's or compact's failure to provide a disposal site.

New York, which generates a large share of the nation's low-level radioactive waste, complied with the 1985 laws requirements for siting and financing of disposal facilities by selecting five potential disposal sites. But residents in two of the counties selected as disposal sites filed suit and were later joined by New York State authorities. They argued that the 1985 amendments were unconstitutional and intruded on states' rights as guaranteed by the Tenth Amendment. The Court of Appeals for the Second Circuit, however, rejected that argument and New York appealed to the Supreme Court.

The Court's decision was six to three; the majority's opinion was announced by Justice O'Connor. Justices White and Stevens delivered separate opinions, in part concurring and in part dissenting, in which Justice Blackmun joined.

Justice O'CONNOR delivers the opinion of the Court.

[T]he Tenth Amendment "states but a truism that all is retained which has not been surrendered." *United States v. Darby*, 312 U.S. 100 (1941). . . . This has been the Court's consistent understanding: "The States unquestionably do retain a significant measure of sovereign authority . . . to the extent that the Constitution has not divested them of their original powers and transferred those powers to the Federal Government." *Garcia v. San Antonio Metropolitan Transit Authority*, [469 U.S. 528 (1985)].

Congress exercises its conferred powers subject to the limitations contained in the Constitution. Thus, for example, under the Commerce Clause Congress may regulate publishers engaged in interstate commerce, but Congress is constrained in the exercise of that power by the First Amendment. The Tenth Amendment likewise restrains the power of Congress, but this limit is not derived from the text of the Tenth Amendment itself, which, as we have discussed, is essentially a tautology. Instead, the Tenth Amendment confirms that the power of the Federal Government is subject to limits that may, in a given instance, reserve power to the States. The Tenth Amendment thus directs us to determine, as in this case, whether an incident of state sovereignty is protected by a limitation on an Article I power. . . .

[The federal] framework has been sufficiently flexible over the past two centuries to allow for enormous changes in the nature of government. The Federal Government undertakes activities today that would have been unimaginable to the Framers in two senses; first, because the Framers would not have conceived that any government would conduct such activities; and second, because the Framers would not have believed that the Federal Government, rather than the States, would assume such responsibilities. Yet the powers conferred upon the Federal Government by the Constitution were phrased in language broad enough to allow for the expansion of the Federal Government's role. Among the provisions of the Constitution that have been particularly important in this regard, three concern us here.

First, the Constitution allocates to Congress the power "to regulate Commerce . . . among the several States." Art. I, Sec. i, cl. . . . Second, the Constitution authorizes Congress "to pay the Debts and provide for the . . . general Welfare of the United States." Art. I, Sec. 8, cl. . . . The Court's broad construction of Congress' power under the Commerce and Spending Clauses has of course been guided, as it has with respect to Congress' power generally, by the Constitution's Necessary and Proper Clause, which authorizes Congress "to make all Laws which shall be necessary and proper for carrying into Execution the foregoing Powers." U.S. Const., Art. I., Sec. 8, cl. 18.

Finally, the Constitution provides that "the Laws of the United States . . . shall be the supreme Law of the Land . . . any Thing in the Constitution or Laws of any State to the Contrary notwithstanding." U.S. Const., Art. VI, cl. 2. . . .

The actual scope of the Federal Government's authority with respect to the States has changed over the years, therefore, but the constitutional structure underlying and limiting that authority has not. In the end, just as a cup may be half empty or half full, it makes no difference whether one views the question at issue in this case as one of ascertaining the limits of the power delegated to the Federal Government under the affirmative provisions of the Constitution or one of discerning the core of sovereignty retained by the States under the Tenth Amendment. Either way, we must determine whether any of the three challenged provisions of the Low-Level Radioactive Waste Policy Amendments Act of 1985 oversteps the boundary between federal and state authority. . . .

Most of our recent cases interpreting the Tenth Amendment have concerned the authority of Congress to subject state governments to generally applicable laws. The Court's jurisprudence in this area has traveled an unsteady path. See *Maryland v. Wirtz*, 392 U.S. 183 (1968) (state schools and hospitals are subject to Fair Labor Standards Act); *National League of Cities v. Usery*, 426 U.S. 833 (1976) (overruling *Wirtz*) (state employers are not subject to Fair Labor Standards Act); *Garcia v. San Antonio Metropolitan Transit Authority*, 469 U.S. 528 (1985) (overruling *National League of Cities*) (state employers are once again subject to Fair Labor Standards Act). This case presents no occasion to apply or revisit the holdings of any of these cases, as this is not a case in which Congress has subjected a State to the same legislation applicable to private parties. Cf. *FERC v. Mississippi*, 456 U.S. 742 (1982).

This case instead concerns the circumstances under which Congress may use the States as implements of regulation; that is, whether Congress may direct or otherwise motivate the States to regulate in a particular field or a particular way. Our cases have established a few principles that guide our resolution of the issue.

As an initial matter, Congress may not simply "commandeer the legislative processes of the States by directly compelling them to enact and enforce a federal regulatory program." *Hodel v. Virginia Surface Mining & Reclamation Assn., Inc.*, 452 U.S. 264 (1981). . . .

While Congress has substantial powers to govern the Nation directly, including in areas of intimate concern to the States, the Constitution has never been understood to confer upon Congress the ability to require the States to govern according to Congress' instructions. . . .

This is not to say that Congress lacks the ability to encourage a State to regulate in a particular way, or that Congress may not hold out incentives to the States as a method of influencing a State's policy choices. Our cases have identified a variety of methods, short of outright coercion, by which Congress may urge a State to adopt a legislative program consistent with federal interests. Two of these methods are of particular relevance here.

First, under Congress' spending power, "Congress may attach conditions on the receipt of federal funds." *South Dakota v. Dole*, 483 U. S. [203 (1987)]. . . .

Second, where Congress has the authority to regulate private activity under the Commerce Clause, we have recognized Congress' power to offer States the choice of regulating that activity according to federal standards or having state law pre-empted by federal regulation. . . .

By contrast, where the Federal Government compels States to regulate, the accountability of both state and federal officials is diminished. If the citizens of New York, for example, do not consider that making provision for the disposal of radioactive waste is in their best interest, they may elect state officials who share their view. That view can always be pre-empted under the Supremacy Clause if it is contrary to the national view, but in such a case it is the Federal Government that makes the decision in full view of the public, and it will be federal officials that suffer the consequences if the decision turns out to be detrimental or unpopular. But where the Federal Government directs the States to regulate, it may be state officials who will bear the brunt of public disapproval, while the federal officials who devised the regulatory program may remain insulated from the electoral ramifications of their decision. Accountability is thus diminished when, due to federal coercion, elected state officials cannot regulate in accordance with the views of the local electorate in matters not pre-empted by federal regulation.

With these principles in mind, we turn to the three challenged provisions of the Low-Level Radioactive Waste Policy Amendments Act of 1985.

The first set of incentives works in three steps. First, Congress has authorized States with disposal sites to impose a surcharge on radioactive waste received from other States. Second, the Secretary of Energy collects a portion of this surcharge and places the money in an escrow account. Third, States achieving a series of milestones receive portions of this fund.

The first of these steps is an unexceptionable exercise of Congress' power to authorize the States to burden interstate commerce. . . .

The second step, the Secretary's collection of a percentage of the surcharge, is no more than a federal tax on interstate commerce, which petitioners do not claim to be an invalid exercise of either Congress' commerce or taxing power.

The third step is a conditional exercise of Congress' authority under the Spending Clause: Congress has placed conditions—the achievement of the milestones—on the receipt of federal funds. . . .

. . .

. . . This third so-called "incentive" offers States, as an alternative to regulating pursuant to Congress' direction, the option of taking title to and possession of the low level radioactive waste generated within their borders and becoming liable for all damages waste generators suffer as a result of the States' failure to do so promptly. In this provision, Congress has crossed the line distinguishing encouragement from coercion. . . .

The take title provision offers state governments a "choice" of either accepting ownership of waste or regulating according to the instructions of Congress. . . . Because an instruction to state governments to take title to waste, standing alone, would be beyond the authority of Congress, and because a direct order to regulate, standing alone, would also be beyond the authority of Congress, it follows that Congress lacks the power to offer the States a choice between the two. Unlike the first two sets of incentives, the take title incentive does not represent the conditional exercise of any congressional power enumerated in the Constitution. In this provision, Congress has not held out the threat of exercising its spending power or its commerce power; it has instead held out the threat, should the States not regulate according to one federal instruction, of simply forcing the States to submit to another federal instruction. A choice between two unconstitutionally coercive regulatory techniques is no choice at all. Either way, "the Act commandeers the legislative processes of the States by directly compelling them to enact and enforce a federal regulatory program," *Hodel v. Virginia Surface Mining & Reclamation Assn., Inc.*, an outcome that has never been understood to lie within the authority conferred upon Congress by the Constitution. . . .

The take title provision appears to be unique. No other federal statute has been cited which offers a state government no option other than that of implementing legislation enacted by Congress. Whether one views the take title provision as lying outside Congress' enumerated powers, or as infringing upon the core of state sovereignty reserved by the Tenth Amendment, the provision is inconsistent with the federal structure of our Government established by the Constitution. . . .

. . . The Constitution permits both the Federal Government and the States to enact legislation regarding the disposal of low level radioactive waste. The Constitution enables the Federal Government to pre-empt state regulation contrary to federal interests, and it permits the Federal Government to hold out incentives to the States as a means of encouraging them to adopt suggested regulatory schemes. It does not, however, authorize Congress simply to direct the States to provide for the disposal of the radioactive waste generated within their borders. While there may be many constitutional methods of achieving regional self-sufficiency in radioactive waste disposal, the method Congress has chosen is not one of them. The judgment of the Court of Appeals is accordingly

Affirmed in part and reversed in part.

Justice WHITE, with whom Justices BLACKMUN and STEVENS join, concurring and dissenting in part.

. . .

My disagreement with the Court's analysis begins at the basic descriptive level of how the legislation at issue in this case came to be enacted. . . . To read the Court's version of events, one would think that Congress was the sole proponent of a solution to the Nation's low-level radioactive waste problem. Not so. The Low-Level Radioactive Waste Policy Act of 1980 (1980 Act), and its amendatory Act of 1985, resulted from the efforts of state leaders to achieve a state-based set of remedies to the waste problem. They sought not federal pre-emption or intervention, but rather congressional sanction of interstate compromises they had reached. . . .

In my view, New York's actions subsequent to enactment of the 1980 and 1985 Acts fairly indicate its approval of the interstate agreement process embodied in those laws within the meaning of Art. I, Sec. 10, cl. 3, of the Constitution, which provides that "no State shall, without the Consent of Congress, . . . enter into any Agreement or Compact with another State." First, the States—including New York—worked through their Governors to petition Congress for the 1980 and 1985 Acts. As I have attempted to demonstrate, these statutes are best understood as the products of collective state action, rather than as impositions placed on States by the Federal Government. Second, New York acted in compliance with the requisites of both statutes in key respects, thus signifying its assent to the agreement achieved among the States as codified in these laws. . . .

The Court announces that it has no occasion to revisit such decisions as *Gregory v. Ashcroft*, [111 S.Ct. 2395] (1991); *South Carolina v. Baker*, 485 U.S. 505 (1988); *Garcia v. San Antonio Metropolitan Transit Authority*, 469 U.S. 528 (1985); *EEOC v. Wyoming*, 460 U.S. 226 (1983); and *National League of*

Cities v. Usery, 426 U.S. 833 (1976), because "this is not a case in which Congress has subjected a State to the same legislation applicable to private parties." Although this statement sends the welcome signal that the Court does not intend to cut a wide swath through our recent Tenth Amendment precedents, it nevertheless is unpersuasive. I have several difficulties with the Court's analysis in this respect: it builds its rule around an insupportable and illogical distinction in the types of alleged incursions on state sovereignty; it derives its rule from cases that do not support its analysis; it fails to apply the appropriate tests from the cases on which it purports to base its rule; and it omits any discussion of the most recent and pertinent test for determining the take title provision's constitutionality.

The Court's distinction between a federal statute's regulation of States and private parties for general purposes, as opposed to a regulation solely on the activities of States, is unsupported by our recent Tenth Amendment cases. In no case has the Court rested its holding on such a distinction. Moreover, the Court makes no effort to explain why this purported distinction should affect the analysis of Congress' power under general principles of federalism and the Tenth Amendment. The distinction, facilely thrown out, is not based on any defensible theory. Certainly one would be hard-pressed to read the spirited exchanges between the Court and dissenting Justices in *National League of Cities,* and in *Garcia v. San Antonio Metropolitan Transit Authority,* as having been based on the distinction now drawn by the Court. An incursion on state sovereignty hardly seems more constitutionally acceptable if the federal statute that "commands" specific action also applies to private parties. The alleged diminution in state authority over its own affairs is not any less because the federal mandate restricts the activities of private parties. . . .

Though I disagree with the Court's conclusion that the take title provision is unconstitutional, I do not read its opinion to preclude Congress from adopting a similar measure through its powers under the Spending or Commerce Clauses. . . . Congress could, in other words, condition the payment of funds on the State's willingness to take title if it has not already provided a waste disposal facility. . . .

Similarly, should a State fail to establish a waste disposal facility by the appointed deadline (under the statute as presently drafted, January 1, 1996, Congress has the power pursuant to the Commerce Clause to regulate directly the producers of the waste. . . .

Finally, our precedents leave open the possibility that Congress may create federal rights of action in the generators of low-level radioactive waste against persons acting under color of state law for their failure to meet certain functions designated in federal-state programs.

Justice STEVENS concurred in part and dissented in part.

C. JUDICIAL FEDERALISM

In important and wide-ranging rulings the Rehnquist Court sharply cut back the opportunities for inmates in state prisons to pursue *habeas corpus* appeals in federal courts.[1] In the process the Court overturned *Fay v. Noia,* 372 U.S. 391 (1963), which had held that federal courts could consider the petitions of prison inmates who had failed to properly appeal their cases in state courts, so long as they had not "deliberately bypassed" the appellate system in state courts. Writing for the Court in *Coleman v. Thompson,* 111 S.Ct. 2546 (1991), however, Justice O'Connor took exactly the opposite view in laying down a new rule under which almost any failure by a prison convict to satisfy a state's appellate procedures will result in his or her forfeiting the right to file a *habeas corpus* petition in federal courts. Robert Coleman, a death-row inmate, had appealed his state *habeas corpus* petition to the Virginia Supreme Court, which dismissed it because his attorney filed it three days after the state's thirty-day time limit for filing such petitions. O'Connor held that that constituted a "procedural default" that barred any further federal court review of Coleman's appeals of his conviction. Justice O'Connor observed that

[t]his is a case about federalism. It concerns the respect that federal courts owe the States and the States' procedural rules when reviewing the claims of state prisoners in federal *habeas corpus.*

This Court will not review a question of federal law decided by a state court if the decision of that court rests on a state law ground that is independent of the federal question and adequate to support the judgment. . . .

In the *habeas* context, the application of the independent and adequate state ground doctrine is grounded in concerns of comity and federalism. Without the rule, a federal district court would be able to do in *habeas* what this Court could not do on direct review; *habeas* would offer state prisoners whose custody was supported by independent and adequate state grounds an end run around the limits of this Court's jurisdiction and a means to undermine the State's interest in enforcing its laws. . . .

In *Michigan v. Long,* 463 U.S. 1032 (1983) . . . [the Court ruled that] a state court that wishes to look to federal law for guidance or as an alternative holding while still relying on an independent and adequate state ground can avoid the presumption by stating "clearly and expressly that [its decision] is . . . based on bona fide separate, adequate, and independent grounds." . . . *Long* [involved the direct review of a state supreme court decision. By contrast] the problem of ambiguous

---

[1]In *Ylst v. Nunnemaker,* 111 S.Ct. 2590 (1991), for example, the Court reaffirmed its new rule, announced in *Coleman v. Thompson,* 111 S.Ct. 2546 (1991), when holding that a state court's unexplained denial of a writ of *habeas corpus* petition is not sufficient, for the purposes of federal review, to lift a procedural bar imposed on direct appeal to federal courts of a state prisoner's conviction. See also *Kenney v. Tampayo-Reyes,* 112 S.Ct. 1715 (1992), discussed in "The Development of Law: Rulings on Plea Bargaining and Effective Counsel," at page 203.

state court decisions in the application of the independent and adequate state ground doctrine in a federal *habeas* case [was first addressed] in *Harris v. Reed,* 489 U.S. 255 (1989). *Harris,* a state prisoner, filed a petition for state postconviction relief, alleging that his trial counsel had rendered ineffective assistance. The state trial court dismissed the petition, and the Appellate Court of Illinois affirmed. In its order, the Appellate Court referred to the Illinois rule that " 'those [issues] which could have been presented [on direct appeal], but were not, are considered waived.' " In *Harris* [the Court] applied in federal *habeas* the presumption this Court adopted in *Long* for direct review cases. . . . After *Harris,* federal courts on *habeas corpus* review of state prisoner claims, like this Court on direct review of state court judgments, will presume that there is no independent and adequate state ground for a state court decision when the decision "fairly appears to rest primarily on federal law, or to be interwoven with the federal law, and when the adequacy and independence of any possible state law ground is not clear from the face of the opinion." . . .

In all cases in which a state prisoner has defaulted his federal claims in state court pursuant to an independent and adequate state procedural rule, federal *habeas* review of the claims is barred unless the prisoner can demonstrate cause for the default and actual prejudice as a result of the alleged violation of federal law, or demonstrate that failure to consider the claims will result in a fundamental miscarriage of justice. *Fay* [*v. Noia,* 372 U.S. 391 (1963)] was based on a conception of federal/state relations that undervalued the importance of state procedural rules. . . . We now recognize the important interest in finality served by state procedural rules, and the significant harm to the States that results from the failure of federal courts to respect them. Cf. *McCleskey v. Zant* (1991).

In a dissenting opinion, joined by Justices Marshall and Stevens, Justice Blackmun charged that the majority was on a "crusade" to deny state prisoners access to federal court. *Coleman,* observed the justice, "marks the nadir of the Court's recent *habeas* jurisprudence."

In addition, the Rehnquist Court has redrawn the lines of judicial federalism in other ways that further reduce federal courts' supervisory role over both the enforcement of federal legislation and decisions of state courts. Writing for the Court in *Sue Suter v. Artist M.,* 112 S.Ct. 1360 (1992), Chief Justice Rehnquist held that abused and neglected children do not have an implied right to sue in federal courts to enforce provisions of the Adoption Assistance and Child Welfare Act of 1980. That act requires, as a condition of receiving federal funding for children's foster care and adoption services, that states "make reasonable efforts" to prevent child abuse and neglect. A federal appellate court agreed that foster children could sue state officials to force compliance with the statute and to stop lengthy delays in the assignment of case workers. But, when reversing that decision, Rehnquist construed the statute to "not unambiguously confer an enforceable right" on the children and held that it was up to federal agencies, not private citizens or federal courts, to ensure states' compliance with the statute. In his words, "[t]he term 'reasonable efforts' in this context is at least as plausibly read to impose only a rather generalized duty on the state, to be enforced not by private individuals, but by the secretary" of the Department of Health and

Human Services. Dissenting Justices Blackmun and Stevens, however, criticized the majority's "unexplained disregard for established law" and "plainly inconsistent" ruling in light of other past decisions.

In its 1992–1993 term the Court had the opportunity to substantially cut back on federal courts' *habeas corpus* review of claims of *Miranda* and Fifth Amendment violations. In a sweeping opinion in *Stone v. Powell*, 428 U.S. 465 (1976) (Vol. 2, Ch. 7), the Burger Court held that prisoners could no longer file for a writ of *habeas corpus* in federal courts for review of their convictions in state courts that they claimed were based on illegally obtained evidence in violation of the Fourth Amendment's exclusionary rule. And in *Withrow v. Williams*, 113 S.Ct. 1745 (1993) (see page 198), Michigan prosecutors asked the Court to extend that ruling to requests for federal *habeas corpus* review of state prisoners' claims of *Miranda* violations. A bare majority of the Court, however, declined to extend *Stone v. Powell* on the ground that *Stone* dealt with *habeas* review of cases involving violations of the exclusionary rule—a rule which the Court deems not to be "a personal constitutional right," but only a prudential rule aimed at deterring illegal searches and seizures. By contrast, in his opinion for the Court Justice Souter held that *Miranda* protects "a fundamental trial right" that justifies federal *habeas* review. Chief Justice Rehnquist and Justices O'Connor, Scalia, and Thomas dissented.

On the same day *Withrow* came down, though, another bare majority affirmed a more rigorous standard for federal courts setting aside convictions of state prisoners who claim violations of their *Miranda* rights. This time writing for the majority, Chief Justice Rehnquist ruled that when exercising *habeas* review federal courts may set aside convictions only if the errors made at trial in not honoring *Miranda* have a "substantial and injurious effect or influence in determining the jury's verdict." In doing so, the chief justice rejected the less stringent standard of whether the error was "harmless beyond a reasonable doubt." As a result, prisoners must show that they suffered "actual prejudice" due to a state trial court's errors. Here, in *Brecht v. Abrahamson*, 113 S.Ct. 1710 (1993), Justices White, Souter, Blackmun, and O'Connor dissented.

D. STATE COURTS AND STATE CONSTITUTIONAL LAW

State supreme courts continue to assert independent state grounds in recognizing civil rights and liberties that are broader than or unprotected by the U.S. Supreme Court's interpretation of the Bill of Rights and the Fourteenth Amendment. (For further discussion, see Vol. 1, Ch. 7.) In 1992, for instance, the Court of Appeals of Maryland, in *Derricott v. State of Maryland*, 611 A.2d 592 (1992), refused to extend recent Fourth

Amendment rulings on "unreasonable searches and seizures" (see Vol. 2, Ch. 7), when holding that under state law police may not search a car stopped for speeding simply because the driver fits a drug courier's profile. State supreme courts in Pennsylvania and Georgia, in *Commonwealth of Pennsylvania v. Edmunds,* 526 Pa. 374 (1991), and *Gary v. State of Georgia,* 262 Ga. 573 (1992), respectively, ruled that the "good faith" exception to the exclusionary rule is not applicable as a matter of state law, contrary to *United States v. Leon,* 468 U.S. 902 (1984), and *Massachusetts v. Sheppard,* 468 U.S. 981 (1984) (in Vol. 2, Ch. 7). In *Commonwealth of Kentucky v. Wasson,* 842 S.W.2d 487 (1992) (at page 25), Kentucky's supreme court emphatically declined to follow the controversial ruling in *Bowers v. Hardwick,* 478 U.S. 186 (1986) (in Vol. 2, Ch. 11), when striking down its state law banning homosexual sodomy on the basis of state guarantees for privacy and equal protection of the law.

8

REPRESENTATIVE
GOVERNMENT, VOTING
RIGHTS, AND
ELECTORAL POLITICS

B. VOTING RIGHTS AND THE
REAPPORTIONMENT REVOLUTION

In the last three terms, the Rehnquist Court confronted a large number of challenges under the Voting Rights Act of 1965 to systems of electing state judges and to devising voting districts. The Court had not previously confronted the question of whether judicial elections are subject to provisions of the Voting Rights Act or reviewed various systems for electing state judges. Some or all of the judges in forty-one states are elected, and in the late 1980s the judicial election systems in Georgia, Louisiana, and Texas were attacked in the lower federal courts.

The litigation grew out of changes made in 1982 by Congress when amending the Voting Rights Act. Section 2 of the act specifies that "[n]o voting qualification or prerequisite to voting or standard, practice, or procedure shall be imposed or applied by any State or political subdivision in a manner which results in a denial or abridgement of the right of any citizen of the United States to vote on account of race or color." "Vote" and "voting" are further defined in the act to "include all action necessary to make a vote effective in any primary, special, or general election . . . with respect to candidates for public or party office." In 1982, Congress amended the act so as to reverse a ruling of the Supreme Court, in *City of Mobile v. Bolden*, 446 U.S. 55 (1980), that had construed the act to require proof of a "discriminatory intent" for establishing a violation of the Voting Rights Act. Instead of a "discriminatory intent" test, Congress wrote into law a "results test" under which minority voters simply must show that they had less opportunity than other residents in

74

a district to elect representatives and public officials. In addition, the 1982 amendments substituted *representatives* for *legislators* in the act. And that invited the question of whether *representatives* includes elected state judges and provided a basis for challenging state judicial election systems.

Under Section 5 of the Voting Rights Act, southern states and portions of some northern states must obtain approval from the Department of Justice (DOJ) for all post-1964 changes in state election laws. In 1988 a group of black voters challenged Georgia's judicial-election system, pointing out that only five of that state's 135 trial judges were black. A three-judge federal district court ruled against Georgia, and on that basis the DOJ declared that the state's judicial election system was discriminatory in diluting the strength of black voters by requiring candidates to attain a majority, rather than a mere plurality, vote and by requiring them to run for specific judgeships in multijudge districts. In a separate lawsuit black and Hispanic citizens challenged the at-large system for electing district judges in a number of Texas's metropolitan counties; at-large elections tend to work against electing minority candidates. They pointed out, for example, that in Harris County, Texas's largest district, blacks counted for 18 percent of the voting age population, while only three of the fifty-nine judges (or 5 percent) were black. Although a federal district court held that the Texas judicial election system was subject to the Voting Rights Act, the Court of Appeals for the Fifth Circuit held, by a vote of seven to six, that judicial elections are not covered because judges "do not represent the people, they serve the people," and the Voting Rights Act only guarantees minorities an equal opportunity to elect "representatives of their choice." Likewise, in the Georgia case the state contended that Section 5 did not apply to judicial elections, and even if it did, it should not apply there because while Georgia had created new judgeships since 1964 its electoral system was not new. But, in contrast to the Fifth Circuit, a federal district court rejected those arguments.

The Rehnquist Court thus confronted two separate questions: (1) Do provisions of the Voting Rights Act apply to judicial elections? and (2) if the act applies, what methods of electing state judges run afoul of the act? Without hearing oral arguments on the first, threshold, question, the Rehnquist Court unanimously said yes, and rejected the argument that judicial elections are exempt from provisions of the Voting Rights Act. It did so in a simple one-sentence order that "summarily affirmed" the ruling of the district court, in *Georgia State Board of Elections v. Brooks*, 111 S.Ct. 288 (1990).

By summarily affirming the lower court in the Georgia cases, however, the Rehnquist Court provided no guidance for the Justice Department or lower courts when reviewing challenges to various state judicial election systems. Accordingly, the Court also granted review of several other cases involving attacks on various methods of electing state judges.

Three cases involving Louisiana's judicial elections were granted. Two, *Chisom v. Roemer*, 111 S.Ct. 2354 (1991), and *United States v. Roemer*, 111 S.Ct. 2354 (1991), challenged Louisiana's method of electing justices to its seven-member state supreme court. Five of those justices are elected from single-member districts, while two are elected in at-large elections in a sixth voting district. Black voters in the sixth district argued that the at-large elections diluted their voting strength. They also contended that if the at-large district were divided along parish lines and split into two districts a majority of the black voters in one of those new districts would have a chance to elect a black justice; no black has been elected to the Louisiana state supreme court in this century.

By a vote of six to three in *Chisom*, the Court held that Section 2 of the Voting Rights Act applies to judicial elections. Writing for the majority, Justice Stevens reasoned that if Congress had intended to exclude judicial elections from the coverage of the Voting Rights Act, it would have explicitly said so. The Court's holding in *Wells v. Edwards*, 409 U.S. 1095 (1973), that the "one-person, one-vote" rule was inapplicable to judicial elections, Stevens observed, does not mean that judicial elections are entirely immune from vote dilution claims. *Wells*, he pointed out, rejected a constitutional claim and, therefore, had no relevance to a correct interpretation of the Voting Rights Act, which was enacted to provide additional protection for voting rights not adequately protected by the Constitution itself. In a dissenting opinion that Chief Justice Rehnquist and Justice Kennedy joined, Justice Scalia countered that

Section 2 of the Voting Rights Act is not some all-purpose weapon for well-intentioned judges to wield as they please in the battle against discrimination. It is a statute. I thought we had adopted a regular method for interpreting the meaning of language in a statute: first, find the ordinary meaning of the language in its textual context; and second, using established canons of construction, ask whether there is any clear indication that some permissible meaning other than the ordinary one applies. If not—and especially if a good reason for the ordinary meaning appears plain—we apply that ordinary meaning.

Today, however, the Court adopts a method quite out of accord with that usual practice. It begins not with what the statute says, but with an expectation about what the statute must mean absent particular phenomena ("we are convinced that if Congress had . . . an intent [to exclude judges] Congress would have made it explicit in the statute, or at least some of the Members would have identified or mentioned it at some point in the unusually extensive legislative history," and the Court then interprets the words of the statute to fulfill its expectation. Finding nothing in the legislative history affirming that judges were excluded from the coverage of Sec. 2, the Court gives the phrase "to elect representatives" the quite extraordinary meaning that covers the election of judges.

Finally, in a major and highly divisive ruling with broad political ramifications, a bare majority ruled, in *Shaw v. Reno*, 113 S.Ct. 2816 (1993) (see page 78), that the Fourteenth Amendment forbids racial gerrymandering in the construction of electoral districts, unless the government demonstrates a "compelling reason" for creating a black or Hispanic congressional district that survives the Court's toughest standard of review, or "strict scrutiny" (see Vol. 2, Ch. 12). In 1992, twenty-six new minority-majority districts were created, with the approval of the Bush administration, in order to ensure black and Hispanic representation in Congress. Justice O'Connor's opinion for the Court left numerous questions unanswered, but moved each of the four dissenters— Justices Blackmun, Souter, Stevens, and White—to file separate dissenting opinions.

THE DEVELOPMENT OF LAW:

Other Rulings Interpreting the Voting Rights Act

Case	Ruling
Houston Lawyers' Association v. Texas Attorney General, 111 S.Ct. 2376 (1991)	By the same six-to-three lineup as in *Chisom v. Roemer,* 111 S.Ct. 2354 (1991), the Court held that Section 2 of the Voting Rights Act applied to Texas's elections of state trial court judges. Justice Stevens wrote for the majority and Justice Scalia for the dissenters.
Presley v. Etowah County Commission, 112 S.Ct. 820 (1992)	By a six-to-three vote the Court gave local governments greater freedom to change their political structure and organization without obtaining prior approval from the Department of Justice under Section 5 of the Voting Rights Act. After the election of a black commissioner in 1987, the white-majority

county commission changed its system of allocating money, from one in which each commissioner had full authority over funds allocated to his or her district, to a common fund under the control of the voting majority on the commission. Writing for the majority, Justice Kennedy held that the county did not have to obtain prior Department of Justice approval because the change did not involve "voting changes" covered by the act. The Voting Rights Act, according to Justice Kennedy, covers only four kinds of "voting changes": (1) changes in the manner of voting, such as switching from single-district to at-large elections; (2) changes in candidacy qualifications; (3) changes in voter registration; and (4) changes affecting the creation or abolition of an elected office. Each of these kinds of changes relates directly to the electoral process, whereas Justice Kennedy deemed changes in the internal operations of an elected body to have no direct relation to voting. Justices Stevens, Blackmun, and White dissented.

Growe, Secretary of	Unanimously reversing a district court decision that
State of Minnesota v.	imposed a reapportionment plan creating a
Emison,	minority-dominated state sentate district in
113 S.Ct. 1075	Minnesota's legislature, the Court held that federal
(1993)	courts must defer to state courts when parallel
	lawsuits challenging redistricting plans are pending.

Minnesota Democrats had favored a redistricting plan approved by state courts, while Republicans backed another plan advanced in federal courts. "The Constitution leaves with the states primary responsibility for apportionment," observed Justice Scalia in his opinion for the Court, which emphasized that federal courts "must neither affirmatively obstruct state reapportionment nor permit federal litigation to be used to impede it." As such, the ruling further advanced the Rehnquist Court's broader interests in curbing federal court jurisdiction and in reinforcing state when reconsidering issues of judicial federalism.

	Unanimously reversing a lower court ruling that
Voinovich v. Quilter,	struck down the creation of black-majority voting
113 S.Ct. 1149	districts, the Court held that states are free to design
(1993)	reapportionment plans that include majority-minority
	districts so long as the end result does not violate the
	Voting Rights Act by "diminishing or abridging the

voting strength of the protected class." Here, Ohio Democrats challenged a Republican-sponsored plan that Democrats claimed packed minorities into voting districts that already elected black state legislators, while diluting blacks' voting strength in other predominantly white districts. Writing for the Court, Justice O'Connor observed that "[T]he practice challenged here, the creation of majority-minority districts, does not invariably minimize or maximize minority voting strength. Instead, it can have either effect or neither. On the one hand, creating majority-black districts necessarily leaves fewer black voters and therefore diminishes black-voter influence in predominantly white districts. On the other hand, the creation of majority-black districts can enhance the influence of black voters. Placing black voters in a district in which they constitute a sizeable and therefore 'safe' majority ensures that they are able to elect their candidate of choice. Which effect the practice has, if any at all, depends entirely on the facts and circumstances of each case."

Shaw v. Reno

113 S.Ct. 2816 (1993)

After the 1990 census, North Carolina became eligible for a twelfth congressional seat. But in order to comply with Section 5 of the Voting Rights Act of 1965, which requires a covered jurisdiction to obtain federal authorization for changes in its election practices and procedures, North Carolina submitted to the Department of Justice a congressional reapportionment plan with one majority-black district. The Bush administration's Department of Justice, however, objected to the state's initial plan because a second congressional district could have been created to give blacks greater voting strength in the state's south-central and south-eastern region. North Carolina's general assembly thus revised its plan to include a second majority-black district in the north-central region. That new district stretched approximately 160 miles along Interstate 85 and for much of its length was no wider than the I-85 corridor. The constitutionality of that district was in turn attacked by several white voters, including a Duke University law school professor. A three-judge district court dismissed the complaint on the ground that, under *United Jewish Organizations of Williamsburgh, Inc. v. Carey,* 430 U.S. 144 (1977), favoring minority voters was not discriminatory in the constitutional sense and that the plan did not proportionally underrepresent white voters statewide. That decision was appealed to the Supreme Court, which granted *certiorari.*

The Court's decision was five to four, with the majority's opinion announced by Justice O'Connor and dissents by Justices White, Blackmun, Stevens, and Souter.

Justice O'CONNOR delivers the opinion of the Court.

An understanding of the nature of appellants' claim is critical to our resolution of the case. In their complaint, appellants did not claim that the General Assembly's reapportionment plan unconstitutionally "diluted" white voting strength. They did not even claim to be white. Rather, appellants' complaint alleged that the deliberate segregation of voters into separate districts on the basis of race violated their constitutional right to participate in a "color-blind" electoral process.

Despite their invocation of the ideal of a "color-blind" Constitution, see *Plessy v. Ferguson,* 163 U.S. 537 (1896) (HARLAN, J., dissenting), appellants appear to concede that race-conscious redistricting is not always unconstitutional. That concession is wise: This Court never has held that race-conscious state decisionmaking is impermissible in all circumstances. What appellants object to is redistricting legislation that is so extremely irregular on its face that it rationally can be viewed only as an effort to segregate the races for purposes of voting, without regard for traditional districting principles and without sufficiently compelling justification. For the reasons that follow, we conclude that appellants have stated a claim upon which relief can be granted under the Equal Protection Clause. . . .

Classifications of citizens solely on the basis of race "are by their very nature odious to a free people whose institutions are founded upon the doctrine of equality." *Hirabayashi v. United States,* 320 U.S. 81 (1943). They threaten to stigmatize individuals by reason of their membership in a racial group and to incite racial hostility. Accordingly, we have held that the Fourteenth Amendment requires state legislation that expressly distinguishes among citizens because of their race to be narrowly tailored to further a compelling governmental interest. See, e.g., *Wygant v. Jackson Bd. of Ed.,* 476 U.S. 267 (1986).

These principles apply not only to legislation that contains explicit racial distinctions, but also to those "rare" statutes that, although race-neutral, are, on their face, "unexplainable on grounds other than race." *Arlington Heights v. Metropolitan Housing Development Corp.,* 429 U.S. 252 (1977). . . .

The Court applied the same reasoning to the "uncouth twenty-eight-sided" municipal boundary line at issue in *Gomillion* [*v. Lightfoot,* 364 U.S. 339 (1960)]. Although the statute that redrew the city limits of Tuskegee was race-neutral on its face, plaintiffs alleged that its effect was impermissibly to remove from the city virtually all black voters and no white voters. . . .

The Court extended the reasoning of *Gomillion* to congressional districting in *Wright v. Rockefeller,* 376 U.S. 52 (1964). At issue in *Wright* were four districts contained in a New York apportionment statute. The plaintiffs alleged that the statute excluded nonwhites from one district and concentrated them in the other three. Every member of the Court assumed that the plaintiffs' allegation that the statute "segregated eligible voters by race and place of origin" stated a constitutional claim. The Justices disagreed only as to whether the plaintiffs had carried their burden of proof at trial. The dissenters thought the unusual shape of the district lines could "be explained only in racial terms." The majority, however, accepted the District Court's finding that the plaintiffs had failed to establish that the districts were in fact drawn on racial lines. Although the boundary lines were somewhat irregular, the majority reasoned, they were not so bizarre as to permit of no other conclusion. Indeed, because most of the nonwhite voters lived together in one area, it would have been difficult to construct voting districts without concentrations of nonwhite voters.

Wright illustrates the difficulty of determining from the face of a single-member districting plan that it purposefully distinguishes between voters on the basis of race. A reapportionment statute typically does not classify persons at all; it classifies tracts of land, or addresses. Moreover, redistricting differs from other kinds of state decisionmaking in that the legislature always is aware of race when it draws district lines, just as it is aware of age, economic status, religious and political persuasion, and a variety of other demographic factors. That sort of race consciousness does not lead inevitably to impermissible race discrimination. As *Wright* demonstrates, when members of a racial group live together in one community, a reapportionment plan that concentrates members of the group in one district and excludes them from others may reflect wholly legitimate purposes. The district lines may be drawn, for example, to provide for compact districts of contiguous territory, or to maintain the integrity of political subdivisions.

The difficulty of proof, of course, does not mean that a racial gerrymander, once established, should receive less scrutiny under the Equal Protection Clause than other state legislation classifying citizens by race. Moreover, it seems clear to us that proof sometimes will not be difficult at all. In some exceptional cases, a reapportionment plan may be so highly irregular that, on its face, it rationally cannot be understood as anything other than an effort to "segregate . . . voters" on the basis of race. *Gomillion,* in which a tortured municipal boundary line was drawn to exclude black voters, was such a case. So, too, would be a case in which a State concentrated a dispersed minority population in a single district by disregarding traditional districting principles such as compactness, contiguity, and respect for political subdivisions. We emphasize that these criteria are important not because they are constitutionally required—they are not—but because they are objective factors that may serve to defeat a claim that a district has been gerrymandered on racial lines. . . .

Put differently, we believe that reapportionment is one area in which appearances do matter. A reapportionment plan that includes in one district individuals who belong to the same race, but who are otherwise widely separated by geographical and political boundaries, and who may have little in common with one another but the color of their skin, bears an uncomfortable resemblance to political apartheid. It reinforces the perception that members of the same racial group—regardless of their age, education, economic status, or the community in which they live—think alike, share the same political interests, and will prefer the same candidates at the polls. We have rejected such perceptions elsewhere as impermissible racial stereotypes. . . .

For these reasons, we conclude that a plaintiff challenging a reapportionment statute under the Equal Protection Clause may state a claim by alleging that the legislation, though race-neutral on its face, rationally cannot be understood as anything other than an effort to separate voters into different districts on the basis of race, and that the separation lacks sufficient justification. It is unnecessary for us to decide whether or how a reapportionment plan that, on its face, can be explained in nonracial terms successfully could be challenged. Thus, we express no view as to whether "the intentional creation of majority-minority districts, without more" always gives rise to an equal protection claim. We hold only that, on the facts of this case, plaintiffs have stated a claim sufficient to defeat the state appellees' motion to dismiss. . . . It is [also] for these reasons that race-based districting by our state legislatures demands close judicial scrutiny. . . .

Justice WHITE, with whom Justices BLACKMUN and STEVENS join, dissenting.

The facts of this case mirror those presented in *United Jewish Organizations of Williamsburgh, Inc. v. Carey*, 430 U.S. 144 (1977), where the Court rejected a claim that creation of a majority-minority district violated the Constitution, either as a per se matter or in light of the circumstances leading to the creation of such a district. Of particular relevance, five of the Justices reasoned that members of the white majority could not plausibly argue that their influence over the political process had been unfairly cancelled, or that such had been the State's intent. Accordingly, they held that plaintiffs were not entitled to relief under the Constitution's Equal Protection Clause. On the same reasoning, I would affirm the district court's dismissal of appellants' claim in this instance.

The Court today chooses not to overrule, but rather to sidestep, *United Jewish Organizations of Williamsburgh*. It does so by glossing over the striking similarities, focusing on surface differences, most notably the (admittedly unusual) shape of the newly created district, and imagining an entirely new cause of action. Because the holding is limited to such anomalous circumstances, it perhaps will not substantially hamper a State's legitimate efforts to redistrict in favor of racial minorities. Nonetheless, the notion that North Carolina's plan, under which whites remain a voting majority in a disproportionate number of congressional districts, and pursuant to which the State has sent its first black representatives since Reconstruction to the United States Congress, might have violated appellants' constitutional rights is both a fiction and a departure from settled equal protection principles. Seeing no good reason to engage in either, I dissent. . . .

Justice BLACKMUN, dissenting.

I . . . agree that the conscious use of race in redistricting does not violate the Equal Protection Clause unless the effect of the redistricting plan is to deny a particular group equal access to the political process or to minimize its voting strength unduly. It is particularly ironic that the case in which today's majority chooses to abandon settled law and to recognize for the first time this "analytically distinct" constitutional claim is a challenge by white voters to the plan under which North Carolina has sent black representatives to Congress for the first time since Reconstruction. I dissent.

Justice STEVENS, dissenting.

For the reasons stated by Justice WHITE, the decision of the District Court should be affirmed. I add these comments to emphasize that the two critical facts in this case are undisputed: first, the shape of District 12 is so bizarre that it must have been drawn for the purpose of either advantaging or disadvantaging a cognizable group of voters; and, second, regardless of that shape, it was drawn for the purpose of facilitating the election of a second black representative from North Carolina.

These unarguable facts, which the Court devotes most of its opinion to proving, give rise to three constitutional questions: Does the Constitution impose a requirement of contiguity or compactness on how the States may draw their electoral districts? Does the Equal Protection Clause prevent a State from drawing district boundaries for the purpose of facilitating the election of a member of an identifiable group of voters? And, finally, if the answer to the second question is generally "No," should it be different when the favored group is defined by race? Since I have already written at length about these questions, my negative answer to each can be briefly explained.

The first question is easy. There is no independent constitutional requirement of compactness or contiguity, and the Court's opinion (despite its many references to the shape of District 12) does not suggest otherwise. . . .

As for the second question, I believe that the Equal Protection Clause is violated when the State creates the kind of uncouth district boundaries seen in *Karcher v. Daggett*, 462 U.S. 725 (1983), *Gomillion v. Lightfoot*, 364 U.S. 339 (1960), and this case, for the sole purpose of making it more difficult for members of a minority group to win an election. The duty to govern impartially is abused when a group with power over the electoral process defines electoral boundaries solely to enhance its own political strength at the expense of any weaker group. That duty, however, is not violated when the majority acts to facilitate the election of a member of a group that lacks such power because it remains underrepresented in the state legislature—whether that group is defined by political affiliation, by common economic interests, or by religious, ethnic, or racial characteristics. The difference between constitutional and unconstitutional gerrymanders has nothing to do with whether they are based on assumptions about the groups they affect, but whether their purpose is to enhance the power of the group in control of the districting process at the expense of any minority group, and thereby to strengthen the unequal distribution of electoral power. . . .

Finally, we must ask whether otherwise permissible redistricting to benefit an underrepresented minority group becomes impermissible when the minority group is defined by its race. The Court today answers this question in the affirmative, and its answer is wrong. If it is permissible to draw boundaries to provide adequate representation for rural voters, for union members, for Hasidic Jews, for Polish Americans, or for Republicans, it necessarily follows that it is permissible to do the same thing for members of the very minority group whose history in the United States gave birth to the Equal Protection Clause. A contrary conclusion could only be described as perverse.

Justice SOUTER, dissenting.

Until today, the Court has analyzed equal protection claims involving race in electoral districting differently from equal protection claims involving other forms of governmental conduct, and before turning to the different regimes of analysis it will be useful to set out the relevant respects in which such districting differs from the characteristic circumstances in which a State might otherwise consciously consider race. Unlike other contexts in which we have addressed the State's conscious use of race, see, e.g., *Richmond v. J. A. Croson Co.*, 488 U.S. 469 (1989) [city contracting]; *Wygant v. Jackson Bd. of Ed.*, 476 U.S. 267 (1986) [teacher layoffs], electoral districting calls for decisions that nearly always require some consideration of race for legitimate reasons where there is a racially mixed population. As long as members of racial groups have the commonality of interest implicit in our ability to talk about concepts like "minority voting strength," and "dilution of minority votes," *Thornburg v. Gingles*, 478 U.S. 30 (1986), and as long as racial bloc voting takes place, legislators will have to take race into account in order to avoid dilution of minority voting strength in the districting plans they adopt. One need look no further than the Voting Rights Act to understand that this may be required, and we have held that race may constitutionally be taken into account in order to comply with that Act. *United Jewish Organizations of Williamsburgh, Inc. v. Carey*, 430 U.S. 144 (1977).

A second distinction between districting and most other governmental decisions in which race has figured is that those other decisions using racial criteria characteristically occur in circumstances in which the use of race to the advantage of one person is necessarily at the obvious expense of a member of a different race. Thus, for example, awarding government contracts on a racial basis excludes certain firms from competition on racial grounds. See *Richmond v. J. A. Croson Co.*, supra. . . . . In districting, by contrast, the mere placement of an individual in one district instead of another denies no one a right or benefit provided to others. All citizens may register, vote, and be represented. . . .

A consequence of this categorical approach is the absence of any need for further searching "scrutiny" once it has been shown that a given districting decision has a purpose and effect falling within one of those categories. If a cognizable harm like dilution or the abridgment of the right to participate in the electoral process is shown, the districting plan violates the Fourteenth Amendment. If not, it does not. Under this approach, in the absence of an allegation of such cognizable harm, there is no need for further scrutiny because a gerrymandering claim cannot be proven without the element of harm. . . .

The Court offers no adequate justification for treating the narrow category of bizarrely shaped district claims differently from other districting claims. The only justification I can imagine would be the preservation of "sound districting principles," such as compactness and contiguity. But as Justice WHITE points out, and as the Court acknowledges, we have held that such principles are not constitutionally required, with the consequence that their absence cannot justify the distinct constitutional regime put in place by the Court today. . . .

I respectfully dissent.

C. CAMPAIGNS AND ELECTIONS

The Court has recently confronted several challenges to state and federal regulations campaigns and elections, (See the cases summarized in "The Development of Law: Rulings on Campaigns and Elections.") In particular, the Court revisited the issue of how and on what basis the line between bribery and campaign contributions should be drawn in *McCormick v. United States*, 111 S.Ct. 1807 (1991). At issue was whether federal prosecutors may use, and on what evidentiary basis, federal extortion laws to prosecute and punish state-elected officials who allegedly extort bribery money but who claim they were merely soliciting campaign contributions. A former West Virginia state legislator, Robert McCormick, appealed his conviction for violating federal law by soliciting money a week before a state primary election from a group of foreign doctors, who repeatedly failed to qualify for medical licenses and who sought special legislation enabling them to practice in the state. McCormick received five cash contributions, totaling $5,250, in violation of state laws limiting campaign contributions to $50. In addition, he failed to report the money on his campaign disclosure forms and his state and federal income tax returns. Both federal prosecutors and McCormick's attorney agreed that campaign contributions do not constitute extortion without evidence of out-and-out vote selling. But McCormick's attorney argued that the logic and evidence used to convict him would potentially render every lawmaker who solicits campaign contributions a federal felon.

By a six-to-three vote overturning McCormick's conviction, the Rehnquist Court made it harder for federal prosecutors to prosecute politicians for extortion in soliciting campaign contributions. Writing for the majority, Justice Byron White held that prosecutors must show that a campaign contributor gave money to a politician in exchange for an "explicit promise" of help. "Money," as Justice White put it, "is constantly being solicited on behalf of candidates, who run on platforms and who claim support on the basis of their views and what they intend to do or have done." Regardless of "[w]hatever ethical considerations and appearances may indicate," he ruled that it would be "unrealistic" to hold that legislators commit extortion when they do something for constituents who have donated money to their campaigns in response to their solicitations. "To hold otherwise," White concluded, "would open to prosecution not only conduct that has long been thought to be well within the law but also conduct that in a very real sense is unavoidable so long as election campaigns are financed by private contributions or expenditures, as they have been from the beginning of the nation."

By contrast, dissenting in *McCormick*, Justice Stevens, joined by Justices Blackmun and O'Connor, argued that the majority's interpretation of federal extortion law, known as the Hobbs Act, was unrealistic. "Subtle extortion is just as wrongful—and probably much more common—than the kind of express understanding that the Court's opinion seems to require," observed Stevens, when likening McCormick's solicitations "to a known thug's offer to protect a storekeeper against the risk of severe property damage in exchange for a cash consideration. Neither the legislator nor the thug needs to make an explicit promise to get his message across."

THE DEVELOPMENT OF LAW

Rulings on Campaigns and Elections

Case	Ruling
Renne v. Greary, 111 S.Ct. 2331 (1991)	By a six-to three vote, the Court held that a challenge to a state law banning political parties from endorsing candidates in nonpartisan elections for judgeships and local government positions was nonjusticiable. Justices Blackmun, Marshall, and White dissented.
Burson v. Freeman, 112 S.Ct. 1846 (1992)	By a four-to-three vote, with Justice Thomas not participating, the Court upheld Tennessee law forbidding the display and distribution of campaign materials, along with the solicitation of votes, near

polling places on election day, while permitting other forms of speech there. Justices O'Connor, Souter, and Stevens dissented.

Norman v. Reed,   Struck down an ordinance requiring new political
112 S.Ct. 698   parties to gather 50,000 signatures on nominating
(1992)   petitions to place their candidates on ballots for local
                      offices, whereas for other statewide offices only
                      25,000 signatures were required. With only Justice
                      Scalia dissenting, the Court reaffirmed citizens' First
and Fourteenth Amendments rights to form political parties and deemed the ordinance to lack a "compelling state interest."

Burdick v. Takuski,   By a six-to-three vote, the Court upheld Hawaii's law
112 S.Ct. 2988   prohibiting write-in votes in state elections as
(1992)   imposing reasonable burdens on citizens' First and
                       Fourteenth Amendment rights. Justices Blackmun,
                       Kennedy, and Stevens dissented.

VOLUME TWO

3

ECONOMIC RIGHTS AND AMERICAN CAPITALISM

THE REHNQUIST COURT signaled in 1987 that it might move in the direction of extending greater protection to private property under the Fifth Amendment's "takings clause," which provides that "private property [shall not] be taken for public use, without just compensation." Writing for a bare majority in *Nollan v. California Coastal Commission,* 483 U.S. 825 (1987) (see Vol. 2, Ch. 3), Justice Scalia struck down a land-use regulation requiring beachfront-property owners to provide public easement across their property to the beach, as it constituted a taking of property without just compensation. Another ruling in *First English Evangelical Lutheran Church v. County of Los Angeles,* 482 U.S. 304 (1987) (see Vol. 2, Ch. 3), invalidated a regulation prohibiting rebuilding in designated flood lands. Both decisions encouraged property-rights groups to challenge the constitutionality of local ordinances, environmental legislation, and other land-use controls. By contrast, environmentalists, preservationists, and urban planners warned that the Court's activist interpretation of the takings clause would make more difficult the enforcement of laws protecting environmental and wildlife preserves, historic buildings, and other zoning laws because of the high costs of compensation for property owners.

During its 1991 term, the Rehnquist Court revisited land-use regulations in several cases.[1] In the leading case, *Lucas v. South Carolina Coastal*

---

[1] See also *Yee v. The City of Escondido, California,* 112 S.Ct. 1522 (1992), holding that a rent-control ordinance did not amount to a takings per se. Writing for the Court, Justice O'Connor distinguished two kinds of takings clause cases: (1) those in which the govern-

Council, 112 S.Ct. 2886 (1992), the owner of beachfront property appealed a decision of the South Carolina Supreme Court that upheld a regulation barring the rebuilding of houses on the shoreline. Two years before that zoning restriction, which aimed to preserve the beach and sand dunes as a storm barrier, David H. Lucas had purchased two oceanfront lots for nearly $1 million, and he argued that the building restriction denied him the use of his property without just compensation. When rejecting Lucas's claim, the South Carolina Supreme Court relied heavily on a 1987 Supreme Court ruling, in *Keystone Bituminous Coal Association v. DeBenedictis,* 480 U.S. 470 (1987), that no Fifth Amendment "takings" occurs when landowners are deprived of all economic use of their property because states and localities may enact laws that "prevent serious public harm."

Although property-rights advocates opposed to new environmental regulations looked for a sweeping decision in *Lucas,* by a six-to-three vote the Court handed down a very narrow ruling. The majority neither reversed *DeBendictis* nor decided whether Lucas was entitled to compensation. Instead, the Court remanded the case to the state courts to determine whether Lucas had been deprived of all economic value of his land and whether the state's building restrictions would be justified as preventing public harms or nuisances.

Writing for the majority in *Lucas,* Justice Scalia held, on the one hand, that property owners who suffer total economic loss of the value of their land may have a takings claim. Historically, the Court recognized takings claims only when the government actually took physical possession of a property, as in an eminent domain proceeding. But more recently, in cases like *Nollan* and *Lucas,* the Court has recognized regulatory takings requiring the government to pay compensation when its regulations diminish the value of private property. In *Lucas,* Scalia held that it is not enough for government to defend its environmental, land-use, and zoning regulations as in the public interest. It must also defend them as necessary to avoid a public harm or the "harmful or noxious use" of private property; thus a property owner might be denied a permit to run a landfill operation because it would result in the flooding of nearby land. Because the state courts failed to identify the public nuisances that would justify the building restrictions imposed by the Beachfront Management Act, the Court remanded the case for further consideration.

Justice Scalia's opinion, on the other hand, limited its takings clause analysis to apply only when property owners were totally deprived of the

---

ment has actually physically taken private property for public use and (2) those challenging regulations of the use of private property. The former generally requires compensation of the owners and "courts to apply a clear rule," whereas the latter requires courts to assess the purpose and economic effects of the regulations. And O'Connor reaffirmed that "[s]tates have broad power to regulate housing conditions in general and the landlord-tenant relationship in particular." The Court also rejected a taking clause challenge in *General Motors v. Romein,* 112 S.Ct. 1105 (1992).

economic value of their land. As he put it, "When the owner of real property has been called upon to sacrifice *all* economically beneficial uses in the name of the common good, that is, to leave his property economically idle, he has suffered a taking." That, however, significantly limited Scalia's ruling because, as dissenting Justice Stevens observed, "A landowner whose property is diminished in value 95 percent recovers nothing, while an owner whose property is diminished 100 percent recovers the land's full value." Since most environmental and land-use regulations do not deprive property owners of all economic use or value of their property, Scalia's analysis in *Lucas* is severely limited. Justices Souter and Kennedy concurred in separate opinions, while Justices Blackmun and Stevens dissented separately.

4

THE NATIONALIZATION
OF THE BILL OF RIGHTS

B. THE RISE AND RETREAT OF THE "DUE
PROCESS REVOLUTION"

In recent years the Rehnquist Court has rebuffed several attempts to have it broadly read the Fourteenth Amendment's due process clause so as to extend procedural safeguards for individuals and to legitimate new substantive liberty interests; (see Vol. 2, Ch. 4) and "The Development of Law: Rulings on Substantive and Procedural Due Process." However, in *Foucha v. United States,* 112 S.Ct. 1780 (1992) (see page 96), Justice White sharply divided the Court when commanding a bare majority for asserting substantive and procedural due process protection under the Fourteenth Amendment. There he struck down Louisiana's law permitting the continued institutionalization of an individual who was criminally acquitted by reason of insanity and who subsequently regained sanity but was still deemed to pose a potential threat to society. Chief Justice Rehnquist and Justice Scalia joined a bitter dissent by Justice Thomas denouncing the majority's due process analysis, while Justice Kennedy dissented separately.

THE DEVELOPMENT OF LAW
Rulings on Substantive and Procedural Due Process

Case	Ruling
Sigert v. Gilley, 111 S.Ct. 1789 (1991) Vote 6:3	By a six-to-three vote, the Court reaffirmed the holding in *Paul v. Davis,* 424 U.S. 693 (1976), that injury to a person's reputation violates neither a liberty interest protected by the due process clauses, nor the constitutional right of privacy. Justices Blackmun, Marshall, and Stevens dissented.
Pacific Mutual Life Insurance Company v. Haslip, 111 S.Ct. 1032 (1991) Vote 8:1	Rejected a Fourteenth Amendment substantive due process challenge to the common law method for assessing punitive damages against corporations for the fraudulent activities of their employees. Justice O'Connor dissented.
Collins v. Harker Heights, 112 S.Ct. 1061 (1992) Vote 9:0	Unanimously rejected the claims of the survivors of a city's sanitation worker that the Fourteenth Amendment embraces the right of workers to be free from "unreasonable risk of harm."
Reno v. Flores, 113 S.Ct. 1439 (1993) Vote 7:2	By a seven-to-two vote, the Court rejected a substantive due process challenge to the Immigration and Naturalization Service's policy of placing children entering the country illegally in detention centers, and releasing them only to parents or close relatives, pending their deportation hearings. Writing for the majority, Justice Scalia rejected out of hand

the claim that the children should be placed in private, rather than governmental, child care centers. That novel claim, in the majority's view, could not be considered "so rooted in the traditions and conscience of our people as to be ranked as fundamental." In separate concurrences, Justices O'Connor and Souter stressed that children do have constitutionally protected interests in freedom from institutional confinement, but that the INS's program satisfied the requirements of due process. By contrast, dissenting Justices Stevens and Blackmun argued that the government should have to establish not only that its detention policy was necessary but also that alternative, less restrictive, policies were unworkable.

*TXO Production
Corporation v. Alliance
Resources Corporation,*
113 S.Ct. 2711
(1993)

Vote 6:3

For the third time in five years, the Court revisited
the issue of whether large punitive damage awards
violate due process. At issue was a jury's punitive
damage award, along with $19,000 in actual
damages, to Alliance Resources, after the company
countersued TXO Production Corporation for filing
suit against it in order to force Alliance Resources to
sell mineral rights to TXO. A jury found that TXO's initial suit was frivolous
and awarded $10 million in punitive damages—approximately 526 times the
amount of actual damages. Although upholding the award and rejecting a
substantive due process challenge, the Court was badly splintered. Justice
Stevens's opinion for the Court commanded only a plurality, with only Chief
Justice Rehnquist and Justice Blackmun joining in its entirety. He reaffirmed
the position, in *Pacific Mutual Life Insurance v. Haslip,* 111 S.Ct. 1032 (1991),
that the Court could not "draw a mathematical bright line" between
constitutionally acceptable and unacceptable jury awards. Instead of focusing
on the disparity between punitive and compensatory awards, Justice Stevens
maintained that the Court should focus on the general "reasonableness" of
an award. Here, TXO's "bad faith" and "larger pattern of fraud, trickery,
and deceit" justified the jury's award. In a concurrence Justice Kennedy
rejected that analysis and argued instead for an approach focusing on the
jury's motivations in making large punitive awards—whether a jury was
impassioned and prejudiced or demonstrated a "rational concern for
deterrence and retribution." In another concurrence, joined by Justice
Thomas, Justice Scalia dismissed out of hand all claims that the due process
clause confers an unenumerated constitutional right to a substantively correct
"reasonableness" determination of a jury's award. By contrast, as in *Haslip,*
Justice O'Connor dissented, though now joined by Justices White and Souter.
Justice O'Connor continued to maintain that the Court should scrutinize
large punitive damages awards, and that here the state courts had
inadequately reviewed the jury's award.

Foucha v. United States
112 S.Ct. 1780 (1992)

In 1984 after being charged with burglary, Terry Foucha, a seventeen-
year-old high-school dropout, was examined by two doctors who determined he was not mentally fit to stand trial. On that basis, a state trial
court ruled he was not guilty by reason of insanity and ordered him
committed to the East Feliciana Forensic Facility, a state institution for
the criminally insane.

In 1988 East Feliciana's superintendent convened a panel to determine whether Foucha could be released without presenting a danger to himself or others. After that panel recommended his release, however, the trial judge appointed another panel, composed of the two doctors who had originally examined Foucha. Although finding him no longer mentally ill, this panel concluded he was antisocial and posed "a menace to himself or others if released." Whereupon, the trial judge declared Foucha dangerous and under a state law ordered him returned to the mental institution. The Louisiana State Supreme Court affirmed, holding that Foucha failed to prove he was not dangerous and that the Court's decisions in *Jones v. United States,* 463 U.S. 354 (1983), and *United States v. Salerno,* 481 U.S. 739 (1987), did not require his release. Nor were the Fourteenth Amendment's due process and equal protection guarantees violated, ruled the state high court, by the state's civil confinement of individuals acquitted of criminal charges on the basis of insanity, who subsequently regained sanity but are still deemed potentially dangerous.

Foucha's attorney appealed to the Supreme Court, arguing that the Fourteenth Amendment barred Louisiana from institutionally confining Foucha until he provided "clear and convincing evidence" that he was no longer dangerous. The state's lawyers countered that Foucha was a continuing threat to society and his involuntary confinement was an analogous form of "preventive detention," which was upheld in *Jones* and *Salerno.*

The Court's decision was five to four, with the majority's opinion announced by Justice White. Justice O'Connor, concurred in part. Justices Kennedy and Thomas dissented, and were joined by Cheif Justice Rehnquist and Justice Scalia.

Justice WHITE delivers the opinion of the Court with respect to parts I and II, which Justices BLACKMUN, STEVENS, O'CONNOR, and SOUTER join, and an opinion with respect to part III, which Justices BLACKMUN, STEVENS, and SOUTER join.

. . .

II

Addington v. Texas, 441 U.S. 418 (1979), held that to commit an individual to a mental institution in a civil proceeding, the State is required by the Due Process Clause to prove by clear and convincing evidence the two statutory preconditions to commitment: that the person sought to be committed is mentally ill and that he requires hospitalization for his own welfare and protection of others. Proof beyond reasonable doubt was not required, but proof by preponderance of the evidence fell short of satisfying due process.

When a person charged with having committed a crime is found not guilty by reason of insanity, however, a State may commit that person without satisfying the *Addington* burden with respect to mental illness and dangerousness. *Jones v. United States,* [463 U.S. 354 (1983)]. Such a verdict, we observed in *Jones,* "establishes two facts: (i) the defendant committed an act that constitutes a criminal offense, and (ii) he committed the act because of mental illness," an illness that the defendant adequately proved in this context by a preponderance of the evidence. From these two facts, it could be properly inferred that at the time of the verdict, the defendant was still mentally ill and dangerous and hence could be committed.

We held, however, that "the committed acquittee is entitled to release when he has recovered his sanity or is no longer dangerous," i.e., the acquittee may be held as long as he is both mentally ill and dangerous, but no longer. We relied on *O'Connor v. Donaldson,* 422 U.S. 563 (1975), which held as a matter of due process that it was unconstitutional for a State to continue to confine a harmless, mentally ill person. Even if the initial commitment was permissible, "it could not constitutionally continue after that basis no longer existed." In the summary of our holdings in our opinion we stated that "the Constitution permits the Government, on the basis of the insanity judgment, to confine him to a mental institution until such time as he has regained his sanity or is no longer a danger to himself or society." *Jones.* The court below was in error in characterizing the above language from *Jones* as merely an interpretation of the pertinent statutory law in the District of Columbia and as having no constitutional significance. In this case, Louisiana does not contend that Foucha was mentally ill at the time of the trial court's hearing. Thus the basis for holding Foucha in a psychiatric facility as an insanity acquittee has disappeared, and the State is no longer entitled to hold him on that basis. *O'Connor.*

The State, however, seeks to perpetuate Foucha's confinement at Feliciana on the basis of his antisocial personality which, as evidenced by his conduct at the facility, the court found rendered him a danger to himself or others. There are at least three difficulties with this position. First, even if his continued confinement were constitutionally permissible, keeping Foucha against his will in a mental institution is improper absent a determination in civil commitment proceedings of current mental illness and dangerousness. . . . Due process requires that the nature of commitment bear some reasonable relation to the purpose for which the individual is committed. Here, according to the testimony given at the hearing in the trial court, Foucha is not suffering from a mental disease or illness. If he is to be held, he should not be held as a mentally ill person.

Second, if Foucha can no longer be held as an insanity acquittee in a mental hospital, he is entitled to constitutionally adequate procedures to establish the grounds for his confinement. *Jackson v. Indiana,* [406 U.S. 715 (1972)], indicates as much. . . .

Third, "the Due Process Clause contains a substantive component that bars certain arbitrary, wrongful government actions regardless of the fairness of the procedures used to implement them." *Zinermon v. Burch,*

494 U.S. 113 (1990). Freedom from bodily restraint has always been at the core of the liberty protected by the Due Process Clause from arbitrary governmental action.

A State, pursuant to its police power, may of course imprison convicted criminals for the purposes of deterrence and retribution. But there are constitutional limitations on the conduct that a State may criminalize. Here, the State has no such punitive interest. As Foucha was not convicted, he may not be punished. Here, Louisiana has by reason of his acquittal exempted Foucha from criminal responsibility as [its state law] requires.

The State may also confine a mentally ill person if it shows "by clear and convincing evidence that the individual is mentally ill and dangerous," *Jones*. Here, the State has not carried that burden; indeed, the State does not claim that Foucha is now mentally ill. . . .

. . .

Justice O'CONNOR concurred in part in a separate opinion.

Justice KENNEDY, joined by Chief Justice REHNQUIST, dissented.

Justice THOMAS, with whom the CHIEF JUSTICE and Justice SCALIA join, dissenting.

. . .

The Court today concludes that Louisiana has denied Foucha both procedural and substantive due process. In my view, each of these conclusions is wrong. I shall discuss them in turn. . . .

In my view, there was no procedural due process violation in this case. [T]he Louisiana Code of Criminal Procedure afford[s] insanity acquittees the opportunity to obtain release by demonstrating at regular intervals that they no longer pose a threat to society. These provisions also afford judicial review of such determinations. Pursuant to these procedures, and based upon testimony of experts, the Louisiana courts determined not to release Foucha at this time because the evidence did not show that he ceased to be dangerous. Throughout these proceedings, Foucha was represented by state-appointed counsel. I see no plausible argument that these procedures denied Foucha a fair hearing on the issue involved or that Foucha needed additional procedural protections.

The Court next concludes that Louisiana's statutory scheme must fall because it violates Foucha's substantive due process rights. I disagree. Until today, I had thought that the analytical framework for evaluating substantive due process claims was relatively straightforward. Certain substantive rights we have recognized as "fundamental"; legislation trenching upon these is subjected to "strict scrutiny," and generally will be invalidated unless the State demonstrates a compelling interest and narrow tailoring. Such searching judicial review of state legislation, however, is the exception, not the rule, in our democratic and federal system; we have consistently emphasized that "the Court has no license to invalidate legislation which it thinks merely arbitrary or unreasonable." *Regents of University of Michigan v. Ewing*, 474 U.S. 214 (1985). Except in the unusual case where a fundamental right is infringed, then, federal judicial scrutiny of the substance of state legislation under the Due Process Clause of the Fourteenth Amendment is not exacting. See, e.g., *Bowers v. Hardwick*, 478 U.S. 186 (1986).

In striking down Louisiana's scheme as a violation of substantive rights guaranteed by the Due Process Clause, the Court today ignores this well-established analytical framework. First, the Court never explains if we are dealing here with a fundamental right, and, if so, what right. Second, the Court never discloses what standard of review applies. Indeed, the Court's opinion is contradictory on both these critical points. . . .

Finally, I see no basis for holding that the Due Process Clause per se prohibits a State from continuing to confine in a "mental institution"— the federal constitutional definition of which remains unclear—an insanity acquittee who has recovered his sanity. As noted above, many States have long provided for the continued detention of insanity acquittees who remain dangerous. Neither Foucha nor the Court present any evidence that these States have traditionally transferred such persons from mental institutions to other detention facilities. Therefore, there is simply no basis for this Court to recognize a "fundamental right" for a sane insanity acquittee to be transferred out of a mental facility. . . .

5

FREEDOM OF EXPRESSION AND ASSOCIATION

A. JUDICIAL APPROACHES TO THE FIRST AMENDMENT

Along with *Rust v. Sullivan*, 111 S.Ct. 1759 (1991) (see page 43), the Rehnquist Court also signaled that it might reassess prior First Amendment rulings bearing on "fighting words," "symbolic speech," and "speech plus conduct" (see Vol. 2, Ch. 5). It did so in granting *R.A.V. v. City of St. Paul, Minnesota*, 112 S.Ct. 2538 (1992) (see page 108). *R.A.V.* provided the Court with its first opportunity to rule on the constitutionality of so-called hate-crime and hate-speech laws that have recently been adopted in more than thirty states, as well as by numerous colleges, universities, and localities.

In a wide-ranging ruling, the Court unanimously invalidated the St. Paul, Minnesota, hate-speech law. In announcing the decision Justice Scalia held that even within the category of fighting words—a category of speech that has traditionally been deemed to fall outside of the scope of First Amendment protection—government may not bar or penalize the expression of some but not other words, based on their content. "The government," Scalia said, may not regulate the "use of 'fighting words' in connection with other ideas—to express hostility, for example, on the basis of political affiliation, union membership, or homosexuality. . . . The First Amendment does not permit St. Paul to impose special prohibitions on those speakers who express views on disfavored subjects." Yet only Chief Justice Rehnquist and Justices Kennedy, Souter, and Thomas agreed with Scalia's analysis and joined his opinion. In concurring opinions that read like dissents, Justices Blackmun, Stevens, and White, whom O'Connor joined, accused the majority of rewriting First Amendment doctrine. As White emphasized, "Under the majority's view, a narrowly drawn, content-based ordinance could never pass constitutional muster if the object of that legislation could be accomplished by banning a wider category of speech. This appears to be a general renunciation of strict scrutiny review, a fundamental tool of First Amendment analysis." Ironically, as White points out, the majority's approach invites broader—rather than narrower—prohibitions of speech. Accordingly, the four concurring justices would have overturned the ordinance as "fatally overbroad because it criminalizes not only unprotected expression but expression protected by the First Amendment."

Despite unanimity on the result in *R.A.V.*, the fragmentation of the justices and disagreements with the reasoning offered by Scalia in his opinion contributed, perhaps, to the Court's willingness to revisit the controversy over hate-speech laws in its 1992 term. In any event, political controversy has continued to brew over the enactment and enforcement of hate-speech laws. In 1990, Congress passed the Hate Crimes Statistics Act, and pursuant to that act the FBI reported that in 1991 there were 4,558 hate crimes—including 1,614 acts of intimidation, 1,301 incidents of vandalism, 1,569 assaults, and 12 murders.

In *Wisconsin v. Mitchell*, 113 S.Ct. 2194 (1993) (see page 137), the Court unanimously upheld a very different kind of hate-speech law than that it struck down in *R.A.V.* Unlike St. Paul's ordinance which criminalized certain kinds of expressions of bias, Wisconsin's law (and those in twenty-seven other states) mandates longer sentences for individuals convicted of assault or vandalism when the crime was committed and the victim was selected out of racial, religious, gender, or ethnic bias.

In addition, in a sweeping opinion that commanded in parts only four other votes, Chief Justice Rehnquist held that the First Amendment's protection against prior restraints does not bar the prosecution under the Racketeer Influenced and Corrupt Organizations (RICO) Act of an owner of a chain of adult bookstores, nor the forfeiture of his businesses and real estate. At the same time, the Court rejected the federal government's argument that the Eighth Amendment's ban on excessive bail and fines was not a barrier to such forfeitures (see Chapter 9 for a further discussion of that issue). Still, the ruling on the First Amendment in *Alexander v. United States*, 113 S.Ct. 2766 (1993) (see page 118), provoked bitter dissents from Justices Kennedy and Souter, who were joined by Justice Blackmun and Stevens.

Finally, the Court unanimously held that school districts may not deny religious groups, and permit nonreligious groups, access to school facilities for meetings at the end of the school day, in *Lamb's Chapel v. Center Moriches Union Free School District*, 113 S.Ct. 2141 (1993) (in Chapter 6). In did so on the grounds that the school district denied Lamb's Chapel's First Amendment right of free speech, as well as held that allowing

Lamb's Chapel to show films related to family values and child rearing
would not violate the First Amendment's (dis)establishment clause.

Rust v. Sullivan

111 S.Ct. 1759 (1991)

In 1970, Congress enacted Title X of the Public Health Service Act,
providing federal funding for family planning services and authorizing
the secretary of the Department of Health, Education, and Welfare (now
the Department of Health and Human Services [HHS]) to make grants
to public and private organizations engaged in family planning projects
and to promulgate regulations for the administration of those grants.
Section 1008 of the act also provided that "[n]one of the funds appropriated under this subchapter shall be used in programs where abortion
is a method of family planning." In 1988, the Reagan administration's
secretary of the HHS set down new regulations attaching three principal
conditions to the award of a grant of federal funds under Title X. First,
the regulations specify that a "Title X project may not provide counseling concerning the use of abortion as a method of family planning or
provide referral for abortion as a method of family planning." Second,
the regulations broadly prohibit grant recipients from engaging in activities that "encourage, promote or advocate abortion as a method of
family planning." Forbidden activities include lobbying for legislation
that would increase the availability of abortion, developing or dis-
seminating materials advocating abortion as a method of family planning, providing speakers to promote abortion, using legal action to make
abortion available, and paying dues to any group that advocates abortion. Finally, the regulations require organizations that are engaged in
family planning and receive federal funding to be organized so that they
are "physically and financially separate" from prohibited abortion activities.

HHS's new regulations were immediately challenged in federal court
by Dr. Irving Rust and several other doctors and recipients of federal
funding family planning projects. They sued on behalf of themselves and
their patients on several grounds: that the regulations were not authorized by Title X and that they violate the First and Fifth Amendment
rights of doctors and clients. A federal district court, however, summarily
decided in favor of the secretary of HHS, and a panel of the Court of
Appeals for the Second Circuit affirmed that decision. Rust thereupon
appealed to the Supreme Court. By a vote of five-to-four the Rehnquist
Court upheld the ban on abortion counseling. Subsequently, under
pressure from Congress to revise its regulations and after months of

negotiations, the Bush administration's HHS issued a new regulation allowing doctors, but not nurses or clinic counselors, to advise women on abortion. However, on November 3, 1992, the day of the presidential election, a three-judge panel (coincidentally composed of Democratic appointees) on the Court of Appeals for the District of Columbia Circuit overturned that revised regulation. It did so, notably in an unpublished disposition in *National Family Planning and Reproductive Health Association, Inc. v. Sullivan,* on the grounds that the administration failed to comply with the Administrative Procedure Act's requirement that agencies provide an opportunity for public "notice and comment" before enacting new federal regulations. Two days after his inauguration, President Bill Clinton fulfilled a campaign promise and repealed the Reagan/Bush administrations' ban on abortion counseling by organizations receiving federal funding.

The Court's decision was five to four, with Chief Justice Rehnquist announcing the majority's opinion. Justice Marshall joined Justice Blackmun's dissent, as did in part Justices Stevens and O'Connor, who also delivered dissenting opinions.

Chief Justice REHNQUIST delivers the opinion of the Court.

We need not dwell on the plain language of the statute because we agree with every court to have addressed the issue that the language is ambiguous. The language of Sec. 1008—that "[n]one of the funds appropriated under this subchapter shall be used in programs where abortion is a method of family planning"—does not speak directly to the issues of counseling, referral, advocacy, or program integrity. If a statute is "silent or ambiguous with respect to the specific issue, the question for the court is whether the agency's answer is based on a permissible construction of the statute." *Chevron v. Natural Resources Defense Council,* 467 U.S. 837 (1984). . . .

The broad language of Title X plainly allows the Secretary's construction of the statute. By its own terms, Sec. 1008 prohibits the use of Title X funds "in programs where abortion is a method of family planning." Title X does not define the term "method of family planning," nor does it enumerate what types of medical and counseling services are entitled to Title X funding. Based on the broad directives provided by Congress in Title X in general and Sec. 1008 in particular, we are unable to say that the Secretary's construction of the prohibition in Sec. 1008 to require a ban on counseling, referral, and advocacy within the Title X project, is impermissible. . . .

There is no question but that the statutory prohibition contained in Sec. 1008 is constitutional. In *Maher v. Roe,* [432 U.S. 464 (1977)], we upheld a state welfare regulation under which Medicaid recipients received payments for services related to childbirth, but not for nontherapeutic abortions. The Court rejected the claim that this unequal subsidization worked a violation of the Constitution. We held that the government may "make a value judgment favoring childbirth over abortion, and . . . implement that judgment by the allocation of public funds." . . .

To hold that the Government unconstitutionally discriminates on the basis of viewpoint when it chooses to fund a program dedicated to advance certain permissible goals, because the program in advancing those goals necessarily discourages alternate goals, would render numerous government programs constitutionally suspect. When Congress established a National Endowment for Democracy to encourage other countries to adopt democratic principles, it was not constitutionally required to fund a program to encourage competing lines of political philosophy such as Communism and Fascism. Petitioners' assertions ultimately boil down to the position that if the government chooses to subsidize one protected right, it must subsidize analogous counterpart rights. But the Court has soundly rejected that proposition. . . .

By requiring that the Title X grantee engage in abortion-related activity separately from activity receiving federal funding, Congress has . . . not denied it the right to engage in abortion-related activities. Congress has merely refused to fund such activities out of the public fisc, and the Secretary has simply required a certain degree of separation from the Title X project in order to ensure the integrity of the federally funded program.

The same principles apply to petitioners' claim that the regulations abridge the free speech rights of the grantee's staff. Individuals who are voluntarily employed for a Title X project must perform their duties in accordance with the regulation's restrictions on abortion counseling and referral. . . .

We turn now to petitioners' argument that the regulations violate a woman's Fifth Amendment right to choose whether to terminate her pregnancy. We recently reaffirmed the long-recognized principle that " 'the Due Process Clauses generally confer no affirmative right to governmental aid, even where such aid may be necessary to secure life, liberty, or property interests of which the government itself may not deprive the individual.' " *Webster* [*v. Reproductive Health Services,* 492 U.S. 490 (1989)] quoting *DeShaney v. Winnebago County Dept. of Social Services,* 489 U.S. 189 (1989). . . .

That the regulations do not impermissibly burden a woman's Fifth Amendment rights is evident from the line of cases beginning with *Maher* and *McRae* and culminating in our most recent decision in *Webster.* Just as Congress' refusal to fund abortions in *McRae* left "an indigent woman with at least the same range of choice in deciding whether to obtain a medically necessary abortion as she would have had if Congress had chosen to subsidize no health care costs at all," and "Missouri's refusal to allow public employees to perform abortions in public hospitals leaves a pregnant woman with the same choices as if the State had chosen not to operate any public hospitals," *Webster,* Congress' refusal to fund abortion counseling and advocacy leaves a pregnant woman with the same choices as if the government had chosen not to fund family-planning services at all. The difficulty that a woman encounters when a Title X project does not provide abortion counseling or referral leaves her in no different position than she would have been if the government had not enacted Title X. . . .

Justice BLACKMUN, with whom Justice MARSHALL joins, with whom Justice STEVENS joins as to parts II and III, and with whom Justice O'CONNOR joins as to part I, dissenting.

Until today, the Court never has upheld viewpoint-based suppression of speech simply because that suppression was a condition upon the acceptance of public funds. Whatever may be the Government's power to condition the receipt of its largess upon the relinquishment of constitutional rights, it surely does not extend to a condition that suppresses the recipient's cherished freedom of speech based solely upon the content or viewpoint of that speech. *Speiser v. Randall,* 357 U.S. 513 (1958) ("To deny an exemption to claimants who engage in certain forms of speech is in effect to penalize them for such speech. . . . The denial is 'frankly aimed at the suppression of dangerous ideas,' " quoting *American Communications Assn. v. Douds,* 339 U.S. 382 (1950)). This rule is a sound one. . . .

The Regulations are also clearly viewpoint-based. While suppressing speech favorable to abortion with one hand, the Secretary compels anti-abortion speech with the other. . . .

[I]t is of no small significance that the speech the Secretary would suppress is truthful information regarding constitutionally protected conduct of vital importance to the listener. One can imagine no legitimate governmental interest that might be served by suppressing such information. . . .

Contrary to the majority's characterization, this is not a case in which individuals seek government aid in exercising their fundamental rights. The Fifth Amendment right asserted by petitioners is the right of a pregnant woman to be free from affirmative governmental interference in her decision. *Roe v. Wade* and its progeny are not so much about a medical procedure as they are about a woman's fundamental right to self-determination. Those cases serve to vindicate the idea that "liberty," if it means anything, must entail freedom from governmental domination in making the most intimate and personal of decisions. By suppressing medically pertinent information and injecting a restrictive ideological message unrelated to considerations of maternal health, the government places formidable obstacles in the path of Title X clients' freedom of choice and thereby violates their Fifth Amendment rights.

Justice STEVENS, dissenting.

In my opinion, the Court has not paid sufficient attention to the language of the controlling statute or to the consistent interpretation accorded the statute by the responsible cabinet officers during four different Presidencies and 18 years.

The relevant text of the "Family Planning Services and Population Research Act of 1970" has remained unchanged since its enactment. The preamble to the Act states that it was passed:

> To promote public health and welfare by expanding, improving, and better coordinating the family planning services and population research activities of the Federal Government, and for other purposes.

The declaration of congressional purposes emphasizes the importance of educating the public about family planning services. . . . In contrast to the statutory emphasis on making relevant information readily available to the public, the statute contains no suggestion that Congress intended to authorize the suppression or censorship of any information by any Government employee or by any grant recipient.

Section 6 of the Act authorizes the provision of federal funds to support the establishment and operation of voluntary family planning projects. The section also empowers the Secretary to promulgate regulations imposing conditions on grant recipients to ensure that "such grants will be effectively utilized for the purposes for which made." Sec. 300a-4(b). Not a word in the statute, however, authorizes the Secretary to impose any restrictions on the dissemination of truthful information or professional advice by grant recipients.

The word "prohibition" is used only once in the Act. Section 6, which adds to the Public Health Service Act the new Title X, covering the subject of population research and voluntary planning programs, includes the following provision:

PROHIBITION OF ABORTION
SEC. 1008. None of the funds appropriated under this title shall be used in programs where abortion is a method of family planning.

Read in the context of the entire statute, this prohibition is plainly directed at conduct, rather than the dissemination of information or advice, by potential grant recipients.

The original regulations promulgated in 1971 by the Secretary of Health, Education and Welfare so interpreted the statute. . . . Conforming to the language of the governing statute, the regulations provided that "[t]he project will not provide abortions as a method of family planning." Like the statute itself, the regulations prohibited conduct, not speech. . . .

The entirely new approach adopted by the Secretary in 1988 was not, in my view, authorized by the statute. The new regulations did not merely reflect a change in a policy determination that the Secretary had been authorized by Congress to make. Rather, they represented an assumption of policymaking responsibility that Congress had not delegated to the Secretary. In a society that abhors censorship and in which policymakers have traditionally placed the highest value on the freedom to communicate, it is unrealistic to conclude that statutory authority to regulate conduct implicitly authorized the Executive to regulate speech.

Justice O'CONNOR, dissenting.

In this case, we need only tell the Secretary that his regulations are not a reasonable interpretation of the statute; we need not tell Congress that it cannot pass such legislation. If we rule solely on statutory grounds, Congress retains the power to force the constitutional question by legislating more explicitly. It may instead choose to do nothing. That decision should be left to Congress; we should not tell Congress what it cannot do before it has chosen to do it.

R.A.V. v. City of St. Paul, Minnesota
112 S.Ct. 2538 (1992)

Robert A. Viktora, a white teenager, and several other white youths burned a cross after midnight on the lawn of the only black family in a St. Paul, Minnesota, neighborhood. He was subsequently arrested and charged with violating a 1989 city ordinance making it a crime to place on public or private property a burning cross, swastika, or other symbol likely to arouse "anger, alarm, or resentment in others on the basis of race, color, creed, religion, or gender." A state juvenile court, however, dismissed the complaint on the grounds that the ordinance was overly broad and unconstitutional. But the Minnesota State Supreme Court reversed upon concluding that the ordinance applied only to conduct "outside First Amendment protection." In determining that the ordinance only prohibited "fighting words," or speech that threatens "imminent lawless action"—categories of speech that have historically fallen outside of the scope of the First Amendment—the state court observed that "[t]he burning of a cross is itself an unmistakable symbol of violence and hatred based on virulent notions of racial supremacy. It is the responsibility, even the obligation, of diverse communities to confront such notions in whatever form they appear." The state high court also distinguished St. Paul's ordinance from Texas's flag-burning law, which was struck down by a bare majority in *Texas v. Johnson,* 491 U.S. 397 (1989) (see Vol. 2, Ch. 5). St. Paul did not ban cross burning per se, the Minnesota court reasoned, "but only those displays that one knows or should know will create anger, alarm, or resentment based on racial, ethnic, gender, or religious bias." Robert A. Viktora appealed that ruling to the Supreme Court.

The Court's decision was unanimous; Justice Scalia announced the opinion. Justice O'Connor joined Justice White's concurrence, as did Justices Blackmun and Stevens who also delivered concurring opinions

Justice SCALIA delivers the opinion of the Court.

The First Amendment generally prevents government from proscribing speech, see, e.g., *Cantwell v. Connecticut,* 310 U.S. 296 (1940), or even expressive conduct, see, e.g., *Texas v. Johnson,* 491 U.S. 397, 406 (1989), because of disapproval of the ideas expressed. Content-based regulations are presumptively invalid. From 1791 to the present, however, our society, like other free but civilized societies, has permitted restrictions upon the content of speech in a few limited areas, which are "of such slight social value as a step to truth that any benefit that may be derived from them is clearly outweighed by the social interest in order and morality." *Chaplinsky* [*v. New Hampshire,* 315 U.S. 568 (1942)]. We have recognized that "the freedom of speech" referred to by the First Amendment does not include a freedom to disregard these traditional limitations. Our decisions since the 1960's have narrowed the scope of the traditional categorical exceptions for defamation, and for obscenity, but a limited categorical approach has remained an important part of our First Amendment jurisprudence.

We have sometimes said that these categories of expression are "not within the area of constitutionally protected speech," or that the "protection of the First Amendment does not extend" to them. Such statements must be taken in context, however, and are no more literally true than is the occasionally repeated shorthand characterizing obscenity "as not being speech at all." What they mean is that these areas of speech can, consistently with the First Amendment, be regulated because of their constitutionally proscribable content (obscenity, defamation, etc.)—not that they are categories of speech entirely invisible to the Constitution, so that they may be made the vehicles for content discrimination unrelated to their distinctively proscribable content. Thus, the government may proscribe libel; but it may not make the further content discrimination of proscribing only libel critical of the government. . . .

The proposition that a particular instance of speech can be proscribable on the basis of one feature (e.g., obscenity) but not on the basis of another (e.g., opposition to the city government) is commonplace, and has found application in many contexts. We have long held, for example, that nonverbal expressive activity can be banned because of the action it entails, but not because of the ideas it expresses—so that burning a flag in violation of an ordinance against outdoor fires could be punishable, whereas burning a flag in violation of an ordinance against dishonoring the flag is not. Similarly, we have upheld reasonable "time, place, or manner" restrictions, but only if they are "justified without reference to the content of the regulated speech." *Ward v. Rock Against Racism,* 491 U.S.

781 (1989). And just as the power to proscribe particular speech on the basis of a noncontent element (e.g., noise) does not entail the power to proscribe the same speech on the basis of a content element; so also, the power to proscribe it on the basis of one content element (e.g., obscenity) does not entail the power to proscribe it on the basis of other content elements.

In other words, the exclusion of "fighting words" from the scope of the First Amendment simply means that, for purposes of that Amendment, the unprotected features of the words are, despite their verbal character, essentially a "nonspeech" element of communication. Fighting words are thus analogous to a noisy sound truck: Each is, as Justice Frankfurter recognized, a "mode of speech," *Niemotko v. Maryland*, 340 U.S. 268 (1951); both can be used to convey an idea; but neither has, in and of itself, a claim upon the First Amendment. As with the sound truck, however, so also with fighting words: The government may not regulate use based on hostility—or favoritism—towards the underlying message expressed. . . .

Even the prohibition against content discrimination that we assert the First Amendment requires is not absolute. It applies differently in the context of proscribable speech than in the area of fully protected speech. The rationale of the general prohibition, after all, is that content discrimination "raises the specter that the Government may effectively drive certain ideas or viewpoints from the marketplace," *Simon & Schuster [Inc. v. Members of the New York State Crime Victims Board*, 112 S.Ct. 501] (1992). But content discrimination among various instances of a class of proscribable speech often does not pose this threat.

When the basis for the content discrimination consists entirely of the very reason the entire class of speech at issue is proscribable, no significant danger of idea or viewpoint discrimination exists. Such a reason, having been adjudged neutral enough to support exclusion of the entire class of speech from First Amendment protection, is also neutral enough to form the basis of distinction within the class. To illustrate: A State might choose to prohibit only that obscenity which is the most patently offensive in its prurience—i.e., that which involves the most lascivious displays of sexual activity. But it may not prohibit, for example, only that obscenity which includes offensive political messages. And the Federal Government can criminalize only those threats of violence that are directed against the President—since the reasons why threats of violence are outside the First Amendment (protecting individuals from the fear of violence, from the disruption that fear engenders, and from the possibility that the threatened violence will occur) have special force when applied to the person of the President. . . . But the Federal Government may not criminalize only those threats against the President that mention his policy on aid to inner cities. And to take a final example, a State may choose to regulate price advertising in one industry but not in others, because the risk of fraud (one of the characteristics of commercial speech that justifies depriving it of full First Amendment protection, see *Virginia Pharmacy Bd. v. Virginia Citizens Consumer Council, Inc.,* 425 U.S. 748 (1976)) is in its view greater there.

Another valid basis for according differential treatment to even a content-defined subclass of proscribable speech is that the subclass happens to be associated with particular "secondary effects" of the speech, so that the regulation is "justified without reference to the content of the . . . speech," *Renton v. Playtime Theatres, Inc.,* 475 U.S. 41 (1986). A State could, for example, permit all obscene live performances except those involving minors. Moreover, since words can in some circumstances violate laws directed not against speech but against conduct (a law against treason, for example, is violated by telling the enemy the nation's defense secrets), a particular content-based subcategory of a proscribable class of speech can be swept up incidentally within the reach of a statute directed at conduct rather than speech. Where the government does not target conduct on the basis of its expressive content, acts are not shielded from regulation merely because they express a discriminatory idea or philosophy. . . .

Applying these principles to the St. Paul ordinance, we conclude that, even as narrowly construed by the Minnesota Supreme Court, the ordinance is facially unconstitutional. Although the phrase in the ordinance, "arouses anger, alarm, or resentment in others," has been limited by the Minnesota Supreme Court's construction to reach only those symbols or displays that amount to "fighting words," the remaining, unmodified terms make clear that the ordinance applies only to "fighting words" that insult, or provoke violence, "on the basis of race, color, creed, religion, or gender." Displays containing abusive invective, no matter how vicious or severe, are permissible unless they are addressed to one of the specified disfavored topics. Those who wish to use "fighting words" in connection with other ideas—to express hostility, for example, on the basis of political affiliation, union membership, or homosexuality—are not covered. The First Amendment does not permit St. Paul to impose special prohibitions on those speakers who express views on disfavored subjects. In its practical operation, moreover, the ordinance goes even beyond mere content discrimination, to actual viewpoint discrimination. Displays containing some words—odious racial epithets, for example—would be prohibited to proponents of all views. But "fighting words" that do not themselves invoke race, color, creed, religion, or gender—aspersions upon a person's mother, for example—would seemingly be usable ad libitum in the placards of those arguing in favor of racial, color, etc. tolerance and equality, but could not be used by that speaker's opponents. One could hold up a sign saying, for example, that all "anti-Catholic bigots" are misbegotten; but not that all "papists" are, for that would insult and provoke violence "on the basis of religion." St. Paul has no such authority to license one side of a debate to fight freestyle, while requiring the other to follow Marquis of Queensbury Rules.

What we have here, it must be emphasized, is not a prohibition of fighting words that are directed at certain persons or groups (which would be facially valid if it met the requirements of the Equal Protection Clause); but rather, a prohibition of fighting words that contain (as the Minnesota Supreme Court repeatedly emphasized) messages of "bias-motivated" hatred and in particular, as applied to this case, messages "based on virulent notions of racial supremacy." . . .

The content-based discrimination reflected in the St. Paul ordinance comes within neither any of the specific exceptions to the First Amendment prohibition we discussed earlier, nor within a more general exception for content discrimination that does not threaten censorship of ideas. It assuredly does not fall within the exception for content discrimination based on the very reasons why the particular class of speech at issue (here, fighting words) is proscribable. As explained earlier, the reason why fighting words are categorically excluded from the protection of the First Amendment is not that their content communicates any particular idea, but that their content embodies a particularly intolerable (and socially unnecessary) mode of expressing whatever idea the speaker wishes to convey. St. Paul has not singled out an especially offensive mode of expression—it has not, for example, selected for prohibition only those fighting words that communicate ideas in a threatening (as opposed to a merely obnoxious) manner. Rather, it has proscribed fighting words of whatever manner that communicate messages of racial, gender, or religious intolerance. Selectivity of this sort creates the possibility that the city is seeking to handicap the expression of particular ideas. That possibility would alone be enough to render the ordinance presumptively invalid, but St. Paul's comments and concessions in this case elevate the possibility to a certainty. . . .

Let there be no mistake about our belief that burning a cross in someone's front yard is reprehensible. But St. Paul has sufficient means at its disposal to prevent such behavior without adding the First Amendment to the fire.

The judgment of the Minnesota Supreme Court is reversed, and the case is remanded for proceedings not inconsistent with this opinion.

It is so ordered.

Justice WHITE, with whom Justice BLACKMUN and Justice O'CONNOR join, and with whom Justice STEVENS joins except as to Part I(A), concurring in the judgment.

I agree with the majority that the judgment of the Minnesota Supreme Court should be reversed. However, our agreement ends there.

[T]he majority casts aside long-established First Amendment doctrine without the benefit of briefing and adopts an untried theory. This is hardly a judicious way of proceeding, and the Court's reasoning in reaching its result is transparently wrong.

I (A)

Today, . . . the Court announces that earlier Courts did not mean their repeated statements that certain categories of expression are "not within the area of constitutionally protected speech." The present Court submits that such clear statements "must be taken in context" and are not "literally true."

To the contrary, those statements meant precisely what they said: The categorical approach is a firmly entrenched part of our First Amendment jurisprudence. Indeed, the Court in *Roth* [*v. United States,* 354 U.S. 476 (1952)], reviewed the guarantees of freedom of expression in effect at the time of the ratification of the Constitution and concluded, "in light of this history, it is apparent that the unconditional phrasing of the First Amendment was not intended to protect every utterance."

In its decision today, the Court points to "nothing . . . in this Court's precedents warranting disregard of this longstanding tradition." Nevertheless, the majority holds that the First Amendment protects those narrow categories of expression long held to be undeserving of First Amendment protection—at least to the extent that lawmakers may not regulate some fighting words more strictly than others because of their content. The Court announces that such content-based distinctions violate the First Amendment because "the government may not regulate use based on hostility—or favoritism—towards the underlying message expressed." Should the government want to criminalize certain fighting words, the Court now requires it to criminalize all fighting words.

To borrow a phrase, "Such a simplistic, all-or-nothing-at-all approach to First Amendment protection is at odds with common sense and with our jurisprudence as well." It is inconsistent to hold that the government may proscribe an entire category of speech because the content of that speech is evil, . . . but that the government may not treat a subset of that category differently without violating the First Amendment; the content of the subset is by definition worthless and undeserving of constitutional protection.

The majority's observation that "fighting words are quite expressive indeed" is no answer. Fighting words are not a means of exchanging views, rallying supporters, or registering a protest; they are directed against individuals to provoke violence or to inflict injury. Therefore, a ban on all fighting words or on a subset of the fighting words category would restrict only the social evil of hate speech, without creating the danger of driving viewpoints from the marketplace.

Therefore, the Court's insistence on inventing its brand of First Amendment underinclusiveness puzzles me. The overbreadth doctrine has the redeeming virtue of attempting to avoid the chilling of protected expression, but the Court's new "underbreadth" creation serves no desirable function. Instead, it permits, indeed invites, the continuation of expressive conduct that in this case is evil and worthless in First Amendment terms, until the city of St. Paul cures the underbreadth by adding to its ordinance a catch-all phrase such as "and all other fighting words that may constitutionally be subject to this ordinance."

Any contribution of this holding to First Amendment jurisprudence is surely a negative one, since it necessarily signals that expressions of violence, such as the message of intimidation and racial hatred conveyed by burning a cross on someone's lawn, are of sufficient value to outweigh the social interest in order and morality that has traditionally placed such fighting words outside the First Amendment. Indeed, by characterizing "fighting words as a form of debate," the majority legitimates hate speech as a form of public discussion.

Furthermore, the Court obscures the line between speech that could be regulated freely on the basis of content (i.e., the narrow categories of expression falling outside the First Amendment) and that which could be regulated on the basis of content only upon a showing of a compelling state interest (i.e., all remaining expression). By placing fighting words, which the Court has long held to be valueless, on at least equal constitutional footing with political discourse and other forms of speech that we have deemed to have the greatest social value, the majority devalues the latter category.

I (B)

In a second break with precedent, the Court refuses to sustain the ordinance even though it would survive under the strict scrutiny applicable to other protected expression. Assuming, arguendo, that the St. Paul ordinance is a content-based regulation of protected expression, it nevertheless would pass First Amendment review under settled law upon a showing that the regulation "is necessary to serve a compelling state interest and is narrowly drawn to achieve that end." *Simon & Schuster.* St. Paul has urged that its ordinance, in the words of the majority, "helps to ensure the basic human rights of members of groups that have historically been subjected to discrimination. . . ." The Court expressly concedes that this interest is compelling and is promoted by the ordinance. Nevertheless, the Court treats strict scrutiny analysis as irrelevant to the constitutionality of the legislation. . . .

Although the First Amendment does not apply to categories of unprotected speech, such as fighting words, the Equal Protection Clause requires that the regulation of unprotected speech be rationally related to a legitimate government interest. A defamation statute that drew distinctions on the basis of political affiliation or "an ordinance prohibiting only those legally obscene works that contain criticism of the city government," would unquestionably fail rational basis review.

Turning to the St. Paul ordinance and assuming arguendo, as the majority does, that the ordinance is not constitutionally overbroad, there is no question that it would pass equal protection review. The ordinance proscribes a subset of "fighting words," those that injure "on the basis of race, color, creed, religion, or gender." This selective regulation reflects the City's judgment that harms based on race, color, creed, religion, or gender are more pressing public concerns than the harms caused by other fighting words. In light of our Nation's long and painful experience with discrimination, this determination is plainly reasonable. Indeed, as the majority concedes, the interest is compelling. . . .

Although I disagree with the Court's analysis, I do agree with its conclusion: The St. Paul ordinance is unconstitutional. However, I would decide the case on overbreadth grounds. . . .

Justice BLACKMUN concurring in the judgment.

. . .

I see no First Amendment values that are compromised by a law that prohibits hoodlums from driving minorities out of their homes by burning crosses on their lawns, but I see great harm in preventing the people of Saint Paul from specifically punishing the race-based fighting words that so prejudice their community. I concur in the judgment, however, because I agree with Justice WHITE that this particular ordinance reaches beyond fighting words to speech protected by the First Amendment.

Justice STEVENS, with whom Justice WHITE and Justice BLACKMUN join as to Part I, concurring in the judgment.

[M]y colleagues today wrestle with two broad principles: first, that certain "categories of expression [including 'fighting words'] are not within the area of constitutionally protected speech;" and second, that "content-based regulations [of expression] are presumptively invalid." Although in past opinions the Court has repeated both of these maxims, it has—quite rightly—adhered to neither with the absolutism suggested by my colleagues. Thus, while I agree that the St. Paul ordinance is unconstitutionally overbroad for the reasons stated in Part II of Justice WHITE's opinion, I write separately to suggest how the allure of absolute principles has skewed the analysis of both the majority and concurring opinions.

I

The Court today revises this categorical approach. It is not, the Court rules, that certain "categories" of expression are "unprotected," but rather that certain "elements" of expression are wholly "proscribable." To the Court, an expressive act, like a chemical compound, consists of more than one element. Although the act may be regulated because it contains a proscribable element, it may not be regulated on the basis of another (nonproscribable) element it also contains. Thus, obscene antigovernment speech may be regulated because it is obscene, but not because it is antigovernment. It is this revision of the categorical approach that allows the Court to assume that the St. Paul ordinance proscribes only fighting words, while at the same time concluding that the ordinance is invalid because it imposes a content-based regulation on expressive activity.

As an initial matter, the Court's revision of the categorical approach seems to me something of an adventure in a doctrinal wonderland, for the concept of "obscene antigovernment" speech is fantastical. The category of the obscene is very narrow; to be obscene, expression must be found by the trier of fact to "appeal to the prurient interest, . . . depict or describe, in a patently offensive way, sexual conduct, [and] taken as a whole, lack serious literary, artistic, political or scientific value." *Miller v. California,* 413 U.S. 15 (1973). "Obscene antigovernment" speech, then, is a contradiction in terms: If expression is antigovernment, it does not "lack serious . . . political . . . value" and cannot be obscene. . . .

I am, however, even more troubled by the second step of the Court's analysis—namely, its conclusion that the St. Paul ordinance is an unconstitutional content-based regulation of speech. Drawing on broadly worded dicta, the Court establishes a near-absolute ban on content-based regulations of expression and holds that the First Amendment prohibits the regulation of fighting words by subject matter. Thus, while the Court rejects the "all-or-nothing-at-all" nature of the categorical approach, it promptly embraces an absolutism of its own: within a particular "proscribable" category of expression, the Court holds, a government must either proscribe all speech or no speech at all. This aspect of the Court's ruling fundamentally misunderstands the role and constitutional status of content-based regulations on speech, conflicts with the very nature of First Amendment jurisprudence, and disrupts well-settled principles of First Amendment law. . . .

Our First Amendment decisions have created a rough hierarchy in the constitutional protection of speech. Core political speech occupies the highest, most protected position; commercial speech and nonobscene, sexually explicit speech are regarded as a sort of second-class expression; obscenity and fighting words receive the least protection of all. Assuming that the Court is correct that this last class of speech is not wholly "unprotected," it certainly does not follow that fighting words and obscenity receive the same sort of protection afforded core political speech. Yet in ruling that proscribable speech cannot be regulated based on subject matter, the Court does just that. Perversely, this gives fighting words greater protection than is afforded commercial speech. . . .

In sum, the central premise of the Court's ruling—that "content-based regulations are presumptively invalid"—has simplistic appeal, but lacks support in our First Amendment jurisprudence. To make matters worse, the Court today extends this overstated claim to reach categories of hitherto unprotected speech and, in doing so, wreaks havoc in an area of settled law. Finally, although the Court recognizes exceptions to its new principle, those exceptions undermine its very conclusion that the St.

Paul ordinance is unconstitutional. Stated directly, the majority's position cannot withstand scrutiny.

II

Although I agree with much of Justice WHITE's analysis, I do not join Part I-A of his opinion because I have reservations about the "categorical approach" to the First Amendment. . . .

[T]his approach sacrifices subtlety for clarity and is, I am convinced, ultimately unsound. As an initial matter, the concept of "categories" fits poorly with the complex reality of expression. Few dividing lines in First Amendment law are straight and unwavering, and efforts at categorization inevitably give rise only to fuzzy boundaries. Our definitions of "obscenity," illustrate this all too well. The quest for doctrinal certainty through the definition of categories and subcategories is, in my opinion, destined to fail.

Moreover, the categorical approach does not take seriously the importance of context. The meaning of any expression and the legitimacy of its regulation can only be determined in context. Whether, for example, a picture or a sentence is obscene cannot be judged in the abstract, but rather only in the context of its setting, its use, and its audience. . . .

Perhaps sensing the limits of such an all-or-nothing approach, the Court has applied its analysis less categorically than its doctrinal statements suggest. The Court has recognized intermediate categories of speech (for example, for indecent nonobscene speech and commercial speech) and geographic categories of speech (public fora, limited public fora, nonpublic fora) entitled to varying levels of protection. The Court has also stringently delimited the categories of unprotected speech. While we once declared that "libelous utterances [are] not . . . within the area of constitutionally protected speech, *Beauharnais v. Illinois,* 343 U.S. 250 (1952), our rulings in *New York Times Co. v. Sullivan,* 376 U.S. 253 (1964); *Gertz v. Robert Welch, Inc.,* 418 U.S. 323 (1974), and *Dun & Bradstreet, Inc. v. Greenmoss Builders, Inc.,* 472 U.S. 749 (1985), have substantially qualified this broad claim. Similarly, we have consistently construed the "fighting words" exception set forth in *Chaplinsky* narrowly. . . . In short, the history of the categorical approach is largely the history of narrowing the categories of unprotected speech.

This evolution, I believe, indicates that the categorical approach is unworkable and the quest for absolute categories of "protected" and "unprotected" speech ultimately futile. . . .

III

. . . Unlike the Court, I do not believe that all content-based regulations are equally infirm and presumptively invalid; unlike Justice WHITE, I do not believe that fighting words are wholly unprotected by the First Amendment. To the contrary, I believe our decisions establish a more complex and subtle analysis, one that considers the content and context of the regulated speech, and the nature and scope of the restriction on speech. Applying this analysis and assuming arguendo (as the Court does) that the St. Paul ordinance is not overbroad, I conclude that such a selective, subject-matter regulation on proscribable speech is constitutional. . . .

In sum, the St. Paul ordinance (as construed by the Court) regulates expressive activity that is wholly proscribable and does so not on the basis of viewpoint, but rather in recognition of the different harms caused by such activity. Taken together, these several considerations persuade me that the St. Paul ordinance is not an unconstitutional content-based regulation of speech. Thus, were the ordinance not overbroad, I would vote to uphold it.

Alexander v. United States,
113 S.Ct. 2766 (1993)

An owner of more than a dozen adult bookstores and theaters, Ferris Alexander, was tried and convicted on seventeen counts of selling pornographic materials and three counts of violating the Racketeer Influenced and Corrupt Organizations (RICO) Act. For the obscenity charges he was sentenced to six years in prison and fined $100,000, as well as ordered to pay the cost of prosecution and incarceration. In addition, the federal government successfully sought the forfeiture of Alexander's businesses and real estate under the RICO Act, and a federal district court ultimately ordered him to forfeit his wholesale and retail businesses, along with almost $9 million acquired through those businesses. Alexander appealed to the Supreme Court, arguing that the application of RICO's forfeiture provisions constituted a prior restraint on free speech in violation of the First Amendment, as well as ran afoul of the Eighth Amendment's prohibition against "cruel and unusual punishment" and "excessive fines."

The Court's decision was, in part, five to four, with the majority's opinion announced by Chief Justice Rehnquist. Justice Kennedy's dissent was joined by Justices Blackmun and Stevens, and in part by Justice Souter. Justice Souter delivered a separate opinion in part concurring and in part dissenting.

Chief Justice REHNQUIST delivers the opinion of the Court.

Practically speaking, petitioner argues, the effect of the RICO forfeiture order here was no different from the injunction prohibiting the publication of expressive material found to be a prior restraint in *Near v.*

Minnesota ex rel. Olson, 283 U.S. 697 (1931). As petitioner puts it, the forfeiture order imposed a complete ban on his future expression because of previous unprotected speech. We disagree. . . .

The term prior restraint is used "to describe administrative and judicial orders forbidding certain communications when issued in advance of the time that such communications are to occur." Temporary restraining orders and permanent injunctions—i.e., court orders that actually forbid speech activities—are classic examples of prior restraints. This understanding of what constitutes a prior restraint is borne out by our cases, even those on which petitioner relies. In *Near v. Minnesota ex rel. Olson,* we invalidated a court order that perpetually enjoined the named party, who had published a newspaper containing articles found to [be in violation of] a state nuisance statute, from producing any future "malicious, scandalous and defamatory" publication. *Near,* therefore, involved a true restraint on future speech—a permanent injunction. . . .

By contrast, the RICO forfeiture order in this case does not forbid petitioner from engaging in any expressive activities in the future, nor does it require him to obtain prior approval for any expressive activities. It only deprives him of specific assets that were found to be related to his previous racketeering violations. Assuming, of course, that he has sufficient untainted assets to open new stores, restock his inventory, and hire staff, petitioner can go back into the adult entertainment business tomorrow, and sell as many sexually explicit magazines and videotapes as he likes, without any risk of being held in contempt for violating a court order. . . .

No doubt the monetarily large forfeiture in this case may induce cautious booksellers to practice self-censorship and remove marginally protected materials from their shelves out of fear that those materials could be found obscene and thus subject them to forfeiture. . . .

[But, the] petitioner's position boils down to this: stiff criminal penalties for obscenity offenses are consistent with the First Amendment; so is the forfeiture of expressive materials as punishment for criminal conduct; but the combination of the two somehow results in a violation of the First Amendment. We reject this counter-intuitive conclusion, which in effect would say that the whole is greater than the sum of the parts.

Petitioner also argues that the forfeiture order in this case—considered atop his 6-year prison term and $100,000 fine—is disproportionate to the gravity of his offenses and therefore violates the Eighth Amendment, either as a "cruel and unusual punishment" or as an "excessive fine." . . . Unlike the Cruel and Unusual Punishments Clause, which is concerned with matters such as the duration or conditions of confinement, "the Excessive Fines Clause limits the Government's power to extract payments, whether in cash or in kind, as punishment for some offense." *Austin v. United States,* [113 S.Ct. 2801] (1993). The in personam criminal forfeiture at issue here is clearly a form of monetary punishment no different, for Eighth Amendment purposes, from a traditional "fine." Accordingly, the forfeiture in this case should be analyzed under the Excessive Fines Clause. . . . It is so ordered.

Justice KENNEDY, with whom Justices BLACKMUN and STEVENS join, and with whom Justice SOUTER joins in part, dissenting.

The Court today embraces a rule that would find no affront to the First Amendment in the Government's destruction of a book and film business and its entire inventory of legitimate expression as punishment for a single past speech offense. Until now I had thought one could browse through any book or film store in the United States without fear that the proprietor had chosen each item to avoid risk to the whole inventory and indeed to the business itself. This ominous, onerous threat undermines free speech and press principles essential to our personal freedom. . . .

The fundamental defect in the majority's reasoning is a failure to recognize that the forfeiture here cannot be equated with traditional punishments such as fines and jail terms. Noting that petitioner does not challenge either the 6-year jail sentence or the $100,000 fine imposed against him as punishment for his RICO convictions, the majority ponders why RICO's forfeiture penalty should be any different. The answer is that RICO's forfeiture penalties are different from traditional punishments by Congress' own design as well as in their First Amendment consequences....

The First Amendment is a rule of substantive protection, not an artifice of categories. The admitted design and the overt purpose of the forfeiture in this case are to destroy an entire speech business and all its protected titles, thus depriving the public of access to lawful expression. This is restraint in more than theory. It is censorship all too real.

Relying on the distinction between prior restraints and subsequent punishments, the majority labels the forfeiture imposed here a punishment and dismisses any further debate over the constitutionality of the forfeiture penalty under the First Amendment. Our cases do recognize a distinction between prior restraints and subsequent punishments, but that distinction is neither so rigid nor so precise that it can bear the weight the Court places upon it to sustain the destruction of a speech business and its inventory as a punishment for past expression. . . .

To be sure, the term prior restraint is not self-defining. . . . [Yet, as] our First Amendment law has developed, we have not confined the application of the prior restraint doctrine to its simpler forms, outright licensing or censorship before speech takes place. In considering governmental measures deviating from the classic form of a prior restraint yet posing many of the same dangers to First Amendment freedoms, we have extended prior restraint protection with some latitude, toward the end of declaring certain governmental actions to fall within the presumption of invalidity. This approach is evident in *Near v. Minnesota ex rel. Olson,* the leading case in which we invoked the prior restraint doctrine to invalidate a state injunctive decree. . . .

One wonders what today's majority would have done if faced in *Near* with a novel argument to extend the traditional conception of the prior restraint doctrine. In view of the formalistic approach the Court advances today, the Court likely would have rejected Near's pleas on the theory that to accept his argument would be to "blur the line separating prior restraints from subsequent punishments to such a degree that it would be impossible to determine with any certainty whether a particular measure is a prior restraint or not." In so holding the Court would have ignored, as the Court does today, that the applicability of First Amendment analysis to a governmental action depends not alone upon the name by which the action is called, but upon its operation and effect on the suppression of speech. *Near*. . . .

The operation and effect of RICO's forfeiture remedies is different from a heavy fine or a severe jail sentence because RICO's forfeiture provisions are different in purpose and kind from ordinary criminal sanctions. The government's stated purpose under RICO, to destroy or incapacitate the offending enterprise, bears a striking resemblance to the motivation for the state nuisance statute the Court struck down as an impermissible prior restraint in *Near*. The purpose of the state statute in *Near* was "not punishment, in the ordinary sense, but suppression of the offending newspaper or periodical." . . . The particular nature of Ferris Alexander's activities ought not blind the Court to what is at stake here. Under the principle the Court adopts, any bookstore or press enterprise could be forfeited as punishment for even a single obscenity conviction. . . .

What is at work in this case is not the power to punish an individual for his past transgressions but the authority to suppress a particular class of disfavored speech. The forfeiture provisions accomplish this in a direct way by seizing speech presumed to be protected along with the instruments of its dissemination, and in an indirect way by threatening all who engage in the business of distributing adult or sexually explicit materials with the same disabling measures. . . . I dissent from the judgment and from the opinion of the Court.

Justice SOUTER concurring in the judgment in part and dissenting in part.

I agree with the Court that petitioner has not demonstrated that the forfeiture at issue here qualifies as a prior restraint as we have traditionally understood that term. I also agree with the Court that the case should be remanded for a determination whether the forfeiture violated the Excessive Fines Clause of the Eighth Amendment. Nonetheless, I agree with Justice KENNEDY that the First Amendment forbids the forfeiture of petitioner's expressive material in the absence of an adjudication that it is obscene or otherwise of unprotected character, and therefore I join [that part] of his dissenting opinion.

B. OBSCENITY, PORNOGRAPHY, AND OFFENSIVE SPEECH

The Rehnquist Court revisited the controversy over nude dancing in *Barnes v. Glen Theatre, Inc.*, 111 S.Ct. 2456 (1991) (see page 123). *Barnes* involved a challenge to Indiana's public decency law for violating nude dancers' right to freedom of expression. The case presented an opportunity to reconsider a 1981 ruling by the Burger Court, in *Schad v. Borough of Mount Ephraim,* 452 U.S. 61 (1981), that gave some First Amendment protection to nude dancing performances. In *Schad* the Burger Court struck down a law prohibiting nude dancers in places of adult entertainment, while also upholding a state's power to ban nude dancing in places that sell liquor on the basis of the Twenty-first Amendment, which empowers states to regulate liquor. In *Barnes* the Rehnquist Court faced a challenge to Indiana's public indecency law requiring "nude" dancers to wear pasties and G-strings.

In the end, the Rehnquist Court was badly split in upholding Indiana's public decency law over First Amendment objections. In announcing the Court's decision for a bare majority, Chief Justice Rehnquist's plurality opinion was joined only by Justices Kennedy and O'Connor. Applying the test for "symbolic speech" set forth in *United States v. O'Brien,* 391 U.S. 367 (1968) (see Vol. 2, Ch. 5), the chief justice rejected the First Amendment claim made that this case was entitled to special scrutiny and concluded that Indiana's law was clearly within its constitutional authority in promoting "social order and morality." In separate concurring opinions, however, Justices Scalia and Souter explained their reasons for upholding the law. According to Scalia, Indiana's was a general law regulating conduct and not specifically directed at expression and, therefore, was not subject to normal First Amendment scrutiny and should be upheld on the grounds that moral opposition to nudity supplies a rational basis for the prohibition of totally nude dancing. In contrast, Souter deemed the nude dancing at issue here to be subject to a degree of First Amendment protection and that *O'Brien*'s test was appropriate, but he reasoned, unlike Rehnquist, that the state's interests in preventing the secondary effects of adult-entertainment establishments—prostitution, sexual assaults, and other criminal activity—warranted the law's enforcement against nude dancing. Dissenting Justice White's opinion commanded the votes of Justices Blackmun, Marshall, and Stevens.

The Court, however, refused to revisit the issue of "dial-a-porn" in denying review to *Dial Information Services Corporation of New York v. Barr,* 112 S.Ct. 966 (1992). Three years earlier, the Rehnquist Court unanimously struck down a 1988 congressional statute banning indecent telephone dial-a-porn services and held that only hard-core obscene messages could be outlawed. In refusing to hear *Barr,* the Court left standing a lower court decision upholding another congressional enactment, passed in response to *Sable Communications v. Federal Communications Commission,* 492 U.S. 115 (1989), that requires telephone companies to block access to sexually explicit messages unless customers ask, in advance and in writing, to receive them.

In its 1993 term the Court will consider whether a child pornography law, banning the "exhibition of the genitals or pubic area," is unconstitutionally vague and overly broad in *Knox v. United States* (No. 92-1183). In upholding a conviction for receiving through the mail videotapes of young women engaged in "sexually explicit conduct," the Court of Appeals for the Third Circuit ruled that the law was not overly broad or vague even when applied here to videotapes in which the young women were wearing clothes.

Barnes v. Glen Theatre, Inc.

111 S.Ct. 2456 (1991)

The Kitty Kat Lounge and the Glen Theatre, located in South Bend, Indiana, are adult-entertainment establishments. Both were subject to the state's public decency law, requiring "nude" dancers to wear pasties and a G-string. Owners and dancers at the Kitty Kat Lounge wanted to present "totally nude dancing"; the dancers worked on commission—receiving a 100 percent commission on the first sixty dollars in drink sales during their performances—and wanted to dance nude because they claimed they would make more money. The Glen Theatre provided adult entertainment through written and printed materials, movie showings, and live entertainment at an enclosed "bookstore." The live entertainment at the bookstore consisted in nude and seminude showings of the female body through glass panels in booths, in which customers insert coins into a timing mechanism that permits them to watch the dancers. The owners and dancers of Glen Theatre also contended that they could make more money if totally nude dancing were allowed, and they sought in federal district court an injunction against the enforcement of Indiana's public indecency statute. The district court found that the statute was "overly broad," but the Court of Appeals for the Seventh Circuit reversed and remanded the case with instructions to consider whether the statute violated the First Amendment as specifically applied to nude dancers. On remand, the district court concluded that "the type of dancing these plaintiffs wish to perform is not expressive activity" protected by the First Amendment, but the Seventh Circuit again reversed the lower court; this time the appellate court held that nonobscene nude dancing performed for entertainment is expression protected by the First Amendment. That decision was, then, appealed to the Supreme Court.

The Court's decision was five to four, with Chief Justice Rehnquist announcing the majority's opinion. Justices Scalia and Souter each concurred. Justices Marshall, Blackmun, and Stevens joined a dissent by Justice White.

Chief Justice REHNQUIST delivers the opinion of the Court.

. . .

Indiana, of course, has not banned nude dancing as such, but has pro-scribed public nudity across the board. The Supreme Court of Indiana has construed the Indiana statute to preclude nudity in what are essen-tially places of public accommodation such as the Glen Theatre and the Kitty Kat Lounge. . . . Respondents contend that while the state may license establishments such as the ones involved here, and limit the geographical area in which they do business, it may not in any way limit the performance of the dances within them without violating the First Amendment. The petitioner contends, on the other hand, that Indiana's restriction on nude dancing is a valid "time, place or manner" restriction under cases such as *Clark v. Community for Creative Non-Violence,* 468 U.S. 288 (1984).

The "time, place, or manner" test was developed for evaluating restric-tions on expression taking place on public property which had been dedicated as a "public forum," *Ward v. Rock Against Racism,* 491 U.S. 781 (1989), although we have on at least one occasion applied it to conduct occurring on private property. See *Renton v. Playtime Theatres, Inc.,* 475 U.S. 41 (1986). In *Clark* we observed that this test has been interpreted to embody much the same standards as those set forth in *United States v. O'Brien,* 391 U.S. 367 (1968), and we turn, therefore, to the rule enun-ciated in *O'Brien.*

[In] *O'Brien* [the Court observed that]

> we think it clear that a government regulation is sufficiently justified if it is within the constitutional power of the Government; if it furthers an important or substantial governmental interest; if the governmental interest is unrelated to the suppression of free expression; and if the incidental restriction on alleged First Amendment free-doms is no greater than is essential to the furtherance of that interest.

Applying the four-part *O'Brien* test enunciated above, we find that In-diana's public indecency statute is justified despite its incidental limita-tions on some expressive activity. The public indecency statute is clearly within the constitutional power of the State and furthers substantial governmental interests.

Justice SCALIA concurring.

I agree that the judgment of the Court of Appeals must be reversed. In my view, however, the challenged regulation must be upheld, not because it survives some lower level of First-Amendment scrutiny, but because, as a general law regulating conduct and not specifically directed at expres-sion, it is not subject to First-Amendment scrutiny at all. . . .

The purpose of Indiana's nudity law would be violated, I think, if 60,000 fully consenting adults crowded into the Hoosierdome to display their genitals to one another, even if there were not an offended innocent in the crowd. Our society prohibits, and all human societies have prohibited, certain activities not because they harm others but because they are considered, in the traditional phrase, "contra bonos mores," i.e., immoral. In American society, such prohibitions have included, for example, sadomasochism, cockfighting, bestiality, suicide, drug use, prostitution, and sodomy. While there may be great diversity of view on whether various of these prohibitions should exist (though I have found few ready to abandon, in principle, all of them) there is no doubt that, absent specific constitutional protection for the conduct involved, the Constitution does not prohibit them simply because they regulate "morality." See *Bowers v. Hardwick*, 478 U.S. 186 (1986) (upholding prohibition of private homosexual sodomy enacted solely on "the presumed belief of a majority of the electorate in [the jurisdiction] that homosexual sodomy is immoral and unacceptable"). . . .

Since the Indiana regulation is a general law not specifically targeted at expressive conduct, its application to such conduct does not in my view implicate the First Amendment. . . .

This is not to say that the First Amendment affords no protection to expressive conduct. Where the government prohibits conduct precisely because of its communicative attributes, we hold the regulation unconstitutional. See, e.g., *United States v. Eichman*, 496 U.S. 310 (1990) (burning flag); *Texas v. Johnson*, 491 U.S. 397 (1989) (same); *Spence v. Washington*, 418 U.S. 405 (1974) (defacing flag); *Tinker v. Des Moines Independent Community School District*, 393 U.S. 503 (1969) (wearing black arm bands); *Brown v. Louisiana*, 383 U.S. 131 (1966) (participating in silent sit-in); *Stromberg v. California*, 283 U.S. 359 (1931) (flying a red flag). In each of the foregoing cases, we explicitly found that suppressing communication was the object of the regulation of conduct. Where that has not been the case, however—where suppression of communicative use of the conduct was merely the incidental effect of forbidding the conduct for other reasons—we have allowed the regulation to stand. *O'Brien.* . . .

Justice SOUTER concurring.

I . . . write separately to rest my concurrence in the judgment, not on the possible sufficiency of society's moral views to justify the limitations at issue, but on the State's substantial interest in combating the secondary effects of adult entertainment establishments of the sort typified by respondents' establishments. . . .

In *Renton v. Playtime Theatres, Inc.*, 475 U.S. 41 (1986), we upheld a city's zoning ordinance designed to prevent the occurrence of harmful secondary effects, including the crime associated with adult entertainment. . . .

In light of *Renton*'s recognition that legislation seeking to combat the secondary effects of adult entertainment need not await localized proof of those effects, the State of Indiana could reasonably conclude that forbidding nude entertainment of the type offered at the Kitty Kat

Lounge and the Glen Theatre's "bookstore" furthers its interest in preventing prostitution, sexual assault, and associated crimes.

Justice WHITE, with whom Justices MARSHALL, BLACKMUN, and STEVENS join, dissenting.

The Court's analysis is erroneous in several respects. Both the Court and Justice SCALIA in his concurring opinion overlook a fundamental and critical aspect of our cases upholding the States' exercise of their police powers. None of the cases they rely upon, including *O'Brien* and *Bowers v. Hardwick,* 478 U.S. 186 (1986), involved anything less than truly general proscriptions on individual conduct. In *O'Brien,* for example, individuals were prohibited from destroying their draft cards at any time and in any place, even in completely private places such as the home. Likewise, in *Bowers,* the State prohibited sodomy, regardless of where the conduct might occur, including the home as was true in that case. The same is true of cases like *Employment Division, Oregon Dept. of Human Resources v. Smith* (1990), which, though not applicable here because it did not involve any claim that the peyote users were engaged in expressive activity, recognized that the State's interests in the use of illegal drugs extends even into the home. By contrast, in this case Indiana does not suggest that its statute applies to, or could be applied to, nudity wherever it occurs, including the home. We do not understand the Court or Justice SCALIA to be suggesting that Indiana could constitutionally enact such an intrusive prohibition, nor do we think such a suggestion would be tenable in light of our decision in *Stanley v. Georgia,* 394 U.S. 557 (1969), in which we held that States could not punish the mere possession of obscenity in the privacy of one's own home.

We are told by the Attorney General of Indiana that the Indiana Supreme Court held that the statute at issue here cannot and does not prohibit nudity as a part of some larger form of expression meriting protection when the communication of ideas is involved. Petitioners also state that the evils sought to be avoided by applying the statute in this case would not obtain in the case of theatrical productions, such as *Salome* or *Hair.* Neither is there any evidence that the State has attempted to apply the statute to nudity in performances such as plays, ballets, or operas.

Thus, the Indiana statute is not a general prohibition of the type we have upheld in prior cases. As a result, the Court's and Justice SCALIA's simple references to the State's general interest in promoting societal order and morality is not sufficient justification for a statute which concededly reaches a significant amount of protected expressive activity. Instead, in applying the *O'Brien* test, we are obligated to carefully examine the reasons the State has chosen to regulate this expressive conduct in a less than general statute. In other words, when the State enacts a law which draws a line between expressive conduct which is regulated and nonexpressive conduct of the same type which is not regulated, *O'Brien* places the burden on the State to justify the distinctions it has made. . . .

Since the State permits the dancers to perform if they wear pasties and G-strings but forbids nude dancing, it is precisely because of the distinctive, expressive content of the nude dancing performances at issue in this case that the State seeks to apply the statutory prohibition. It is only because nude dancing performances may generate emotions and feelings of eroticism and sensuality among the spectators that the State seeks to regulate such expressive activity, apparently on the assumption that creating or emphasizing such thoughts and ideas in the minds of the spectators may lead to increased prostitution and the degradation of women. But generating thoughts, ideas, and emotions is the essence of communication. The nudity element of nude dancing performances cannot be neatly pigeonholed as mere "conduct" independent of any expressive component of the dance. . . .

[E]ven if there were compelling interests, the Indiana statute is not narrowly drawn. If the State is genuinely concerned with prostitution and associated evils, as Justice SOUTER seems to think, or the type of conduct that was occurring in *California v. LaRue*, 409 U.S. 109 (1972), it can adopt restrictions that do not interfere with the expressiveness of nonobscene nude dancing performances. For instance, the State could perhaps require that, while performing, nude performers remain at all times a certain minimum distance from spectators, that nude entertainment be limited to certain hours, or even that establishments providing such entertainment be dispersed throughout the city. Likewise, the State clearly has the authority to criminalize prostitution and obscene behavior. Banning an entire category of expressive activity, however, generally does not satisfy the narrow tailoring requirement of strict First Amendment scrutiny. Furthermore, if nude dancing in barrooms, as compared with other establishments, is the most worrisome problem, the State could invoke its Twenty-first Amendment powers and impose appropriate regulation. *New York State Liquor Authority v. Bellanca*, 452 U.S. 714 (1981) (per curiam).

C. LIBEL

An important ruling on libel was handed down in *Masson v. The New Yorker Magazine*, 111 S.Ct. 2419 (1991). *Masson* raised a complicated question of whether actual malice may be inferred in a libel suit by a public figure based on evidence of fabricated quotations. Writing for the Court, Justice Kennedy held that the First Amendment does not in libel suits provide a shield for writers who fabricate quotations.

Masson v. The New Yorker Magazine
111 S.Ct. 2419 (1991)

Mr. Jeffrey Masson, a psychologist, was hired in 1980 as the projects director of the Sigmund Freud Archives. Subsequently, his research led him to challenge Freud's reasons for abandoning his "seduction theory," a controversial theory about adult emotional disorders rooted in childhood sexual abuse. His discussion of his research resulted in his dismissal from the archives in 1981. A year later Janet Malcolm interviewed Mr. Masson about the controversy, compiling more than forty hours of taped interviews. Her two-part article was published in 1983 in *The New Yorker* and republished as a book.

Mr. Masson sued Ms. Malcolm, *The New Yorker*, and the publisher for defamation. He charged that certain direct quotations were altered or fabricated, and all seriously damaged his reputation. Ms. Malcolm, for instance, quoted him as saying that if he had remained at the archives it "would have been a center of scholarship, but it would also have been a place of sex, women, and fun." That quote, however, did not appear in transcripts of the interviews. Nonetheless, a federal district court found for Ms. Malcolm, and a three-judge panel of the U.S. Court of Appeals for the Ninth Circuit by a two-to-one vote affirmed that decision. The majority held that actual malice could not be inferred if the word changes did not "alter the substantive content" or were "rational interpretations" of Mr. Masson's unambiguous statements. By contrast, dissenting Judge Alex Kozinski argued, "The right to deliberately alter quotations is not, in my view, a concomitant of a free press. . . . As I see it, when a writer uses quotation marks in reporting what someone else has said, she is representing that those are the speaker's own words or something very close to them." Mr. Masson appealed the decision of the Ninth Circuit to the Supreme Court, which granted review.

The Court's decision was seven to two. The majority's opinion was announced by Justice Kennedy. A separate opinion, in part dissenting and in part concurring, was delivered by Justice White and joined by Justice Scalia.

Justice KENNEDY delivers the opinion of the Court.

The First Amendment limits [states'] libel law in various respects. When, as here, the plaintiff is a public figure, he cannot recover unless he proves by clear and convincing evidence that the defendant published the defamatory statement with actual malice, i.e., with "knowledge that it was false or with reckless disregard of whether it was false or not." *New*

York Times Co. v. Sullivan, 376 U.S. 254 (1964). Mere negligence does not suffice. . . .

Actual malice under the *New York Times* standard should not be confused with the concept of malice as an evil intent or a motive arising from spite or ill will. We have used the term actual malice as a shorthand to describe the First Amendment protections for speech injurious to reputation and we continue to do so here. But the term can confuse as well as enlighten. In this respect, the phrase may be an unfortunate one. In place of the term actual malice, it is better practice that jury instructions refer to publication of a statement with knowledge of falsity or reckless disregard as to truth or falsity. This definitional principle must be remembered in the case before us. . . .

A fabricated quotation may injure reputation in at least two senses, either giving rise to a conceivable claim of defamation. First, the quotation might injure because it attributes an untrue factual assertion to the speaker. An example would be a fabricated quotation of a public official admitting he had been convicted of a serious crime when in fact he had not.

Second, regardless of the truth or falsity of the factual matters asserted within the quoted statement, the attribution may result in injury to reputation because the manner of expression or even the fact that the statement was made indicates a negative personal trait or an attitude the speaker does not hold. . . .

The work at issue here, however, as with much journalistic writing, provides the reader no clue that the quotations are being used as a rhetorical device or to paraphrase the speaker's actual statements. To the contrary, the work purports to be nonfiction, the result of numerous interviews. . . .

The constitutional question we must consider here is whether, in the framework of a summary judgment motion, the evidence suffices to show that respondents acted with the requisite knowledge of falsity or reckless disregard as to truth or falsity. This inquiry in turn requires us to consider the concept of falsity; for we cannot discuss the standards for knowledge or reckless disregard without some understanding of the acts required for liability. We must consider whether the requisite falsity inheres in the attribution of words to the petitioner which he did not speak.

In some sense, any alteration of a verbatim quotation is false. But writers and reporters by necessity alter what people say, at the very least to eliminate grammatical and syntactical infelicities. If every alteration constituted the falsity required to prove actual malice, the practice of journalism, which the First Amendment standard is designed to protect, would require a radical change, one inconsistent with our precedents and First Amendment principles. Petitioner concedes this absolute definition of falsity in the quotation context is too stringent, and acknowledges that "minor changes to correct for grammar or syntax" do not amount to falsity for purposes of proving actual malice. We agree, and must determine what, in addition to this technical falsity, proves falsity for purposes of the actual malice inquiry. . . .

We reject the idea that any alteration beyond correction of grammar or syntax by itself proves falsity in the sense relevant to determining actual malice under the First Amendment. An interviewer who writes from notes often will engage in the task of attempting a reconstruction of the speaker's statement. That author would, we may assume, act with knowledge that at times she has attributed to her subject words other than those actually used. Under petitioner's proposed standard, an author in this situation would lack First Amendment protection if she reported as quotations the substance of a subject's derogatory statements about himself. . . .

We conclude that a deliberate alteration of the words uttered by a plaintiff does not equate with knowledge of falsity for purposes of *New York Times Co. v. Sullivan,* and *Gertz v. Robert Welch, Inc.,* unless the alteration results in a material change in the meaning conveyed by the statement. The use of quotations to attribute words not in fact spoken bears in a most important way on that inquiry, but it is not dispositive in every case.

Deliberate or reckless falsification that comprises actual malice turns upon words and punctuation only because words and punctuation express meaning. Meaning is the life of language. And, for the reasons we have given, quotations may be a devastating instrument for conveying false meaning. In the case under consideration, readers of *In the Freud Archives* may have found Malcolm's portrait of petitioner especially damning because so much of it appeared to be a self-portrait, told by petitioner in his own words. And if the alterations of petitioner's words gave a different meaning to the statements, bearing upon their defamatory character, then the device of quotations might well be critical in finding the words actionable. . . .

We apply these principles to the case before us. . . . The record contains substantial . . . evidence which, in a light most favorable to petitioner, would support a jury determination under a clear and convincing standard that Malcolm deliberately or recklessly altered the quotations.

First, many of the challenged passages resemble quotations that appear on the tapes, except for the addition or alteration of certain phrases, giving rise to a reasonable inference that the statements have been altered. Second, Malcolm had the tapes in her possession and was not working under a tight deadline. Unlike a case involving hot news, Malcolm cannot complain that she lacked the practical ability to compare the tapes with her work in progress. Third, Malcolm represented to the editor-in-chief of *The New Yorker* that all the quotations were from the tape recordings. Fourth, Malcolm's explanations of the time and place of unrecorded conversations during which petitioner allegedly made some of the quoted statements have not been consistent in all respects. Fifth, petitioner suggests that the progression from typewritten notes, to manuscript, then to galleys provides further evidence of intentional alteration.

Justice WHITE, with whom Justice SCALIA joined, concurred in part and dissented in part.

D. COMMERCIAL SPEECH

During the Burger Court years (1969–1986), greater First Amendment protection was accorded commercial speech, though often over the sharp dissent of Justice Rehnquist (see Vol. 2, Ch. 5). In its 1992 term, the Rehnquist Court signaled that it might reassess the commercial speech doctrine in granting three cases review. In *Cincinnati v. Discovery Network*, 113 S.Ct. 1505 (1993), however, the majority struck down an ordinance that barred news racks on public sidewalks for free magazines and papers containing primarily advertisements, for example, for real estate and education courses. Writing for the majority in a narrow holding, Justice Stevens held that Cincinnati "seriously underestimate[d]" the First Amendment's protection for commercial speech and that the city's ban, which would have required removing 62 of 2,000 vending machines on city sidewalks, lacked a "reasonable fit" with the city's regulatory goal of reducing litter. But, joined by Justices White and Thomas, dissenting Chief Justice Rehnquist reiterated his view that commercial speech should receive less constitutional protection than other, noncommercial speech. As he put it, "every news rack that is removed from the city's sidewalks marginally enhances the safety of its streets and esthetics of its cityscape." By contrast, concurring Justice Blackmun urged his colleagues to reassess the commercial speech doctrine and to firmly establish that "truthful, noncoercive commercial speech concerning lawful activities is entitled to full First Amendment protection."

In *Edenfield v. Fane*, 113 S.Ct. 1793 (1993), the Court affirmed an Eleventh Circuit holding that the Supreme Court's precedents permitting states to ban soliciting by lawyers should not apply to certified public accountants (CPAs) since "[s]olicitation by a CPA does not entail the coercive force of the personal presence of a trained advocate." Writing for the majority, Justice Kennedy reaffirmed the First Amendment's protection of commercial speech and solicitations that are neither fraudulent nor deceptive. In doing so, he distinguished prior rulings that limited protection for attorneys' solicitations on the ground that "a CPA is not 'a professional trained in the art of persuasion' " and that CPAs solicit business in ways conducive to long-term relationships with their clients, rather than engaging in "high pressure sales tactics." Although Chief Justice Rehnquist has been a vigorous critic of the Court's extension of First Amendment protection to commercial speech, he sided with the majority. Only Justice O'Connor dissented, finding "no constitutional difference between a rule prohibiting in-person solicitation by attorneys, and a rule prohibiting in-person solicitation by certified public accountants (CPA's). The attorney's rhetorical power derives not only from his specific training in the art of persuasion, but more generally from his professional expertise. His certified status as an expert in a complex subject matter—the law—empowers the attorney to overawe inexpert clients. CPA's have an analogous power."

Finally, in *United States v. Edge Broadcasting Company*, 113 S.Ct. 2696 (1993), the Rehnquist Court considered federal limitations on lottery-related advertisements. Under federal law, lottery advertisements are generally prohibited, but broadcasters may advertise state-run lotteries on stations licensed in a state that conducts lotteries. A North Carolina company, Edge Broadcasting Company, challenged the application of those restrictions because it wanted to broadcast advertisements for Virginia's lottery. Broadcasting close to the Virginia and North Carolina border, approximately 90 percent of Edge's listeners reside in the former state, though it is licensed in the latter. A federal district and appellate court held that the restrictions as applied to Edge failed to directly advance the government's interests, but the Rehnquist Court reversed.

Writing for the majority in *Edge Broadcasting Company*, Justice White applied the four-factor test for commercial speech set forth in *Central Hudson Gas & Electric Corp. v. Public Service Commission of New York*, 447 U.S. 557 (1980): (1) whether the speech concerns lawful activity and is not misleading; (2) whether the asserted governmental interest is substantial; and, if so, (3) whether the regulation directly advances the asserted governmental interest; and (4) whether the regulation is not more extensive than necessary to serve the interest. The restrictions on lottery advertisements were deemed permissible in *Central Hudson* and the Court found that they were properly applied to Edge Broadcasting because they advanced the federal government's interest in supporting nonlottery states' antigambling policies and did so in an effective and nonexcessive way, thus satisfying the third and fourth factors setout in *Central Hudson*. In reversing the lower court's decision, the Court concluded that even though only about 10 percent of Edge's listeners resided in North Carolina, the restriction on Edge's broadcasting of Virginia lottery advertisements was not "ineffective" or "marginal" to advancing North Carolina's antigambling policy. Justices Stevens and Blackmun dissented.

E. FREEDOM OF THE PRESS

Two cases on the Court's 1990 plenary docket raised questions involving state regulations that allegedly posed direct or indirect prior restraints on the freedom of the press. One, *Cohen v. Cowles Media Co.*, 111 S.Ct. 2513 (1991), raised an issue bearing on indirect prior restraints on the press. *Cohen* posed the question of whether newspapers may be sued for disclosing the names of their confidential sources. Dan Cohen, a political consultant, was fired from his job after two newspapers identified him as the confidential source of damaging information about the criminal record of another candidate. He had been promised anonymity by reporters, but their editors overrode their objections to naming him and revised their stories so as to point up the fact that Cohen was the source of the damaging information. Cohen sued for breach of contract and a jury awarded him $700,000. The Minnesota Supreme Court, however, overturned that award when holding that the First Amendment's guarantee for freedom of the press outweighed "the common law interest in protecting a promise of anonymity."

By a five-to-four vote, the Court held that the First Amendment does not provide a shield against suits for damages, under state promissory estoppel law, for a newspaper's breach of a promise of confidentiality. Writing for the bare majority, Justice White observed that

> generally applicable laws do not offend the First Amendment simply because their enforcement against the press has incidental effects on its ability to gather and report the news. . . . [T]ruthful information sought to be published must have been lawfully acquired. The press may not with impunity break and enter an office or dwelling to gather news. Neither does the First Amendment relieve a newspaper reporter of the obligation shared by all citizens to respond to a grand jury subpoena and answer questions relevant to a criminal investigation, even though the reporter might be required to reveal a confidential source. The press, like others interested in publishing, may not publish copyrighted material without obeying the copyright laws. Similarly, the media must obey the National Labor Relations Act, and the Fair Labor Standards Act; may not restrain trade in violation of the antitrust laws; and must pay nondiscriminatory taxes. It is therefore beyond dispute that "[t]he publisher of a newspaper has no special immunity from the application of general laws. He has no special privilege to invade the rights and liberties of others." Accordingly, enforcement of such general laws against the press is not subject to stricter scrutiny than would be applied to enforcement against other persons or organizations.

In *Cohen*, dissenting Justice Blackmun, joined by Justice Marshall, contended that the First Amendment protects "the reporting of truthful information regarding a political campaign." In a separate dissenting opinion, joined by Justices Blackmun, Marshall, and O'Connor, Justice Souter contended that the "general applicability" of laws should not be dispositive of the First Amendment claims and deemed it necessary to balance the competing claims and interests in the case. According to Justice Souter, "There can be no doubt that the fact of Cohen's identity expanded the universe of information relevant to the choice faced by Minnesota voters in that State's 1982 gubernatorial election, the publication of which was thus of the sort quintessentially subject to strict First Amendment protection."

In *Leathers v. Medlock*, 111 S.Ct. 1438 (1991), the Court dealt with the question of whether states that impose taxes on cable television must also apply the levy to similar communications services, such as the unscrambling of satellite signals. The Arkansas Supreme Court ruled that the state's 4 percent tax on cable television services was permissible only if it did not discriminate in favor of similar forms of mass communications, while exempting newspapers and magazines from the sales tax. By a seven-to-two vote in *Leathers,* the justices upheld Arkansas's tax on cable television companies. In her opinion for the Court, Justice O'Connor reaffirmed that states may neither single out the press as a whole for special taxes nor discriminate among different kinds of media on the basis of content or for the purpose of censorship. Nonetheless, O'Connor held that states may apply general taxes to some kinds of media, and not others, so long as the taxes do not discriminate "on the basis of ideas." Dissenting Justices Marshall and Blackmun criticized the majority for failing to pay adequate attention to the First Amendment claims that the state was unconstitutionally bestowing financial benefits and burdens on different kinds of media. In Justice Marshall's words, "Even when structured in a manner that is content neutral, a scheme that imposes different burdens on like-situated members of the press violates the First Amendment because it poses the risk that the state might abuse this power."

In its 1991 term, however, in *Simon & Schuster, Inc. v. Members of the New York State Crime Victims Board,* 112 S.Ct. 501 (1991), the Rehnquist Court struck down New York's "Son-of-Sam" law. The law was adopted to prevent criminals from profiting from their notoriety and the sale of stories of their criminal activities. In 1977, David Berkowitz, a serial killer popularly known as the "Son of Sam," murdered five women and later agreed to publish his story of terror for a substantial advance on royalties. New York's legislature immediately responded by passing its Son-of-Sam law, requiring publishers to deposit with the Victims Control Board all royalties and earnings from their contracts with accused or convicted criminals. The board in turn was authorized to hold the money for five years, during which time victims could bring civil actions against a convicted defendant, and to make payments to victims of a crime. The act also covered individuals who were not criminally charged, tried, and convicted, but who admitted committing crimes in a book or other commercial communications. In 1987, the Victims Control Board notified Simon & Schuster that it had violated the law by not turning over its contract with and the royalties owed Henry Hill, who retold his life in organized crime in *Wiseguy*. Attorneys for Simon &

Schuster and Hill countered that New York's law violated the First Amendment's guarantee for freedom of speech and press.

Relying on *Leathers* in her opinion for the Court in *Simon & Schuster,* Justice O'Connor struck down New York's law as "presumptively inconsistent with the First Amendment" for imposing "a financial burden on speakers because of the content of their speech." "In the context of financial regulation," O'Connor underscored, "the Government's ability to impose content-based burdens on speech raises the specter that the Government may effectively drive certain ideas or viewpoints from the marketplace. The First Amendment presumptively places this sort of discrimination beyond the power of the Government." Nor did the Court find New York's statute either to serve a "compelling state interest" or to have been "narrowly drawn to achieve that end." Justice O'Connor thus concluded that

[a]s a means of ensuring that victims are compensated from the proceeds of crime, the Son of Sam law is significantly overinclusive. . . . In addition, the statute's broad definition of "person convicted of a crime" enables the Board to escrow the income of any author who admits in his work to having committed a crime, whether or not the author was ever actually accused or convicted. These two provisions combine to encompass a potentially very large number of works. Had the Son of Sam law been in effect at the time and place of publication, it would have escrowed payment for such works as *The Autobiography of Malcolm X,* which describes crimes committed by the civil rights leader before he became a public figure; *Civil Disobedience,* in which Thoreau acknowledges his refusal to pay taxes and recalls his experience in jail; and even the *Confessions of Saint Augustine,* in which the author laments "my past foulness and the carnal corruptions of my soul," one instance of which involved the theft of pears from a neighboring vineyard.

In separate opinions in *Simon & Schuster,* Justices Blackmun and Kennedy concurred. Notably, the latter justice took strong exception to the Court's "balancing approach" to the First Amendment and the state's interests. In Justice Kennedy's words,

Here a law is directed to speech alone where the speech in question is not obscene, not defamatory, not words tantamount to an act otherwise criminal, not an impairment of some other constitutional right, not an incitement to lawless action, and not calculated or likely to bring about imminent harm the State has the substantive power to prevent. No further inquiry is necessary to reject the State's argument that the statute should be upheld.

F. REGULATING THE BROADCAST MEDIA

The Federal Communications Commission (FCC) began in 1987 to enforce more strictly regulations against "indecent" radio and television broadcasts, and the following year Congress passed legislation, sponsored by Senator Jesse Helms (R–NC), that completely banned "inde-cent" broadcasts. The regulations were defended as necessary to protect children and the privacy of unsuspecting adult listeners, but were at-tacked for being too broad and for having a chilling effect on innovative programming and free speech. In *Federal Communications Commission v. Pacifica Foundation,* 438 U.S. 726 (1978) (see Vol. 2, Ch. 5), the Burger Court had upheld the FCC's power to ban "indecent" broadcasts over First Amendment objections. Nevertheless, a federal appellate court struck down Congress's 1988 legislation and the Rehnquist Court de-clined to review that decision in *Federal Communications Commission v. Action for Children's Television,* 112 S.Ct. 1282 (1992), leaving the lower court's ruling overturning the legislation intact. In the process of litigating the case, the FCC modified its regulations to allow the broadcast of such materials after 8 P.M. and before 6 A.M. In 1992, the FCC fined Infinity Broadcasting Company an unprecedented $600,000 for airing several indecent broadcasts, which were deemed to be "patently offensive," by the highly popular shock-radio commentator Howard Stern.

G. FAIR TRIAL/FREE PRESS CONTROVERSIES

The most important recent ruling bearing on a defendant's Sixth Amendment right to obtain an impartial jury trial and the "fair trial/free press" controversy came in *Mu'Min v. Virginia,* 111 S.Ct. 1899 (1991) (see page 000). Writing for a bare majority, Chief Justice Rehnquist held that in a murder case that had received substantial pretrial publicity the Sixth Amendment does not require judges to question potential jurors about what information each has seen or read about the crime.

H. SYMBOLIC SPEECH AND SPEECH-PLUS-CONDUCT

One year after striking down St. Paul, Minnesota's law punishing "hate speech" in *R.A.V. v. St. Paul, Minnesota* (see page 108), the Rehn-quist Court turned its attention to the laws in twenty-eight states that provide for enhanced sentences for individuals convicted of assault and battery or vandalism when the victim was selected out of racial, religious, gender, or ethnic bias. In rejecting a challenge to enhanced sentencing for "hate speech" accompanying a crime in *Wisconsin v. Mitchell,* 113 S.Ct. 2194 (1993) (see page 137), the Court unanimously upheld Wiscon-sin's law and dismissed the claim that such laws deny or have a chilling effect on First Amendment–protected speech-plus-conduct. Other re-cent rulings are summarized below in "The Development of Law: Rul-ings on Symbolic Speech and Speech-Plus-Conduct."

THE DEVELOPMENT OF LAW
Rulings on Symbolic Speech and Speech-Plus-Conduct

Case	Ruling
Forsyth County v. The Nationalist Movement, 112 S.Ct. 2395 (1992)	By a five-to-four vote, the Court struck down an ordinance imposing a fee of up to $1000 per day for parades and rallies, which had been adopted after a clash between civil rights demonstrators and Ku Klux Klan members. Writing for the majority, Justice Blackmun found that (1) the ordinance gave "unbridled discretion" to administrators, (2) it

discriminated against groups on the basis of the content of their speech since unpopular groups might be penalized by having to pay higher fees, and (3) the $1000 ceiling on fees was irrelevant in light of competing First Amendment values. Chief Justice Rehnquist and Justices Scalia, Thomas, and White dissented.

International Society for Krishna Consciousness v. Lee, 112 S.Ct. 2701 (1992)	In a plurality opinion joined by Justices O'Connor, Scalia, Thomas, and White, Chief Justice Rehnquist upheld a ban on all soliciting in government run airports and ruled that airports are not "public forums." However, in a concurring opinion Justice Kennedy deemed airports to constitute a First Amendment–protected forum, whereas in a separate

concurrence Justice O'Connor expressed strong disagreement with the view that airports are "public forums." On that score Justices Blackmun, Souter, and Stevens dissented. But those three justices were joined by Kennedy and O'Connor in voting to strike down the ordinance's prohibition of leafleting in airports. In sum, by a five-to-four vote the Court held that airports are not "public forums"; by a six-to-three vote upheld bans on solicitations; and by a five-to-four vote struck down the prohibition on leafleting.

Wisconsin v. Mitchell

113 S.Ct. 2194 (1993)

One evening in 1989 Todd Mitchell and several other black men and youths were talking about a scene in the movie *Mississippi Burning,* in which a white man beats a young black. Later, as the group moved outside to the street, Mitchell asked them, "Do you all feel hyped up to move on some white people?" Shortly thereafter a young white boy appeared on the other side of the street. And as he walked by, Mitchell counted "one, two, three" and said: "There goes a white boy; go get him!" After rushing the boy, Mitchell and the others beat him unconscious and stole his tennis shoes.

Subsequently, Mitchell was convicted of battery, which carries a maximum sentence of two years imprisonment. But under Wisconsin's "hate-speech" law an enhanced sentence may be given whenever the defendant "intentionally selects the person against whom the crime . . . is committed . . . because of the race, religion, color, disability, sexual orientation, national origin or ancestry of that person." Accordingly, Mitchell was sentenced to four years imprisonment. His challenge to the state's "hate-speech" law was initially unsuccessful, but on appeal the state supreme court agreed that the law violated "the First Amendment directly by punishing what the legislature has deemed to be offensive thought." But that ruling was appealed by the state and the Supreme Court granted review.

The Court's decision was unanimous. Chief Justice Rehnquist announced the opinion.

Chief Justice REHNQUIST delivers the opinion of the Court.

The State argues that the statute does not punish bigoted thought, as the Supreme Court of Wisconsin said, but instead punishes only conduct. While this argument is literally correct, it does not dispose of Mitchell's First Amendment challenge. To be sure, our cases reject the "view that an apparently limitless variety of conduct can be labeled 'speech' whenever the person engaging in the conduct intends thereby to express an idea." *United States v. O'Brien,* 391 U.S. 367 (1968); accord, *R.A.V. [v. City of St. Paul, Minnesota,* 112 S.Ct. 2538 (1922)]. Thus, a physical assault is not by any stretch of the imagination expressive conduct protected by the First Amendment. See *Roberts v. United States Jaycees,* 468 U.S. 609 (1984) ("Violence or other types of potentially expressive activities that produce special harms distinct from their communicative impact . . . are entitled to no constitutional protection").

But the fact remains that under the Wisconsin statute the same criminal conduct may be more heavily punished if the victim is selected because of his race or other protected status than if no such motive obtained. Thus, although the statute punishes criminal conduct, it enhances the maximum penalty for conduct motivated by a discriminatory point of view more severely than the same conduct engaged in for some other reason or for no reason at all. Because the only reason for the enhancement is the defendant's discriminatory motive for selecting his victim, Mitchell argues (and the Wisconsin Supreme Court held) that the statute violates the First Amendment by punishing offenders' bigoted beliefs.

Traditionally, sentencing judges have considered a wide variety of factors in addition to evidence bearing on guilt in determining what sentence to impose on a convicted defendant. Thus, in many States the commission of a murder, or other capital offense, for pecuniary gain is a separate aggravating circumstance under the capital-sentencing statute. . . .

[But] Mitchell argues that the Wisconsin penalty-enhancement statute is invalid because it punishes the defendant's discriminatory motive, or reason, for acting. But motive plays the same role under the Wisconsin statute as it does under federal and state antidiscrimination laws, which we have previously upheld against constitutional challenge.

Nothing in our decision last Term in *R.A.V.* compels a different result here. That case involved a First Amendment challenge to a municipal ordinance prohibiting the use of " 'fighting words' that insult, or provoke violence, 'on the basis of race, color, creed, religion or gender.' " Because the ordinance only proscribed a class of "fighting words" deemed particularly offensive by the city—i.e., those "that contain . . . messages of 'bias-motivated' hatred"—we held that it violated the rule against content-based discrimination. But whereas the ordinance struck down in *R.A.V.* was explicitly directed at expression (i.e., "speech" or "messages,") the statute in this case is aimed at conduct unprotected by the First Amendment. . . .

Finally, there remains to be considered Mitchell's argument that the Wisconsin statute is unconstitutionally overbroad because of its "chilling effect" on free speech. Mitchell argues (and the Wisconsin Supreme Court agreed) that the statute is "overbroad" because evidence of the defendant's prior speech or associations may be used to prove that the defendant intentionally selected his victim on account of the victim's protected status. Consequently, the argument goes, the statute impermissibly chills free expression with respect to such matters by those concerned about the possibility of enhanced sentences if they should in the future commit a criminal offense covered by the statute. We find no merit in this contention.

The sort of chill envisioned here is far more attenuated and unlikely than that contemplated in traditional "overbreadth" cases. We must conjure up a vision of a Wisconsin citizen suppressing his unpopular bigoted opinions for fear that if he later commits an offense covered by the statute, these opinions will be offered at trial to establish that he selected his victim on account of the victim's protected status, thus qualifying him for penalty-enhancement. To stay within the realm of rationality, we must surely put to one side minor misdemeanor offenses covered by the statute, such as negligent operation of a motor vehicle, for it is difficult, if not impossible, to conceive of a situation where such offenses would be racially motivated. We are left, then, with the prospect of a citizen suppressing his bigoted beliefs for fear that evidence of such beliefs will be introduced against him at trial if he commits a more serious offense against person or property. This is simply too speculative a hypothesis to support Mitchell's overbreadth claim. . . .

For the foregoing reasons, we hold that Mitchell's First Amendment rights were not violated by the application of the Wisconsin penalty-enhancement provision in sentencing him. The judgment of the Supreme Court of Wisconsin is therefore reversed, and the case is remanded for further proceedings not inconsistent with this opinion.

6

FREEDOM FROM AND OF RELIGION

A. THE (DIS)ESTABLISHMENT OF RELIGION

In its 1989 term the Rehnquist Court made a major shift in its approach toward the First Amendment's free exercise clause. And in its 1990 term the Court signaled that it might be prepared to reconsider the approach to the establishment clause taken in the 1970s and 1980s, and overturn precedents in that area as well. In *Employment Division, Department of Human Resources of Oregon v. Smith*, 494 U.S. 872 (1990) (see Vol. 2, Ch. 6), the Rehnquist Court abandoned the quarter-century-old test set forth by the Warren Court in *Sherbert v. Verner*, 374 U.S. 398 (1963) (see Vol. 2, Ch. 6). Whereas the Rehnquist Court signaled its shift toward upholding laws even though they adversely affect individuals' freedom of religious exercise in *Oregon v. Smith*, in granting oral arguments during its 1991 term in *Lee v. Weisman*, 112 S.Ct. 2649 (1992) (see page 143), the justices indicated that they might reconsider the three-prong test, set forth by the Burger Court in *Lemon v. Kurtzman*, 403 U.S. 603 (1971) (see Vol. 2, Ch. 6), for determining whether states and localities run afoul of the establishment clause. A number of the justices have long criticized *Lemon*. In particular, Chief Justice Rehnquist and Justice Scalia have pushed for a greater accommodation of religion by government and allowing states and localities more latitude in promoting religion, despite the objections of those challenging governmental policies and practices under the establishment clause (see Vol. 2, Ch. 6).

In *Lee v. Weisman* a bare majority declined to reconsider *Lemon*, however. Justice Kennedy announced the decision because he cast the deciding vote in a ruling that otherwise split the justices four to four. The school district's supervision of graduation ceremonies, according to

Kennedy, "places public pressure, as well as peer pressure, on attending students to stand as a group or, at least, maintain respectful silence during the Invocation and Benediction." And he concluded that under any of the Court's First Amendment tests "the government may not coerce anyone to support or participate in religion or its exercise." Kennedy's opinion, though, held out the possibility that government may endorse religion in other ways and that he might join the four dissenters here in other cases that allow governmental involvement with religion outside of public schools, as with official displays of crèches and other religious symbols. In that regard, his analysis conceded too much for the four other justices—Justices Souter, O'Connor, Blackmun, and Stevens—in the majority. In separate concurrences, those four justices emphasized that in their view government may no more endorse religion than, as in *Lee,* coerce participation in a religious practice. By contrast, the four dissenters—Chief Justice Rehnquist and Justices Scalia, Thomas, and White—derided Kennedy's analysis of the psychological coercion of students forced to attend benedictions as "psychology practiced by amateurs."

In its 1992–1993 term, the Rehnquist Court again declined to reexamine and to jettison the *Lemon* test in *Lamb's Chapel v. Center Moriches Union Free School District,* 113 S.Ct. 2141 (1993) (see page 150). There, the Court unanimously held that the denial by a Long Island, New York, school district of a religious group's use of public school facilities for meetings after school hours violated the First Amendment's guarantee for free speech. In addition, writing for the Court Justice White held that permitting religious groups to show films on school grounds at the end of the school day did not run afoul of either *Lemon* or the First Amendment's (dis)establishment clause. In a sharply worded concurring opinion, joined by Justice Thomas and embraced by Justice Kennedy, Justice Scalia criticized the Court's continued reliance on *Lemon.*

Notable also is what the Rehnquist Court now permits under the *Lemon* test and allowed by declining to review *Jones v. Clear Creek Independent School District,* 977 F.2d 963 (1992). In response to the Court's ruling in *Lee v. Weisman,* evangelical churches and supports have pushed student organizations to have voluntary prayers at graduation ceremonies. In this way they sought to evade the ruling in *Lee v. Weisman,* which barred school-sponsored prayers at graduation ceremonies. The Clear Creek Independent School District, near Houston, Texas, adopted the policy that "use of an invocation and/or benediction at high school graduation exercise shall rest with the discretion of the graduating senior class" and that "the invocation and benediction shall be nonsectarian and nonproselytizing in nature." Merritt Jones and his family challenged the constitutionality of that policy as a violation of the First Amendment (dis)establishment clause. But the Court of Appeals for the Fifth Circuit upheld that school district's policy as consistent with not only *Lemon*'s three-prong test but also *Lee v. Weisman.* In denying review of that ruling and in unanimously deciding *Lamb's Chapel,* the Rehnquist Court underscored its renewed accommodationist and nonpreferentialist approach to church-state controversies, as well as unwillingness to discard *Lemon* without first reaching agreement on a new standard for determining the boundaries of the separation of church and state.

Finally, in *Zobrest v. Catalina Foothills School District*, 113 S.Ct. 2462 (1993) (see page 153), a bare majority of the Rehnquist Court held that the First Amendment's (dis)establishment clause does not bar public funding for a sign-language interpreter for a deaf student who wanted to attend a religious school. Justices Blackmun, Stevens, Souter, and O'Connor dissented.

Lee v. Weisman

112 S.Ct. 2649 (1992)

Daniel Weisman, who is Jewish and the father of two school students in Providence, Rhode Island, initially objected to the middle and high schools' allowing prayers during its commencement ceremonies when his first daughter graduated. He renewed his complaints when his second daughter graduated. At that graduation ceremony, Rabbi Leslie Gutterman offered an invocation thanking God "for the legacy of America where diversity is celebrated," and a benediction in which he observed, "O God, we are grateful for the learning which we have celebrated on this joyous commencement. . . . We give thanks to you, Lord, for keeping us alive, sustaining us and allowing us to reach this special, happy occasion." Subsequently, Weisman sued school officials and federal district and appellate courts ruled that mentioning God during public-school graduation ceremonies violates the First Amendment establishment clause. In appealing that decision, attorneys for the school board countered that such prayers do not constitute governmental endorsement or promotion of religion. Moreover, in a brief supporting the school board, the Bush administration asked the justices to abandon the three-prong test established in *Lemon v. Kurtzman*, 403 U.S. 603 (1971) (see Vol. 2, Ch. 6). Under that test, laws and government practices run afoul of the establishment clause if they (1) fail to have a secular purpose or (2) have the primary effect of advancing religion or (3) promote "an excessive government entanglement with religion." There the district and appellate courts concluded that the graduation prayers constituted an "advancement of religion." And the Bush administration urged the Court to "jettison the framework erected by *Lemon* in circumstances where, as here, the practice under assault is a non-coercive, ceremonial acknowledgement of the heritage of a deeply religious people."

The Court's decision was five to four. The majority's opinion was announced by Justice Kennedy. Justices Blackmun and Souter's concurrences were joined by Justices Stevens and O'Connor. Justice Scalia's dissent was joined by Chief Justice Rehnquist and Justices White and Thomas.

Justice KENNEDY delivers the opinion of the Court.

This case does not require us to revisit the difficult questions dividing us in recent cases, questions of the definition and full scope of the principles governing the extent of permitted accommodation by the State for the religious beliefs and practices of many of its citizens. See *Allegheny County v. Greater Pittsburgh ACLU,* 492 U.S. 573 (1989); *Wallace v. Jaffree,* 472 U.S. 38 (1985); *Lynch v. Donnelly,* 465 U.S. 668 (1984). For without reference to those principles in other contexts, the controlling precedents as they relate to prayer and religious exercise in primary and secondary public schools compel the holding here that the policy of the city of Providence is an unconstitutional one. We can decide the case without reconsidering the general constitutional framework by which public schools' efforts to accommodate religion are measured. Thus we do not accept the invitation of petitioners and amicus the United States to reconsider our decision in *Lemon v. Kurtzman,* [403 U.S. 602 (1971)]. The government involvement with religious activity in this case is pervasive, to the point of creating a state-sponsored and state-directed religious exercise in a public school. Conducting this formal religious observance conflicts with settled rules pertaining to prayer exercises for students, and that suffices to determine the question before us.

The principle that government may accommodate the free exercise of religion does not supersede the fundamental limitations imposed by the Establishment Clause. It is beyond dispute that, at a minimum, the Constitution guarantees that government may not coerce anyone to support or participate in religion or its exercise, or otherwise act in a way which establishes a [state] religion or religious faith, or tends to do so." *Lynch.* The State's involvement in the school prayers challenged today violates these central principles. . . .

We need not look beyond the circumstances of this case to see the phenomenon at work. The undeniable fact is that the school district's supervision and control of a high school graduation ceremony places public pressure, as well as peer pressure, on attending students to stand as a group or, at least, maintain respectful silence during the Invocation and Benediction. This pressure, though subtle and indirect, can be as real as any overt compulsion. Of course, in our culture standing or remaining silent can signify adherence to a view or simple respect for the views of others. And no doubt some persons who have no desire to join a prayer have little objection to standing as a sign of respect for those who do. But for the dissenter of high school age, who has a reasonable perception that she is being forced by the State to pray in a manner her conscience will not allow, the injury is no less real. There can be no doubt that for many, if not most, of the students at the graduation, the act of standing or remaining silent was an expression of participation in the Rabbi's prayer. That was the very point of the religious exercise. It is of little comfort to a dissenter, then, to be told that for her the act of standing or remaining in silence signifies mere respect, rather than participation. What matters is that, given our social conventions, a reasonable dissenter in this milieu could believe that the group exercise signified her own participation or approval of it. . . .

The injury caused by the government's action, and the reason why Daniel and Deborah Weisman object to it, is that the State, in a school setting, in effect required participation in a religious exercise. It is, we concede, a brief exercise during which the individual can concentrate on joining its message, meditate on her own religion, or let her mind wander. But the embarrassment and the intrusion of the religious exercise cannot be refuted by arguing that these prayers, and similar ones to be said in the future, are of a de minimis character. To do so would be an affront to the Rabbi who offered them and to all those for whom the prayers were an essential and profound recognition of divine authority. And for the same reason, we think that the intrusion is greater than the two minutes or so of time consumed for prayers like these. . . .

Inherent differences between the public school system and a session of a State Legislature distinguish this case from *Marsh v. Chambers*, 463 U.S. 783 (1983). The considerations we have raised in objection to the invocation and benediction are in many respects similar to the arguments we considered in *Marsh*. But there are also obvious differences. The atmosphere at the opening of a session of a state legislature where adults are free to enter and leave with little comment and for any number of reasons cannot compare with the constraining potential of the one school event most important for the student to attend. The influence and force of a formal exercise in a school graduation are far greater than the prayer exercise we condoned in *Marsh*. The *Marsh* majority in fact gave specific recognition to this distinction and placed particular reliance on it in upholding the prayers at issue there. Today's case is different. At a high school graduation, teachers and principals must and do retain a high degree of control over the precise contents of the program, the speeches, the timing, the movements, the dress, and the decorum of the students. In this atmosphere the state-imposed character of an invocation and benediction by clergy selected by the school combine to make the prayer a state-sanctioned religious exercise in which the student was left with no alternative but to submit. . . .

For the reasons we have stated, the judgment of the Court of Appeals is Affirmed.

Justice BLACKMUN, with whom Justice STEVENS and Justice O'CONNOR join, concurring.

The Court holds that the graduation prayer is unconstitutional because the State "in effect required participation in a religious exercise." Although our precedents make clear that proof of government coercion is not necessary to prove an Establishment Clause violation, it is sufficient. Government pressure to participate in a religious activity is an obvious indication that the government is endorsing or promoting religion.

But it is not enough that the government restrain from compelling religious practices: it must not engage in them either. The Court repeatedly has recognized that a violation of the Establishment Clause is not predicated on coercion. The Establishment Clause proscribes public schools from "conveying or attempting to convey a message that religion or a particular religious belief is favored or preferred," *County of Allegheny v. ACLU* (1989), even if the schools do not actually "impose pressure upon a student to participate in a religious activity." *Westside Community Bd. of Ed. v. Mergens,* 496 U.S. 226 (1990) (KENNEDY, J., concurring).

There is no doubt that attempts to aid religion through government coercion jeopardize freedom of conscience. . . .

Our decisions have gone beyond prohibiting coercion, however, because the Court has recognized that "the fullest possible scope of religious liberty," *Schempp,* entails more than freedom from coercion. The Establishment Clause protects religious liberty on a grand scale; it is a social compact that guarantees for generations a democracy and a strong religious community—both essential to safeguarding religious liberty. . . .

Justice SOUTER, with whom Justice STEVENS and Justice O'CONNOR join, concurring.

. . .

That government must remain neutral in matters of religion does not foreclose it from ever taking religion into account. The State may "accommodate" the free exercise of religion by relieving people from generally applicable rules that interfere with their religious callings. See, e.g., *Corporation of Presiding Bishop of Church of Jesus Christ of Latter-Day Saints v. Amos,* 483 U.S. 327 (1987); see also *Sherbert v. Verner,* 374 U.S. 398 (1963). Contrary to the views of some, such accommodation does not necessarily signify an official endorsement of religious observance over disbelief. . . .

Whatever else may define the scope of accommodation permissible under the Establishment Clause, one requirement is clear: accommodation must lift a discernible burden on the free exercise of religion. Concern for the position of religious individuals in the modern regulatory state cannot justify official solicitude for a religious practice unburdened by general rules; such gratuitous largesse would effectively favor religion over disbelief. By these lights one easily sees that, in sponsoring the graduation prayers at issue here, the State has crossed the line from permissible accommodation to unconstitutional establishment.

Justice SCALIA, with whom the CHIEF JUSTICE, Justice WHITE, and Justice THOMAS join, dissenting.

. . .

From our Nation's origin, prayer has been a prominent part of governmental ceremonies and proclamations. The Declaration of Independence, the document marking our birth as a separate people, "appealed to the Supreme Judge of the world for the rectitude of our intentions" and avowed "a firm reliance on the protection of divine Providence." In his first inaugural address, after swearing his oath of office on a Bible, George Washington deliberately made a prayer a part of his first official act as President. . . . Such supplications have been a characteristic feature of inaugural addresses ever since. . . .

[A] tradition of Thanksgiving Proclamations—with their religious theme of prayerful gratitude to God—has been adhered to by almost every President. . . .

The Court presumably would separate graduation invocations and benedictions from other instances of public "preservation and transmission of religious beliefs" on the ground that they involve "psychological coercion." I find it a sufficient embarrassment that our Establishment Clause jurisprudence regarding holiday displays, has come to "require scrutiny more commonly associated with interior decorators than with the judiciary." *American Jewish Congress v. Chicago*, 827 F. 2d 120 (Easterbrook, J., dissenting). But interior decorating is a rock-hard science compared to psychology practiced by amateurs. A few citations of "research in psychology" that have no particular bearing upon the precise issue here, cannot disguise the fact that the Court has gone beyond the realm where judges know what they are doing. The Court's argument that state officials have "coerced" students to take part in the invocation and benediction at graduation ceremonies is, not to put too fine a point on it, incoherent.

The Court identifies two "dominant facts" that it says dictate its ruling that invocations and benedictions at public-school graduation ceremonies violate the Establishment Clause. Neither of them is in any relevant sense true.

The Court declares that students' "attendance and participation in the [invocation and benediction] are in a fair and real sense obligatory." But what exactly is this "fair and real sense"? According to the Court, students at graduation who want "to avoid the fact or appearance of participation," in the invocation and benediction are psychologically obligated by "public pressure, as well as peer pressure, . . . to stand as a group or, at least, maintain respectful silence" during those prayers. This assertion—the very linchpin of the Court's opinion—is almost as intriguing for what it does not say as for what it says. It does not say, for example, that students are psychologically coerced to bow their heads, place their hands in a Drer-like prayer position, pay attention to the prayers, utter "Amen," or in fact pray. (Perhaps further intensive psychological research remains to be done on these matters.) It claims only that students are psychologically coerced "to stand . . . or, at least, maintain respectful silence." Both halves of this disjunctive (both of which must amount to the fact or appearance of participation in prayer if the Court's analysis is to survive on its own terms) merit particular attention.

To begin with the latter: The Court's notion that a student who simply sits in "respectful silence" during the invocation and benediction (when all others are standing) has somehow joined—or would somehow be perceived as having joined—in the prayers is nothing short of ludicrous. We indeed live in a vulgar age. But surely "our social conventions" have not coarsened to the point that anyone who does not stand on his chair and shout obscenities can reasonably be deemed to have assented to everything said in his presence. Since the Court does not dispute that students exposed to prayer at graduation ceremonies retain (despite "subtle coercive pressures") the free will to sit, there is absolutely no basis for the Court's decision. It is fanciful enough to say that "a reasonable dissenter," standing head erect in a class of bowed heads, "could believe that the group exercise signified her own participation or approval of it." It is beyond the absurd to say that she could entertain such a belief while pointedly declining to rise.

But let us assume the very worst, that the nonparticipating graduate is "subtly coerced" . . . to stand! Even that half of the disjunctive does not remotely establish a "participation" (or an "appearance of participation") in a religious exercise. The Court acknowledges that "in our culture standing . . . can signify adherence to a view or simple respect for the views of others." (Much more often the latter than the former, I think, except perhaps in the proverbial town meeting, where one votes by standing.) But if it is a permissible inference that one who is standing is doing so simply out of respect for the prayers of others that are in progress, then how can it possibly be said that a "reasonable dissenter . . . could believe that the group exercise signified her own participation or approval"? Quite obviously, it cannot. I may add, moreover, that maintaining respect for the religious observances of others is a fundamental civic virtue that government (including the public schools) can and should cultivate—so that even if it were the case that the displaying of such respect might be mistaken for taking part in the prayer, I would deny that the dissenter's interest in avoiding even the false appearance of participation constitutionally trumps the government's interest in fostering respect for religion generally.

The opinion manifests that the Court itself has not given careful consideration to its test of psychological coercion. For if it had, how could it observe, with no hint of concern or disapproval, that students stood for the Pledge of Allegiance, which immediately preceded Rabbi Gutterman's invocation? The government can, of course, no more coerce political orthodoxy than religious orthodoxy. *West Virginia Board of Education v. Barnette,* 319 U.S. 624 (1943). Moreover, since the Pledge of Allegiance has been revised since *Barnette* to include the phrase "under God," recital of the Pledge would appear to raise the same Establishment Clause issue

as the invocation and benediction. If students were psychologically coerced to remain standing during the invocation, they must also have been
psychologically coerced, moments before, to stand for (and thereby, in
the Court's view, take part in or appear to take part in) the Pledge. Must
the Pledge therefore be barred from the public schools (both from graduation ceremonies and from the classroom)? In *Barnette* we held that a
public-school student could not be compelled to recite the Pledge; we did
not even hint that she could not be compelled to observe respectful
silence—indeed, even to stand in respectful silence—when those who
wished to recite it did so. Logically, that ought to be the next project for
the Court's bulldozer. . . .

The deeper flaw in the Court's opinion does not lie in its wrong answer
to the question whether there was state-induced "peer-pressure" coercion; it lies, rather, in the Court's making violation of the Establishment
Clause hinge on such a precious question. The coercion that was a
hallmark of historical establishments of religion was coercion of religious
orthodoxy and of financial support by force of law and threat of penalty.
Typically, attendance at the state church was required; only clergy of the
official church could lawfully perform sacraments; and dissenters, if tolerated, faced an array of civil disabilities. . . .

Our religion-clause jurisprudence has become bedeviled (so to speak)
by reliance on formulaic abstractions that are not derived from, but
positively conflict with, our long-accepted constitutional traditions. Fore-
most among these has been the so-called *Lemon* test, see *Lemon v. Kurtzman,*
403 U.S. 602 (1971), which has received well-earned criticism from many
members of this Court. The Court today demonstrates the irrelevance of
Lemon by essentially ignoring it, and the interment of that case may be the
one happy byproduct of the Court's otherwise lamentable decision. Un-
fortunately, however, the Court has replaced *Lemon* with its psycho-
coercion test, which suffers the double disability of having no roots
whatever in our people's historic practice, and being as infinitely expand-
able as the reasons for psychotherapy itself. . . .

The reader has been told much in this case about the personal interest
of Mr. Weisman and his daughter, and very little about the personal
interests on the other side. They are not inconsequential. . . .

The narrow context of the present case involves a community's celebration of one of the milestones in its young citizens' lives, and it is a bold
step for this Court to seek to banish from that occasion, and from
thousands of similar celebrations throughout this land, the expression of
gratitude to God that a majority of the community wishes to make. The
issue before us today is not the abstract philosophical question whether
the alternative of frustrating this desire of a religious majority is to be
preferred over the alternative of imposing "psychological coercion," or a
feeling of exclusion, upon nonbelievers. Rather, the question is whether
a mandatory choice in favor of the former has been imposed by the
United States Constitution. As the age-old practices of our people show,
the answer to that question is not at all in doubt. . . . For the foregoing
reasons, I dissent.

Lamb's Chapel v. Center Moriches Union Free School District

113 S.Ct. 2141 (1993)

Under New York law, local school boards may adopt regulations permitting the after-hours use of school property for ten specified purposes, but not including meetings for religious purposes. The Center Moriches Union Free School District adopted, pursuant to state law, regulations allowing social, civic, and recreational uses of its schools (Rule 10), but prohibiting use by any group for religious purposes (Rule 7). Subsequently, the school district refused two requests by Lamb's Chapel, an evangelical church, to use school facilities for a religious-oriented film series on family values and child-rearing on the ground that the film appeared to be church related. Lamb's Chapel filed suit in federal district Court, claiming that the school district had violated the First Amendment's guarantee for freedom of speech and religious exercise. The district court granted summary judgment to the school district, and an appellate court affirmed, on the ground that school property was a "limited public forum" open only for designated purposes and that the exclusion of the Church's film series was a reasonable and neutral-viewpoint restriction. Lamb's Chapel thereupon appealed to the Supreme Court, which granted review and reversed the lower court.

The Court's decision was unanimous, with the opinion announced by Justice White. Concurring opinions were delivered by Justice Scalia, with whom Justice Thomas joined, and by Justice Kennedy.

Justice WHITE delivered the opinion of the Court.

There is no question that the [School] District, like the private owner of property, may legally preserve the property under its control for the use to which it is dedicated. It is also common ground that the District need not have permitted after-hours use of its property for any of the uses permitted by the state education law. The District, however, did open its property for two of the 10 uses permitted by [state law]. The Church argued below that because under Rule 10 of the rules issued by the District, school property could be used for "social, civic, and recreational" purposes, the District had opened its property for such a wide variety of communicative purposes that restrictions on communicative uses of the property were subject to the same constitutional limitations as restrictions in traditional public fora such as parks and sidewalks. Hence, its view was that subject matter or speaker exclusions on District property were required to be justified by a compelling state interest and to be narrowly drawn to achieve that end. Both the District Court and the

Court of Appeals rejected this submission, which is also presented to this Court. . . . We need not rule on this issue, however, for even if the courts below were correct in this respect—and we shall assume for present purposes that they were—the judgment below must be reversed.

With respect to public property that is not a designated public forum open for indiscriminate public use for communicative purposes, we have said that "control over access to a nonpublic forum can be based on subject matter and speaker identity so long as the distinctions drawn are reasonable in light of the purpose served by the forum and are viewpoint neutral." *Cornelius v. NAACP Legal Defense and Ed. Fund, Inc.,* 473 U.S. 788 (1985). The Court of Appeals appeared to recognize that the total ban on using District property for religious purposes could survive First Amendment challenge only if excluding this category of speech was reasonable and viewpoint neutral. The court's conclusion in this case was that Rule 7 met this test. We cannot agree with this holding, for Rule 7 was unconstitutionally applied in this case.

The Court of Appeals thought that the application of Rule 7 in this case was viewpoint neutral because it had been and would be applied in the same way to all uses of school property for religious purposes. That all religions and all uses for religious purposes are treated alike under Rule 7, however, does not answer the critical question whether it discriminates on the basis of viewpoint to permit school property to be used for the presentation of all views about family issues and child-rearing except those dealing with the subject matter from a religious standpoint.

There is no suggestion from the courts below or from the District or the State that a lecture or film about child-rearing and family values would not be a use for social or civic purposes otherwise permitted by Rule 10. That subject matter is not one that the District has placed off limits to any and all speakers. Nor is there any indication in the record before us that the application to exhibit the particular film involved here was or would have been denied for any reason other than the fact that the presentation would have been from a religious perspective. In our view, denial on that basis was plainly invalid under our holding in *Cornelius,* that "although a speaker may be excluded from a nonpublic forum if he wishes to address a topic not encompassed within the purpose of the forum . . . or if he is not a member of the class of speakers for whose special benefit the forum was created . . . the government violates the First Amendment when it denies access to a speaker solely to suppress the point of view he espouses on an otherwise includible subject."

The film involved here no doubt dealt with a subject otherwise permissible under Rule 10, and its exhibition was denied solely because the film dealt with the subject from a religious standpoint. The principle that has emerged from our cases "is that the First Amendment forbids the government to regulate speech in ways that favor some viewpoints or ideas at the expense of others." *City Council of Los Angeles v. Taxpayers for Vincent,* 466 U.S. 789 (1984). That principle applies in the circumstances of this case. . . .

The District, as a respondent, would save its judgment below on the ground that to permit its property to be used for religious purposes would be an establishment of religion forbidden by the First Amendment. This Court suggested in *Widmar v. Vincent*, 454 U.S. 263 (1981), that the interest of the State in avoiding an Establishment Clause violation "may be [a] compelling" one justifying an abridgment of free speech otherwise protected by the First Amendment; but the Court went on to hold that permitting use of University property for religious purposes under the open access policy involved there would not be incompatible with the Court's Establishment Clause cases.

We have no more trouble than did the *Widmar* Court in disposing of the claimed defense on the ground that the posited fears of an Establishment Clause violation are unfounded. The showing of this film would not have been during school hours, would not have been sponsored by the school, and would have been open to the public, not just to church members. The District property had repeatedly been used by a wide variety of private organizations. Under these circumstances, as in Widmar, there would have been no realistic danger that the community would think that the District was endorsing religion or any particular creed, and any benefit to religion or to the Church would have been no more than incidental. As in *Widmar*, permitting District property to be used to exhibit the film involved in this case would not have been an establishment of religion under the three-part test articulated in *Lemon v. Kurtzman*, 403 U.S. 602 (1971): The challenged governmental action has a secular purpose, does not have the principal or primary effect of advancing or inhibiting religion, and does not foster an excessive entanglement with religion. . . .

Justice KENNEDY concurred in an opinion expressing agreement with Justice SCALIA's rejection of the majority's reliance on *Lemon*.

Justice SCALIA, with whom Justice THOMAS joins, concurring in the judgment.

I . . . agree with the Court that allowing Lamb's Chapel to use school facilities poses "no realistic danger" of a violation of the Establishment Clause, but I cannot accept most of its reasoning in this regard. The Court explains that . . . access to school property would not violate the three-part test articulated in *Lemon v. Kurtzman*, 403 U.S. 602 (1971).

As to the Court's invocation of the *Lemon* test: Like some ghoul in a late-night horror movie that repeatedly sits up in its grave and shuffles abroad, after being repeatedly killed and buried, *Lemon* stalks our Establishment Clause jurisprudence once again, frightening the little children and school attorneys of Center Moriches Union Free School District. Its most recent burial, only last Term, was, to be sure, not fully six-feet under: our decision in *Lee v. Weisman*, [112 S.Ct. 2649] (1992), conspicuously avoided using the supposed "test" but also declined the invitation to repudiate it. Over the years, however, no fewer than five of the currently sitting Justices have, in their own opinions, personally driven pencils through the creature's heart (the author of today's opinion repeatedly), and a sixth has joined an opinion doing so. See, e.g., *Weisman* (SCALIA, J., joined by, inter alios, THOMAS, J., dissenting); *Allegheny County v. American Civil Liberties Union, Greater Pittsburgh Chapter,* 492 U.S. 573 (1989) (KENNEDY, J., concurring in judgment in part and dissenting in part); *Corporation of Presiding Bishop of Church of Jesus Christ of Latter-day Saints v. Amos,* 483 U.S. 327, 346-349 (1987) (O'CONNOR, J., concurring); *Wallace v. Jaffree,* 472 U.S. 38 (1985) (REHNQUIST, J., dissenting); id. (WHITE, J., dissenting); *School Dist. of Grand Rapids v. Ball,* 473 U.S. 373 (1985) (WHITE, J., dissenting); *Widmar v. Vincent,* 454 U.S. 263 (1981) (WHITE, J., dissenting); *New York v. Cathedral Academy,* 434 U.S. 125 (1977) (WHITE, J., dissenting); *Roemer v. Maryland Bd. of Public Works,* 426 U.S. 736 (1976) (WHITE, J., concurring in judgment); *Committee for Public Education & Religious Liberty v. Nyquist,* 413 U.S. 756 (1973) (WHITE, J., dissenting).

The secret of the *Lemon* test's survival, I think, is that it is so easy to kill. It is there to scare us (and our audience) when we wish it to do so, but we can command it to return to the tomb at will. See, e.g., *Lynch v. Donnelly,* 465 U.S. 668 (1984) [noting instances in which Court has not applied *Lemon* test]. When we wish to strike down a practice it forbids, we invoke it, see, e.g., *Aguilar v. Felton,* 473 U.S. 402 (1985) [striking down state remedial education program administered in part in parochial schools]; when we wish to uphold a practice it forbids, we ignore it entirely, see *Marsh v. Chambers,* 463 U.S. 783 (1983) [upholding state legislative chaplains]. Sometimes, we take a middle course, calling its three prongs "no more than helpful signposts," *Hunt v. McNair,* 413 U.S. 734, 741 (1973). Such a docile and useful monster is worth keeping around, at least in a somnolent state; one never knows when one might need him.

For my part, I agree with the long list of constitutional scholars who have criticized *Lemon* and bemoaned the strange Establishment Clause geometry of crooked lines and wavering shapes its intermittent use has produced. I will decline to apply *Lemon*—whether it validates or invalidates the government action in question—and therefore cannot join the opinion of the Court today.

Zobrest v. Catalina Foothills School District
113 S.Ct. 2462 (1993)

The parents of James Zobrest, a deaf child, sued the Catalina Foothills School District after it refused to provide a sign-language interpreter to accompany James Zobrest to classes at a Roman Catholic high school. They alleged that the Individuals with Disabilities Education Act (IDEA) and the First Amendment's free exercise clause required the school district to provide the interpreter and that the amendment's (dis)establishment clause did not present an insurmountable barrier. After a federal district and appellate court disagreed, the Zobrests appealed to the Supreme Court, which granted *certiorari*.

The Court's decision was five to four; the majority's opinion was announced by Chief Justice Rehnquist. Justice Blackmun's dissent was joined by Justice Souter and in part by Justices Stevens and O'Connor. Justice O'Connor, joined by Justice Stevens, also delivered a dissenting opinion.

Chief Justice REHNQUIST delivered the opinion of the Court.

We have never said that "religious institutions are disabled by the First Amendment from participating in publicly sponsored social welfare programs." *Bowen v. Kendrick,* 487 U.S. 589 (1988). For if the Establishment Clause did bar religious groups from receiving general government benefits, then "a church could not be protected by the police and fire departments, or have its public sidewalk kept in repair." *Widmar v. Vincent,* 454 U.S. 263 (1981). Given that a contrary rule would lead to such absurd results, we have consistently held that government programs that neutrally provide benefits to a broad class of citizens defined without reference to religion are not readily subject to an Establishment Clause challenge just because sectarian institutions may also receive an attenuated financial benefit. Nowhere have we stated this principle more clearly than in *Mueller v. Allen,* 463 U.S. 388 (1983), and *Witters v. Washington Dept. of Services for Blind,* 474 U.S. 481 (1986), two cases dealing specifically with government programs offering general educational assistance.

In *Mueller,* we rejected an Establishment Clause challenge to a Minnesota law allowing taxpayers to deduct certain educational expenses in computing their state income tax, even though the vast majority of those deductions (perhaps over 90%) went to parents whose children attended sectarian schools. Two factors, aside from States' traditionally broad taxing authority, informed our decision. We noted that the law "permits all parents—whether their children attend public school or private—to deduct their children's educational expenses." We also pointed out that under Minnesota's scheme, public funds become available to sectarian schools "only as a result of numerous private choices of individual parents of school-age children," thus distinguishing *Mueller* from our other cases involving "the direct transmission of assistance from the State to the schools themselves."

Witters was premised on virtually identical reasoning. In that case, we upheld against an Establishment Clause challenge the State of Washington's extension of vocational assistance, as part of a general state program, to a blind person studying at a private Christian college to become a pastor, missionary, or youth director. Looking at the statute as a whole, we observed that "any aid provided under Washington's program that ultimately flows to religious institutions does so only as a result of the genuinely independent and private choices of aid recipients." The program, we said, "creates no financial incentive for students to undertake sectarian education." We also remarked that, much like the law in *Mueller,* "Washington's program is 'made available generally without regard to the sectarian-nonsectarian, or public-nonpublic nature of the institution benefited.' " In light of these factors, we held that Washington's program—even as applied to a student who sought state assistance so that he could become a pastor—would not advance religion in a manner inconsistent with the Establishment Clause.

That same reasoning applies with equal force here. . . . Respondent contends, however, that this case differs from *Mueller* and *Witters,* in that petitioners seek to have a public employee physically present in a sectarian school to assist in James' religious education. In light of this distinction, respondent argues that this case more closely resembles *Meek v. Pittenger,* 421 U.S. 349 (1975), and *School Dist. of Grand Rapids v. Ball,* 473 U.S. 373 (1985). In *Meek,* we struck down a statute that provided "massive aid" to private schools—more than 75% of which were church related—through a direct loan of teaching material and equipment. The material and equipment covered by the statute included maps, charts, and tape recorders. . . . *Ball* similarly involved two public programs that provided services on private school premises; there, public employees taught classes to students in private school classrooms. We found that those programs likewise violated the Constitution, relying largely on *Meek.* According to respondent, if the government could not provide educational services on the premises of sectarian schools in *Meek* and *Ball,* then it surely cannot provide James with an interpreter on the premises of Salpointe.

Respondent's reliance on *Meek* and *Ball* is misplaced for two reasons. First, the programs in *Meek* and *Ball*—through direct grants of government aid—relieved sectarian schools of costs they otherwise would have borne in educating their students. For example, the religious schools in *Meek* received teaching material and equipment from the State, relieving them of an otherwise necessary cost of performing their educational function. "This kind of direct aid," we determined, "is indistinguishable from the provision of a direct cash subsidy to the religious school." The extension of aid to petitioners, however, does not amount to "an impermissible 'direct subsidy' " of Salpointe. For Salpointe is not relieved of an expense that it otherwise would have assumed in educating its students. . . .

Second, the task of a sign-language interpreter seems to us quite different from that of a teacher or guidance counselor. . . . Nothing in this record suggests that a sign-language interpreter would do more than accurately interpret whatever material is presented to the class as a whole. . . . James' parents have chosen of their own free will to place him in a pervasively sectarian environment. The sign-language interpreter they have requested will neither add to nor subtract from that environment, and hence the provision of such assistance is not barred by the Establishment Clause. . . .

Justice BLACKMUN, with whom Justice SOUTER joins, and with
whom Justice STEVENS and Justice O'CONNOR join as to Part I,
dissenting.

I disagree both with the Court's decision to reach this question and
with its disposition on the merits. I therefore dissent. . . .

At Salpointe [High School, a private Roman Catholic school], where
the secular and the sectarian are "inextricably intertwined," governmental assistance to the educational function of the school necessarily entails
governmental participation in the school's inculcation of religion. A state-
employed sign-language interpreter would be required to communicate
the material covered in religion class, the nominally secular subjects that
are taught from a religious perspective, and the daily Masses at which
Salpointe encourages attendance for Catholic students. In an environment so pervaded by discussions of the divine, the interpreter's every
gesture would be infused with religious significance. Indeed, petitioners
willingly concede this point: "That the interpreter conveys religious messages is a given in the case." *Brief for Petitioners.* By this concession, petitioners would seem to surrender their constitutional claim.

The majority attempts to elude the impact of the record by offering
three reasons why this sort of aid to petitioners survives Establishment
Clause scrutiny. First, the majority observes that provision of a sign-
language interpreter occurs as "part of a general government program
that distributes benefits neutrally to any child qualifying as 'handicapped'
under the IDEA, without regard to the 'sectarian-nonsectarian, or public-
nonpublic' nature of the school the child attends." Second, the majority
finds significant the fact that aid is provided to pupils and their parents,
rather than directly to sectarian schools. And, finally, the majority opines
that "the task of a sign-language interpreter seems to us quite different
from that of a teacher or guidance counselor."

But the majority's arguments are unavailing. As to the first two, even
a general welfare program may have specific applications that are constitutionally forbidden under the Establishment Clause. For example, a
general program granting remedial assistance to disadvantaged schoolchildren attending public and private, secular and sectarian schools alike
would clearly offend the Establishment Clause insofar as it authorized the
provision of teachers. See *Aguilar v. Felton,* 473 U.S. 402 (1985); *Grand
Rapids School District v. Ball,* 473 U.S. 373 (1985); *Meek v. Pittenger,* 421 U.S.
349 (1975). Such a program would not be saved simply because it sup-
plied teachers to secular as well as sectarian schools. Nor would the fact
that teachers were furnished to pupils and their parents, rather than
directly to sectarian schools, immunize such a program from Establishment Clause scrutiny. The majority's decision must turn, then, upon the
distinction between a teacher and a sign-language interpreter. . . .

[O]ur cases make clear that government crosses the boundary when it
furnishes the medium for communication of a religious message. If petitioners receive the relief they seek, it is beyond question that a state-

employed sign-language interpreter would serve as the conduit for petitioner's religious education, thereby assisting Salpointe in its mission of religious indoctrination. But the Establishment Clause is violated when a sectarian school enlists "the machinery of the State to enforce a religious orthodoxy." *Lee v. Weisman,* [112 S.Ct. 2649] (1992). . . .

[The majority's] distinction between the provision of funds and the provision of a human being is not merely one of form. It goes to the heart of the principles animating the Establishment Clause. As Amicus Council on Religious Freedom points out, the provision of a state-paid sign-language interpreter may pose serious problems for the church as well as for the state. Many sectarian schools impose religiously based rules of conduct, as Salpointe has in this case. A traditional Hindu school would be likely to instruct its students and staff to dress modestly, avoiding any display of their bodies. And an orthodox Jewish yeshiva might well forbid all but kosher food upon its premises. To require public employees to obey such rules would impermissibly threaten individual liberty, but to fail to do so might endanger religious autonomy. For such reasons, it long has been feared that "a union of government and religion tends to destroy government and to degrade religion." *Engel v. Vitale,* 370 U.S. 421 (1962). The Establishment Clause was designed to avert exactly this sort of conflict.

Justice O'CONNOR, joined by Justice STEVENS, dissented in a separate opinion, expressing her view that the Court should have simply decided the statutory question and remanded the case, rather than reaching out to address the First Amendment's (dis)establishment clause.

B. FREE EXERCISE OF RELIGION

Whether governments may ban animal sacrifices in religious ceremonies was at issue in *Church of Lukumi Babalu Aye v. City of Hialeah,* 113 S.Ct. 2217 (1993) (see page 158). But the case is also significant because it is the first case granted review that raises a First Amendment free-exercise claim since the Rehnquist Court signaled that it would no longer overturn generally applicable laws that burden religious minorities and gave governments greater leeway in restricting religious practices in *Employment Division, Department of Human Resources of Oregon v. Smith,* 494 U.S. 872 (1990) (see Vol. 2, Ch. 6). Lawyers for the Church of Lukumi Babalu Aye challenged the constitutionality of a new ordinance adopted by the city of Hialeah, Florida, banning animal sacrifices and effectively prohibiting the practice of Santeria. Santeria, which is practiced in the Caribbean and in parts of the United States by Cuban refugees and others, sacrifices animals at birth, marriage, and death rites, as well as in ceremonies to cure the sick and to initiate new members. An estimated 50,000 to 60,000 followers of Santeria live in South Florida. And church attorneys claimed that Hialeah violated their First Amendment freedom of religious exercise by specifically prohibiting animal sacrifices for religious purposes. But Hialeah's attorneys countered, and a federal district court agreed, that on the basis of the Court's ruling in *Employment Division, Department of Human Resources of Oregon v. Smith*, 494 U.S. 872 (1990) (see Vol. 2, Ch. 6), the city could legitimately ban animal sacrifice and that the burden imposed on the practice of Santeria was only "an incidental effect of a generally applicable and otherwise valid provision prohibiting animal sacrifice." Remarkably, a unanimous Court struck down Hialeah's restrictions, though notably Justices Souter, Blackmun and O'Connor in concurring opinions expressed their disagreement with the Court's continued reliance on *Smith* and urged reconsideration of that ruling.

Church of the Lukumi Babalu Aye v. City of Hialeah
113 S.Ct. 2217 (1993)

In 1987, the Church of the Lukumi Babalu Aye leased land in Hialeah, Florida, and announced plans to establish a church, school, and cultural center there, which would bring its practice of Santeria, including the ritual sacrifice of animals, into the open. Santeria originated in the nineteenth century with the Yoruba people of eastern Africa who were brought as slaves to Cuba and other parts of the Caribbean. Santeria teaches that individuals have a destiny from God, but a destiny only fulfilled with the aid of spirits, or orishas, symbolized through the iconography of Catholic saints and who depend for survival on animal sacrifice. The practice of animal sacrifice is part of rituals performed at birth, marriage, and death rites; for the cure of the sick; at initiation ceremonies, and at an annual celebration. Chickens, pigeons, doves, ducks, guinea pigs, goats, sheep, and turtles are sacrificed by the cutting of the carotid arteries in the neck. The animals are then cooked and eaten, except after healing and death rituals. Approximately 50,000 to 60,000 people follow Santeria in South Florida.

The church's announcement sparked immediate controversy and public outcry over the sacrifice of animals. As a result, Hialeah's city council passed several ordinances prohibiting animal sacrifice, including:

Resolution 87-66, expressing "concern" over religious practices inconsistent with public morals, peace, or safety, and declaring the city's "commitment" to prohibiting such practices;

Ordinance 87-40, punishing "whoever . . . unnecessarily or cruelly . . . kills any animal";

Ordinance 87-52, which defines "sacrifice" as "to unnecessarily kill
. . . an animal in a . . . ritual . . . not for the primary purpose of food
consumption," and prohibits the "possession, sacrifice, or slaughter" of
an animal if it is killed in "any type of ritual" and there is an intent to use
it for food, but exempts" any licensed [food] establishment" if the killing
is otherwise permitted by law;

Ordinance 87-71, prohibiting the sacrifice of animals; and

Ordinance 87-72, which defines "slaughter" as "the killing of animals for
food," and prohibits slaughter outside of areas zoned for slaughterhouses,
but includes an exemption for "small numbers of hogs and/or cattle"
when exempted by state law.

Church attorneys immediately attacked the constitutionality of the
ordinances for abrogating the First Amendment's guarantee of free exercise of religion. After a federal district and appellate court upheld the
ordinance, the Church appealed to the Supreme Court.

The Court's decision was unanimous, with Justice Kennedy announcing the opinion. Concurring opinions were delivered by Justice Scalia,
who was joined by Chief Justice Rehnquist; by Justice Souter; and by
Justice Blackmun, who was joined by Justice O'Connor.

Justice KENNEDY delivers the opinion for the Court with respect to
Parts I, III, and IV, which Chief Justice REHNQUIST and Justices
WHITE, STEVENS, SCALIA, SOUTER, and THOMAS join; Part
II-B, which Chief Justice REHNQUIST and Justices WHITE, STE-
VENS, SCALIA, and THOMAS join; Parts II-A-1 and II-A-3, which
Chief Justice REHNQUIST and Justices STEVENS, SCALIA, and
THOMAS join; and Part II-A-2, which Justice Stevens joins.

We invalidate the challenged enactments and reverse the judgment of
the Court of Appeals. . . .

II

In addressing the constitutional protection for free exercise of religion,
our cases establish the general proposition that a law that is neutral and
of general applicability need not be justified by a compelling governmental interest even if the law has the incidental effect of burdening a particular religious practice. *Employment Div., Dept. of Human Resources of Oregon v.
Smith,* [492 U.S. 872 (1992)]. Neutrality and general applicability are
interrelated, and, as becomes apparent in this case, failure to satisfy one
requirement is a likely indication that the other has not been satisfied. A
law failing to satisfy these requirements must be justified by a compelling
governmental interest and must be narrowly tailored to advance that

interest. These ordinances fail to satisfy the *Smith* requirements. We begin by discussing neutrality.

[*A*] At a minimum, the protections of the Free Exercise Clause pertain if the law at issue discriminates against some or all religious beliefs or regulates or prohibits conduct because it is undertaken for religious reasons. See, e.g., *Braunfeld v. Brown,* 366 U.S. 599 (1961). . . .

[*1*] Although a law targeting religious beliefs as such is never permissible, if the object of a law is to infringe upon or restrict practices because of their religious motivation, the law is not neutral, *Smith;* and it is invalid unless it is justified by a compelling interest and is narrowly tailored to advance that interest. There are, of course, many ways of demonstrating that the object or purpose of a law is the suppression of religion or religious conduct. To determine the object of a law, we must begin with its text, for the minimum requirement of neutrality is that a law not discriminate on its face. A law lacks facial neutrality if it refers to a religious practice without a secular meaning discernible from the language or context. Petitioners contend that three of the ordinances fail this test of facial neutrality because they use the words "sacrifice" and "ritual," words with strong religious connotations. We agree that these words are consistent with the claim of facial discrimination, but the argument is not conclusive. The words "sacrifice" and "ritual" have a religious origin, but current use admits also of secular meanings. The ordinances, furthermore, define "sacrifice" in secular terms, without referring to religious practices.

We reject the contention advanced by the city that our inquiry must end with the text of the laws at issue. Facial neutrality is not determinative. The Free Exercise Clause, like the Establishment Clause, extends beyond facial discrimination. The Clause "forbids subtle departures from neutrality," *Gillette v. United States,* 401 U.S. 437 (1971), and "covert suppression of particular religious beliefs." Official action that targets religious conduct for distinctive treatment cannot be shielded by mere compliance with the requirement of facial neutrality. . . .

The record in this case compels the conclusion that suppression of the central element of the Santeria worship service was the object of the ordinances. First, though use of the words "sacrifice" and "ritual" does not compel a finding of improper targeting of the Santeria religion, the choice of these words is support for our conclusion. There are further respects in which the text of the city council's enactments discloses the improper attempt to target Santeria. Resolution 87-66, adopted June 9, 1987, recited that "residents and citizens of the City of Hialeah have expressed their concern that certain religions may propose to engage in practices which are inconsistent with public morals, peace or safety," and "reiterated" the city's commitment to prohibit "any and all [such] acts of any and all religious groups." No one suggests, and on this record it cannot be maintained, that city officials had in mind a religion other than Santeria.

It becomes evident that these ordinances target Santeria sacrifice when the ordinances' operation is considered. . . . It is a necessary conclusion that almost the only conduct subject to [Hialeah's] Ordinances is the religious exercise of Santeria church members. The texts show that they were drafted in tandem to achieve this result. . . .

The legitimate governmental interests in protecting the public health and preventing cruelty to animals could be addressed by restrictions stopping far short of a flat prohibition of all Santeria sacrificial practice. If improper disposal, not the sacrifice itself, is the harm to be prevented, the city could have imposed a general regulation on the disposal of organic garbage. It did not do so. . . .

Under similar analysis, narrower regulation would achieve the city's interest in preventing cruelty to animals. With regard to the city's interest in ensuring the adequate care of animals, regulation of conditions and treatment, regardless of why an animal is kept, is the logical response to the city's concern, not a prohibition on possession for the purpose of sacrifice. The same is true for the city's interest in prohibiting cruel methods of killing. . . . If the city has a real concern that other methods are less humane, however, the subject of the regulation should be the method of slaughter itself, not a religious classification that is said to be some general relation to it. . . .

[B] We turn next to a second requirement of the Free Exercise Clause, the rule that laws burdening religious practice must be of general applicability. *Smith*. . . .

The principle that government, in pursuit of legitimate interests, cannot in a selective manner impose burdens only on conduct motivated by religious belief is essential to the protection of the rights guaranteed by the Free Exercise Clause. The principle underlying the general applicability requirement has parallels in our First Amendment jurisprudence. In this case we need not define with precision the standard used to evaluate whether a prohibition is of general application, for these ordinances fall well below the minimum standard necessary to protect First Amendment rights.

Respondent claims that Ordinances 87-40, 87-52, and 87-71 advance two interests: protecting the public health and preventing cruelty to animals. The ordinances are underinclusive for those ends. They fail to prohibit nonreligious conduct that endangers these interests in a similar or greater degree than Santeria sacrifice does. The underinclusion is substantial, not inconsequential. Despite the city's proffered interest in preventing cruelty to animals, the ordinances are drafted with care to forbid few killings but those occasioned by religious sacrifice. Many types of animal deaths or kills for nonreligious reasons are either not prohibited or approved by express provision. For example, fishing—which occurs in Hialeah—is legal. Extermination of mice and rats within a home is also permitted. . . .

The ordinances are also underinclusive with regard to the city's interest in public health, which is threatened by the disposal of animal carcasses in open public places and the consumption of uninspected meat. Neither interest is pursued by respondent with regard to conduct that is not motivated by religious conviction. The health risks posed by the improper disposal of animal carcasses are the same whether Santeria sacrifice or some nonreligious killing preceded it. The city does not, however, prohibit hunters from bringing their kill to their houses, nor does it regulate disposal after their activity. Despite substantial testimony at trial that the same public health hazards result from improper disposal of garbage by restaurants, restaurants are outside the scope of the ordinances. Improper disposal is a general problem that causes substantial health risks, but which respondent addresses only when it results from religious exercise.

The ordinances are underinclusive as well with regard to the health risk posed by consumption of uninspected meat. Under the city's ordinances, hunters may eat their kill and fishermen may eat their catch without undergoing governmental inspection. Likewise, state law requires inspection of meat that is sold but exempts meat from animals raised for the use of the owner and "members of his household and nonpaying guests and employees." The asserted interest in inspected meat is not pursued in contexts similar to that of religious animal sacrifice. . . .

We conclude, in sum, that each of Hialeah's ordinances pursues the city's governmental interests only against conduct motivated by religious belief. The ordinances "have every appearance of a prohibition that society is prepared to impose upon [Santeria worshippers] but not upon itself." *The Florida Star v. B.J.F.*, 491 U.S. 524 (1989) (SCALIA, J., concurring in part and concurring in judgment). This precise evil is what the requirement of general applicability is designed to prevent.

III

A law burdening religious practice that is not neutral or not of general application must undergo the most rigorous of scrutiny. To satisfy the commands of the First Amendment, a law restrictive of religious practice must advance " 'interests of the highest order' " and must be narrowly tailored in pursuit of those interests. The compelling interest standard that we apply once a law fails to meet the Smith requirements is not "watered . . . down" but "really means what it says." *Smith.* A law that targets religious conduct for distinctive treatment or advances legitimate governmental interests only against conduct with a religious motivation will survive strict scrutiny only in rare cases. It follows from what we have already said that these ordinances cannot withstand this scrutiny.

First, even were the governmental interests compelling, the ordinances are not drawn in narrow terms to accomplish those interests. . . . Respondent has not demonstrated, moreover, that, in the context of these ordinances, its governmental interests are compelling. . . . The laws here in question were enacted contrary to these constitutional principles, and they are void.

Justice SCALIA, with whom Chief Justice REHNQUIST joins, concurring in part and concurring in the judgment.

The Court analyzes the "neutrality" and the "general applicability" of the Hialeah ordinances in separate sections (Parts II-A and II-B, respectively), and allocates various invalidating factors to one or the other of those sections. If it were necessary to make a clear distinction between the two terms, I would draw a line somewhat different from the Court's. But I think it is not necessary, and would frankly acknowledge that the terms are not only "interrelated," but substantially overlap. . . .

In my view, the defect of lack of neutrality applies primarily to those laws that by their terms impose disabilities on the basis of religion (e.g., a law excluding members of a certain sect from public benefits); whereas the defect of lack of general applicability applies primarily to those laws which, though neutral in their terms, through their design, construction, or enforcement target the practices of a particular religion for discriminatory treatment. But certainly a law that is not of general applicability (in the sense I have described) can be considered "nonneutral"; and certainly no law that is nonneutral (in the relevant sense) can be thought to be of general applicability. Because I agree with most of the invalidating factors set forth in Part II of the Court's opinion, and because it seems to me a matter of no consequence under which rubric ("neutrality," Part II-A, or "general applicability," Part II-B) each invalidating factor is discussed, I join the judgment of the Court and all of its opinion except section 2 of Part II-A.

I do not join that section because it departs from the opinion's general focus on the object of the laws at issue to consider the subjective motivation of the lawmakers, i.e., whether the Hialeah City Council actually intended to disfavor the religion of Santeria. As I have noted elsewhere, it is virtually impossible to determine the singular "motive" of a collective legislative body, and this Court has a long tradition of refraining from such inquiries. . . .

Justice SOUTER, concurring in part and concurring in the judgment.

This case turns on a principle about which there is no disagreement, that the Free Exercise Clause bars government action aimed at suppressing religious belief or practice. The Court holds that Hialeah's animal-sacrifice laws violate that principle, and I concur in that holding without reservation.

Because prohibiting religious exercise is the object of the laws at hand, this case does not present the more difficult issue addressed in our last free-exercise case, *Smith,* which announced the rule that a "neutral, generally applicable" law does not run afoul of the Free Exercise Clause even when it prohibits religious exercise in effect. The Court today refers to that rule in dicta, and despite my general agreement with the Court's opinion I do not join Part II, where the dicta appear, for I have doubts about whether the *Smith* rule merits adherence. I write separately to explain why the *Smith* rule is not germane to this case and to express my view that, in a case presenting the issue, the Court should re-examine the rule *Smith* declared. . . .

[T]his is far from a representative free-exercise case. While, as the Court observes, the Hialeah City Council has provided a rare example of a law actually aimed at suppressing religious exercise, *Smith* was typical of our free-exercise cases, involving as it did a formally neutral, generally applicable law. The rule *Smith* announced, however, was decidedly untypical of the cases involving the same type of law. Because *Smith* left those prior cases standing, we are left with a free-exercise jurisprudence in tension with itself, a tension that should be addressed, and that may legitimately be addressed, by reexamining the *Smith* rule in the next case that would turn upon its application. . . .

The *Smith* rule, in my view, may be reexamined consistently with principles of *stare decisis*. To begin with, the *Smith* rule was not subject to "full-dress argument" prior to its announcement. . . . The *Smith* rule's vitality as precedent is limited further by the seeming want of any need of it in resolving the question presented in that case. Justice O'CONNOR reached the same result as the majority by applying, as the parties had requested, "our established free exercise jurisprudence," and the majority never determined that the case could not be resolved on the narrower ground, going instead straight to the broader constitutional rule. But the Court's better practice, one supported by the same principles of restraint that underlie the rule of *stare decisis*, is not to " 'formulate a rule of constitutional law broader than is required by the precise facts to which it is to be applied.' " *Ashwander v. TVA*, 297 U.S. 288 (1936) (BRANDEIS, J., concurring). I am not suggesting that the *Smith* Court lacked the power to announce its rule, I think a rule of law unnecessary to the outcome of a case, especially one not put into play by the parties, approaches without more the sort of "dicta . . . which may be followed if sufficiently persuasive but which are not controlling." *Humphrey's Executor v. United States*, 295 U.S. 602 (1935). . . .

The considerations of full-briefing, necessity, and novelty thus do not exhaust the legitimate reasons for reexamining prior decisions, or even for reexamining the *Smith* rule. One important further consideration warrants mention here, however, because it demands the reexamination I have in mind. *Smith* presents not the usual question of whether to follow a constitutional rule, but the question of which constitutional rule to follow, for *Smith* refrained from overruling prior free-exercise cases that contain a free-exercise rule fundamentally at odds with the rule *Smith* declared. *Smith,* indeed, announced its rule by relying squarely upon the precedent of prior cases. Since that precedent is nonetheless at odds with the *Smith* rule, as I have discussed above, the result is an intolerable tension in free-exercise law which may be resolved, consistently with principles of *stare decisis,* in a case in which the tension is presented and its resolution pivotal.

While the tension on which I rely exists within the body of our extant case law, a rereading of that case law will not, of course, mark the limits of any enquiry directed to reexamining the *Smith* rule, which should be reviewed in light not only of the precedent on which it was rested but also of the text of the Free Exercise Clause and its origins. As for text, *Smith* did not assert that the plain language of the Free Exercise Clause compelled its rule, but only that the rule was "a permissible reading" of the Clause. Suffice it to say that a respectable argument may be made that the pre-*Smith* law comes closer to fulfilling the language of the Free Exercise Clause than the rule *Smith* announced. . . .

Nor did *Smith* consider the original meaning of the Free Exercise Clause, though overlooking the opportunity was no unique transgression. Save in a handful of passing remarks, the Court has not explored the history of the Clause since its early attempts in 1879 and 1890, see *Reynolds v. United States,* 98 U.S. [245 (1879)], attempts that recent scholarship makes clear were incomplete. The curious absence of history from our free-exercise decisions creates a stark contrast with our cases under the Establishment Clause, where historical analysis has been so prominent. . . .

Our cases now present competing answers to the question when government, while pursuing secular ends, may compel disobedience to what one believes religion commands. The case before us is rightly decided without resolving the existing tension, which remains for another day when it may be squarely faced.

Justice BLACKMUN, with whom Justice O'CONNOR joins, concurring.

I write separately to emphasize that the First Amendment's protection of religion extends beyond those rare occasions on which the government explicitly targets religion (or a particular religion) for disfavored treatment, as is done in this case. In my view, a statute that burdens the free exercise of religion "may stand only if the law in general, and the State's refusal to allow a religious exemption in particular, are justified by a compelling interest that cannot be served by less restrictive means." *Smith* (dissenting opinion). The Court, however, applies a different test. It applies the test announced in *Smith,* under which "a law that is neutral and of general applicability need not be justified by a compelling governmental interest even if the law has the incidental effect of burdening a particular religious practice." I continue to believe that *Smith* was wrongly decided, because it ignored the value of religious freedom as an affirmative individual liberty and treated the Free Exercise Clause as no more than an antidiscrimination principle. Thus, while I agree with the result the Court reaches in this case, I arrive at that result by a different route.

When a law discriminates against religion as such, as do the ordinances in this case, it automatically will fail strict scrutiny under *Sherbert v. Verner,* 374 U.S. 398 (1963) [holding that governmental regulation that imposes a burden upon religious practice must be narrowly tailored to advance a compelling state interest]. This is true because a law that targets religious practice for disfavored treatment both burdens the free exercise of religion and, by definition, is not precisely tailored to a compelling governmental interest.

Thus, unlike the majority, I do not believe that "[a] law burdening religious practice that is not neutral or not of general application must undergo the most rigorous of scrutiny." In my view, regulation that targets religion in this way, ipso facto, fails strict scrutiny. It is for this reason that a statute that explicitly restricts religious practices violates the First Amendment. . . .

7

THE FOURTH
AMENDMENT
GUARANTEE AGAINST
UNREASONABLE
SEARCHES AND SEIZURES

A. REQUIREMENTS FOR A WARRANT AND
REASONABLE SEARCHES AND SEIZURES

In a number of rulings on the Fourth Amendment's guarantee against "unreasonable searches and seizures," the Rehnquist Court continued down the road toward returning more authority to states and localities in establishing their criminal procedure policies and practices. The Court has not been as deferential to states' police powers and law enforcement interests since before the Warren Court (1953–1969), which revolutionized criminal justice by nationalizing principal guarantees of the Bill of Rights (see Vol. 2, Ch. 4). Indeed, the majority on the Rehnquist Court is both more deferential to federalism (see Vol. 1, Ch. 7) and less concerned about supervising, or maintaining uniform, national standards for protecting the rights of the accused than even the conservative Burger Court (1969–1986).

The five-to-four ruling in *County of Riverside v. McLaughlin,* 111 S.Ct. 1661 (1991) (see page 168), is notable in this regard. Writing for the majority, Justice O'Connor reinterpreted a Burger Court holding, in *Gerstein v. Pugh,* 420 U.S. 103 (1975), that required state and local authorities to provide defendants "promptly" with a fair and reliable determination of the probable cause for their warrantless arrest. O'Connor concluded that states may hold individuals who have been arrested without a warrant, for up to forty-eight hours without a hearing to determine whether police had probable cause to an arrest and incarcerate an individual. Notably, in dissent Justice Scalia sharply criticized the majority for its reinterpretation of *Gerstein* and departure from the common law and constitutional jurisprudence underlying the adoption of the Fourth

Amendment in 1791. In a separate opinion, Justices Blackmun, Marshall, and Stevens also dissented.

In two cases in its 1992 term the Court dealt with questions involving the seizure of private property.[1] *Soldal v. Cook County,* 113 S.Ct. 538 (1992), raised the question of whether the Fourth Amendment applies to the seizure and removal of a mobile home from a trailer park by the landowner, who removed the mobile home without an eviction order, while police prevented the homeowner from interfering with the eviction. In an appellate court's view, Edward Soldal's home had not been "seized" for the purposes of the Fourth Amendment because the police had not seized his mobile home, and Soldal's Fourth Amendment–protected privacy interests had not been invaded since his home had not been entered and "the privacy of its interior [remained] uncompromised and undisturbed." Unanimously reversing the lower court ruling, the Rehnquist Court rejected such a narrow reading of the amendment's protection for private property. Writing for the Court, Justice White observed that

> [a] "seizure" of property . . . occurs when "there is some meaningful interference with an individual's possessory interests in that property." *United States v. Jacobsen,* 466 U.S. 109 (1984). In addition, we have emphasized that "at the very core" of the Fourth Amendment "stands the right of a man to retreat into his own home." *Silverman v. United States,* 365 U.S. 505 (1961). As a result of the state action in this case, the Soldals' domicile was not only seized, it literally was carried away, giving a new meaning to the term "mobile home." We fail to see how being unceremoniously dispossessed of one's home in the manner alleged to have occurred here can be viewed as anything but a seizure invoking the protection of the Fourth Amendment.

County of Riverside v. McLaughlin
111 S.Ct. 1661 (1991)

Donald McLaughlin was arrested without a warrant and imprisoned for two days in the Riverside County Jail without a hearing before a judge to establish the probable cause for his arrest. He later filed a class action suit in federal district court seeking injunctive and declaratory relief.

[1] The other case involving the seizure of private property grew out of the government's "drug war." In *United States v. A Parcel of Land,* 113 S.Ct. 1126 (1993), Justice Stevens construed the Comprehensive Drug Abuse Prevention and Control Act to exempt from forfeiture the property of owners who purchased the property with a gift of money that was unknown to them the result of drug trafficking. Here, the Court barred the government from seizing a house purchased by a woman with a gift of $240,000 from her live-in lover, who was subsequently convicted of drug trafficking. Chief Justice Rehnquist and Justices Kennedy and White dissented.

McLaughlin charged that the County of Riverside ran afoul of *Gerstein v. Pugh*, 420 U.S. 103 (1975), in failing to provide "prompt" judicial hearings and determinations of the probable cause for arresting, without a warrant, persons like himself. And he requested an order requiring the County of Riverside to provide "arrestees, arrested without warrants, prompt probable cause, bail and arraignment hearings." Riverside combined such determinations with arraignment proceedings, which it required to be conducted within two days of arrest, excluding weekends and holidays. The district court subsequently issued a preliminary injunction requiring all persons arrested without a warrant in the county to be provided with a probable cause determination within thirty-six hours of their arrest, unless there were exigent circumstances. The Court of Appeals for the Ninth Circuit affirmed, and the County of Riverside appealed to the Supreme Court.

The Court's decision was five to four, with Justice O'Connor delivering the majority's opinion. Dissenting opinions were delivered by Justice Marshall, who was joined by Justices Blackmun and Stevens, and by Justice Scalia.

Justice O'CONNOR delivers the opinion of the Court.

In *Gerstein v. Pugh*, 420 U.S. 103 (1975), this Court held that the Fourth Amendment requires a prompt judicial determination of probable cause as a prerequisite to an extended pretrial detention following a warrantless arrest.

This case requires us to define what is "prompt" under *Gerstein*. . . .

In *Gerstein*, this Court held unconstitutional Florida procedures under which persons arrested without a warrant could remain in police custody for 30 days or more without a judicial determination of probable cause. In reaching this conclusion we attempted to reconcile important competing interests. On the one hand, States have a strong interest in protecting public safety by taking into custody those persons who are reasonably suspected of having engaged in criminal activity, even where there has been no opportunity for a prior judicial determination of probable cause. On the other hand, prolonged detention based on incorrect or unfounded suspicion may unjustly "imperil [a] suspect's job, interrupt his source of income, and impair his family relationships." We sought to balance these competing concerns by holding that States "must provide a fair and reliable determination of probable cause as a condition for any significant pretrial restraint of liberty, and this determination must be made by a judicial officer either before or promptly after arrest." Id. . . .

Gerstein held that probable cause determinations must be prompt—not immediate. The Court explained that "flexibility and experimentation" were "desirab[le]"; that "[t]here is no single preferred pretrial procedure"; and that "the nature of the probable cause determination usually will be shaped to accord with a State's pretrial procedure viewed as a whole." The Court of Appeals and the dissent disregard these statements, relying instead on selective quotations from the Court's opinion. As we have explained, *Gerstein* struck a balance between competing interests; a proper understanding of the decision is possible only if one takes into account both sides of the equation. . . .

In our view, the Fourth Amendment permits a reasonable postponement of a probable cause determination while the police cope with the everyday problems of processing suspects through an overly burdened criminal justice system.

But flexibility has its limits; *Gerstein* is not a blank check. . . .

Our task in this case is to articulate more clearly the boundaries of what is permissible under the Fourth Amendment. Although we hesitate to announce that the Constitution compels a specific time limit, it is important to provide some degree of certainty so that States and counties may establish procedures with confidence that they fall within constitutional bounds. Taking into account the competing interests articulated in *Gerstein,* we believe that a jurisdiction that provides judicial determinations of probable cause within 48 hours of arrest will, as a general matter, comply with the promptness requirement of *Gerstein.* For this reason, such jurisdictions will be immune from systemic challenges.

This is not to say that the probable cause determination in a particular case passes constitutional muster simply because it is provided within 48 hours. Such a hearing may nonetheless violate *Gerstein* if the arrested individual can prove that his or her probable cause determination was delayed unreasonably. Examples of unreasonable delay are delays for the purpose of gathering additional evidence to justify the arrest, a delay motivated by ill will against the arrested individual, or delay for delay's sake. In evaluating whether the delay in a particular case is unreasonable, however, courts must allow a substantial degree of flexibility. . . .

Where an arrested individual does not receive a probable cause determination within 48 hours, the calculus changes. In such a case, the arrested individual does not bear the burden of proving an unreasonable delay. Rather, the burden shifts to the government to demonstrate the existence of a bona fide emergency or other extraordinary circumstance.

The fact that in a particular case it may take longer than 48 hours to consolidate pretrial proceedings does not qualify as an extraordinary circumstance. Nor, for that matter, do intervening weekends. A jurisdiction that chooses to offer combined proceedings must do so as soon as is reasonably feasible, but in no event later than 48 hours after arrest.

Justice MARSHALL, with whom Justices BLACKMUN and STEVENS joined, dissented in a separate opinion.

Justice SCALIA dissenting.

. . .

It was the purpose of the Fourth Amendment to put this matter beyond time, place and judicial predilection, incorporating the traditional common-law guarantees against unlawful arrest. . . .

In my view, absent extraordinary circumstances, it is an "unreasonable seizure" within the meaning of the Fourth Amendment for the police, having arrested a suspect without a warrant, to delay a determination of probable cause for the arrest either (1) for reasons unrelated to arrangement of the probable-cause determination or completion of the steps incident to arrest, or (2) beyond 24 hours after the arrest. Like the Court, I would treat the time limit as a presumption; when the 24 hours are exceeded the burden shifts to the police to adduce unforeseeable circumstances justifying the additional delay.

B. EXCEPTIONS TO THE WARRANT REQUIREMENT

In a series of rulings, the Rehnquist Court adopted a narrow reading of the Fourth Amendment's proscription against "unreasonable searches and seizures." *California v. Hodari D.,* 111 S.Ct. 1547 (1991) posed an inexorable question given the Court's prior rulings on the permissibility of police officers' stopping and frisking individuals for whom they have probable cause or a reasonable suspicion of being engaged in criminal activities. Specifically, here the question presented was whether police made an unlawful "seizure" when they chased a man who ran away at the sight of them, and then recovered abandoned evidence (drugs), which was used at trial. By a seven-to-two vote, the Rehnquist Court held that even though police did not have a "reasonable suspicion" for them to question or detain Hodari D., the abandoned evidence seized by the police could still be used against the defendant at trial.

Writing for the Court, Justice Scalia held that Hodari D. had not been "seized" within the meaning of the Fourth Amendment. On his view, criminal suspects are seized for Fourth Amendment purposes only at the point at which officers either use physical force or the suspect complies with their "show of authority." "We do not think it desirable," as he put it, "to stretch the Fourth Amendment beyond its words. . . . Street pursuits always place the public at some risk, and compliance with police orders to stop should therefore be encouraged. . . . Since policemen do not command 'Stop!' expecting to be ignored, or give chase hoping to be outrun, it fully suffices to apply the deterrent to their genuine, successful seizures."

In a footnote, Scalia further added that states need not bother to show that police even had a "reasonable suspicion" to justify their pursuit of an individual fleeing from them, because they need not meet that standard within the context of an individual fleeing their presence. "That it would be unreasonable to stop, for brief inquiry, young men who scatter in panic upon the mere sighting of the police is not self-evident, and arguably contradicts proverbial common sense," he noted, quoting the biblical saying "The wicked flee when no man pursueth."

The facts in *Hodari D.* are important because they are replayed virtually every day in urban areas of the country. Hodari D., a teenager, was standing with several other youths around a car in a high-crime area of Oakland, California. At some point, they spotted an unmarked police car approaching and started running away. With the police in chase, Hodari D. tossed away a small rock of crack cocaine, which the police subsequently recovered. Seconds later Hodari was tackled to ground by a police officer; he was found to be also carrying a pager and $130 in cash. At a preliminary hearing, Hodari D.'s attorney argued that the cocaine had to be excluded at his trial because it was obtained in violation of the Fourth Amendment. The trial judge disagreed, but was overturned by a state appellate court, which relied on the Court's previous rulings that police must have "reasonable suspicion" to stop and question people.

The two dissenters in *Hodari D.*, Justices Stevens and Marshall, called the majority's ruling "profoundly unwise" and "seriously flawed." They charged the Court with encouraging "unlawful displays of force that will frighten countless innocent citizens into surrendering whatever privacy rights they may still have." Justice Stevens, moreover, complained that the majority's interpretation of what constitutes a seizure under the Fourth Amendment would allow a police officer to "fire his weapon at an innocent citizen and not implicate the Fourth Amendment—as long as he misses his target." In contrast with the majority's view, a seizure according to Stevens "occurs whenever an objective evaluation of a police officer's show of force conveys the message that the citizen is not entirely free to leave." Here, in Hodari's case, he said, "the officer's show of force—taking the form of a head-on chase—adequately conveyed" that message.

In its 1992 term the Rehnquist Court was invited to approve yet another exception—a "plain feel" exception—to the Fourth Amendment's warrant requirement in *Minnesota v. Dickerson,* 113 S.Ct. 2130 (1993) (see page 173). Here, Minnesota appealed a ruling of its state supreme court that rejected such an exception, and argued that a "plain feel exception" was analogous to the "plain view" exception and a logical extension of *Terry v. Ohio,* 392 U.S. 1 (1968) (see Vol. 2, Ch. 7), which held that police may stop and frisk individuals who they suspect are engaged in criminal activities. Although finding that in this case the police went too far in squeezing a small object in the pocket of a suspect's jacket, the Court expanded *Terry*'s stop-and-frisk exception to include searches and seizures of "nonthreatening contraband," as well as weapons, that are immediately identifiable by touch during a police patdown of a suspect.

Minnesota v. Dickerson
113 S.Ct. 2130 (1993)

One evening in 1989 two Minneapolis police officers patrolling the city in an unmarked squad car noticed Timothy Dickerson leaving an apartment building. They had previously responded to complaints of drug sales in the building and considered it a "crack house." Dickerson was walking toward the police but upon spotting the squad car abruptly turned in the opposite direction. One of the police officers watched as Dickerson entered an alley, and based upon his seemingly evasive actions and the fact that he had just left a building known for cocaine traffic, the officers decided to stop him. Pulling their squad car into the alley, they ordered Dickerson to stop and submit to a patdown search. That search revealed no weapons, but the officer conducting the search felt a small lump in Dickerson's nylon jacket, reached into a pocket, and retrieved a small plastic bag containing one-fifth of one gram of crack cocaine. Dickerson was immediately arrested and charged with the possession of a controlled substance.

Before his trial Dickerson's attorney moved to suppress the cocaine, but the trial judge, after concluding that the officers were justified under *Terry v. Ohio*, 392 U.S. 1 (1968), in stopping and frisking Dickerson, rejected the motion on the ground that the officer's search of Dickerson's pocket was analogous to the "plain-view" exception. The trial court's decision, however, was reversed by an appellate court and that decision was affirmed by the state supreme court, which agreed that the police overstepped *Terry* in seizing the cocaine and "declined to adopt the plain feel exception" to the Fourth Amendment's warrant requirement. Minnesota appealed to the Supreme Court, which granted review and affirmed the state supreme court's ruling.

The Court's decision was six to three, with Justice White announcing the majority's opinion. Justice Scalia concurred. In a separate opinion joined by Justices Blackmun and Thomas, Chief Justice Rehnquist in part concurred and in part dissented.

Justice WHITE delivers the opinion of the Court.

Terry [*v. Ohio*, 392 U.S. 1 (1968)] held that "when an officer is justified in believing that the individual whose suspicious behavior he is investigating at close range is armed and presently dangerous to the officer or to others," the officer may conduct a patdown search "to determine whether the person is in fact carrying a weapon." Rather, a protective search—permitted without a warrant and on the basis of reasonable suspicion less than probable cause—must be strictly "limited to that which is necessary for the discovery of weapons which might be used to harm the officer or others nearby." If the protective search goes beyond what is necessary to determine if the suspect is armed, it is no longer valid under *Terry* and its fruits will be suppressed. *Sibron v. New York*, 392 U.S. 40 (1968).

These principles were settled 25 years ago when, on the same day, the Court announced its decisions in *Terry* and *Sibron*. The question presented today is whether police officers may seize nonthreatening contraband detected during a protective patdown search of the sort permitted by *Terry*. We think the answer is clearly that they may, so long as the officer's search stays within the bounds marked by *Terry*.

We have already held that police officers, at least under certain circumstances, may seize contraband detected during the lawful execution of a *Terry* search. In *Michigan v. Long*, [463 U.S. 1032 (1983)], for example, police approached a man who had driven his car into a ditch and who appeared to be under the influence of some intoxicant. As the man moved to reenter the car from the roadside, police spotted a knife on the floorboard. The officers stopped the man, subjected him to a patdown search, and then inspected the interior of the vehicle for other weapons. During the search of the passenger compartment, the police discovered an open pouch containing marijuana and seized it. This Court upheld the validity of the search and seizure under *Terry*. The Court held first that, in the context of a roadside encounter, where police have reasonable suspicion based on specific and articulable facts to believe that a driver may be armed and dangerous, they may conduct a protective search for weapons not only of the driver's person but also of the passenger compartment of the automobile. Of course, the protective search of the vehicle, being justified solely by the danger that weapons stored there could be used against the officers or bystanders, must be "limited to those areas in which a weapon may be placed or hidden." The Court then held: "If, while conducting a legitimate *Terry* search of the interior of the automobile, the officer should, as here, discover contraband other than weapons, he clearly cannot be required to ignore the contraband, and the Fourth Amendment does not require its suppression in such circumstances."

The Court in *Long* justified this latter holding by reference to our cases under the "plain-view" doctrine. If, however, the police lack probable cause to believe that an object in plain view is contraband without conducting some further search of the object—i.e., if "its incriminating character [is not] 'immediately apparent' "—the plain-view doctrine cannot justify its seizure. *Arizona v. Hicks*, 480 U.S. 321 (1987).

We think that this doctrine has an obvious application by analogy to cases in which an officer discovers contraband through the sense of touch during an otherwise lawful search. The rationale of the plain-view doctrine is that if contraband is left in open view and is observed by a police officer from a lawful vantage point, there has been no invasion of a legitimate expectation of privacy and thus no "search" within the meaning of the Fourth Amendment—or at least no search independent of the initial intrusion that gave the officers their vantage point. The warrantless seizure of contraband that presents itself in this manner is deemed justified by the realization that resort to a neutral magistrate under such circumstances would often be impracticable and would do little to promote the objectives of the Fourth Amendment. The same can be said of tactile discoveries of contraband. If a police officer lawfully pats down a suspect's outer clothing and feels an object whose contour or mass makes its identity immediately apparent, there has been no invasion of the suspect's privacy beyond that already authorized by the officer's search for weapons; if the object is contraband, its warrantless seizure would be justified by the same practical considerations that inhere in the plain view context. . . .

It remains to apply these principles to the facts of this case. Respondent has not challenged the finding made by the trial court and affirmed by both the Court of Appeals and the State Supreme Court that the police were justified under *Terry* in stopping him and frisking him for weapons. Thus, the dispositive question before this Court is whether the officer who conducted the search was acting within the lawful bounds marked by *Terry* at the time he gained probable cause to believe that the lump in respondent's jacket was contraband. . . . The Minnesota Supreme Court, after "a close examination of the record," held that the officer's own testimony "belies any notion that he 'immediately' " recognized the lump as crack cocaine. Rather, the court concluded, the officer determined that the lump was contraband only after "squeezing, sliding and otherwise manipulating the contents of the defendant's pocket"—a pocket which the officer already knew contained no weapon.

Under the State Supreme Court's interpretation of the record before it, it is clear that the court was correct in holding that the police officer in this case overstepped the bounds of the "strictly circumscribed" search for weapons allowed under *Terry*. Where, as here, "an officer who is executing a valid search for one item seizes a different item," this Court rightly "has been sensitive to the danger . . . that officers will enlarge a specific authorization, furnished by a warrant or an exigency, into the equivalent of a general warrant to rummage and seize at will." *Texas v. Brown*, 460 U.S. [730 (1983)] (STEVENS, J., concurring in judgment). Here, the officer's continued exploration of respondent's pocket after having concluded that it contained no weapon was unrelated to "the sole justification of the search [under *Terry*:] . . . the protection of the police officer and others nearby." It therefore amounted to the sort of evidentiary search that *Terry* expressly refused to authorize, and that we have condemned in subsequent cases. . . .

Justice SCALIA, concurring.

My problem with the present case is that I am not entirely sure that the physical search—the "frisk"—that produced the evidence at issue here complied with [the Fourth Amendment's] constitutional standard. The decision of ours that gave approval to such searches, *Terry v. Ohio,* 392 U.S. 1 (1968), made no serious attempt to determine compliance with traditional standards, but rather, according to the style of this Court at the time, simply adjudged that such a search was "reasonable" by current estimations.

There is good evidence, I think, that the "stop" portion of the *Terry* "stop-and-frisk" holding accords with the common law—that it had long been considered reasonable to detain suspicious persons for the purpose of demanding that they give an account of themselves.

I am unaware, however, of any precedent for a physical search of a person thus temporarily detained for questioning. Sometimes, of course, the temporary detention of a suspicious character would be elevated to a full custodial arrest on probable cause—as, for instance, when a suspect was unable to provide a sufficient accounting of himself. At that point, it is clear that the common law would permit not just a protective "frisk," but a full physical search incident to the arrest. When, however, the detention did not rise to the level of a full-blown arrest (and was not supported by the degree of cause needful for that purpose), there appears to be no clear support at common law for physically searching the suspect. I frankly doubt, moreover, whether the fiercely proud men who adopted our Fourth Amendment would have allowed themselves to be subjected, on mere suspicion of being armed and dangerous, to such indignity. . . .

On the other hand, even if a "frisk" prior to arrest would have been considered impermissible in 1791, perhaps it was considered permissible by 1868, when the Fourteenth Amendment (the basis for applying the Fourth Amendment to the States) was adopted. Or perhaps it is only since that time that concealed weapons capable of harming the interrogator quickly and from beyond arm's reach have become common—which might alter the judgment of what is "reasonable" under the original standard. But technological changes were no more discussed in *Terry* than was the original state of the law.

If I were of the view that *Terry* was (insofar as the power to "frisk" is concerned) incorrectly decided, I might—even if I felt bound to adhere to that case—vote to exclude the evidence incidentally discovered, on the theory that half a constitutional guarantee is better than none. I might also vote to exclude it if I agreed with the original-meaning-is-irrelevant, good-policy-is-constitutional-law school of jurisprudence that the *Terry* opinion represents. As a policy matter, it may be desirable to permit "frisks" for weapons, but not to encourage "frisks" for drugs by admitting evidence other than weapons.

I adhere to original meaning, however. And though I do not favor the mode of analysis in *Terry,* I cannot say that its result was wrong. Constitutionality of the "frisk" in the present case was neither challenged nor argued. Assuming, therefore, that the search was lawful, I agree with the Court's premise that any evidence incidentally discovered in the course of it would be admissible, and join the Court's opinion in its entirety.

Chief Justice REHNQUIST, with whom Justices BLACKMUN and THOMAS joined, concurred in part and dissented in part, explaining that in their view the state supreme court's decision should be vacated and the case remanded for further consideration in light of the Court's decision because it remained unclear from the record whether the officer's search was within the bounds of *Terry v. Ohio.*

C. THE SPECIAL PROBLEMS OF AUTOMOBILES IN A MOBILE SOCIETY

In its 1990 term, the Rehnquist Court handed down a number of decisions bearing on police searches and seizures of automobile occupants and their belongings. In *Florida v. Bostick,* 111 S.Ct. 2382 (1991), by a six-to-three vote the justices upheld random police questioning of bus and train passengers.

Bostick originated with the "war on drugs" as waged in Broward County, Florida. There, sheriff's department officers routinely board buses at scheduled stops and ask passengers for permission to search their luggage. As it happened, two officers boarded a bus on which Terrance Bostick was traveling and, without reasonable suspicion or probable cause, questioned him and other passengers at a scheduled bus stop. They asked for his consent to search two of his bags and advised him of his right to deny consent, but he contested both that he was in a position to deny their request and that he in fact consented to their search. In any event, police searched his bags, and upon finding some cocaine, they arrested him. At a pretrial hearing he unsuccessfully moved to suppress the introduction of the cocaine as evidence on the grounds that it had been seized in violation of his Fourth Amendment rights. And Bostick later pled guilty but reserved the right to appeal the trial court's denial of his motion to suppress the contraband. An appellate court affirmed the trial court's denial of his motion, but deemed it important enough to certify the question for decision by the Florida Supreme Court, which in turn concluded that Bostick had been unlawfully seized because a reasonable passenger in his situation would not have felt free to leave the bus to avoid questioning by the police. The state supreme court ruled that "an impermissible seizure result[s] when police mount a drug search on buses during scheduled stops and question boarded passengers without articulable reasons for doing so, thereby obtaining consent to search the passengers' luggage." The state, thereupon, appealed that decision to the U.S. Supreme Court.

Writing for the Court, Justice O'Connor reaffirmed that "the Fourth Amendment permits police officers to approach individuals at random in airport lobbies and other public places to ask them questions and to request consent to search their luggage, so long as a reasonable person would understand that he or she could refuse to cooperate." And O'Connor found no basis for distinguishing random searches and seizures in airport terminals from those in buses and trains. In her words:

Our cases make it clear that a seizure does not occur simply because a police officer approaches an individual and asks a few questions. So long as a reasonable person would feel free "to disregard the police and go about his business," *California v. Hodari D.*, 499 U.S. — (1991), the encounter is consensual and no reasonable suspicion is required. The encounter will not trigger Fourth Amendment scrutiny unless it loses its consensual nature. The Court made precisely this point in *Terry v. Ohio*, 392 U.S. 1 (1968).

Since *Terry*, we have held repeatedly that mere police questioning does not constitute a seizure. . . . There is no doubt that if this same encounter had taken place before Bostick boarded the bus or in the lobby of the bus terminal, it would not rise to the level of a seizure. The Court has dealt with similar encounters in airports and has found them to be "the sort of consensual encounter[s] that implicat[e] no Fourth Amendment interest." *Florida v. Rodriguez*, 469 U.S. 1 (1984). We have stated that even when officers have no basis for suspecting a particular individual, they may generally ask questions of that individual, see *INS v. Delgado*, 466 U.S. 210, 216 (1984); ask to examine the individual's identification, *United States v. Mendenhall*, 446 U.S. 544 (1980); and request consent to search his or her luggage—as long as the police do not convey a message that compliance with their requests is required. . . .

[The] mere fact that Bostick did not feel free to leave the bus does not mean that the police seized him. Bostick was a passenger on a bus that was scheduled to depart. He would not have felt free to leave the bus even if the police had not been present. Bostick's movements were "confined" in a sense, but this was the natural result of his decision to take the bus; it says nothing about whether or not the police conduct at issue was coercive.

Concluding, Justice O'Connor also rejected Bostick's claim that he was "seized" because no reasonable person would freely consent to a search of luggage that he or she knows contains drugs. That argument, observed O'Connor, could not "prevail because the 'reasonable person' test presupposes an innocent person."

Dissenting in *Bostick*, Justices Marshall, Blackmun and Stevens countered,

[T]he Fourth Amendment clearly condemns the suspicionless, dragnet-style sweep of intrastate or interstate buses. Withdrawing this particular weapon from the government's drug-war arsenal would hardly leave the police without any means of combatting the use of buses as instrumentalities of the drug trade. The police would remain free, for example, to approach passengers whom they have a reasonable, articulable basis to suspect of criminal wrongdoing. Alternatively, they could continue to confront passengers without suspicion so long as they took simple steps, like advising the passengers confronted of their right to decline to be questioned, to dispel the aura of coercion and intimidation that pervades such encounters. There is no reason to expect that such requirements would render the Nation's buses law-enforcement-free zones.

In two other rulings, the Court dealt with police searches of containers found in automobiles when they are not armed with search warrants. In *Florida v. Jimeno*, 111 S.Ct. 1801 (1991), with only Justices Marshall and Stevens dissenting, the Court ruled that if a driver of an automobile is stopped by police and gives permission to search the car, the police do not need a search warrant to open any containers found inside the automobile. Writing for the majority, Chief Justice Rehnquist observed,

The touchstone of the Fourth Amendment is reasonableness. *Katz v. United States,* 389 U.S. 347 (1967). The Fourth Amendment does not proscribe all state-initiated searches and seizures; it merely proscribes those which are unreasonable. Thus, we have long approved consensual searches because it is no doubt reasonable for the police to conduct a search once they have been permitted to do so. *Schneckloth v. Bustamonte,* 412 U.S. 218 (1973). The standard for measuring the scope of a suspect's consent under the Fourth Amendment is that of "objective" reasonableness—what would the typical reasonable person have understood by the exchange between the officer and the suspect? The question before us, then, is whether it is reasonable for an officer to consider a suspect's general consent to a search of his car to include consent to examine a paper bag lying on the floor of the car. We think that it is.

By contrast, Justice Marshall, along with Justice Stevens, dissented in *Jimeno* and reaffirmed his dissent almost twenty years earlier, in *Schneckloth v. Bustamonte,* 412 U.S. 218 (1973) (see Vol. 2, Ch. 7), where he criticized the majority on the Burger Court for asserting "practical interests in efficacious law enforcement as the basis for not requiring the police to take meaningful steps to establish the basis of an individual's consent."

In *California v. Acevedo*, 111 S.Ct. 1982 (1991) (see page 180) the Rehnquist Court went much further and overturned Burger Court rulings that had held that police must under most circumstances obtain a search warrant in order to search containers found in the trunks of automobiles. In *United States v. Chadwick,* 433 U.S. 1 (1977), and *Arkansas v. Sanders,* 442 U.S. 753 (1979), the Court barred warrantless searches of closed containers found in cars unless police have either a warrant or, at least, probable cause to search the car itself. Notably, in those seven-to-two decisions, Justices Blackmun and Rehnquist dissented. In *Acevedo,* those two justices were then joined by every one of Reagan's and Bush's appointees; Justices White, Marshall and Stevens dissented. Writing for the Court's present majority, Justice Blackmun overturned the Burger Court's precedents, claiming that it "confused courts and police and impeded effective law enforcement." The Court's prior line drawing and rulings on warrantless searches of containers found in automobiles were indeed confusing and cross-cutting (see Vol. 2, Ch. 7). On the one hand, the Court had held that police needed no warrant to search containers in cars if they had probable cause to search a car. On the other hand, under other rulings of the Court, police could not open containers that they suspected of containing contraband if they did not have probable cause to search a car in the first place. In announcing the Court's decision in *Acevedo,* Blackmun held that "[t]he protections of the Fourth Amendment must not turn on such coincidences." But note that the dissenters charge that the majority " 'cured' [this 'anomaly'] at the expense of creating a more serious paradox": without a warrant police may not search a briefcase carried by its owner when walking down a street, but now may do so when the owner places the briefcase in the locked trunk of his car.

California v. Acevedo

111 S.Ct. 1982 (1991)

In October 1987, police in Santa Ana, California, received a telephone call from a federal drug-enforcement agent in Hawaii, informing them that he had seized a package of marijuana that was to have been delivered by Federal Express to a house in Santa Ana. It was decided that the agent would send the package to the police instead and they would take it to the local Federal Express office and arrest the person who claimed it. A few days later, Jamie Daza claimed the package and then drove to his apartment, taking the package in with him. While still staked-out at his apartment an hour later, police observed Daza leave to throw away the box and paper that had contained the marijuana into a trash bin. At that point, one of the officers left the scene to get a search warrant, but before the officer returned police saw Richard St. George leave the apartment carrying a blue knapsack that appeared to be half full. The officers stopped him as he was driving off, searched the knapsack, and found twelve pounds of marijuana. A little later, Charles Acevedo arrived at the apartment and, after about ten minutes, reappeared carrying a brown paper bag that looked full. Acevedo walked to a silver Honda in the parking lot and placed the bag in the trunk of the car and started the car's engine. Fearing the loss of evidence, officers in a marked police car stopped him and subsequently, without a warrant, opened the trunk and the bag and found marijuana.

Acevedo was charged with possession of marijuana. At his trial he moved to suppress the introduction of the marijuana as evidence against him on the ground that it was obtained in violation of his Fourth Amendment rights. After his motion was denied, he pleaded guilty and, after his conviction and sentence, appealed the court's denial of his motion to suppress the marijuana as evidence. A state appellate court concluded that the marijuana should have been suppressed on the grounds that the officers had probable cause to believe that the paper bag contained drugs but lacked probable cause to suspect that Acevedo's car, itself, otherwise contained contraband. Because the officers' probable cause was directed specifically at the bag, the court held that the case was controlled by *United States v. Chadwick*, 433 U.S. 1 (1977), which held that under similar circumstances police needed a warrant to search a large trunk placed in the back of a car, rather than by *United States v. Ross*, 456 U.S. 798 (1982), which had upheld a warrantless search of containers in the trunk of a car that police had probable cause to believe was being used by a drug dealer (see Vol. 2, Ch. 7). Although the court agreed that the officers could seize the paper bag, it held that, under *Chadwick*, they could not open the bag without first obtaining a warrant for that purpose. Subsequently, the state of California appealed that ruling to the state supreme court, which denied review, and to the Supreme Court, which granted review.

The Court's decision was six to three; Justice Blackmun announced the majority opinion, with which Justice Scalia concurred. Justice White delivered a dissenting opinion, as did Justice Stevens, who was joined by Justice Marshall.

Justice BLACKMUN delivers the opinion of the Court.

. . . In *Carroll* [*v. United States*], 267 U.S. 132 (1925) this Court . . . held that a warrantless search of an automobile based upon probable cause to believe that the vehicle contained evidence of crime in the light of an exigency arising out of the likely disappearance of the vehicle did not contravene the Warrant Clause of the Fourth Amendment.

The Court refined the exigency requirement in *Chambers v. Maroney*, 399 U.S. 42 (1970), when it held that the existence of exigent circumstances was to be determined at the time the automobile is seized. . . . Following *Chambers*, if the police have probable cause to justify a warrantless seizure of an automobile on a public roadway, they may conduct either an immediate or a delayed search of the vehicle.

In *United States v. Ross*, 456 U.S. 798, decided in 1982, we held that a warrantless search of an automobile under the *Carroll* doctrine could include a search of a container or package found inside the car when such a search was supported by probable cause. . . . In *Ross*, therefore, we clarified the scope of the *Carroll* doctrine as properly including a "probing search" of compartments and containers within the automobile so long as the search is supported by probable cause.

In addition to this clarification, *Ross* distinguished the *Carroll* doctrine from the separate rule that governed the search of closed containers. The Court had announced this separate rule, unique to luggage and other closed packages, bags, and containers, in *United States v. Chadwick,* 433 U.S. 1 (1977). In *Chadwick,* federal narcotics agents had probable cause to believe that a 200-pound double-locked footlocker contained marijuana. The agents tracked the locker as the defendants removed it from a train and carried it through the station to a waiting car. As soon as the defendants lifted the locker into the trunk of the car, the agents arrested them, seized the locker, and searched it. In this Court . . . the United States urged that the search of movable luggage could be considered analogous to the search of an automobile. The Court rejected this argument because, it reasoned, a person expects more privacy in his luggage and personal effects than he does in his automobile. . . .

In *Arkansas v. Sanders,* 442 U.S. 753 (1979), the Court extended *Chadwick*'s rule to apply to a suitcase actually being transported in the trunk of a car. In *Sanders,* the police had probable cause to believe a suitcase contained marijuana. They watched as the defendant placed the suitcase in the trunk of a taxi and was driven away. The police pursued the taxi for several blocks, stopped it, found the suitcase in the trunk, and searched it. Although the Court had applied the *Carroll* doctrine to searches of integral parts of the automobile itself, indeed, in *Carroll,* contraband whiskey was in the upholstery of the seats, it did not extend the doctrine to the warrantless search of personal luggage "merely because it was located in an automobile lawfully stopped by the police." Again, the *Sanders* majority stressed the heightened privacy expectation in personal luggage and concluded that the presence of luggage in an automobile did not diminish the owner's expectation of privacy in his personal items.

In *Ross,* the Court endeavored to distinguish between *Carroll,* which governed the *Ross* automobile search, and *Chadwick,* which governed the *Sanders* automobile search. It held that the *Carroll* doctrine covered searches of automobiles when the police had probable cause to search an entire vehicle but that the *Chadwick* doctrine governed searches of luggage when the officers had probable cause to search only a container within the vehicle. Thus, in a *Ross* situation, the police could conduct a reasonable search under the Fourth Amendment without obtaining a warrant, whereas in a *Sanders* situation, the police had to obtain a warrant before they searched. . . .

The facts in this case closely resemble the facts in *Ross.* . . . This Court in *Ross* rejected *Chadwick*'s distinction between containers and cars. . . . [But w]e now must decide the question deferred in *Ross:* whether the Fourth Amendment requires the police to obtain a warrant to open the sack in a movable vehicle simply because they lack probable cause to search the entire car. We conclude that it does not. . . .

We now agree that a container found after a general search of the automobile and a container found in a car after a limited search for the container are equally easy for the police to store and for the suspect to hide or destroy. In fact, we see no principled distinction in terms of either the privacy expectation or the exigent circumstances between the paper bag found by the police in *Ross* and the paper bag found by the police here. Furthermore, by attempting to distinguish between a container for which the police are specifically searching and a container which they come across in a car, we have provided only minimal protection for privacy and have impeded effective law enforcement. . . .

We conclude that it is better to adopt one clear-cut rule to govern automobile searches and eliminate the warrant requirement for closed containers set forth in *Sanders*. The interpretation of the *Carroll* doctrine set forth in *Ross* now applies to all searches of containers found in an automobile. In other words, the police may search without a warrant if their search is supported by probable cause.

Justice SCALIA concurred in a separate opinion.

Justice WHITE dissented in a separate opinion.

Justice STEVENS, with whom Justice MARSHALL joins, dissenting.

. . .

In its opinion today, the Court recognizes that the police did not have probable cause to search respondent's vehicle and that a search of any-thing but the paper bag that respondent had carried from Daza's apart-ment and placed in the trunk of his car would have been unconstitutional. Moreover, as I read the opinion, the Court assumes that the police could not have made a warrantless inspection of the bag before it was placed in the car. Finally, the Court also does not question the fact that, under our prior cases, it would have been lawful for the police to seize the container and detain it (and respondent) until they obtained a search warrant. Thus, all of the relevant facts that governed our decisions in *Chadwick* and *Sanders* are present here whereas the relevant fact that justified the vehicle search in *Ross* is not present. The Court does not attempt to identify any exigent circumstances that would justify its refusal to apply the general rule against warrantless searches. Instead, it ad-vances these three arguments: First, the rules identified in the foregoing cases are confusing and anomalous. Second, the rules do not protect any significant interest in privacy. And, third, the rules impede effective law enforcement. None of these arguments withstands scrutiny.

THE "CONFUSION"

In the nine years since *Ross* was decided, the Court has considered three cases in which the police had probable cause to search a particular container and one in which they had probable cause to search two vehicles. The decisions in all four of those cases were perfectly straightforward and provide no evidence of confusion in the state or lower federal courts.

In *United States v. Place,* 462 U.S. 696 (1983), we held that, although reasonable suspicion justifies the temporary detention of an airline passenger's luggage, the seizure in that particular case was unreasonable because of the prolonged delay in ascertaining the existence of probable cause. . . . In *Oklahoma v. Castleberry,* 471 U.S. 146 (1985), police officers had probable cause to believe the defendant carried narcotics in blue suitcases in the trunk of his car. After arresting him, they opened the trunk, seized the suitcases, and searched them without a warrant. The state court held that the search was invalid. . . . This Court affirmed by an equally divided court. 471 U.S. 146 (1985). In the case the Court decides today, the California Court of Appeal also had no difficulty applying the critical distinction. . . .

In the case in which the police had probable cause to search two vehicles, *United States v. Johns,* 469 U.S. 478 (1985), we rejected the respondent's reliance on *Chadwick* with a straightforward explanation of why that case, unlike *Ross,* did not involve an exception to the warrant requirement. We first expressed our agreement with the Court of Appeals that the Customs officers who had conducted the search had probable cause to search the vehicles. We then explained:

> Under the circumstances of this case, respondents' reliance on *Chadwick* is misplaced. . . . *Chadwick* . . . did not involve the exception to the warrant requirement recognized in *Carroll v. United States,* because the police had no probable cause to believe that the automobile, as contrasted to the footlocker, contained contraband. This point is underscored by our decision in *Ross,* which held that notwithstanding *Chadwick* police officers may conduct a warrantless search of containers discovered in the course of a lawful vehicle search. Given our conclusion that the Customs officers had probable cause to believe that the pickup trucks contained contraband, *Chadwick* is simply inapposite.

The decided cases thus provide no support for the Court's concern about "confusion." The Court instead relies primarily on predictions that were made by Justice Blackmun in his dissenting opinions in *Chadwick* and *Sanders.* The Court, however, cites no evidence that these predictions have in fact materialized or that anyone else has been unable to understand the "inherent opaqueness," of this uncomplicated issue. . . .

To the extent there was any "anomaly" in our prior jurisprudence, the Court has "cured" it at the expense of creating a more serious paradox. For, surely it is anomalous to prohibit a search of a briefcase while the owner is carrying it exposed on a public street yet to permit a search once the owner has placed the briefcase in the locked trunk of his car. . . .

THE PRIVACY ARGUMENT

The Court's statement that *Chadwick* and *Sanders* provide only "minimal protection to privacy," is also unpersuasive. Every citizen clearly has an interest in the privacy of the contents of his or her luggage, briefcase, handbag or any other container that conceals private papers and effects from public scrutiny. That privacy interest has been recognized repeatedly in cases spanning more than a century. Under the Court's holding today, the privacy interest that protects the contents of a suitcase or a briefcase from a warrantless search when it is in public view simply vanishes when its owner climbs into a taxicab. . . .

THE BURDEN ON LAW ENFORCEMENT

. . .

In the years since *Ross* was decided, the Court has heard argument in 30 Fourth Amendment cases involving narcotics. In all but one, the government was the petitioner. All save two involved a search or seizure without a warrant or with a defective warrant. And, in all except three, the Court upheld the constitutionality of the search or seizure. In the meantime, the flow of narcotics cases through the courts has steadily and dramatically increased. . . . No impartial observer could criticize this Court for hindering the progress of the war on drugs. On the contrary, decisions like the one the Court makes today will support the conclusion that this Court has become a loyal foot soldier in the Executive's fight against crime. Even if the warrant requirement does inconvenience the police to some extent, that fact does not distinguish this constitutional requirement from any other procedural protection secured by the Bill of Rights. It is merely a part of the price that our society must pay in order to preserve its freedom. . . .

I respectfully dissent.

D. OTHER GOVERNMENTAL SEARCHES IN THE ADMINISTRATIVE STATE

In its 1991 term the Rehnquist Court signaled that it was in no mood to reconsider challenges to mandatory drug testing of public employees. In a pair of rulings, in *National Treasury Employees v. Von Raab*, 489 U.S. 656 (1989), and *Skinner v. Railway Labor Executives' Association*, 489 U.S. 602 (1989) (see Vol. 2, Ch. 7), the Court upheld drug-testing programs for employees of the U.S. Customs Service who were involved in serious accidents. More than forty federal agencies now conduct drug tests under an executive order for a drug-free federal workplace. Carl Willner, an attorney in the antitrust division of the Department of Justice (DOJ), challenged the DOJ's drug-testing requirement as a violation of his Fourth Amendment guarantee against unreasonable searches and seizures. In 1990, a federal district court ruled that "suspicionless testing" of employees was unconstitutional and should be limited to only public employees in jobs "affecting public safety, and those working directly with aspects of drug enforcement." But a three-judge panel of the Court of Appeals for the District of Columbia Circuit reversed and the Rehnquist Court denied review to an appeal of that ruling in *Willner v. Barr,* 112 S.Ct. 669 (1992).

E. THE EXCLUSIONARY RULE

With one exception, in the first five terms of Rehnquist's chief justice-ship, the Court has not reexamined the Fourth Amendment's contro-versial exclusionary rule, which requires the exclusion at trial of evi-dence that police have obtained illegally. That the Rehnquist Court has not reexamined or, as some conservatives anticipated, jettisoned the rule is in part due to the course the Court has charted with respect to the Fourth Amendment more generally. In cases such as *California v. Hodari D.* (1991) (see page 171), a majority of the Rehnquist Court has avoided ruling on the exclusionary rule by simply holding that police had not technically undertaken a "search" under the Fourth Amend-ment, and hence the exclusionary rule did not apply to the evidence that they obtained.

But in its 1992 term the Rehnquist Court granted review of the government's appeal of decision by the Court of Appeals for the Ninth Circuit in *United States v. Padilla,* 113 S.Ct. 1936 (1993). The appellate court had held that the exclusionary rule protects people from arbitrary invasions of their privacy and extended the rule to bar the use of evi-dence against Xavier Padilla, an alleged drug-ring leader, that stemmed from an illegal search of a car driven by Luis Arciniega, a drug trafficker who worked with Padilla. Without even a reasonable suspicion that Arciniega was carrying contraband and in violation of the Fourth Amendment, police stopped his Cadillac on an interstate highway and subsequently discovered a trunkload of cocaine. Arciniega in turn was persuaded by police to continue delivering cocaine to Padilla, and when he made his next delivery, the police arrested Jorge and Maria Padilla in a motel room. Maria Padilla then led police to her husband, Xavier. Xavier's attorneys argued that the evidence against him should be ex-cluded at trial because the original search of Arciniega's car was illegal, and that he had a Fourth Amendment–protected privacy interest that had been breached by the police. The Ninth Circuit agreed, but in appealing its decision solicitor general Kenneth Starr countered that the Fourth Amendment exclusionary rule applies only to a person whose rights were infringed at the time of an illegal search, but not to persons who were not present at the time of the search. In a brief, unsigned opinion, the Court unanimously embraced Starr's position and reversed the lower Court decision, rejecting its expansion of the exclusionary rule to include a "co-conspirator exception."

In deciding *Padilla*, the Court rejected the lower court's exception stating that the exclusionary rule does not extend to those not present at the time of the illegal search.

8

THE FIFTH AMENDMENT GUARANTEE AGAINST SELF-ACCUSATION

A. COERCED CONFESSIONS AND POLICE INTERROGATIONS

While the Rehnquist Court declined to overturn the landmark ruling in *Miranda v. Arizona* (1966) (see Vol. 2, Ch. 8) in *Minnick v. Mississippi* (1990) (see Vol. 2, Ch. 8), it continued its retrenchment in the constitutional protection accorded criminal defendants with several other rulings. In *Arizona v. Fulminante,* 111 S.Ct. 1246 (1991) (see page 190), the Rehnquist Court significantly undercut a 1967 Warren Court ruling in *Chapman v. California,* 386 U.S. 18 (1967). *Chapman* drew a line on the extension of the so-called harmless error doctrine—under which appellate courts will not reverse the judgments of trial courts on the ground that minor procedural errors were made during a trial. (All fifty states have harmless error statutes and federal legislation provides that federal appellate courts should not reverse lower court decisions for "errors or defects which do not affect the substantial rights of the parties" in a suit.) In *Chapman,* adverse comments by the prosecutor and trial judge about a defendant's refusal to testify in his own defense at trial were held not to be constitutionally harmless errors. Writing for the Court, with only Justice Harlan dissenting, Justice Black also ruled that "before a federal constitutional error can be held harmless, [an appellate court] must be able to declare a belief that it was harmless beyond a reasonable doubt." Moreover, Justice Black noted that three kinds of constitutional errors were not subject to the harmless error doctrine, namely, when a defendant submits to a coerced confession, faces a criminal trial without the assistance of counsel, and is tried before a biased judge. As a result of

Chapman, prosecutorial use of coerced confessions were not considered harmless errors and invariably resulted in reversals of defendants' convictions. But five members of the Rehnquist Court held otherwise in *Fulminante.*

Fulminante bitterly divided the justices. Although Justice White delivered the opinion announcing the Court's decision, Chief Justice Rehnquist commanded four other votes for holding that the admission at trial of coerced confessions may be excused as a harmless error if it can be shown that other evidence, obtained independently of the confession, was also used at trial and was adequate to support a guilty verdict. Justice Souter provided the key vote in joining the four Reagan appointees to form a majority on that issue. But the lineup of the justices changed and was complicated by their stands on other questions presented in the case as well. Notably, Justice White's opinion commanded a majority of the Court on two other aspects of the ruling. White deemed the circumstances of Fulminante's confession to constitute a coerced confession, whereas Justices Rehnquist, O'Connor, Kennedy, and Souter disagreed. On that issue, Justice Scalia joined White's opinion, which also was joined by Justices Blackmun, Marshall, and Stevens. Moreover, on the final question of whether the use of Fulminante's confession was harmless beyond a reasonable doubt, White commanded a majority for affirming the judgment of the Arizona Supreme Court and remanding the case for a new trial at which Fulminante's confession may not be used against him. On that question White was joined by Blackmun, Marshall, Stevens, and Kennedy; Rehnquist, O'Connor, and Scalia dissented; and Souter refused to indicate whether or how he voted on that issue.

In *McNeil v. Wisconsin,* 111 S.Ct. 2204 (1991) (see page 194), the Court confronted an issue growing out of the intersection of the Fifth Amendment right against self-incrimination and the Sixth Amendment right to counsel. The question in *McNeil* was whether police violate a suspect's Fifth Amendment *Miranda* right if they question him about a crime when his court-appointed lawyer in another criminal case is not present. In that case, Paul McNeil was in police custody and had previously appeared in court with his attorney on another charge when he was subsequently questioned about a different crime without the presence of his attorney. Thus the narrow question posed was whether a suspect's Sixth Amendment right to counsel *implicitly* carries with it the Fifth Amendment right, as construed in *Miranda,* not to be questioned about any other crime in the absence of a suspect's attorney.

Two other decisions handed down during the 1992 term also dealt with federal courts' review of *Miranda* violations. Both were decided by bare majorities, yet ran in opposite directions. In *Brecht v. Abrahamson,* 111 S.Ct. 1710 (1993), the Court announced a new rule for federal courts when setting aside convictions on *habeas* review of cases involving state courts' errors in observing an accused's *Miranda* rights. Todd Brecht was convicted of first-degree murder after admitting that he shot the victim, but also claiming that it was an accident. The trial judge allowed the prosecution to impeach his testimony by pointing out that Brecht failed to say the shooting was accidental prior to receiving his *Miranda* warnings and by emphasizing his post-*Miranda* silence, which ran afoul of *Doyle v. Ohio*, 426 U.S. 610 (1976). A state appeals court deemed the impeachment of Brecht's testimony prejudicial, but the Wisconsin supreme court reversed. The state supreme court held that the trial court's error was "harmless beyond a reasonable doubt"—the "harmless error" standard set forth in *Chapman v. California*, 386 U.S. 18 (1967). A federal district court in turn disagreed and overturned the conviction. That ruling was then reversed by the Court of Appeals for the Seventh Circuit, which applied the less rigorous standard laid down in *Kotteakos v. United States*, 328 U.S. 750 (1946). Applying *Kotteakos*'s standard of whether a trial error has a "substantial and injurious effect or influence in determining the jury's verdict," the appellate court upheld Brecht's conviction. Brecht appealed but the Supreme Court affirmed and, as in *Arizona v. Fulminante* (see page 190), refused to extend *Chapman*'s "harmless error" standard. Delivering an opinion that commanded only the votes of Justices Kennedy, Scalia, Stevens, and Thomas, Chief Justice Rehnquist held that on *habeas* review federal courts may set aside convictions only when trial errors involving violations of *Miranda* have a "substantial and injurious effect or influence" that results in "actual prejudice." Justices White, Blackmun, O'Connor, and Souter each filed dissenting opinions.

In *Withrow v. Williams*, 113 S.Ct. 1745 (1993) (see page 198), however, another bare majority declined to extend the ruling in *Stone v. Powell*, 428 U.S. 465 (1976) (Vol. 2, Ch. 7) so as to withdraw federal *habeas corpus* jurisdiction from cases involving state prisoners' claims of *Miranda* violations. In *Stone v. Powell*, the Court held that the landmark ruling on the Fourth Amendment's exclusionary rule, in *Mapp v. Ohio*, 367 U.S. 643 (1961) (Vol. 2, Ch. 7), did not recognize "a personal constitutional right," rather merely a prudential rule geared toward deterring illegal searches and seizures. And on that basis *Stone* held that prisoners could no longer file for a writ of *habeas corpus* in federal courts for review of convictions in state courts that they claimed were based on illegally obtained evidence. Notably, writing for the majority in *Withrow* Justice Souter refused to extend *Stone*'s reasoning and ruled that *Miranda* guarantees "a fundamental trial right" justifying federal *habeas* review. *Withrow* thus underscores the Court's differing evaluation of *Mapp*'s exclusionary rule and *Miranda*'s safeguards, and the continuing division within the Rehnquist Court over *Miranda*. In *Withrow*, Chief Justice Rehnquist and Justices O'Connor, Scalia, and Thomas dissented.

As the Court has refined and made exceptions to *Miranda*, it has also invited confusion in lower federal and state courts. Yet under the direction of Chief Justice Rehnquist, the Court annually grants review to fewer cases than during the Burger Court years (1969–1986), prompting Justice White, among others, to dissent from the denial of *certiorari* and to argue that the Court ought to resolve the conflicting standards and confusion created by its rulings. *Mueller v. Virginia,* 113 S.Ct. 1880 (1993), is one such case in which Justice White, joined by Justices Blackmun and Souter, dissented from the majority's refusal to provide further guidance for abiding by *Miranda.* In *Edwards v. Arizona,* 451 U.S. 477 (1981) (see Vol. 2, Ch. 8), the Court held that a suspect who invokes the right to counsel during a police interrogation may not be further interrogated until his attorney is present. But courts have basically split three ways over how to apply the so-called *Edwards* rule: (1) some have held that all police questioning must cease once a suspect requests an attorney; (2) others have tried to define a threshold for determining when the suspect's request triggers *Edwards* and *Miranda*'s right to the presence of an attorney; and, finally, (3) still other courts have held that police questioning must stop when when a suspect's equivocal statements may "arguably" be construed as a request for the presence of counsel.

Mueller v. Virginia presented an opportunity to clarify the confusion engendered by *Edwards.* Here, Everett Mueller was tried, convicted, and sentenced to death for the abduction and murder of a young girl. At his trial and over the objections of his attorney, a confession made by Mueller in the absence of counsel was admitted into evidence against him. After being read his *Miranda* rights, Mueller had asked police whether "I need an attorney here." With a shrug, police responded, "You're just talking to us," and continued their interrogation which led Mueller to confess to the crime. The Virginia supreme court upheld the trial court's admission into evidence of that confession on the ground that Mueller's question "did not constitute an unambiguous request for counsel," and therefore did fall under *Edwards.* Dissenting from the denial of Mueller's appeal of that decision, Justice White explained that because "a substantial number of criminal defendants who are identically situated in the eyes of the Constitution have received and will continue to receive dissimilar treatment because of the different approaches taken by the lower courts, I would grant *certiorari.*"

Arizona v. Fulminante

111 S.Ct. 1246 (1991)

While serving time in a federal prison for another crime, Oreste C. Fulminante made an incriminating confession to a fellow inmate, Anthony Sarivola, who was actually an informer for the Federal Bureau of Investigation (FBI). He did so because the informer offered to protect him from violence in the prison, but only on the condition that he give him a full account of the murder of Fulminante's eleven-year-old stepdaughter. Fulminante agreed and told Sarivola how he had murdered his stepdaughter. His confession to Sarivola, along with another, less detailed confession made to Sarivola's wife after his release from prison, was later introduced as evidence against him in a trial for murdering his stepdaughter. Following his conviction, Fulminante's attorney appealed to the Arizona Supreme Court, which overturned the conviction. Based on rulings of the Supreme Court of the United States, the state supreme court found that Fulminante's confession was involuntary and coerced, that the use of the confession at his trial was not a harmless error, and thus Fulminante was entitled to a retrial. The state then appealed that decision to the Supreme Court, which granted review.

The Court's decision was five to four and five to three. The justices were extraordinarily divided on the opinion announced by Justice White, who commanded only a bare majority on just two of the three issues presented. A separate opinion, in part dissenting and commanding another majority on the central issue, by Chief Justice Rehnquist was joined by Justice O'Connor and in parts by Justices Kennedy, Souter, and Scalia. Justice White's opinion held (1) that Fulminante's confession was coerced and (2) that its use as evidence against him at trial was not harmless beyond a reasonable doubt. His opinion on both of those issues was joined by Justices Blackmun, Marshall, and Stevens. And White commanded a bare majority by picking up the vote of Justice Scalia on (1) and the vote of Justice Kennedy on (2). On the latter issue, Chief Justice Rehnquist and Justices O'Connor and Scalia dissented, and Justice Souter failed to indicate whether or how he voted on that issue. The separate opinion by Chief Justice Rehnquist in turn commanded four votes (O'Connor, Kennedy, Souter, and Scalia) for another bare majority holding that (3) the admission at trial of coerced confessions may be excused as a harmless error if there is other evidence that adequately supports a guilty verdict.

Justice WHITE delivers the opinion of the Court.

Although the question is a close one, we agree with the Arizona Supreme Court's conclusion that Fulminante's confession was coerced. . . . Accepting the Arizona court's finding, permissible on this record, that there was a credible threat of physical violence, we agree with its conclusion that Fulminante's will was overborne in such a way as to render his confession the product of coercion.

Four of us, Justices MARSHALL, BLACKMUN, STEVENS, and myself, would affirm the judgment of the Arizona Supreme Court on the ground that the harmless-error rule is inapplicable to erroneously admitted coerced confessions. We thus disagree with the Justices who have a contrary view.

The majority today abandons what until now the Court has regarded

as the "axiomatic [proposition] that a defendant in a criminal case is
deprived of due process of law if his conviction is founded, in whole or
in part, upon an involuntary confession, without regard for the truth or
falsity of the confession, and even though there is ample evidence aside
from the confession to support the conviction." *Jackson v. Denno*, 378 U.S.
368 (1964). . . .

In extending to coerced confessions the harmless-error rule of *Chapman v.
United States*, 386 U.S. 18 (1967), the majority declares that because the
Court has applied that analysis to numerous other "trial errors," there is no
reason that it should not apply to an error of this nature as well. The four of
us remain convinced, however, that we should abide by our cases that have
refused to apply the harmless-error rule to coerced confessions, for a
coerced confession is fundamentally different from other types of erroneously admitted evidence to which the rule has been applied. . . .

Chapman specifically noted three constitutional errors that could not be
categorized as harmless error: using a coerced confession against a defendant in a criminal trial, depriving a defendant of counsel, or trying a
defendant before a biased judge. The majority attempts to distinguish the
use of a coerced confession from the other two errors listed in *Chapman*
first by distorting the decision in *Payne v. Arkansas* [356 U.S. 560 (1958)]
and then by drawing a meaningless dichotomy between "trial errors" and
"structural defects" in the trial process. . . .

The search for truth is indeed central to our system of justice, but
"certain constitutional rights are not, and should not be, subject to harmless-error analysis because those rights protect important values that are
unrelated to the truth-seeking function of the trial." *Rose v. Clark*, 478 U.S.
570 (1986). The right of a defendant not to have his coerced confession
used against him is among those rights, for using a coerced confession
"abort[s] the fair trial process and "render[s] a trial fundamentally unfair." *Id.*

For the foregoing reasons the four of us would adhere to the consistent
line of authority that has recognized as a basic tenet of our criminal
justice system, before and after both *Miranda* and *Chapman*, the prohibition against using a defendant's coerced confession against him at his
criminal trial. *Stare decisis* is "of fundamental importance to the rule of
law," *Welch v. Texas Highways and Public Transp.*, 483 U.S. 468 (1987); the
majority offers no convincing reason for overturning our long line of
decisions requiring the exclusion of coerced confessions.

Since five Justices have determined that harmless-error analysis applies
to coerced confessions, it becomes necessary to evaluate under that ruling
the admissibility of Fulminante's confession to Sarivola. . . . Five of us are
of the view that the State has not carried its burden and accordingly affirm
the judgment of the court below reversing petitioner's conviction. . . .

Our review of the record leads us to conclude that the State has failed
to meet its burden of establishing, beyond a reasonable doubt, that the
admission of Fulminante's confession to Anthony Sarivola was harmless
error. Three considerations compel this result.

First, the transcript discloses that both the trial court and the State recognized that a successful prosecution depended on the jury believing the two confessions. Absent the confessions, it is unlikely that Fulminante would have been prosecuted at all. . . .

Second, the jury's assessment of the confession to Donna Sarivola could easily have depended in large part on the presence of the confession to Anthony Sarivola. Absent the admission at trial of the first confession, the jurors might have found Donna Sarivola's story unbelievable. . . .

Third, the admission of the first confession led to the admission of other evidence prejudicial to Fulminante. For example, the State introduced evidence that Fulminante knew of Sarivola's connections with organized crime in an attempt to explain why Fulminante would have been motivated to confess to Sarivola in seeking protection. Absent the confession, this evidence would have had no relevance and would have been inadmissible at trial. . . .

Finally, . . . it is clear that the presence of the confession also influenced the sentencing phase of the trial. Under Arizona law, the trial judge is the sentencer. . . .

In declaring that Fulminante "acted with an especially heinous and depraved state of mind," the sentencing judge relied solely on the two confessions. Although the sentencing judge might have reached the same conclusions even without the confession to Anthony Sarivola, it is impossible to say so beyond a reasonable doubt. . . . Because a majority of the Court has determined that Fulminante's confession to Anthony Sarivola was coerced and because a majority has determined that admitting this confession was not harmless beyond a reasonable doubt, we agree with the Arizona Supreme Court's conclusion that Fulminante is entitled to a new trial at which the confession is not admitted. Accordingly the judgment of the Arizona Supreme Court is

Affirmed.

Chief Justice REHNQUIST, with whom Justice O'CONNOR joins, Justice KENNEDY and Justice SOUTER join as to parts I and II, and Justice SCALIA joins as to parts II and III, concurring as to part II, and dissenting as to parts I and III.

. . .

II

Since this Court's landmark decision in *Chapman v. California*, 386 U.S. 18 (1967), in which we adopted the general rule that a constitutional error does not automatically require reversal of a conviction, the Court has applied harmless-error analysis to a wide range of errors and has recognized that most constitutional errors can be harmless. . . .

The admission of an involuntary confession—a classic "trial error"—is markedly different from the other two constitutional violations referred to in the *Chapman* footnote as not being subject to harmless-error analysis. One of those cases, *Gideon v. Wainwright*, 372 U.S. 335 (1963), involved the total deprivation of the right to counsel at trial. The other, *Turney v. Ohio*, 273 U.S. 510 (1927), involved a judge who was not impartial. These are structural defects in the constitution of the trial mechanism, which defy analysis by "harmless-error" standards. The entire conduct of the trial from beginning to end is obviously affected by the absence of counsel for a criminal defendant, just as it is by the presence on the bench of a judge who is not impartial. Since our decision in *Chapman*, other cases have added to the category of constitutional errors which are not subject to harmless error the following: unlawful exclusion of members of the defendant's race from a grand jury, *Vasquez v. Hillery*, 474 U.S. 254 (1986); the right to self-representation at trial, *McKaskle v. Wiggins*, 465 U.S. 168 (1984); and the right to public trial, *Waller v. Georgia*, 467 U.S. 39 (1984). Each of these constitutional deprivations is a similar structural defect affecting the framework within which the trial proceeds, rather than simply an error in the trial process itself. . . .

It is evident from a comparison of the constitutional violations which we have held subject to harmless error, and those which we have held not, that involuntary statements or confessions belong in the former category. The admission is a "trial error," similar in both degree and kind to the erroneous admission of other types of evidence. The evidentiary impact of an involuntary confession, and its effect upon the composition of the record, is indistinguishable from that of a confession obtained in violation of the Sixth Amendment—of evidence seized in violation of the Fourth Amendment— or [as in *Chapman*] of a prosecutor's improper comment on a defendant's silence at trial in violation of the Fifth Amendment.

III

I would agree with the finding of the Supreme Court of Arizona in its initial opinion—in which it believed harmless-error analysis was applicable to the admission of involuntary confessions—that the admission of Fulminante's confession was harmless. Indeed, this seems to me to be a classic case of harmless error: a second confession giving more details of the crime that the first was admitted in evidence and found to be free of any constitutional objection.

Justice KENNEDY concurred in a separate opinion.

McNeil v. Wisconsin
111 S.Ct. 2204 (1991)

Paul McNeil was arrested in Omaha, Nebraska, in May 1987, on an outstanding warrant for his arrest on a charge of committing an armed robbery in Wisconsin. Shortly thereafter two deputy sheriffs from Wisconsin arrived at his prison cell to take him back to Wisconsin. Back in Wisconsin, McNeil was charged with armed robbery and appointed an attorney. But while in jail McNeil was visited by a sheriff, who was investigating a second robbery and murder in another part of the state. The sheriff read McNeil his *Miranda* rights and he signed a form waiving them. Under questioning McNeil did not deny knowledge of those crimes, but claimed that he was not involved in them. Two days later, the sheriff returned to McNeil's jail cell, and again, after being advised of his *Miranda* rights, McNeil initialed a form waiving those rights. This time, though, McNeil confessed to having been involved in the robbery and murder, as well as implicating two other men. His statement was typed up by a detective and McNeil initialed every reference to himself and signed every page.

After subsequently questioning one of the men named by McNeil, the sheriff returned to question McNeil, and once again he signed a form waiving his *Miranda* rights. McNeil now claimed that he had lied about the other man's involvement in the crime in order to minimize his own role, and again he signed another statement providing a second incriminating account of the crime. Two days later, he was formally charged with the second robbery and murder, and he was transferred to the county jurisdiction in which those offenses took place.

At a pretrial hearing McNeil unsuccessfully sought to suppress the use of his three incriminating statements. He was then tried and convicted for second-degree murder, attempted first-degree murder, and armed robbery, and sentenced to sixty years in prison. Appealing his conviction and sentence, McNeil claimed that the trial court's refusal to suppress his incriminating statements was a reversible error. McNeil also contended that his courtroom appearance with the public defender assigned to him in connection with his first robbery charge constituted an invocation of the *Miranda* right to counsel, and that any subsequent waiver of that right during police-initiated questioning regarding any offense was invalid. The Wisconsin Supreme Court, however, rejected McNeil's interpretation of the application of *Miranda* and his Fifth and Sixth Amendment rights. McNeil thereupon appealed to the Supreme Court, which granted review.

The Court's decision was six to three; the majority's opinion was announced by Justice Scalia. Justice Kennedy concurred. Justice Stevens's dissent was joined by Justices Marshall and Blackmun.

Justice SCALIA delivers the opinion of the Court.

This case presents the question whether an accused's invocation of his Sixth Amendment right to counsel during a judicial proceeding constitutes an invocation of his *Miranda* right to counsel. . . .

The Sixth Amendment provides that "[i]n all criminal prosecutions, the accused shall enjoy the right . . . to have the Assistance of Counsel for his defense." In *Michigan v. Jackson,* 475 U.S. 625 (1986), we held that once this right to counsel has attached and has been invoked, any subsequent waiver during a police-initiated custodial interview is ineffective. It is undisputed, and we accept for purposes of the present case, that at the time petitioner provided the incriminating statements at issue, his Sixth Amendment right had attached and had been invoked with respect to the [first charge of] armed robbery, for which he had been formally charged.

The Sixth Amendment right, however, is offense-specific. It cannot be invoked once for all future prosecutions, for it does not attach until a prosecution is commenced, that is, " 'at or after the initiation of adversary judicial criminal proceedings—whether by way of formal charge, preliminary hearing, indictment, information, or arraignment.' " *United States v. Gouveia,* 467 U.S. 180 (1984) (quoting *Kirby v. Illinois,* 406 U.S. 682 (1972) (plurality opinion)). And just as the right is offense-specific, so also its *Michigan v. Jackson* effect of invalidating subsequent waivers in police-initiated interviews is offense-specific. . . .

Because petitioner provided the statements at issue here before his Sixth Amendment right to counsel with respect to the [second set of] offenses had been (or even could have been) invoked, that right poses no bar to the admission of the statements in this case.

[McNeil] relies, however, upon a different "right to counsel," found not in the text of the Sixth Amendment, but in this Court's jurisprudence relating to the Fifth Amendment guarantee that "[n]o person . . . shall be compelled in any criminal case to be a witness against himself." In *Miranda v. Arizona,* 384 U.S. 436 (1966), we established a number of prophylactic rights designed to counteract the "inherently compelling pressures" of custodial interrogation, including the right to have counsel present. *Miranda* did not hold, however, that those rights could not be waived. On the contrary, the opinion recognized that statements elicited during custodial interrogation would be admissible if the prosecution could establish that the suspect "knowingly and intelligently waived his privilege against self-incrimination and his right to retained or appointed counsel."

In *Edwards v. Arizona,* 451 U.S. 477 (1981), we established a second layer of prophylaxis for the *Miranda* right to counsel: once a suspect asserts the right, not only must the current interrogation cease, but he may not be approached for further interrogation "until counsel has been made available to him,"—which means, we have most recently held, that counsel must be present, *Minnick v. Mississippi,* [111 S.Ct. 468] (1990). If the police do subsequently initiate an encounter in the absence of counsel (assuming there has been no break in custody), the suspect's statements are presumed involuntary and therefore inadmissible as substantive evidence at trial, even where the suspect executes a waiver and his statements would be considered voluntary under traditional standards. This is "designed to prevent police from badgering a defendant into waiving his previously asserted *Miranda* rights," *Michigan v. Harvey,* 494 U.S. 344

(1990). The *Edwards* rule, moreover, is not offense-specific: once a suspect invokes the *Miranda* right to counsel for interrogation regarding one offense, he may not be reapproached regarding any offense unless counsel is present. *Arizona v. Roberson*, 486 U.S. 675 (1988).

Having described the nature and effects of both the Sixth Amendment right to counsel and the *Miranda-Edwards* "Fifth Amendment" right to counsel, we come at last to the issue here: Petitioner seeks to prevail by combining the two of them. He contends that, although he expressly waived his *Miranda* right to counsel on every occasion he was interrogated, those waivers were the invalid product of impermissible approaches, because his prior invocation of the offense-specific Sixth Amendment right with regard to the [first robbery-] burglary was also an invocation of the nonoffense-specific *Miranda-Edwards* right. We think that is false as a matter of fact and inadvisable (if even permissible) as a contrary-to-fact presumption of policy.

As to the former: The purpose of the Sixth Amendment counsel guarantee—and hence the purpose of invoking it—is to "protec[t] the unaided layman at critical confrontations" with his "expert adversary," the government, after "the adverse positions of government and defendant have solidified" with respect to a particular alleged crime. The purpose of the *Miranda-Edwards* guarantee, on the other hand—and hence the purpose of invoking it—is to protect a quite different interest: the suspect's "desire to deal with the police only through counsel." This is in one respect narrower than the interest protected by the Sixth Amendment guarantee (because it relates only to custodial interrogation) and in another respect broader (because it relates to interrogation regarding any suspected crime and attaches whether or not the "adversarial relationship" produced by a pending prosecution has yet arisen). To invoke the Sixth Amendment interest is, as a matter of fact, not to invoke the *Miranda-Edwards* interest. One might be quite willing to speak to the police without counsel present concerning many matters, but not the matter of prosecution. It can be said, perhaps, that it is likely that one who has asked for counsel's assistance in defending against a prosecution would want counsel present for all custodial interrogation, even interrogation unrelated to the charge. That is not necessarily true, since suspects often believe that they can avoid the laying of charges by demonstrating an assurance of innocence through frank and unassisted answers to questions. But even if it were true, the likelihood that a suspect would wish counsel to be present is not the test for applicability of *Edwards*. The rule of that case applies only when the suspect "ha[s] expressed" his wish for the particular sort of lawyerly assistance that is the subject of *Miranda*. It requires, at a minimum, some statement that can reasonably be construed to be expression of a desire for the assistance of an attorney in dealing with custodial interrogation by the police. . . .

Affirmed.

Justice KENNEDY concurred in a separate opinion.

Justice STEVENS, with whom Justices MARSHALL and BLACKMUN join, dissenting.

The predicate for the Court's entire analysis is the failure of the defendant at the preliminary hearing to make a "statement that can reasonably be construed to be expression of a desire for the assistance of an attorney in dealing with custodial interrogation by the police." If petitioner in this case had made such a statement indicating that he was invoking his Fifth Amendment right to counsel as well as his Sixth Amendment right to counsel, the entire offense-specific house of cards that the Court has erected today would collapse, pursuant to our holding in *Arizona v. Roberson*, 486 U.S. 675 (1988), that a defendant who invokes the right to counsel for interrogation on one offense may not be reapproached regarding any offense unless counsel is present.

Withrow v. Williams
113 S.Ct. 1745 (1993)

Upon arriving at Robert Williams's house, two police officers asked him to go to the police station for questioning about a double murder, and he agreed. After Williams had been searched but not handcuffed, Williams and the officers drove to the station. There Williams was questioned about the crime and, though initially denying any involvement, soon implicated himself. When continuing their questioning, police assured Williams that their only concern was the identity of the "shooter." After consulting each other, the officers decided not to advise Williams of his rights under *Miranda v. Arizona*, 384 U.S. 436 (1966). And when Williams persisted in his denials, one officer rebuffed him, saying:

> You know everything that went down. You just don't want to talk about it. What it's gonna amount to is you can talk about it now and give us the truth and we're gonna check it out and see if it fits or else we're simply gonna charge you and lock you up and you can just tell it to a defense attorney and let him try and prove differently.

That apparently worked, for Williams then admitted he gave the murder weapon to the killer, who in turn called him after the crime and told him where the weapon was discarded. Williams still maintained that he had not been present at the crime scene. But at this point, some forty minutes after police began their questioning, the officers read Williams his *Miranda* rights. Williams waived those rights and subsequently made several more inculpatory statements. Despite his prior denials, Williams admitted that he drove the murderer to and from the scene of the crime, witnessed the murders, and helped dispose of incriminating evidence.

At a pretrial hearing Williams's attorney moved to suppress his responses to the initial interrogation, but the judge held that Williams had been given a timely warning of his *Miranda* rights. Williams was later convicted and given two concurrent life sentences. Subsequently, Williams petitioned for a writ of *habeas corpus,* alleging that his *Miranda* rights were violated. A federal district court agreed that Williams was in custody for *Miranda* purposes when police threatened to "lock [him] up," and thus the trial court should have excluded all statements Williams made from that point until he received the *Miranda* warnings. The Court of Appeals for the Seventh Circuit affirmed and summarily rejected the state's argument that the rule in *Stone v. Powell,* 428 U.S. 465 (1976), should apply to bar *habeas* review of Williams's *Miranda* claim. Michigan appealed and the Supreme Court granted *certiorari.*

The Court's decision was five to four, with Justice Souter announcing the majority's opinion. Separate opinions, in part concurring and in part dissenting, by Justices O'Connor and Scalia were joined by Chief Justice Rehnquist and Justice Thomas, respectively.

Justice SOUTER delivered the opinion of the Court.

In *Stone v. Powell,* 428 U.S. 465 (1976), we held that when a State has given a full and fair chance to litigate a Fourth Amendment claim, federal *habeas* review is not available to a state prisoner alleging that his conviction rests on evidence obtained through an unconstitutional search or seizure. Today we hold that *Stone*'s restriction on the exercise of federal *habeas* jurisdiction does not extend to a state prisoner's claim that his conviction rests on statements obtained in violation of the safeguards mandated by *Miranda v. Arizona,* 384 U.S. 436 (1966). . . .

We have made it clear that *Stone*'s limitation on federal *habeas* relief was not jurisdictional in nature, but rested on prudential concerns counseling against the application of the Fourth Amendment exclusionary rule on collateral review. We recognized that the exclusionary rule, held applicable to the States in *Mapp v. Ohio,* 367 U.S. 643 (1961), "is not a personal constitutional right"; it fails to redress "the injury to the privacy of the victim of the search or seizure" at issue, "for any 'reparation comes too late.' " *Stone* (quoting *Linkletter v. Walker,* 381 U.S. 618 [1965]). The rule serves instead to deter future Fourth Amendment violations, and we reasoned that its application on collateral review would only marginally advance this interest in deterrence. On the other side of the ledger, the costs of applying the exclusionary rule on *habeas* were comparatively great. . . .

In this case, the argument for extending *Stone* falls short. To understand why, a brief review of the derivation of the *Miranda* safeguards, and the purposes they were designed to serve, is in order.

The Self-Incrimination Clause of the Fifth Amendment guarantees that no person "shall be compelled in any criminal case to be a witness against himself." In *Bram v. United States,* 168 U.S. 532 (1897), the Court held that the Clause barred the introduction in federal cases of involuntary confessions made in response to custodial interrogation. We did not recognize the Clause's applicability to state cases until 1964, however, see *Malloy v. Hogan,* 378 U.S. 1, and, over the course of 30 years . . . we analyzed the admissibility of confessions in such cases as a question of due process under the Fourteenth Amendment. Under this approach, we examined the totality of circumstances to determine whether a confession had been " 'made freely, voluntarily and without compulsion or inducement of any sort.' " *Haynes v. Washington,* 373 U.S. 503 (1963) (quoting *Wilson v. United States,* 162 U.S. 613 [1896]). Indeed, we continue to employ the totality-of-circumstances approach when addressing a claim that the introduction of an involuntary confession has violated due process. E.g., *Arizona v. Fulminante* (1991). . . .

Petitioner, supported by the United States as *amicus curiae,* argues that *Miranda*'s safeguards are not constitutional in character, but merely "prophylactic," and that in consequence *habeas* review should not extend to a claim that a state conviction rests on statements obtained in the absence of those safeguards. We accept petitioner's premise for purposes of this case, but not her conclusion. . . .

As we explained in *Stone,* the *Mapp* rule "is not a personal constitutional right," but serves to deter future constitutional violations; although it mitigates the juridical consequences of invading the defendant's privacy, the exclusion of evidence at trial can do nothing to remedy the completed and wholly extrajudicial Fourth Amendment violation. Nor can the *Mapp* rule be thought to enhance the soundness of the criminal process by improving the reliability of evidence introduced at trial. Quite the contrary, as we explained in *Stone,* the evidence excluded under *Mapp* "is typically reliable and often the most probative information bearing on the guilt or innocence of the defendant."

Miranda differs from *Mapp* in both respects. "Prophylactic" though it may be, in protecting a defendant's Fifth Amendment privilege against self-incrimination *Miranda* safeguards "a fundamental trial right." The privilege embodies "principles of humanity and civil liberty, which had been secured in the mother country only after years of struggle," *Bram,* and reflects "many of our fundamental values and most noble aspirations . . ." *Murphy v. Waterfront Comm'n of New York Harbor,* 378 U.S. 52 (1964). . . .

Finally, and most importantly, eliminating review of *Miranda* claims would not significantly benefit the federal courts in their exercise of *habeas* jurisdiction, or advance the cause of federalism in any substantial way. As one *amicus* concedes, eliminating *habeas* review of *Miranda* issues would not prevent a state prisoner from simply converting his barred *Miranda* claim into a due process claim that his conviction rested on an involuntary confession. Indeed, although counsel could provide us with no empirical basis for projecting the consequence of adopting petitioner's position, it seems reasonable to suppose that virtually all *Miranda* claims would simply be recast in this way.

If that is so, the federal courts would certainly not have heard the last of *Miranda* on collateral review. Under the due process approach, as we have already seen, courts look to the totality of circumstances to determine whether a confession was voluntary. We could lock the front door against *Miranda*, but not the back.

We thus fail to see how abdicating *Miranda*'s bright-line (or, at least, brighter-line) rules in favor of an exhaustive totality-of-circumstances approach on *habeas* would do much of anything to lighten the burdens placed on busy federal courts. We likewise fail to see how purporting to eliminate *Miranda* issues from federal *habeas* would go very far to relieve such tensions as *Miranda* may now raise between the two judicial systems. . . .

Justice O'CONNOR, with whom the CHIEF JUSTICE joins, concurring in part and dissenting in part.

Today the Court permits the federal courts to overturn on *habeas* the conviction of a double-murderer, not on the basis of an inexorable constitutional or statutory command, but because it believes the result desirable from the standpoint of equity and judicial administration. Because the principles that inform our *habeas* jurisprudence—finality, federalism, and fairness—counsel decisively against the result the Court reaches, I respectfully dissent from this holding. . . .

The Court identifies a number of differences that, in its view, distinguish this case from *Stone v. Powell.* I am sympathetic to the Court's concerns but find them misplaced nonetheless. . . .

The consideration the Court identifies as being "most important" of all, is an entirely pragmatic one. Specifically, the Court "projects" that excluding *Miranda* questions from *habeas* will not significantly promote efficiency or federalism because some *Miranda* issues are relevant to a statement's voluntariness. It is true that barring *Miranda* claims from *habeas* poses no barrier to the adjudication of voluntariness questions. But that does not make it "reasonable to suppose that virtually all *Miranda* claims [will] simply be recast" and litigated as voluntariness claims. . . .

As the Court emphasizes today, *Miranda*'s prophylactic rule is now 26 years old; the police and the state courts have indeed grown accustomed to it. But it is precisely because the rule is well accepted that there is little further benefit to enforcing it on *habeas*. . . . In my view, *Miranda* imposes such grave costs and produces so little benefit on *habeas* that its continued application is neither tolerable nor justified. . . .

Justice SCALIA, with whom Justice THOMAS joins, concurring in part and dissenting in part.

In my view, both the Court and Justice O'CONNOR disregard the most powerful equitable consideration: that Williams has already had full and fair opportunity to litigate this claim. He had the opportunity to raise it in the Michigan trial court; he did so and lost. He had the opportunity to seek review of the trial court's judgment in the Michigan Court of Appeals; he did so and lost. Finally, he had the opportunity to seek discretionary review of that Court of Appeals judgment in both the Michigan Supreme Court and this Court; he did so and review was denied. The question at this stage is whether, given all that, a federal *habeas* court should now reopen the issue and adjudicate the *Miranda* claim anew. The answer seems to me obvious: it should not. That would be the course followed by a federal *habeas* court reviewing a federal conviction; it mocks our federal system to accord state convictions less respect. . . .

9

THE RIGHTS TO
COUNSEL AND OTHER
PROCEDURAL
GUARANTEES

A. THE RIGHT TO COUNSEL

In *McNeil v. Wisconsin*, 111 S.Ct. 2204 (1991) (see page 194) the
Rehnquist Court drew a sharp distinction between the Sixth Amendment right to counsel and the right to counsel under *Miranda v. Arizona*,
384 U.S. 436 (1966) (in Vol. 2, Ch. 8), when holding that an accused's
invocation of his Sixth Amendment right to counsel during a judicial
proceeding does not simultaneously constitute an invocation of the right
to counsel derived by *Miranda* from the Fifth Amendment's guarantee
against compelled self-incrimination.

B. PLEA BARGAINING AND THE RIGHT TO
EFFECTIVE COUNSEL

THE DEVELOPMENT OF LAW
Other Rulings on Plea Bargaining and Effective Counsel

Case	Ruling
Burns v. United States 111 S.Ct. 2182 (1991) Vote 5:4	In an opinion for a bare majority, Justice Marshall held that a federal district court judge violated the rights of a defendant who agreed to plea guilty to a crime upon an understanding that under federal sentencing guidelines, established by the U.S.

THE DEVELOPMENT OF LAW *(Continued)*

Sentencing Commission, he receive a prison sentence in the range of thirty to thirty-seven months. At the end of his sentencing hearing, however, a federal judge sentenced Burns to sixty months in prison. Justice Marshall held that that sentence was impermissible because Burns had no notice of the possibility of receiving a longer sentence as a result of his guilty plea. The majority held that the lack of notice ran afoul of Congress's objectives in creating the U.S. Sentencing Commission and authorizing it to establish sentencing guidelines and declined to hold that the due process clause mandates a defendant's notification of the possibility that judges may depart from the sentencing guidelines. By contrast, in his first dissenting opinion, Justice Souter contended that the majority had imposed "a procedural requirement neither contemplated by Congress nor warranted by the language of any statute or rule." Chief Justice Rehnquist and Justices White and O'Connor joined in his dissent.

Keeney v. *Tampayo-Reyes* 112 S.Ct. 1715 (1992) Vote 5:4	A bare majority held that a Cuban immigrant, who pled no-contest to a murder charge but later claimed that the Spanish translation of his plea was so poor that he did not understand the basis of his plea bargain agreement, had forfeited the opportunity for federal *habeas corpus* review because his lawyer failed to spell out adequately the important facts supporting

that claim in state court proceedings. In his opinion for the Court, Justice White also overturned a Warren Court ruling, *Townsend v. Sain*, 372 U.S. 293 (1993), which had held that state petitioners forfeit the right to federal *habeas corpus* review only when they or their attorneys purposively fail to support their claims in a "deliberate bypass" of the state courts. Justice Blackmun, Stevens, Kennedy, and O'Connor dissented.

Lockhart v. Fretwell 113 S. Ct. 838 (1993) Vote 7:2	Held that a *habeas corpus* petitioner was not denied his Sixth and Fourteenth Amendment rights to effective counsel during the sentencing phase of a capital felony-murder trail. Writing for the majority, Chief Justice Rehnquist held that a defendant who did not have effective counsel during the sentencing stage of murder trial must show that his attorney's errors

were so serious as to result in an "unfair or unreliable" verdict. Justices Blackmun and Stevens dissented.

Parke v. Raley 113 S.Ct. 517 (1992) Vote 8:0	Rejected a claim by a three-time convicted felon, who was sentenced to five years for robbery and an additional ten years under Kentucky's "persistent felony offender," that he had been denied due process because his first two convictions were the

result of plea bargains and that records of those proceedings were not introduced and thus the state had not shown that his pleas were made knowingly and voluntarily. In writing for the Court, Justice O'Connor affirmed Kentucky's burden-shifting rule in recidivism proceedings that require the defendant to produce evidence justifying the suppression of a prior conviction and guilty plea.

Godinez v. Moran 113 S.Ct. 2680 (1993) Vote 7:2	Writing for the Court, Justice Thomas held that the competency standard for pleading guilty or waiving the right to counsel at trial is the same for standing trial: whether the defendant has "sufficient present ability to consult with his lawyer with a reasonable degree of rational understanding" and a "rational as well as factual understanding of the proceedings

against him." The due process clause does not impose more rigorous standards, though states remain free to adopt more stringent standards. Justice Blackmun, joined by Justice Stevens, dissented.

C. INDICTMENT BY A GRAND JURY

The Rehnquist Court's conservatism when dealing with the rights of the accused and its eagerness to reach out to address issues of interest to its controlling majority were further underscored by a five-to-four ruling on grand jury indictments. Writing for a bare majority in *United States v. Williams*, 112 S.Ct. 1735 (1992), Justice Scalia held that when seeking a grand jury's indictment charging an accused with a criminal offense federal prosecutors need not present exculpatory evidence—facts favorable to the accused which might result in the grand jury's refusal to hand down an indictment. In holding that federal courts have no power to dismiss an indictment because prosecutors withheld "substantially exculpatory evidence" from a grand jury, Scalia emphasized that the role of a grand jury—unlike a trial jury—is to "assess whether there is adequate basis for bringing a criminal charge," not to determine an accused's ultimate guilt or innocence. "Imposing on the prosecutor a legal obligation to present exculpatory evidence in his possession would be incompatible with this system," claimed Scalia, even though prosecutors must turn over such exculpatory evidence to a defendant's attorney before going to trial.

In a sharply worded dissent, Justice Stevens criticized the majority for both improperly addressing a question that had not been raised in either the district or appellate court and deciding it wrongly. Conceding that prosecutor need not "ferret out and present all" favorable evidence, Stevens nonetheless maintained that prosecutors should not be allowed to "mislead the grand jury into believing that there is probable cause to indict by withholding clear evidence to the contrary." In his view, the majority bent over backwards to sanction overzealous prosecution and prosecutorial misconduct. Moreover, Stevens's dissent was joined by Justices Blackmun, O'Connor, and Thomas, in one of the few five-to-four rulings in the 1992 that split Reagan and Bush appointees.

D. RIGHT TO AN IMPARTIAL JURY TRIAL

Given growing racial and ethnic heterogenity in the country's population, perhaps inexorably challenges to the inclusion and exclusion of racial and ethnic minorities in the composition of juries have increased. The Court in turn has confronted a series of challenges to the exclusion of racial and ethnic minorities from juries. But that has also been part of the fallout from its ruling in *Batson v. Kentucky*, 476 U.S. 79 (1986) (see Vol. 2, Ch. 9). *Batson* held that a black defendant could challenge prosecutors' exclusion of blacks from juries by means of peremptory challenges. However, in *Holland v. Illinois*, 493 U.S. 474 (1990), Justice Scalia forged a bare majority for holding that a white defendant's right to an impartial jury under the Sixth Amendment was not violated by the exclusion of all black potential jurors. But then, in *Powers v. Ohio*, 111 S.Ct. 1364 (1991), Justice Kennedy held that prosecutors' use of peremptory challenges to exclude blacks from juries of white defendants violates the equal protection clause. In doing so, he distinguished *Holland* on the basis that the Fourteenth Amendment "prohibits a prosecutor from using the State's peremptory challenges to exclude otherwise qualified and unbiased persons from the . . . jury solely by reason of their race, a practice that forecloses a significant opportunity to participate in civil life." "The suggestion," Kennedy added, "that racial classifications may survive when visited upon all persons is no more authoritative today than the case that advanced the theorem, *Plessy v. Ferguson*, 163 U.S. 537 (1896). The idea has no place in our modern equal protection jurisprudence." Still, Justice Scalia, dissenting along with Chief Justice Rehnquist, claimed that he was "unmoved" by white defendants' claims that their rights are violated when they are tried by all-white juries.

Subsequently, by a six-to-three vote in *Edmonson v. Leesville Concrete, Co.,* 111 S.Ct. 2077 (1991) (see page 261), the Court also extended its ruling in *Batson* to the use of peremptory challenges to exclude blacks from juries in civil trials. And the Court again revisited in *Georgia v. McCollum,* 112 S.Ct. 2348 (1992), the issue of using race as a basis for excluding potential jurors from criminal trials, and further extended the *Batson, Powers,* and *Edmonson* line of rulings. *Batson* barred prosecutors from disqualifying jurors on the basis of race. And, as noted above, *Powers* held that criminal defendants of any race may challenge a prosecutor's racially based peremptory challenges, while *Edmonson* held that lawyers in civil trials may not exclude potential jurors on the basis of race. *Georgia v. McCollum,* thus, raised the issue of whether two white defendants charged with criminally assaulting two blacks could exclude blacks from serving on the jury.

Writing for the majority in *McCollum,* Justice Blackmun held that it was unconstitutional in criminal trials for defendants' attorneys, no less than prosecutors, to exclude jurors on the basis of their race. In his words, it is "an affront to justice to argue that a fair trial includes the right to discriminate against a group of citizens based on their race." As a result, all-white juries in racially charged cases, such as that of the white police officers tried for the beating of motorist Rodney King in Los Angeles, will be more difficult to obtain. At the same time, *McCollum* will also make it more difficult for minority defendants to exclude white jurors in order to secure some minorities on their juries. And that point was not lost on Justice Thomas, who in a concurring opinion warned that "black criminal defendants will rue the day that this Court ventured down this road. . . . Simply stated, securing representation of the defendant's race on the jury may help to overcome racial bias and provide the defendant with a better chance of having a fair trial." Only Justices O'Connor and Scalia dissented. The majority, in Scalia's words, had "destroyed" the ages-old right of criminal defendants to exercise peremptory challenges as they wish, to secure a jury that they consider fair."

In its 1993–1994 term, the Court will again consider a further extension of the *Batson* rule. *J.E.B. v. T.B.,* which is further discussed in Chapter 12, raises the issue of whether the *Batson* rule should be extended to bar prosecutors from eliminating potential jurors solely on the basis of their gender.

Another aspect of the right to an impartial jury that has engaged the Rehnquist Court is that of the parameters of attorneys' *voir dire* examination of potential jurors.[1] In *Morgan v. Illinois,* 112 S.Ct. 2979 (1992) (see page 230), the Rehnquist Court held that counsel for defendants in capital cases must be allowed to ask during *voir dire* examination whether a potential juror would automatically impose the death penalty after the defendant's conviction. Denial of such questioning during jury selection, the Court ruled, violates the Fourteenth Amendment's due process clause.

---

[1] In *Hernandez v. New York,* 111 S.Ct. 1859 (1991), however, the Court upheld a prosecutor's questioning and use of peremptory challenges to exclude Hispanics from a jury. The jurors were excluded not because they were Hispanic, but because the prosecutor claimed that he was "uncertain that they would be able to listen and follow the interpreter" of Spanish-speaking witnesses at trial. "In holding that a race-neutral reason for a peremptory challenge means a reason other than race," Justice Kennedy emphasized that "we do not resolve the more difficult question of the breadth with which the concept of race should be defined for equal protection purposes." Justices Blackmun, Marshall, and Stevens dissented.

In *Mu'Min v. Virginia*, 111 S.Ct. 1899 (1991), the Court addressed the issue of whether a defendant has a constitutional right to closely question prospective jurors about what they have heard or read about the trial in pretrial publicity. The Virginia Supreme Court held that defendants are entitled to know only whether a prospective juror has formed an opinion about the case that would preclude his or her impartiality. Writing for a bare majority, Chief Justice Rehnquist upheld the state supreme court's ruling and observed that

> [u]ndoubtedly, if counsel were allowed to see individual jurors answer questions about exactly what they had read, a better sense of the juror's general outlook on life might be revealed, and such a revelation would be of some use in exercising peremptory challenges. But, since peremptory challenges are not required by the Constitution, *Ross v. Oklahoma*, 487 U.S. 81 (1988), this benefit cannot be a basis for making "content" questions about pretrial publicity a constitutional requirement.

Justice O'Connor concurred, while Justices Marshall, Blackmun, Stevens, and Kennedy dissented.

Finally, in *Sullivan v. Louisiana*, 113 S.Ct. 2078 (1993), the Court unanimously reaffirmed that in criminal cases juries must find the accused guilty beyond a reasonable doubt. Although the Rehnquist Court has expanded the "harmless error doctrine" in other areas—for example, *Arizona v. Fulminante* (1991) (in Chapter 8)—here it declined to hold that a judge's instructions to a jury that it must find the defendant "probably guilty" constituted merely a harmless error. Writing for the Court, Justice Scalia observed, "the Fifth Amendment requirement of proof beyond a reasonable doubt and the Sixth Amendment requirement of a jury verdict are interrelated. It would not satisfy the Sixth Amendment to have a jury determine that the defendant is probably guilty. . . . In other words, the jury verdict required by the Sixth Amendment is a jury verdict of guilty beyond a reasonable doubt."

E. A SPEEDY AND PUBLIC TRIAL

Besides guaranteeing individuals accused of crimes the right "to be informed of the nature and cause of the accusation against" them and the right "to be confronted with the witnesses against" them, the Sixth Amendment also guarantees criminal defendants a "speedy and public trial." Those guarantees convey as well a presumption against trials *in absentia* of the defendant. The Federal Rules of Criminal Procedure, however, permit a waiver of the accused's right to be present at the trial "whenever a defendant initially present is voluntarily absent after the trial has commenced." But in *Crosby v. United States*, 113 S.Ct. 748 (1993), involving an appeal of the government's trial of a defendant *in absentia,* the Court unanimously held that Rule 43 of the Federal Rules of Criminal Procedure forbids the government from putting on trial a defendant who is absent at its beginning.

In *Doggett v. United States,* 112 S.Ct. 2686 (1992), the Court held that the prosecution of an individual who was indicted eight and a half years earlier for importing and conspiring to distribute cocaine violated his Sixth Amendment right to a speedy trial. Marc Doggett had been indicted but left the country before the Drug Enforcement Agency (DEA) could arrest him. The DEA knew that Doggett was later imprisoned in Panama but never followed up on his whereabouts after it learned that he had gone to Colombia. Subsequently, Doggett reentered the country, married, earned a college degree, found gainful employment, and lived openly under his own name. Eight years later the U.S. Marshal's Service located him during a credit check on individuals with outstanding warrants and arrested him. Relying on *Barker v. Wingo,* 407 U.S. 514 (1972), Justice Souter ruled that the government's negligence in bringing Doggett to trial constituted "presumptive prejudice" and violated his Sixth Amendment right to a speedy trial. Chief Justice Rehnquist and Justices O'Connor, Scalia, and Thomas dissented.

F. THE RIGHTS TO BE INFORMED OF CHARGES AND TO CONFRONT ACCUSERS

In the last few years, the Rehnquist Court has taken a number of cases involving the right of defendants to confront their accusers in cases involving alleged rape and sexual abuse of children. *Michigan v. Lucas,* 111 S.Ct. 1743 (1991), was one such case. *Lucas* raised the question of whether a defendant, accused of sexually assaulting his former girlfriend, was denied of his Sixth Amendment right to confront accusors because Michigan's rape-shield law mandates that evidence of past sexual conduct be barred at trial if a defendant fails to give notice at least ten days prior to the trial of its introduction.

In *Lucas,* the Court upheld Michigan's rape-shield law. Writing for the majority, Justice O'Connor held that the defendant's right to confront accusers does not permit courts to adopt per se rules barring trial courts from allowing the introduction at trial of evidence of rape victims' prior sexual relationship with criminal defendants. Nor are states precluded from requiring defendants to give notification within ten days of their arraignment of their plans to present evidence about the alleged victim's past sexual conduct, and on that basis ban in some cases the introduction of such evidence at trial. Michigan's ten-day deadline for such notification is the shortest in the country; the federal rape-shield law requires such notice fifteen days before a trial commences. Justice Blackmun concurred, while Justice Stevens, joined by Justice Marshall, dissented.

The Court also revisited in its 1991 term the question of whether the Sixth Amendment's confrontation clause requires a showing in each case of alleged sexual abuse of children that the victim is unavailable or incapable of testifying before the child's out-of-court statements may be introduced as evidence. Bare majorities in two 1990 cases, *Maryland v. Craig*, 497 U.S.836 (1990), and *Idaho v. Wright*, 497 U.S. 805 (1990) (see Vol. 2, Ch. 9), held that defendants on trial for allegedly sexually abusing children do not have an absolute right to confront their accusers, and that states may shield alleged victims from face-to-face confrontations with defendants by introducing the children's testimony through the use of videotaped statements or closed-circuit television. Left unanswered, though, was whether judges may exclude all testimony by alleged victims who are capable of testifying, and thereby allow juries to determine a defendant's guilt entirely on the basis of hearsay testimony of those who questioned the children out of court.

The Court finally appeared to lay to rest the remaining questions about the use of hearsay evidence in trials for child abuse. In *White v. Illinois*, 112 S.Ct. 736 (1992), the justices unanimously held that the Sixth Amendment's confrontation clause permits, in a trial of a defendant accused of sexually abusing a four-year-old child, the introduction of a victim's "spontaneous declaration" to police and doctors, along with the results of a medical examination. The Court rejected the claim that an accused's right to confront witnesses requires the prosecution either to produce the victim at trial or establish the victim's unavailability. Chief Justice Rehnquist explained that

[g]iven the evidentiary value of such statements, their reliability, and that establishing a generally applicable unavailability rule would have few practical benefits while imposing pointless litigation costs, we see no reason to treat the out-of-court statements in this case differently from those we found admissible in [cases not involving child abuse]. . . . We therefore see no basis . . . for excluding from trial, under the aegis of the Confrontation Clause, evidence embraced within such exceptions to the hearsay rule as those for spontaneous declarations and statements made for medical treatment.

Justice Thomas concurred and registered his "strict constructionist" approach to constitutional interpretation. In an opinion joined by Justice Scalia, Thomas suggested that the Court should reconsider its application of the confrontation clause and that it should not apply it to hearsay evidence per se:

There is virtually no evidence of what the drafters of the Confrontation Clause intended it to mean. . . . The strictest reading would be to construe the phrase "witnesses against him" to confer on a defendant the right to confront and cross-examine only those witnesses who actually appear and testify at trial. . . .

I believe that it is possible to interpret the Confrontation Clause . . . in a manner that is faithful to both the provision's text and history. One possible formulation is as follows: The federal constitutional right of confrontation extends to any witness who actually testifies at trial, but the Confrontation Clause is implicated by extrajudicial statements only insofar as they are contained in formalized testimonial materials, such as affidavits, depositions, prior testimony, or confessions. It was this discrete category of testimonial materials that was historically abused by prosecutors as a means of depriving criminal defendants of the benefit of the adversary process, and under this approach, the Confrontation Clause would not be construed to extend beyond the historical evil to which it was directed.

G. THE GUARANTEE AGAINST DOUBLE JEOPARDY

In *United States v. Felix*, 112 S.Ct. 1377 (1992), the Court held that the Fifth Amendment's double-jeopardy clause is not violated by two separate federal prosecutions of a defendant for the crime of manufacturing illegal drugs and then for conspiracy to manufacture and distribute the same illegal drugs in a different jurisdiction. The Court unanimously agreed that the two prosecutions were not for "the same offense." In Chief Justice Rehnquist's words, "A substantive crime and a conspiracy to commit that crime are not the 'same offense' for double jeopardy purposes, even if they are based on the same underlying incidents, because the essence 'of a conspiracy offense is in the agreement or confederation to commit a crime'" [quoting *United States v. Bayer*, 331 U.S. 532 (1947)].

A bare majority of the Rehnquist Court also overturned another five-to-four ruling, in *Grady v. Corbin*, 495 U.S. 508 (1990), in *United States v. Dixon*, 113 S.Ct. 2849 (1993). In *Grady* a bare majority held that the double-jeopardy clause "bars any subsequent prosecution in which the government, to establish an essential element of an offense charged in that prosecution, will prove conduct that constitutes an offense for which the defendant has already been prosecuted." In doing so, the Court held that the government was barred from prosecuting an individual for vehicular homicide because he had already pleaded guilty to minor traffic offenses in the same accident. But that test barring prosecutions for the "same conduct" drew a bitter dissent from Justice Scalia, and by the time the Court considered *Dixon*, two members—Justices Brennan and Marshall—making up the bare majority in *Grady* were no longer on the bench.

At issue in *Dixon* was whether an individual convicted of defying a judge's order may be criminally prosecuted for the conduct that led to the contempt-of-court citation in the first place. In holding that the double-jeopardy clause does not bar such prosecutions, Justice Scalia's opinion for the Court commanded only four votes. Justice Scalia, on the one hand, reaffirmed the test set forth in *Blockburger v. United States*, 284 U.S. 299 (1932), which inquires whether each offense contains an element not contained in the other; and, if not, whether they are the "same offense" for the purposes of the double-jeopardy clause. He also over-ruled *Grady's* "same conduct" test as inconsistent with the Court's prece-dents and the history of the double-jeopardy clause. Justice Scalia's opinion thus reaffirmed the Court's traditional view of the guarantee against double jeopardy, under which the question is not whether the two prosecutions require proof of the same conduct, but instead whether the two offenses have the same "elements." Still, his opinion prompted no less than four other separate opinions, in part concurring and dissent-ing, from Chief Justice Rehnquist and Justices Blackmun, Souter, and White.

Once again, in its 1993–1994 term, the Court will confront a double jeopardy issue in *Caspari v. Bohlen* (No. 92-1500). At issue is whether a man convicted of robbery and sentenced as a repeat offender in a faulty sentencing hearing may be subjected to a new sentencing hearing with-out violating his right against double jeopardy. The Court of Appeals for the Eighth Circuit held that the double-jeopardy clause applies, and the state appealed.

H. THE GUARANTEE AGAINST EXCESSIVE BAIL AND FINES

In recent years the Court has faced a series of challenges to state and federal laws authorizing the seizure and forfeiture of property of in-dividuals who have been convicted of criminal activities. Forfeitures have become a major weapon in the federal government's so-called drug war. In 1992 alone, the federal government seized $2 billion in property and sold millions more of forfeited property at auction. Besides *Soldal v. Cook County*, 113 S.Ct. 538 (1992), and *United States v. A Parcel of Land*, 113 S.Ct. 1126 (both of which raised Fourth Amendment and statutory questions and are discussed in Chapter 7), the Court confronted two Eighth Amendment challenges to forfeitures under that amendment's guarantee against "excessive fines." And in both of these cases, *Alexander v. United States*, 113 S.Ct. 2766 (1993) (see page 118), and *Austin v. United States*, 113 S.Ct. 2801 (1993), the Court sharply rebuffed the federal government's argument that forfeitures are not punitive but "remedial," and that the guilt or innocence of the property owner is "constitutionally irrelevant."

In *Alexander* (see page 118), a bare majority rejected a First Amend-ment challenge to the forfeiture of an adult-entertainment business under the Racketeer Influenced and Corrupt Organizations (RICO) Act, but unanimously agreed that the case should be remanded back to the lower court for a determination of whether the forfeiture violated the Eighth Amendment ban on "excessive fines." In an even more impor-tant ruling on that provision of the Eighth Amendment in *Austin v. United States*, the Court unanimously held that the guarantee against "excessive fines" requires the government to show a relationship between the seriousness of the offense and the forfeiture of the property.

Richard Austin, after being convicted of selling cocaine, argued that the government's filing of a civil forfeiture complaint against his mobile home and autobody shop abridged the Eighth Amendment. The federal government, however, argued successfully in the lower federal courts that that amendment applies only to criminal proceedings and punishments, and not civil actions, like forfeiture, even though tied to a criminal conviction. Rejecting the government's arguments in his opinion for the Court, Justice Blackmun observed that

[t]he Government argues that [federal provisions authorizing forfeitures] are not punitive but, rather, should be considered remedial in two respects. First, they remove the "instruments" of the drug trade "thereby protecting the community from the threat of continued drug dealing." Second, the forfeited assets serve to compensate the Government for the expense of law enforcement activity and for its expenditure on societal problems such as urban blight, drug addiction, and other health concerns resulting from the drug trade.

In our view, neither argument withstands scrutiny. Concededly, we have recognized that the forfeiture of contraband itself may be characterized as remedial because it removes dangerous or illegal items from society. The Court, however, previously has rejected government's attempt to extend that reasoning to conveyances used to transport illegal liquor. See *One 1958 Plymouth Sedan v. Pennsylvania*, 380 U.S. 693 (1965). In that case it noted: "There is nothing even remotely criminal in possessing an automobile." The same, without question, is true of the properties involved here, and the Government's attempt to characterize these properties as "instruments" of the drug trade must meet the same fate as Pennsylvania's effort to characterize the 1958 Plymouth Sedan as "contraband."

The Government's second argument about the remedial nature of this forfeiture is no more persuasive. We previously have upheld the forfeiture of goods involved in customs violations as "a reasonable form of liquidated damages." *One Lot Emerald Cut Stones v. United States*, 409 U.S. 232 (1972). . . .

Fundamentally, even assuming that [the forfeiture provisions] serve some remedial purpose, the Government's argument must fail. "[A] civil sanction that cannot fairly be said solely to serve a remedial purpose, but rather can only be explained as also serving either retributive or deterrent purposes, is punishment, as we have come to understand the term." In light of the historical understanding of forfeiture as punishment, the clear focus of [the forfeiture provisions] on the culpability of the owner, and the evidence that Congress understood those provisions as serving to deter and to punish, we cannot conclude that forfeiture under Sections 881(a)(4) and (a)(7) [of the U.S. Code] serves solely a remedial purpose. We therefore conclude that forfeiture under these provisions constitutes "payment to a sovereign as punishment for some offense," and, as such, is subject to the limitations of the Eighth Amendment's Excessive Fines Clause.

Justice Blackmun concluded, however, by declining to accept the invitation in *Austin* to lay down guidelines for when the government's seizure of property is unconstitutionally excessive. Instead, as in *Alexander*, the Court remanded *Austin* back to the lower court for reconsideration. As a result, the issue will percolate in the lower federal courts, allowing them to devise their own rules for determining when forfeitures violate the Eighth Amendment, and allowing the Court to eventually revisit the issue of forfeitures and "excessive fines" when it decides to do so.

I. INDIGENTS AND THE CRIMINAL JUSTICE SYSTEM

The Court's major rulings affecting indigents and the criminal justice system are discussed in "The Court's Docket and Screening Cases" (page 21), which deals with the filing of *in forma pauperis* petitions, and in "Cruel and Unusual Punishment," Chapter 10, which discusses death penalty appeals.

10

CRUEL AND UNUSUAL PUNISHMENT

A. NONCAPITAL PUNISHMENT

A bare majority of the Rehnquist Court in *Harmelin v. Michigan*, 111 S.Ct. 2680 (1991), rejected the contention that a mandatory lifetime sentence, without the possibility of parole, for possessing 650 grams of cocaine violated the Eighth Amendment's ban against cruel and unusual punishment. Ronald Harmelin had argued that the sentence was cruel and unusual because it was "significantly disproportionate" to the crime he committed and because the sentencing judge was statutorily required to impose it, without taking into account the particular circumstances of the crime and of the criminal. Although a bare majority of the Court agreed to uphold Harmelin's sentence, the five justices in the majority could not agree on the constitutional analysis supporting the Court's ruling.

In delivering the opinion of the Court in *Harmelin,* the only part of Justice Scalia's opinion joined by four other justices—Chief Justice Rehnquist and Justices Kennedy, Souter, and O'Connor—rejected Harmelin's claim that his sentence was unconstitutional because it was mandatory in nature and trial courts had no opportunity to consider "mitigating factors" when determining it. Severe, mandatory penalties, Scalia held, may be cruel but they are not unusual in the constitutional sense. He did so based on a review of the history and development of early Anglo-American common law, which he said demonstrated that "it [is] most unlikely that the English Cruel and Unusual Punishments Clause was meant to forbid 'disproportionate' punishments. There is even less likelihood that proportionality of punishment was one of the traditional 'rights and privileges of Englishmen' apart from the Declaration of Rights, which happened to be included in the Eighth Amendment." Scalia also rejected Harmelin's claim that the "individualized capital-sentencing doctrine," which has been central to the Court's death penalty jurisprudence, extended outside of the context of capital punishment because there are qualitative differences between death and all other kinds of sentences.

Only Chief Justice Rehnquist, however, joined those portions of Scalia's opinion in which he further contended that the Eighth Amendment contains no requirement that non–death penalty sentences be proportionate to the offense and that prior holdings in *Rummel v. Estelle,* 445 U.S. 263 (1980), and *Solem v. Helm,* 463 U.S. 277 (1983) (see Vol. 2, Ch. 10), suggesting contrariwise should be rejected and overturned. According to Scalia and Rehnquist, there are no adequate textual or historical standards to enable judges to determine whether a particular penalty is disproportional, and the judiciary should simply defer to the wisdom of state legislatures.

Justice Scalia's rejection of the Court's prior rulings and analysis proved too much for the three other justices supporting the result in *Harmelin.* Joined by Justices O'Connor and Souter in a separate concurring opinion, Justice Kennedy reaffirmed the Court's prior rulings that the Eighth Amendment's cruel and unusual punishments clause encompasses a narrow proportionality principle that applies to noncapital sentences.

First, agreeing with Justice Scalia, Justice Kennedy observed that guidelines specifying prison terms for specific crimes involve a substantial penological judgment that generally is properly one for legislatures to make and that reviewing courts should give substantial deference to legislative determinations. Second, he noted that there are a variety of legitimate penological theories—theories such as retribution, deterrence, incapacitation, and rehabilitation—that underlie sentencing laws and the Eighth Amendment does not mandate any one such theory. Third, marked divergences both in sentencing theories and in the length of prescribed prison terms are the inevitable, often beneficial, result of the federal structure, and differing attitudes and perceptions of local conditions may yield different conclusions regarding the appropriate length of terms for particular crimes. Fourth, departing from Justices Scalia and Rehnquist, Kennedy reaffirmed that federal courts have undertaken, and may continue to undertake, proportionality review of noncapital punishment sentences. "All of these principles—the primacy of the legislature, the variety of legitimate penological schemes, the nature of our federal system, and the requirement that proportionality review be guided by objective factors," Kennedy concluded, "inform the final one: the Eighth Amendment does not require strict proportionality between crime and sentence. Rather, it forbids only extreme sentences that are 'grossly disproportionate' to the crime," citing *Solem* and *Weems.*

In light of those principles, Kennedy agreed that Harmelin's sentence was not grossly disproportionate to the crime of possessing more than 650 grams of cocaine. And he characterized Harmelin's suggestion that the crime was nonviolent and victimless was "false to the point of absurdity." The amount of cocaine Harmelin possessed, Kennedy emphasized, had a potential yield of between 32,500 and 65,000 doses, and the state could reasonably conclude that possession of such a large amount of cocaine was momentous enough to warrant the deterrence and retribution of a lifetime sentence without parole. Given the severity of Harmelin's crime, Kennedy further maintained, there is no need to conduct a comparative analysis between his sentence and sentences imposed for other crimes in Michigan and for the same crime in other jurisdictions.

The four dissenters took strong exception to Scalia's and Kennedy's treatment of prior cases, constitutional analysis, and upholding of Harmelin's sentence. Along with Justices Blackmun and Stevens, Justice White countered that

> [t]he Court's capital punishment cases requiring proportionality reject Justice SCALIA's notion that the Amendment bars only cruel and unusual modes or methods of punishment. Under that view, capital punishment—a mode of punishment—would either be completely barred or left to the discretion of the legislature. Yet neither is true. The death penalty is appropriate in some cases and not in others. The same should be true of punishment by imprisonment.

Justices Stevens and Marshall also filed separate dissenting opinions.

The Court considered as well a couple of important questions involving the application of the Eighth Amendment's ban on cruel and unusual punishment to the confinement and treatment of prison inmates. In *Wilson v. Seiter*, 111 S.Ct. 2321 (1991), the justices confronted the question of whether unfit prison living conditions, even in the absence of evidence that prison officials acted maliciously, constitute cruel and unusual punishment. There, Ohio prison officials were accused of being indifferent to miserable prison conditions, ranging from overcrowding to rat-infested kitchens.

In announcing *Wilson*, Justice Scalia held that prisoners claiming that the conditions of their confinement violate the Eighth Amendment must show "a culpable state of mind on the part of prison officials," because the concept of *intent* is implicit in the amendment's ban against cruel and unusual punishment. For prisoners to prevail with claims of an Eighth Amendment violation, Scalia ruled that they must show "deliberate indifference" of prison officials to the conditions of their confinement. In a concurring opinion joined by Justices Blackmun, Marshall, and Stevens, however, Justice White took strong exception to the majority's reinterpretation of prior rulings and charged that its "deliberate indifference" standard was both inconsistent with those rulings and unwise.

In *Hudson v. McMillian*, 112 S.Ct. 995 (1992), however, the Rehnquist

Court went the other way, splitting seven to two in holding that a prison inmate's Eighth Amendment rights were violated by prison guards' use of excessive force. Keith Hudson was punched and kicked by two guards while he remained handcuffed and a supervisor instructed the guards not to "have too much fun." He sustained loosened teeth and a split lip but no "significant injury." After initially winning $800 in damages, Hudson's claims were dismissed by an appellate court on the ground that he failed to show a "significant injury" from "objectively and clearly unnecessary" use of excessive force aimed at "an unnecessary and wanton infliction of pain."

When reversing the lower court's ruling in *Hudson,* Justice O'Connor ruled that the touchstone for the Court's analysis in such cases was "whether force was applied in a good-faith effort to maintain or restore discipline, or maliciously and sadistically to cause harm." O'Connor thereupon distinguished *Whitley v. Albers,* 475 U.S. 312 (1986), which held that an inmate's Eighth Amendment rights were not violated by a prison guard's shooting him during a prison riot. The settled rule, in O'Connor's view, was whether guards "unnecessarily and wanton[ly]" inflict pain. O'Connor, though, rejected the argument that inmates must also show a "significant injury" and refused to extend Justice Scalia's analysis, in *Wilson v. Seiter,* 111 S.Ct. 2321 (1991), requiring alleged wrongdoing to be "objectively harmful enough" to constitute a constitutional violation. That "objective component" of the Eighth Amendment, O'Connor held, was (1) contextually dependent on kind of claim raised and (2) draws "its meaning from evolving standards of decency that mark the progress of a maturing society," citing *Trop v. Dulles,* 356 U.S. 86 (1958). On that basis, O'Connor distinguished *Wilson* and other cases involving conditions-of-confinement claims and whether the denial of inmates' medical needs constitute "cruel and unusual punishment." In such cases, inmates must show "deliberate indifference" of prison authorities and that their deprivations or injuries are "serious." By contrast, inmates claiming constitutional deprivations due to excessive force must show that "prison officials maliciously and sadistically use[d] force to cause harm," though not that they suffered "significant harm." To further require a showing of "significant harm," O'Connor reasoned, would permit "any physical punishment, no matter how diabolic or inhuman, inflicting less than some arbitrary quantity of injury" under the Eighth Amendment.

In a sharply worded dissenting opinion, joined by Justice Scalia, Justice Thomas not only took strong exception to the majority's reliance on the *dicta* in *Trop v. Dulles* that the Eighth Amendment "draw[s] its meaning from evolving standards of decency." He also rejected the Court's conclusions that inmates need not show a significant injury and that the ban against cruel and unusual punishment applies in cases such as *Hudson,* rather than only those challenging prison sentences or other official "punishment." Justice Thomas's opinion underscored that his approach to constitutional interpretation strongly resists expansive readings, and relies heavily on the history, of constitutional guarantees. As Justice Thomas explained,

> Until recent years, the Cruel and Unusual Punishment Clause was not deemed to apply at all to deprivations that were not inflicted as part of the sentence for a crime. For generations, judges and commentators regarded the Eighth Amendment as applying only to torturous punishments meted out by statutes or sentencing judges, and not generally to any hardship that might befall a prisoner during incarceration. . . . Surely prison was not a more congenial place in the early years of the Republic than it is today; nor were our judges and commentators so naive as to be unaware of the often harsh conditions of prison life. Rather, they simply did not conceive of the Eighth Amendment as protecting inmates from harsh treatment. . . .

> Today's expansion of the Cruel and Unusual Punishment Clause beyond all bounds of history and precedent is, I suspect, yet another manifestation of the pervasive view that the Federal Constitution must address all ills in our society. Abusive behavior by prison guards is deplorable conduct that properly evokes outrage and contempt. But that does not mean that it is invariably unconstitutional. The Eighth Amendment is not, and should not be turned into, a National Code of Prison Regulation. To reject the notion that the infliction of concededly "minor" injuries can be considered either "cruel" or "unusual" "punishment" (much less cruel and unusual punishment) is not to say that it amounts to acceptable conduct. Rather, it is to recognize that primary responsibility for preventing and punishing such conduct rests not with the Federal Constitution but with the laws and regulations of the various States.

A majority of the Court, nonetheless, buttressed the ruling in *Hudson v. McMillian* in its 1992–1993 term, with Justices Thomas and Scalia again dissenting. Writing for the Court in *Helling v. McKinney*, 113 S.Ct. 2475 (1993), Justice White held that prison inmate Donald Helling could raise an Eighth Amendment claim against prison authorities who he said showed "deliberate indifference" to his objections to being housed with another cell mate who smoked five packs of cigarettes a day, and thus exposed Helling involuntarily to health risks. As to the amendment's applicability to such conditions of imprisonment, Justice White observed:

> Contemporary standards of decency require no less. In *Estelle* [*v. Gamble*, 429 U.S. 97 (1976)], we concluded that although accidental or inadvertent failure to provide adequate medical care to a prisoner would not violate the Eighth Amendment, "deliberate indifference to serious medical needs of prisoners" violates the Amendment because it constitutes the unnecessary and wanton infliction of pain contrary to contemporary standards of decency. . . .

For the same reasons expressed in their dissenting opinion in *Hudson*, Justices Thomas and Scalia dissented.

B. CAPITAL PUNISHMENT

The Rehnquist Court pressed ahead in the direction of reducing the number of opportunities for appealing death sentences and removing procedural obstacles to executions. Long lamenting and criticizing procedural barriers to the imposition of capital punishment and conducting executions, Chief Justice Rehnquist commands a solid majority for expediting the executions of death-row inmates.

In a major ruling affecting death penalty appeals, the Rehnquist Court sharply curtailed opportunities for death-row inmates and other state prisoners to file multiple challenges to the constitutionality of their sentences. Over the strong objections of three dissenters, in *McCleskey v. Zant,* 111 S.Ct. 1454 (1991), the Court handed down a new standard for lower federal courts under which a prisoner's second or subsequent *habeas corpus* petition must be dismissed except only in exceptional circumstances.

The import and impact of *McCleskey v. Zant* lies in the fact that death-row inmates typically file several successive writ of *habeas corpus* petitions, raising different constitutional claims, in their efforts to overturn their convictions and sentences. Approximately 40 percent of all death sentences have been overturned by lower courts upon finding constitutional errors in the conviction and sentencing of death-row inmates. By limiting lower courts' consideration of successive petitions in *McCleskey v. Zant,* the Rehnquist Court's ruling thus enables states to carry out death sentences more quickly; under federal law, though, there is no limit on the number of *habeas corpus* petitions that may be filed by inmates in federal prisons.

Writing for the majority in *McCleskey v. Zant,* Justice Kennedy redefined the "abuse of the writ" doctrine so as to make it easier for state prosecutors to contest as an abuse of the writ all *habeas corpus* petitions filed after a prisoner's initial one. Under the Court's new definition of abuse of the writ, second and subsequent petitions, raising new constitutional claims, may be dismissed as abusive unless inmates show (1) that there was "cause" for not raising the claim earlier and (2) that the inmate suffered "actual prejudice" from the constitutional error that he claimed occurred in his trial, conviction and sentencing. Under the Court's previous approach, dating from the mid-1960s, second and subsequent petitions were considered abusive only if they contained arguments that an attorney, for strategic or other reasons, deliberately refrained from making an earlier claim or that they were previously omitted due to an attorney's "inexcusable neglect." By contrast, Justice Kennedy held that the failure of an inmate's lawyer to raise a constitutional claim, whether mistakenly or not, would not constitute "cause" for saving the petition from automatic dismissal unless the attorney's representation was so deficient as to amount to "constitutionally ineffective assistance of counsel," a very difficult standard to meet.[1] Kennedy also added that there

---

[1] See *Strickland v. Washington,* 466 U.S. 668 (1984) in Vol. 2, Ch. 9.

must be a "showing of some external impediment preventing counsel from construing or raising a claim" to excuse the failure to do so in an earlier petition. And he predicted that the newly reformulated abuse of the writ standard "should curtail the abusive petitions that in recent years have threatened to undermine the integrity of the *habeas corpus* process."[2]

The majority's action in granting and expediting review of *Payne v. Tennessee*, 111 S.Ct. 1031 (1991), further registers how a series of changes in short succession in the Court's composition may dramatically change the course of constitutional law. In *Booth v. Maryland*, 482 U.S. 496 (1987) (see Vol. 2, Ch. 9), Justice Powell cast the crucial fifth vote for disallowing the use of victim-impact statements. Following Powell's resignation and the confirmation of his successor, Justice Kennedy, the Rehnquist Court reconsidered the issue in *South Carolina v. Gathers*, 490 U.S. 805 (1989). But again, a bare majority voted to bar the use of victim-impact statements. This time, Justice White switched sides and voted to reaffirm *Booth* in deference to its precedential value, while Justice Scalia issued a sharp dissenting opinion arguing that *Booth* was wrongly decided and ought to be overruled. But by a six-to-three vote (with Justice White switching his position again, without explanation) in *Payne v. Tennessee* (see page 226), the Rehnquist Court overturned its earlier rulings in *Booth* and *Gathers*. Chief Justice Rehnquist handed down the Court's opinion holding that the Eighth Amendment does not bar the use of victim-impact statements. Separate concurrences were filed by Justices Scalia, O'Connor, and Souter, and Justices Blackmun, Marshall, and Stevens dissented.

Along with numerous other rulings on capital punishment that generally cut back on opportunities for appeals and for challenging death sentences (see "The Development of Law: Other Recent Rulings of the Rehnquist Court on Capital Punishment"), the Court held in *Morgan v. Illinois*, 112 S.Ct. 2222 (1992) (see page 230), that under the Fourteenth Amendment's guarantee for due process, defendants' attorneys must be permitted to ask potential jurors whether, on the defendants' conviction, they would automatically vote to impose the death penalty.

During its 1993 term the Court will review still other Eighth Amendment challenges to states' sentencing procedures in capital cases. At issue in *State of Tennessee v. Middlebrooks*, for instance, is the permissibility of a sentencing procedure that encourages jurors to vote for the death penalty when the accused is convicted of a murder that was committed along with another felony—here, the kidnapping and torturing of a fourteen-year-old boy. A state court struck down the provision on the ground that it "duplicates," or counts twice against the accused, the elements of a crime.

---

[2] See also *Coleman v. Thompson*, 111 S.Ct. 2546 (1991) (page 70).

THE DEVELOPMENT OF LAW
Other Recent Rulings of the Rehnquist Court on Capital Punishment

Case	Ruling
Perry v. Louisiana 111 S.Ct. 804 (1991) Vote 8:0	Without hearing oral arguments and without Justice Souter's participation, the Rehnquist Court set aside a state supreme court ruling that held that the forced induction of mind-altering drugs on a prisoner, in order to make him well enough to execute, did not violate the Eighth Amendment and remanded the

case for reconsideration in light of its prior decision in *Washington v. Harper*, 111 S.Ct. 1028 (1990) (see Vol. 2, Ch. 4). *Harper* held that mentally ill inmates may be treated with antipsychotic drugs against their will when they are deemed dangerous and the treatment is in their medical interest; whereas in *Perry* mind-altering drugs were given to a death-row inmate for the purpose of making him mentally competent for execution.

Case	Ruling
Parker v. Dugger 111 S.Ct. 731 (1991) Vote 5:4	Writing for a bare majority, Justice O'Connor held that when reviewing a death sentence the Florida state supreme court had erroneously concluded that a trial court had not found any mitigating circumstances and thus denied the defendant's right to individualized sentencing under the Eighth

Amendment. Justice White filed a dissenting opinion, which Chief Justice Rehnquist and Justices Scalia and Kennedy joined, objecting to the majority's "second-guessing" of the state supreme court.

Case	Ruling
Lankford v. Idaho 111 S.Ct. 1723 (1991) Vote 5:4	By a five-to-four vote, the Court held that judges may not impose the death sentence after prosecutors decide not to seek capital punishment. Writing for a bare majority, Justice Stevens held that Lankford's "lack of adequate notice that the judge was contemplating the imposition of the death sentence

created an impermissible risk that the adversary process may have malfunctioned in this case." Dissenting Justice Scalia, however, charged that the majority invited a new defense based on "ignorance of the law." Chief Justice Rehnquist and Justices White and Souter joined in Scalia's dissent.

Case	Ruling
Yates v. Evatt 111 S.Ct. 1884 (1991) Vote 9:0	Writing for the Court, Justice Souter held that a trial judge's impermissible jury instructions may not be considered a "harmless error" and overturned the conviction and death sentence in this case.

THE DEVELOPMENT OF LAW *(Continued)*

Case	Ruling
Schad v. Arizona 111 S.Ct. 2491 (1991) Vote 5:4	The Court addressed the issue of whether a jury, in convicting a defendant of a crime for which death is a possible sentence, must agree unanimously on all elements of the crime. In a plurality opinion, Justice Souter held that Arizona's characterization of a robbery and a murder as a single crime was

permissible and that juries need not unanimously agree on alternative theories of premeditated or felony murder counts. Justice White dissented, along with Justices Blackmun, Marshall, and Stevens.

Case	Ruling
Stringer v. Black 112 S.Ct. 1130 (1992) Vote 6:3	Held that the Court's prior holding in *Maynard v. Cartwright*, 486 U.S. 356 (1988), which invalidated as too vague the use of "especially heinous, atrocious or cruel" nature of a crime as an aggravating factor to be weighed in capital cases, has retroactive application in *habeas corpus* proceedings challenging a

death sentence; Justices Scalia, Souter, and Thomas dissented.

Case	Ruling
Dawson v. Delaware 112 S.Ct. 1093 (1992) Vote 8:1	Writing for the Court, Chief Justice Rehnquist overturned the death sentence of an individual who claimed that his First Amendment right of freedom of association was violated by the prosecution's reference to his membership in a white racist group, the Aryan Brotherhood, as an aggravating factor to

be considered by the jury when deciding whether to impose a death sentence. The majority held that the defendant's membership in the Aryan Brotherhood was not relevant to a showing of his "bad character" and, in any event, such membership is "constitutionally protected." By contrast, dissenting alone Justice Thomas countered that the majority "ignores reality" in disallowing such evidence and rejected as misguided the Court's finding that the prosecution had violated the defendant's First Amendment rights.

Case	Ruling
Morgan v. Illinois, 112 S.Ct. 2222 (1992) Vote 6:3	Held that a defendant's attorney must be permitted to ask prospective jurors whether they would automatically favor the death penalty, in the event that they convict the defendant. By a vote of six to three the justices held that the denial of the defendant's counsel's request to so question potential

jurors violated the Fourteenth Amendment's guarantee for due process. Chief Justice Rehnquist and Justices Scalia and Thomas dissented.

THE DEVELOPMENT OF LAW *(Continued)*

Case	Ruling
Sawyer v. Whitley 112 S.Ct. 2514 (1992) Vote 9:0	Held that a defendant bringing a successive *habeas corpus* claim that he or she was "actually innocent" must show by "clear and convincing evidence" that, but for a constitutional error at the trial and sentencing, no reasonable juror would have found the defendant eligible for the death penalty under applicable state law.

Richmond v. Lewis
113 S.Ct.
528 (1992)

Vote 8:1

Overturned a death sentence on the ground that the trial judge relied on the unconstitutionally vague sentencing factor that the crime committed was "especially heinous, cruel, or depraved." In addition, in her opinion for the Court Justice O'Connor held that the state supreme court had failed to correct for that error by not performing a new sentencing calculus. Justice Scalia dissented.

Arave v. Creech
113 S.Ct.
1534 (1993)

Vote 7:2

Held that Idaho's death penalty statute was not too vague in specifying as an aggravating factor for imposing capital punishment that the defendant commit a crime "with utter disregard for human life." An appellate court had struck down the provision on the ground that judges and juries were not on that basis permitted "to make a principled distinction between those who deserve the death penalty and those who do not." But writing for the majority Justice O'Connor reversed that decision and concluded that state courts had adequately narrowed the criteria to apply to only someone who is a "coldblooded, pitiless slayer." Justices Blackmun and Stevens dissented.

Lockhart v. Fretwell
113 S.Ct.
838 (1993)

Vote 7:2

Chief Justice Rehnquist overturned a writ of *habeas corpus* appeal in holding that a defendant who had ineffective counsel at the sentencing stage of his capital trial must show that his attorney's errors were so grave as to result in an "unfair or unreliable" verdict. Justices Blackmun and Stevens dissented.

Graham v. Collins
113 S.Ct.
892 (1993)

Vote 5:4

For a bare majority Justice White rejected a challenge to a death sentence imposed under a Texas statute, which was subsequently invalidated by the Court in 1989, and dismissed the defendant's claim that under that defunct statute the jury was

THE DEVELOPMENT OF LAW *(Continued)*

Case	Ruling

not able to fully weigh his youth and troubled family background as mitigating factors when deciding to impose the death penalty. Justices Blackmun, O'Connor, Souter, and Stevens dissented.

Herrera v. Collins
113 S.Ct.
853 (1993)

Vote 6:3

Held that a defendant who is sentenced to death and belatedly presents new evidence of his innocence is not ordinarily entitled to a new trial. Writing for the majority, Chief Justice Rehnquist conceded that "truly persuasive" evidence with an "extraordinary high" chance of success might warrant in some cases an exception to that general rule. Rehnquist also rejected Leonel Herrera's argument that Texas's limitation of thirty days for filing for new trials violated the Fourteenth Amendment's due process clause. That limitation on appeals for new trials, in Rehnquist's words, does not "transgress a principle of fundamental fairness rooted in the traditions and conscience of our people." By contrast, dissenting Justice Blackmun, joined by Justices Souter and Stevens, countered that it "shocks the conscience" and is contrary to "any standard of decency" to execute someone who can "show that he is probably innocent."

Johnson v. Texas
113 S.Ct.
2658 (1993)

Vote 5:4

Held that the ruling in *Penry v. Lynaugh,* 492 U.S. 302 (1989) (in Vol. 2, Ch. 10), holding that Texas's capital punishment system at that time failed to give adequate consideration to the defendant's mitigating evidence of mental retardation, did not establish a "new rule" requiring specific consideration of mental retardation as a mitigating circumstance during the sentencing stage of a capital case. Texas's 1991 guidelines for juries in capital cases, requiring them to consider two special issues—(1) whether the accused's actions were committed deliberately and with a reasonable expectation that death would result, and (2) the probability that the accused would commit acts of violence constituting a continuing threat to society—along with any and all mitigating circumstances when imposing a death sentence, are constitutional. Justices O'Connor, Blackmun, Stevens, and Souter dissented.

Payne v. Tennessee
111 S.Ct. 2597 (1991)

Pervis Payne, a borderline retarded man with no previous criminal record, was tried and convicted of stabbing to death a twenty-eight-year-old woman and her two-year-old daughter, as well as attempting to murder her three-year-old son. During closing arguments at his trial, the prosecutor asked the jury to impose the death sentence and told them, "There obviously is nothing you can do for Charisse or Lacie. But there is something you can do for Nicholas. . . . He is going to want to know what type of justice was done." Payne was sentenced to death and his attorney immediately appealed the sentence on the ground that the trial judge impermissibly allowed the prosecution's use of victim-impact statements and failed to comply with the Court's rulings in *Booth v. Maryland,* 482 U.S. 496 (1987) (see Vol. 2, Ch. 9), and *South Carolina v. Gathers,* 490 U.S. 805 (1989). But when the Court granted review, it directed the attorneys to specifically address the question of whether *Booth* and *Gathers* should be overturned, even though neither party had raised that question in their original petition and briefs.

The Court's decision was six to three. Chief Justice Rehnquist announced the majority's opinion, with which Justices O'Connor, Scalia, and Souter each concurred. Justice Blackmun joined dissents by Justices Marshall and Stevens.

Chief Justice REHNQUIST delivers the opinion of the court.

In this case we reconsider our holdings in *Booth v. Maryland,* 482 U.S. 496 (1987), and *South Carolina v. Gathers,* 490 U.S. 805 (1989), that the Eighth Amendment bars the admission of victim impact evidence during the penalty phase of a capital trial. . . .

Booth and *Gathers* were based on two premises: that evidence relating to a particular victim or to the harm that a capital defendant causes a victim's family do not in general reflect on the defendant's "blameworthiness," and that only evidence relating to "blameworthiness" is relevant to the capital sentencing decision. However, the assessment of harm caused by the defendant as a result of the crime charged has understandably been an important concern of the criminal law, both in determining the elements of the offense and in determining the appropriate punishment. Thus, two equally blameworthy criminal defendants may be guilty of different offenses solely because their acts cause differing amounts of harm. . . .

Payne echoes the concern voiced in Booth's case that the admission of victim impact evidence permits a jury to find that defendants whose victims were assets to their community are more deserving of punishment that those whose victims are perceived to be less worthy. As a general matter, however, victim impact evidence is not offered to encourage comparative judgments of this kind—for instance, that the killer of a hardworking, devoted parent deserves the death penalty, but that the murderer of a reprobate does not. It is designed to show instead each victim's "uniqueness as an individual human being," whatever the jury might think the loss to the community resulting from his death might be. . . .

Under our constitutional system, the primary responsibility for defining crimes against state law, fixing punishments for the commission of these crimes, and establishing procedures for criminal trials rests with the States. The state laws respecting crimes, punishments, and criminal procedure are of course subject to the overriding provisions of the United States Constitution. Where the State imposes the death penalty for a particular crime, we have held that the Eighth Amendment imposes special limitations upon that process.

First, there is a required threshold below which the death penalty cannot be imposed. In this context, the State must establish rational criteria that narrow the decisionmaker's judgment as to whether the circumstances of a particular defendant's case meet the threshold. Moreover, a societal consensus that the death penalty is disproportionate to a particular offense prevents a State from imposing the death penalty for that offense.

Second, States cannot limit the sentencer's consideration of any relevant circumstance that could cause it to decline to impose the penalty. In this respect, the State cannot challenge the sentencer's discretion, but must allow it to consider any relevant information offered by the defendant." *McCleskey v. Kemp,* 481 U.S. 279 (1987). But, as we noted in *California v. Ramos,* 463 U.S. 992 (1983), "[b]eyond these limitations . . . the Court has deferred to the State's choice of substantive factors relevant to the penalty determination." . . .

The States remain free, in capital cases, as well as others, to devise new procedures and new remedies to meet felt needs. Victim impact evidence is simply another form or method of informing the sentencing authority about the specific harm caused by the crime in question, evidence of a general type long considered by sentencing authorities. We think the *Booth* Court was wrong in stating that this kind of evidence leads to the arbitrary imposition of the death penalty. In the majority of cases, and in this case, victim impact evidence serves entirely legitimate purposes. In the event that evidence is introduced that is so unduly prejudicial that it renders the trial fundamentally unfair, the Due Process Clause of the Fourteenth Amendment provides a mechanism for relief. . . .

We thus hold that if the State chooses to permit the admission of victim impact evidence and prosecutorial argument on that subject, the Eighth Amendment erects no per se bar. . . .

Stare decisis is not an inexorable command; rather, it "is a principle of policy and not a mechanical formula of adherence to the latest decision." *Helvering v. Hallock,* 309 U.S. 106 (1940). This is particularly true in constitutional cases, because in such cases "correction through legislative action is practically impossible." *Burnet v. Coronado Oil & Gas Co.,* [285 U.S. 393 (1932)] (BRANDEIS, J., dissenting). Considerations in favor of *stare decisis* are at their acme in cases involving property and contract rights, where reliance interests are involved, see *Swift & Co. v. Wickham,* 382 U.S. 111 (1965); *Burnet v. Coronado Oil & Gas Co.,* supra, the opposite is true in cases such as the present one involving procedural and evidentiary rules.

Booth and *Gathers* were decided by the narrowest of margins, over spirited dissents challenging the basic underpinnings of those decisions. . . . Reconsidering these decisions now, we conclude for the reasons heretofore stated, that they were wrongly decided and should be, and now are, overruled. We accordingly affirm the judgment of the Supreme Court of Tennessee.

Affirmed.

Justices O'CONNOR, SCALIA, and SOUTER concurred in separate opinions.

Justice MARSHALL, with whom Justice BLACKMUN joins, dissenting.

Power, not reason, is the new currency of this Court's decisionmaking. . . . Neither the law nor the facts supporting *Booth* and *Gathers* underwent any change in the last four years. Only the personnel of this Court did.

In dispatching *Booth* and *Gathers* to their graves, today's majority ominously suggests that an even more extensive upheaval of this Court's precedents may be in store. Renouncing this Court's historical commitment to a conception of "the judiciary as a source of impersonal and reasoned judgments," *Moragne v. States Marine Lines,* 398 U.S. 375 (1970), the majority declares itself free to discard any principle of constitutional liberty which was recognized or reaffirmed over the dissenting votes of four Justices and with which five or more Justices now disagree. The implications of this radical new exception to the doctrine of *stare decisis* are staggering. The majority today sends a clear signal that scores of established constitutional liberties are now ripe for reconsideration, thereby inviting the very type of open defiance of our precedents that the majority rewards in this case. Because I believe that this Court owes more to its constitutional precedents in general and to *Booth* and *Gathers* in particular, I dissent. . . .

[T]his Court has never departed from precedent without "special justification." *Arizona v. Rumsey,* 467 U.S. 203 (1984). Such justifications include the advent of "subsequent changes or development in the law" that undermine a decision's rationale, *Patterson v. McLean Credit Union,* [491 U.S. 164 (1989)]; the need "to bring [a decision] into agreement with experience and with facts newly ascertained," *Burnet,* supra; and a showing that a particular precedent has become a "detriment to coherence and consistency in the law," *Patterson*.

The majority cannot seriously claim that any of these traditional bases for overruling a precedent applies to *Booth* or *Gathers*. The majority does not suggest that the legal rationale of these decisions has been undercut by changes or developments in doctrine during the last two years. Nor does the majority claim that experience over that period of time has discredited the principle that "any decision to impose the death sentence be, and appear to be, based on reason rather than caprice or emotion," *Gardner v. Florida*, 430 U.S. 349 (1977) (plurality opinion), the larger postulate of political morality on which *Booth* and *Gathers* rest. . . .

It takes little real detective work to discern just what has changed since this Court decided *Booth* and *Gathers:* this Court's own personnel. . . .

In addition, the majority points out, *"Booth* and *Gathers* were decided by the narrowest of margins, over spirited dissents" and thereafter were "questioned by members of the Court." Taken together, these considerations make it legitimate, in the majority's view, to elevate the position of the *Booth* and *Gathers* dissenters into the law of the land.

This truncation of the Court's duty to stand by its own precedents is astonishing. By limiting full protection of the doctrine of *stare decisis* to "cases involving property and contract rights," the majority sends a clear signal that essentially all decisions implementing the personal liberties protected by the Bill of Rights and the Fourteenth Amendment are open to reexamination. Taking into account the majority's additional criterion for overruling—that a case either was decided or reaffirmed by a 5-4 margin "over spirited dissen[t],"—the continued vitality of literally scores of decisions must be understood to depend on nothing more than the proclivities of the individuals who now comprise a majority of this Court.*
See, e.g., *Metro Broadcasting v. FCC,* [497 U.S. 547] (1990) (authority of Federal government to set aside broadcast licenses for minority applicants); *Grady v. Corbin,* [495 U.S. 508] (1990) (right under Double Jeopardy Clause not to be subjected twice to prosecution for same criminal

---

*Based on the majority's new criteria for overruling, these decisions, too, must be included on the "endangered precedents" list: *Rutan v. Republican Party of Illinois,* 497 U.S. 62 (1990) (First Amendment right not to be denied public employment on the basis of party affiliation); *Peel v. Attorney Registration and Disciplinary Comm'n,* 496 U.S. 91 (1990) (First Amendment right to advertise legal specialization); *Zinermon v. Burch,* 494 U.S. 113 (1990) (due process right to procedural safeguards aimed at assuring voluntariness of decision to commit oneself to mental hospital); *James v. Illinois,* 493 U.S. 307 (1990) (Fourth Amendment right to exclusion of illegally obtained evidence introduced for impeachment of defense witness); *Rankin v. McPherson,* 483 U.S. 378 (1987) (First Amendment right of public employee to express views on matter of public importance); *Rock v. Arkansas,* 483 U.S. 44 (1987) (Fifth Amendment and Sixth Amendment right of criminal defendant to provide hypnotically refreshed testimony on his own behalf); *Gray v. Mississippi,* 481 U.S. 648 (1987) (rejecting applicability of harmless-error analysis to Eighth Amendment right not to be sentenced to death by "death qualified" jury); *Maine v. Moulton,* 474 U.S. 159 (1985) (Sixth Amendment right to counsel violated by introduction of statements made to government informant-codefendant in course of preparing defense strategy); *Garcia v. San Antonio Metropolitan Transit Auth.,* 469 U.S. 528 (1985) (rejecting theory that Tenth Amendment provides immunity to states from federal regulation); *Pulliam v. Allen,* 466 U.S. 522 (1984) (right to obtain injunctive relief from constitutional violations committed by judicial officials).

conduct); *Mills v. Maryland,* supra (Eighth Amendment right to jury instructions that do not preclude consideration of nonunanimous mitigating factors in capital sentencing); *United States v. Paradise,* 480 U.S. 149
(1987) (right to promotions as remedy for racial discrimination in government hiring); *Ford v. Wainwright,* 477 U.S. 399 (1986) (Eighth Amendment
right not to be executed if insane); *Thornburgh v. American College of Obstetricians and Gynecologists,* 476 U.S. 747 (1986) (reaffirming right to abortion
recognized in Roe v. Wade, 410 U.S. 113 (1973)); *Aguilar v. Felton,* 473
U.S. 402 (1985) (Establishment Clause bar on governmental financial
assistance to parochial schools).

In my view, this impoverished conception of *stare decisis* cannot possibly
be reconciled with the values that inform the proper judicial function.
Contrary to what the majority suggests, *stare decisis* is important not
merely because individuals rely on precedent to structure their commercial activity but because fidelity to precedent is part and parcel of a
conception of "the judiciary as a source of impersonal and reasoned
judgments." . . .

Justice STEVENS, with whom Justice BLACKMUN joined, dissented in
a separate opinion.

Morgan v. Illinois
112 S.Ct. 2222 (1992)

Derrick Morgan was convicted in Cook County, Illinois, of first-degree
murder and sentenced to death. Prior to his trial, three separate venires
were called before the jury was finally chosen. In accordance with Illinois
law, the trial court, rather than the attorneys, conducted *voir dire* examination of the potential jurors. The prosecution in seeking capital punishment requested the judge to determine whether any potential juror
would in all instances refuse to impose the death penalty upon conviction
of the offense. The trial judge, over opposition from the defense, questioned each venire whether any member had moral or religious principles so strong that he or she could not impose the death penalty "regardless of the facts." Seventeen potential jurors were excused when they
expressed substantial doubts about their ability to follow Illinois law in
deciding whether to impose a sentence of death. All of the jurors eventually empaneled were also asked individually: "Would you automatically
vote against the death penalty no matter what the facts of the case were?"
After seven members of the first venire had been questioned, including
three who eventually became jurors, petitioner's counsel requested the

trial court to ask all prospective jurors the following question: "If you found Derrick Morgan guilty, would you automatically vote to impose the death penalty no matter what the facts are?" The trial court refused this request. Morgan was subsequently convicted and sentenced to death. On appeal, the Illinois Supreme Court affirmed his conviction and sentence, rejecting Morgan's claim that, pursuant to *Ross v. Oklahoma*, 487 U.S. 81 (1988), *voir dire* must include the "life qualifying" or "reverse-*Witherspoon*" question on the request counsel. (In *Witherspoon v. Illinois*, 391 U.S. 510 (1968) (see Vol. 2, Ch. 9), the Court held that it was impermissible to exclude from capital cases potential jurors who opposed the imposition of capital punishment.) Morgan's attorney appealed that ruling to the Supreme Court of the United States.

The Court's decision six to three; Justice White announced the majority's opinion. Justice Scalia's dissent was joined by Chief Justice Rehnquist and Justice Thomas.

Justice WHITE delivers the opinion of the Court.

We decide here whether, during voir dire for a capital offense, a state trial court may, consistent with the Due Process Clause of the Fourteenth Amendment, refuse inquiry into whether a potential juror would automatically impose the death penalty upon conviction of the defendant. . . .

We have emphasized previously that there is not "any one right way for a State to set up its capital sentencing scheme," *Spaziano v. Florida*, 468 U.S. 447 (1984) (citations omitted), and that no State is constitutionally required by the Sixth Amendment or otherwise to provide for jury determination of whether the death penalty shall be imposed on a capital defendant. Illinois has chosen, however, to delegate to the jury this task in the penalty phase of capital trials in addition to its duty to determine guilt or innocence of the underlying crime. The issue, therefore, is whether petitioner is entitled to relief under the Due Process Clause of the Fourteenth Amendment. We conclude that he is. . . .

[O]ur decisions dealing with capital sentencing juries and presenting issues most analogous to that which we decide here today, e.g., *Witherspoon v. Illinois*, 391 U.S. [510 (1968)]; *Adams v. Texas*, 448 U.S. 38 (1980); *Wainwright v. Witt*, 469 U.S. 412 (1985); *Ross v. Oklahoma*, 487 U.S. 81 (1988), have relied on the strictures dictated by the Sixth and Fourteenth Amendments to ensure the impartiality of any jury that will undertake capital sentencing.

Witt held that "the proper standard for determining when a prospective juror may be excused for cause because of his or her views on capital punishment . . . is whether the juror's views would 'prevent or substantially impair the performance of his duties as a juror in accordance with his instructions and his oath.' " Under this standard, it is clear from *Witt* and *Adams*, the progeny of *Witherspoon*, that a juror who in no case would vote for capital punishment, regardless of his or her instructions, is not an impartial juror and must be removed for cause.

Thereafter, in *Ross v. Oklahoma,* a state trial court refused to remove for cause a juror who declared he would vote to impose death automatically if the jury found the defendant guilty. That juror, however, was removed by the defendant's use of a peremptory challenge, and for that reason the death sentence could be affirmed. But in the course of reaching this result, we announced our considered view that because the Constitution guarantees a defendant on trial for his life the right to an impartial jury, the trial court's failure to remove the juror for cause was constitutional error under the standard enunciated in *Witt.* . . .

We reiterate this view today. A juror who will automatically vote for the death penalty in every case will fail in good faith to consider the evidence of aggravating and mitigating circumstances as the instructions require him to do. Indeed, because such a juror has already formed an opinion on the merits, the presence or absence of either aggravating or mitigating circumstances is entirely irrelevant to such a juror. Therefore, based on the requirement of impartiality embodied in the Due Process Clause of the Fourteenth Amendment, a capital defendant may challenge for cause any prospective juror who maintains such views. If even one such juror is empaneled and the death sentence is imposed, the State is disentitled to execute the sentence. . . .

The adequacy of voir dire is not easily the subject of appellate review, but we have not hesitated, particularly in capital cases, to find that certain inquiries must be made to effectuate constitutional protections. . . .

We have also come to recognize that the principles first propounded in *Witherspoon v. Illinois,* the reverse of which are at issue here, demand inquiry into whether the views of prospective jurors on the death penalty would disqualify them from sitting. At its inception, *Witherspoon* conferred no "right" on a State, but was in reality a limitation of a State's making "unlimited challenges for cause to exclude those jurors who might hesitate" to return a verdict imposing death. Upon consideration of the jury in *Witherspoon,* drawn as it was from a venire from which the State struck any juror expressing qualms about the death penalty, we found it self-evident that, in its role as "arbiter of the punishment to be imposed, this jury fell woefully short of that impartiality to which the petitioner was entitled under the Sixth and Fourteenth Amendments." . . .

Witherspoon limited a State's power broadly to exclude jurors hesitant in their ability to sentence a defendant to death, but nothing in that decision questioned the power of a State to execute a defendant sentenced to death by a "jury from which the only veniremen who were in fact excluded for cause were those who made unmistakably clear . . . that they would automatically vote against the imposition of capital punishment without regard to any evidence that might be developed at the trial of the case before them. . . ."

We deal here with petitioner's ability to exercise intelligently his complementary challenge for cause against those biased persons on the venire who as jurors would unwaveringly impose death after a finding of guilt.

Were voir dire not available to lay bare the foundation of petitioner's challenge for cause against those prospective jurors who would always impose death following conviction, his right not to be tried by such jurors would be rendered as nugatory and meaningless as the State's right, in the absence of questioning, to strike those who would never do so.

The only issue remaining is whether the questions propounded by the trial court were sufficient to satisfy petitioner's right to make inquiry. . . .

A defendant on trial for his life must be permitted on voir dire to ascertain whether his prospective jurors function under such misconception. The risk that such jurors may have been empaneled in this case and infected petitioner's capital sentencing "[is] unacceptable in light of the ease with which that risk could have been minimized." Petitioner was entitled, upon his request, to inquiry discerning those jurors who, even prior to the State's case-in-chief, had predetermined the terminating issue of his trial, that being whether to impose the death penalty. . . .

Because the "inadequacy of voir dire" leads us to doubt that petitioner was sentenced to death by a jury empaneled in compliance with the Fourteenth Amendment, his sentence cannot stand.

Justice SCALIA, with whom the CHIEF JUSTICE and Justice THOMAS join, dissenting.

The Court today holds that a juror who will always impose the death penalty for capital murder is not "impartial" in the sense required by the Sixth Amendment; that the Constitution requires that voir dire directed to this specific "bias" be provided upon the defendant's request; and that the more general questions about "fairness" and ability to "follow the law" that were asked during voir dire in this case were inadequate. Because these conclusions seem to me jointly and severally wrong, I dissent. . . .

Even if I agreed with the Court . . . that jurors who will always advocate a death sentence for capital murder are not "impartial" and must be excused for cause, I would not agree with the further conclusion that the Constitution requires a trial court to make specific inquiries on this subject during voir dire. . . .

11

THE RIGHT OF PRIVACY

A. PRIVACY AND REPRODUCTIVE FREEDOM

Besides *Rust v. Sullivan* (see page 103), upholding the Reagan administration's reinterpretation of Title X of the Public Health Service Act to forbid family planning clinics receiving federal funding under the act from discussing abortion with clients, the Rehnquist Court let stand another Reagan administration restriction on free speech and family planning services. It did so in denying review to *Planned Parenthood v. Agency for International Development,* 111 S.Ct. 335 (1991), which challenged a 1984 ban on federal funding of foreign health-care organizations that use money from any source to perform abortions or to provide abortion counseling. Planned Parenthood had argued that the restrictions, which apply to $220 million in family planning grants administered by the Agency for International Development (AID), were "far more sweeping than those upheld in *Rust v. Sullivan* since they apply to every part of an organization, [when] any element of which receives AID funds." Subsequently, after almost a year of negotiations and with a view to the 1992 presidential election, President Bush's Department of Health and Human Services (HHS) revised its 1988 policy barring family planning clinics that receive federal funding from offering counseling on abortion. Bush had earlier vetoed a bill that would have lifted the ban on abortion counseling and Congress was unable to override his veto. Then, in March, HHS moderated its ban to make a narrow exception allowing doctors—but not nurses, counselors, or other clinic personnel—to discuss abortion, even for nonmedical reasons.

However, on election day, November 3, 1992, a three-judge panel (composed of three Democratic appointees) of the Court of Appeals for the District of Columbia Circuit struck down the revised abortion gag-order rule on the ground that the HHS had arbitrarily modified the rule and failed to comply with public notice and comment procedures for agency ruling making. Subsequently, two days after his inauguration and on the twentieth anniversary of the *Roe v. Wade* ruling, President Bill Clinton issued executive orders repealing federal restrictions on abortion counseling, fetal tissue research, and funding for foreign health-care organizations that provide abortions and counseling; Clinton ordered as well the Food and Drug Administration to review its policy, adopted during the Bush presidency, barring the importation of RU-486, the French abortion pill.

The Rehnquist Court had also agreed in 1991 to tackle another case arising from the political controversy over abortion. *Bray v. Alexandria Women's Health Clinic*, 113 S.Ct. 753 (1993), raised the question whether federal courts may enjoin antiabortion protesters from blockading abortion clinics. Operation Rescue and other antiabortion groups had been enjoined from blockading clinics under the Civil Rights Act of 1871, which prohibits conspiracies to deprive people of their civil rights; the law is known as the Ku Klux Klan Act because it was enacted in response to attacks on blacks after the Civil War. According to the National Abortion Federation, between 1987 and 1990 more than 26,000 antiabortion protesters were arrested at over 400 blockades of clinics. *Bray* originated in 1989 when Operation Rescue announced plans to block access to several northern Virginia clinics. A year earlier, antiabortion protesters had successfully blockaded other Virginia clinics and overwhelmed local police. Consequently, the clinics promptly sought a court order enjoining antiabortion activists—including convicted abortion-clinic bomber Michael Bray and his wife, Jayne—from undertaking the blockades. A federal district judge's injunction against the antiabortion protesters was affirmed by an appellate court, and the Brays appealed to the Supreme Court.

Nine months after hearing oral arguments, however, the justices failed to reach agreement and rescheduled arguments for the 1992 term. Finally, in mid-January 1993 the Court handed down its ruling in *Bray*, denying federal jurisdiction over antiabortion protesters under the 1871 law. Writing for the majority, Justice Scalia dismissed out of hand arguments for extending federal jurisdiction:

> Our precedents establish that in order to prove a private conspiracy in violation of [the act], a plaintiff must show, *inter alia*, (1) that "some racial, or perhaps otherwise class-based, invidiously discriminatory animus (lay) behind the conspirators' action," and (2) that the conspiracy "aimed at interfering with rights" that are "protected against private, as well as official, encroachment." We think neither showing has been made in the present case. . . .
>
> To begin with, we reject the [view] . . . that opposition to abortion constitutes discrimination against the "class" of "women seeking abor-

tion." Whatever may be the precise meaning of a "class" . . . the term unquestionably connotes something more than a group of individuals who share a desire to engage in conduct that the defendant disfavors. . . .

[Alexandria Women's Health Clinic's] case comes down, then, to the proposition that intent is legally irrelevant; that since voluntary abortion is an activity engaged in only by women, to disfavor it is *ipso facto* to discriminate invidiously against women as a class. Our cases do not support that proposition. . . .

Respondents' federal claim fails for a second, independent reason: A private conspiracy [under the act] requires an intent to deprive persons of a right guaranteed against private impairment. No intent to deprive of such a right was established here. . . .

The other right alleged by respondents to have been intentionally infringed is the right to abortion. . . . The statute does not apply . . . to private conspiracies that are "aimed at a right that is by definition a right only against state interference," but applies only to such conspiracies as are "aimed at interfering with rights protected against private, as well as official, encroachment." There are few such rights. . . . The right to abortion is not among them. It would be most peculiar to accord it that preferred position, since it is much less explicitly protected by the Constitution than, for example, the right of free speech rejected for such status. . . .

Trespassing upon private property is unlawful in all states, as is, in many states and localities, intentionally obstructing the entrance to private premises. These offenses may be prosecuted criminally under state law, and may also be the basis for state civil damages. They do not, however, give rise to a federal cause of action simply because their objective is to prevent the performance of abortions, any more than they do so (as we have held) when their objective is to stifle free speech.

In an opinion in part concurring and dissenting, Justice Souter advanced a very different interpretation. The statute, in his view, applied to any "conspiracy intended to hobble or overwhelm the capacity of duly constituted state police authorities to secure equal protection of the laws, even when the conspirators' animus is not based on race or a like class characteristic, and even when the ultimate object of the conspiracy is to violate a constitutional guarantee that applies solely against state action." Although rejecting Scalia's analysis, Souter nonetheless concluded that the district court, though finding that the Brays and other activists conspired to block access to the clinics, had failed to expressly hold that the Brays' conspiracy had the "purpose of preventing or hindering the constituted authorities of [Virginia] from giving or securing to all persons within [Virginia] the equal protection of the laws." Accordingly, Souter would have remanded the case back to the lower court for reconsideration of that issue.

In two other dissenting opinions in *Bray,* each joined by Justice Black-

mun, Justices Stevens and O'Connor also took strong exception to
Scalia's reasoning and result. Justice Stevens protested that "the error
that infects the Court's entire opinion is the unstated and mistaken
assumption that this is a case about opposition to abortion. It is not. It
is a case about the exercise of federal power to control an interstate
conspiracy to commit illegal acts." Justice O'Connor adamantly rejected
the majority's interpretation as well:

[The Civil Rights Act of 1871] provides a federal remedy against private conspiracies aimed at depriving any person or class of persons of the "equal protection
of the laws," or of "equal privileges and immunities under the laws." In my view,
respondents' injuries and petitioners' activities fall squarely within the ambit of
this statute. . . . The victims of petitioners' tortious actions are linked by their
ability to become pregnant and by their ability to terminate their pregnancies,
characteristics unique to the class of women. Petitioners' activities are directly
related to those class characteristics and therefore, I believe, are appropriately
described as class based. . . .

In my opinion, petitioners' unlawful conspiracy to prevent the clinics from
serving those women, who are targeted by petitioners by virtue of their class
characteristics, is a group-based, private deprivation of the "equal protection of
the laws." . . . The statute was intended to provide a federal means of redress to
the targets of private conspiracies seeking to accomplish their political and social
goals through unlawful means. Today the Court takes yet another step in restricting the scope of the statute, to the point where it now cannot be applied to a
modern-day paradigm of the situation the statute was meant to address.

Bray was not the only case on the Court's 1992 docket that raised a
question of the applicability of federal statutes to pro-life organizations.
The National Organization for Women (NOW), which has sought in
lower federal courts to use the Racketeer Influenced Corrupt Organization (RICO) Act to stop antiabortion protests and blockades, also
filed an appeal of a lower federal court's decision in *National Organization for Women v. Scheidler,* 765 F. 937 (1991). The RICO statute provides for triple damages and other penalties for those convicted of conspiracy and running "racketeering enterprises"; NOW argues that
antiabortion groups' harassment of doctors, staff, and patients at clinics
amounts to extortion under the RICO statute. While some federal
courts have agreed and the Court declined earlier appeals, the Eighth
Circuit appellate court rejected NOW's arguments, holding instead
that the RICO Act applies only to an "economically motivated enterprise" or to illegal activities that are economically motivated. An appeal of that decision was granted and the Court will hear oral arguments in *National Organization for Women v. Scheidler* (No. 92-780) during
its 1993–1994 term.

The Rehnquist Court's controversial and bitterly divided five-to-four
decision in *Webster v. Reproductive Health Services,* 492 U.S. 4090 (1989) (see
Vol. 2, Ch. 11), invited states and localities to enact more stringent
restrictions on the availability of abortions. A number of states—includ-

ing Pennsylvania, Louisiana, Utah, and the Territory of Guam—passed tougher new laws in anticipation of the Court's possible reversal of *Roe v. Wade*, 410 U.S. 113 (1973) (see Vol. 2, Ch. 11). And the constitutionality of each of those laws was in turn challenged in federal courts. One of the first appeals of a post-*Webster* ruling on states' more restrictive abortion laws to reach the Court was *Planned Parenthood of Southeastern Pennsylvania v. Casey*, 112 S.Ct. 2791 (1992) (see page 240).

Casey fragmented the Court three ways. Four justices—Chief Justice Rehnquist and Justices Scalia, Thomas, and White—voted to uphold all of Pennsylvania's restrictions on abortion and expressly to overrule *Roe v. Wade*. By contrast, *Roe*'s author, Justice Blackmun, would have struck down all of the restrictions, while in a separate opinion in part concurring and dissenting Justice Stevens voted to uphold informed consent and reporting requirements, but to overturn the state's requirements for abortion counseling, a twenty-four-hour waiting period, and spousal notification. The balance on the Court was held by Justices O'Connor, Kennedy, and Souter, who in an extraordinary move issued a joint opinion announcing the Court's decision. They upheld all of Pennsylvania's restrictions, except for the requirement of spousal notification and reporting requirement in that regard. While claiming to reaffirm "the central holding" of *Roe v. Wade*, they rejected much of that decision, including its trimester analysis of permissible and impermissible regulations, as well as overturned portions of the Court's earlier rulings in *Akron v. Akron Center for Reproductive Health, Inc.*, 462 U.S. 416 (1983), and *Thornburgh v. American College of Obstetricians & Gynecologists*, 476 U.S. 747 (1986) (see Vol. 2, Ch. 11). In addition, the plurality embraced an undue burden analysis of a woman's substantive liberty interests, drawing a line on states' most restrictive regulations at the point of viability, as well as proposed a novel theory of *stare decisis* that drew sharp criticism from Chief Justice Rehnquist and Justices Scalia, Thomas, and White. Although an overwhelming majority on the Court in *Casey* abandoned *Roe*'s assertion of a "fundamental right" of women to choose abortion, a bare majority stood against expressly overturning *Roe* and allowing states to ban abortions prior to fetal viability.

Subsequently, the Court by a six-to-three vote and without explanation denied review of *Ada v. Guam Society of Obstetricians & Gynecologists*, 113 S.Ct. 633 (1992). In that case the governor of the Territory of Guam appealed a ruling by the Ninth Circuit that invalidated Guam's 1990 law barring virtually all abortions, except those required by a medical emergency. Justice Scalia, joined by Chief Justice Rehnquist and Justice White, dissented, arguing that the case should be heard because under the Court's overbreadth doctrine not all applications of a statute may be invalid. Scalia saw "no reason why the Guam law would not be constitutional at least in its application to abortions conducted after the point at which the child may live outside the womb." However, those three justices were unable to persuade a fourth justice, as required under the

Court's informal rule of four, to vote for granting review. Justice Thomas, who sided with the three other dissenters in *Casey*, offered no explanation for not voting to grant *Ada*.

As if to underscore the majority's unwillingness to revisit the abortion controversy, the Rehnquist Court also denied an appeal of the Fifth Circuit's upholding of Mississippi's 1991 abortion law. That law requires women seeking an abortion to wait twenty-four hours after giving their consent and having their doctors explain the medical risks of abortion, describe the stages of fetal development, as well as discuss pregnancy prevention and alternatives to abortion, along with notifying them "that the father is liable to assist in the support of her child." In light of the ruling in *Casey*, the appellate court held that these requirements did not unduly burden women, and thus were constitutional, in *Barnes v. Moore*, 970 F.2d 12 (1992), *cert.* denied, 113 S.Ct. 656 (1992). The Court as well denied review of an appeal, in *Edwards v. Sojourner T.*, 113 S.Ct. 1414 (1993), of an appellate court decision striking down Louisiana's 1991 law banning all abortions except those necessary to save a woman's life and in cases of rape or incest, as well as providing prison terms for doctors convicted of performing abortions.

However, the Rehnquist Court may be eventually forced to grant an appeal of a challenge to restrictive abortion laws and to clarify the application of *Casey*'s "undue burden" standard. Notably, in *Fargo Women's Health Organization v. Schafer*, 113 S.Ct. 1669 (1993), over the dissent of Justices Blackmun and Stevens, the Court declined, pending the outcome of lawsuit in the lower courts, to stop North Dakota from enforcing its law requiring women to receive counseling and wait twenty-four hours before obtaining an abortion. But in separate concurring statements accompanying the Court's order, Justices O'Connor and Souter rejected an appellate court's holding that those challenging North Dakota's law had to show that it was unconstitutional in unduly burdening all women seeking an abortion. Fargo Women's Health Organization, though, contended that North Dakota unduly burdens women who must travel great distances from within or outside of the state to North Dakota's only abortion clinic and stay overnight or miss work in order to comply with the state's counseling and waiting-period requirements. At least four justices (Blackmun, O'Connor, Souter, and Stevens) appear to agree that federal courts should give greater scrutiny to the actual impact of restrictive abortion laws on women seeking abortions. In Justice O'Connor's words, "a law restricting abortions constitutes an undue burden, and hence is invalid, if in a large fraction of the cases in which the law is relevant, it will operate as a substantial obstacle to a woman's choice to undergo an abortion." With Justice White's retirement at the end of the 1992–1993 term and confirmation of his successor, the balance on the Court could well shift in the direction of clarifying and making *Casey*'s undue burden test more rigorous on a case-by-case basis.

Planned Parenthood of Southeastern Pennsylvania v. Casey

112. S.Ct. 2791 (1992)

In 1988 and 1989, following the Supreme Court's ruling in *Webster v. Reproductive Health Services,* 492 U.S. 490 (1989) (see Vol. 2, Ch. 11), Pennsylvania amended its state abortion law by enacting more restrictive provisions conditioning access to abortions. Planned Parenthood of Southeastern Pennsylvania immediately challenged the constitutionality of those provisions. Subsequently, the Court of Appeals for the Third Circuit upheld most of those restrictions, except for a spousal notification provision. In doing so, the Third Circuit adopted Justice O'Connor's undue burden analysis, in her dissenting opinion in *Akron v. Akron Center for Reproductive Health, Inc.,* 462 U.S. 416 (1983) (see Vol. 2, Ch. 11). Accordingly, the appellate court gave strict scrutiny to any restriction that unduly burdened women and held that abortion restrictions that do not pose an undue burden are permissible so long as they have a rational basis. And on that basis, the Third Circuit upheld Pennsylvania's requiring women to (1) be informed by doctors about fetal development; (2) give their consent or, if they were minors, obtain parental consent; and (3) wait at least twenty-four hours after giving their informed consent before obtaining an abortion as well as (4) imposing certain reporting and public disclosure requirements on doctors who perform abortions. Despite the fact that virtually identical requirements were struck down by a bare majority of the Burger Court in *Thornburgh v. American College of Obstetricians and Gynecologists,* 476 U.S. 747 (1986) (see Vol. 2, Ch. 11), the Third Circuit noted that the Rehnquist Court had substantially altered its analysis and undercut support for a woman's fundamental right to obtain an abortion in *Webster.* The appellate court, moreover, did not deem any of the above restrictions to constitute an undue burden and, therefore, applied the rational basis test when upholding these requirements. Pennsylvania, however, also required married women to notify their spouses of their desire to obtain an abortion and the appellate court overturned that requirement as an undue burden on women. When strictly scrutinizing that provision, the Third Circuit concluded that it unduly burdened women by potentially exposing them to spousal abuse, violence, and economic duress at the hands of their husbands. Both sides of the abortion controversy appealed the appellate court's decision.

The Court's decision was five to four, but the justices split three-two-four. The opinion was announced by Justices O'Connor, Kennedy, and Souter. Justices Blackmun and Stevens delivered separate opinions in part concurring and in part dissenting. Chief Justice Rehnquist and Justice Scalia joined each other and were joined by Justices Thomas and White.

Justice O'CONNOR, Justice KENNEDY, and Justice SOUTER announce the judgment of the Court and deliver the opinion of the Court with respect to Parts I, II, III, V-A, V-C, and VI, an opinion with respect to Part V-E, in which JUSTICE STEVENS joins, and an opinion with respect to Parts IV, V-B, and V-D.

I

After considering the fundamental constitutional questions resolved by *Roe* [*v. Wade*, 410 U.S. 113 (1973)], principles of institutional integrity, and the rule of *stare decisis*, we are led to conclude this: the essential holding of *Roe v. Wade* should be retained and once again reaffirmed.

It must be stated at the outset and with clarity that *Roe*'s essential holding, the holding we reaffirm, has three parts. First is a recognition of the right of the woman to choose to have an abortion before viability and to obtain it without undue interference from the State. Before viability, the State's interests are not strong enough to support a prohibition of abortion or the imposition of a substantial obstacle to the woman's effective right to elect the procedure. Second is a confirmation of the State's power to restrict abortions after fetal viability, if the law contains exceptions for pregnancies which endanger a woman's life or health. And third is the principle that the State has legitimate interests from the outset of the pregnancy in protecting the health of the woman and the life of the fetus that may become a child. These principles do not contradict one another; and we adhere to each. . . .

. . .

III

A [W]hen this Court reexamines a prior holding, its judgment is customarily informed by a series of prudential and pragmatic considerations designed to test the consistency of overruling a prior decision with the ideal of the rule of law, and to gauge the respective costs of reaffirming and overruling a prior case. Thus, for example, we may ask whether the rule has proved to be intolerable simply in defying practical workability; whether the rule is subject to a kind of reliance that would lend a special hardship to the consequences of overruling and add inequity to the cost of repudiation; whether related principles of law have so far developed as to have left the old rule no more than a remnant of abandoned doctrine; or whether facts have so changed or come to be seen so differently, as to have robbed the old rule of significant application or justification, e.g., *Burnet v. Coronado Oil Gas Co.*, 285 U.S. 393 (1932) (BRANDEIS, J., dissenting). . . .

Although *Roe* has engendered opposition, it has in no sense proven "unworkable," representing as it does a simple limitation beyond which a state law is unenforceable. . . .

We have seen how time has overtaken some of *Roe*'s factual assumptions: advances in maternal health care allow for abortions safe to the mother later in pregnancy than was true in 1973, and advances in neonatal care have advanced viability to a point somewhat earlier. But these facts go only to the scheme of time limits on the realization of competing interests, and the divergences from the factual premises of 1973 have no bearing on the validity of *Roe*'s central holding, that viability marks the earliest point at which the State's interest in fetal life is constitutionally adequate to justify a legislative ban on nontherapeutic abortions. The soundness or unsoundness of that constitutional judgment in no sense turns on whether viability occurs at approximately 28 weeks, as was usual at the time of *Roe*, at 23 to 24 weeks, as it sometimes does today, or at some moment even slightly earlier in pregnancy, as it may if fetal respiratory capacity can somehow be enhanced in the future. Whenever it may occur, the attainment of viability may continue to serve as the critical fact, just as it has done since *Roe* was decided; which is to say that no change in *Roe*'s factual underpinning has left its central holding obsolete, and none supports an argument for overruling it.

B   In a less significant case, *stare decisis* analysis could, and would, stop at the point we have reached. But the sustained and widespread debate *Roe* has provoked calls for some comparison between that case and others of comparable dimension that have responded to national controversies and taken on the impress of the controversies addressed. Only two such decisional lines from the past century present themselves for examination, and in each instance the result reached by the Court accorded with the principles we apply today.

The first example is that line of cases identified with *Lochner v. New York*, 198 U.S. 45 (1905), which imposed substantive limitations on legislation limiting economic autonomy in favor of health and welfare regulation, adopting, in Justice Holmes' view, the theory of laissez-faire. The *Lochner* decisions were exemplified by *Adkins v. Children's Hospital of D.C.*, 261 U.S. 525 (1923), in which this Court held it to be an infringement of constitutionally protected liberty of contract to require the employers of adult women to satisfy minimum wage standards. Fourteen years later, *West Coast Hotel Co. v. Parrish*, 300 U.S. 379 (1937), signalled the demise of *Lochner* by overruling *Adkins*. In the meantime, the Depression had come and, with it, the lesson that seemed unmistakable to most people by 1937, that the interpretation of contractual freedom protected in *Adkins* rested on fundamentally false factual assumptions about the capacity of a relatively unregulated market to satisfy minimal levels of human welfare. . . .

The second comparison that 20th century history invites is with the cases employing the separate-but-equal rule for applying the Fourteenth Amendment's equal protection guarantee. They began with *Plessy v. Ferguson*, 163 U.S. 537 (1896), holding that legislatively mandated racial segregation in public transportation works no denial of equal protection. . . . The *Plessy* Court considered "the underlying fallacy of the plaintiff's argument to consist in the assumption that the enforced separation of the two races stamps the colored race with a badge of inferiority. If this be so, it is not by reason of anything found in the act, but solely because the colored race chooses to put that construction upon it." Whether, as a matter of historical fact, the Justices in the *Plessy* majority believed this or not, this understanding of the implication of segregation was the stated justification for the Court's opinion. But this understanding of the facts and the rule it was stated to justify were repudiated in *Brown v. Board of Education,* 347 U.S. 483 (1954). . . .

The Court in *Brown* addressed these facts of life by observing that whatever may have been the understanding in *Plessy*'s time of the power of segregation to stigmatize those who were segregated with a "badge of inferiority," it was clear by 1954 that legally sanctioned segregation had just such an effect, to the point that racially separate public educational facilities were deemed inherently unequal. Society's understanding of the facts upon which a constitutional ruling was sought in 1954 was thus fundamentally different from the basis claimed for the decision in 1896. While we think *Plessy* was wrong the day it was decided, we must also recognize that the *Plessy* Court's explanation for its decision was so clearly at odds with the facts apparent to the Court in 1954 that the decision to reexamine *Plessy* was on this ground alone not only justified but required.

West Coast Hotel and *Brown* each rested on facts, or an understanding of facts, changed from those which furnished the claimed justifications for the earlier constitutional resolutions. . . . In constitutional adjudication as elsewhere in life, changed circumstances may impose new obligations, and the thoughtful part of the Nation could accept each decision to overrule a prior case as a response to the Court's constitutional duty.

Because the case before us presents no such occasion it could be seen as no such response. Because neither the factual underpinnings of *Roe*'s central holding nor our understanding of it has changed (and because no other indication of weakened precedent has been shown) the Court could not pretend to be reexamining the prior law with any justification beyond a present doctrinal disposition to come out differently from the Court of 1973. . . .

C The examination of the conditions justifying the repudiation of *Adkins* by *West Coast Hotel* and *Plessy* by *Brown* is enough to suggest the terrible price that would have been paid if the Court had not overruled as it did. In the present case, however, as our analysis to this point makes clear, the terrible price would be paid for overruling. Our analysis would not be complete, however, without explaining why overruling *Roe*'s central holding would not only reach an unjustifiable result under principles of *stare decisis,* but would seriously weaken the Court's capacity to exercise the judicial power and to function as the Supreme Court of a Nation dedicated to the rule of law. . . .

The underlying substance of [the Court's] legitimacy is . . . expressed in the Court's opinions, and our contemporary understanding is such that a decision without principled justification would be no judicial act at all. . . . The Court must take care to speak and act in ways that allow people to accept its decisions on the terms the Court claims for them, as grounded truly in principle, not as compromises with social and political pressures having, as such, no bearing on the principled choices that the Court is obliged to make. Thus, the Court's legitimacy depends on making legally principled decisions under circumstances in which their principled character is sufficiently plausible to be accepted by the Nation. . . .

The Court's duty in the present case is clear. In 1973, it confronted the already divisive issue of governmental power to limit personal choice to undergo abortion, for which it provided a new resolution based on the due process guaranteed by the Fourteenth Amendment. Whether or not a new social consensus is developing on that issue, its divisiveness is no less today than in 1973, and pressure to overrule the decision, like pressure to retain it, has grown only more intense. A decision to overrule *Roe*'s essential holding under the existing circumstances would address error, if error there was, at the cost of both profound and unnecessary damage to the Court's legitimacy, and to the Nation's commitment to the rule of law. It is therefore imperative to adhere to the essence of *Roe*'s original decision, and we do so today.

IV

. . .

We conclude that the basic decision in *Roe* was based on a constitutional analysis which we cannot now repudiate. The woman's liberty is not so unlimited, however, that from the outset the State cannot show its concern for the life of the unborn, and at a later point in fetal development the State's interest in life has sufficient force so that the right of the woman to terminate the pregnancy can be restricted.

That brings us, of course, to the point where much criticism has been directed at *Roe,* a criticism that always inheres when the Court draws a specific rule from what in the Constitution is but a general standard. . . . And it falls to us to give some real substance to the woman's liberty to determine whether to carry her pregnancy to full term.

We conclude the line should be drawn at viability, so that before that time the woman has a right to choose to terminate her pregnancy. We adhere to this principle for two reasons. First, as we have said, is the doctrine of *stare decisis.* Any judicial act of line-drawing may seem somewhat arbitrary, but *Roe* was a reasoned statement, elaborated with great care. We have twice reaffirmed it in the face of great opposition. Although we must overrule those parts of *Thornburgh* and *Akron I* which, in our view, are inconsistent with *Roe*'s statement that the State has a legitimate interest in promoting the life or potential life of the unborn, the central premise of those cases represents an unbroken commitment by this Court to the essential holding of *Roe.* It is that premise which we reaffirm today.

The second reason is that the concept of viability, as we noted in *Roe*, is the time at which there is a realistic possibility of maintaining and nourishing a life outside the womb, so that the independent existence of the second life can in reason and all fairness be the object of state protection that now overrides the rights of the woman. Consistent with other constitutional norms, legislatures may draw lines which appear arbitrary without the necessity of offering a justification. But courts may not. We must justify the lines we draw. And there is no line other than viability which is more workable. . . .

The woman's right to terminate her pregnancy before viability is the most central principle of *Roe v. Wade*. It is a rule of law and a component of liberty we cannot renounce. . . .

Though the woman has a right to choose to terminate or continue her pregnancy before viability, it does not at all follow that the State is prohibited from taking steps to ensure that this choice is thoughtful and informed. Even in the earliest stages of pregnancy, the State may enact rules and regulations designed to encourage her to know that there are philosophic and social arguments of great weight that can be brought to bear in favor of continuing the pregnancy to full term and that there are procedures and institutions to allow adoption of unwanted children as well as a certain degree of state assistance if the mother chooses to raise the child herself. "The Constitution does not forbid a State or city, pursuant to democratic processes, from expressing a preference for normal childbirth." *Webster v. Reproductive Health Services* [(1989)]. It follows that States are free to enact laws to provide a reasonable framework for a woman to make a decision that has such profound and lasting meaning. This, too, we find consistent with *Roe*'s central premises, and indeed the inevitable consequence of our holding that the State has an interest in protecting the life of the unborn.

We reject the trimester framework, which we do not consider to be part of the essential holding of *Roe*. . . . The trimester framework suffers from these basic flaws: in its formulation it misconceives the nature of the pregnant woman's interest; and in practice it undervalues the State's interest in potential life, as recognized in *Roe*. . . .

Because we set forth a standard of general application to which we intend to adhere, it is important to clarify what is meant by an undue burden. . . . We give this summary:

(a) To protect the central right recognized by *Roe v. Wade* while at the same time accommodating the State's profound interest in potential life, we will employ the undue burden analysis as explained in this opinion. An undue burden exists, and therefore a provision of law is invalid, if its purpose or effect is to place a substantial obstacle in the path of a woman seeking an abortion before the fetus attains viability.

(b) We reject the rigid trimester framework of *Roe v. Wade*. To promote the State's profound interest in potential life, throughout pregnancy the State may take measures to ensure that the woman's choice is informed, and measures designed to advance this interest will not be invalidated as long as their purpose is to persuade the woman to choose childbirth over abortion. These measures must not be an undue burden on the right.

(c) As with any medical procedure, the State may enact regulations to further the health or safety of a woman seeking an abortion. Unnecessary health regulations that have the purpose or effect of presenting a substantial obstacle to a woman seeking an abortion impose an undue burden on the right.

(d) Our adoption of the undue burden analysis does not disturb the central holding of *Roe v. Wade,* and we reaffirm that holding. Regardless of whether exceptions are made for particular circumstances, a State may not prohibit any woman from making the ultimate decision to terminate her pregnancy before viability.

(e) We also reaffirm *Roe*'s holding that "subsequent to viability, the State in promoting its interest in the potentiality of human life may, if it chooses, regulate, and even proscribe, abortion except where it is necessary, in appropriate medical judgment, for the preservation of the life or health of the mother."

These principles control our assessment of the Pennsylvania statute, and we now turn to the issue of the validity of its challenged provisions.

v

A Because it is central to the operation of various other requirements, we begin with the statute's definition of medical emergency. Under the statute, a medical emergency is "that condition which, on the basis of the physician's good faith clinical judgment, so complicates the medical condition of a pregnant woman as to necessitate the immediate abortion of her pregnancy to avert her death or for which a delay will create serious risk of substantial and irreversible impairment of a major bodily function."

. . . We conclude that, as construed by the Court of Appeals, the medical emergency definition imposes no undue burden on a woman's abortion right.

. . .

B Our prior decisions establish that as with any medical procedure, the State may require a woman to give her written informed consent to an abortion. In this respect, the statute is unexceptional. Petitioners challenge the statute's definition of informed consent because it includes the provision of specific information by the doctor and the mandatory 24-hour waiting period. The conclusions reached by a majority of the Justices in the separate opinions filed today and the undue burden standard adopted in this opinion require us to overrule in part some of the Court's past decisions, decisions driven by the trimester framework's prohibition of all previability regulations designed to further the State's interest in fetal life. . . .

To the extent *Akron I* and *Thornburgh* find a constitutional violation when the government requires, as it does here, the giving of truthful, nonmisleading information about the nature of the procedure, the attendant health risks and those of childbirth, and the "probable gestational age" of the fetus, those cases go too far, are inconsistent with *Roe*'s acknowledgment of an important interest in potential life, and are overruled. . . .

   C   Section 3209 of Pennsylvania's abortion law provides, except in cases of medical emergency, that no physician shall perform an abortion on a married woman without receiving a signed statement from the woman that she has notified her spouse that she is about to undergo an abortion. The woman has the option of providing an alternative signed statement certifying that her husband is not the man who impregnated her; that her husband could not be located; that the pregnancy is the result of spousal sexual assault which she has reported; or that the woman believes that notifying her husband will cause him or someone else to inflict bodily injury upon her. A physician who performs an abortion on a married woman without receiving the appropriate signed statement will have his or her license revoked, and is liable to the husband for damages. . . .

   [T]here are millions of women in this country who are the victims of regular physical and psychological abuse at the hands of their husbands. Should these women become pregnant, they may have very good reasons for not wishing to inform their husbands of their decision to obtain an abortion. Many may have justifiable fears of physical abuse, but may be no less fearful of the consequences of reporting prior abuse to the Commonwealth of Pennsylvania. Many may have a reasonable fear that notifying their husbands will provoke further instances of child abuse; these women are not exempt from Section 3209's notification requirement. Many may fear devastating forms of psychological abuse from their husbands, including verbal harassment, threats of future violence, the destruction of possessions, physical confinement to the home, the withdrawal of financial support, or the disclosure of the abortion to family and friends. These methods of psychological abuse may act as even more of a deterrent to notification than the possibility of physical violence, but women who are the victims of the abuse are not exempt from Section 3209's notification requirement. And many women who are pregnant as a result of sexual assaults by their husbands will be unable to avail themselves of the exception for spousal sexual assault, because the exception requires that the woman have notified law enforcement authorities within 90 days of the assault, and her husband will be notified of her report once an investigation begins. . . .

   The unfortunate yet persisting conditions we document above will mean that in a large fraction of the cases in which Section 3209 is relevant, it will operate as a substantial obstacle to a woman's choice to undergo an abortion. It is an undue burden, and therefore invalid. . . .

   D   We next consider the parental consent provision. . . .

   We have been over most of this ground before. Our cases establish, and we reaffirm today, that a State may require a minor seeking an abortion to obtain the consent of a parent or guardian, provided that there is an adequate judicial bypass procedure. Under these precedents, in our view, the one-parent consent requirement and judicial bypass procedure are constitutional. . . .

E   In [*Planned Parenthood of Central Missouri v.*] *Danforth,* [428 U.S. 552 (1976)], we held that recordkeeping and reporting provisions "that are reasonably directed to the preservation of maternal health and that properly respect a patient's confidentiality and privacy are permissible." We think that under this standard, all the provisions at issue here except that relating to spousal notice are constitutional. . . .

Subsection (12) of the reporting provision requires the reporting of, among other things, a married woman's "reason for failure to provide notice" to her husband. This provision in effect requires women, as a condition of obtaining an abortion, to provide the Commonwealth with the precise information we have already recognized that many women have pressing reasons not to reveal. Like the spousal notice requirement itself, this provision places an undue burden on a woman's choice, and must be invalidated for that reason.

Justice BLACKMUN concurring in part, concurring in the judgment in part, and dissenting in part.

I join parts I, II, III, V-A, V-C, and VI of the joint opinion of Justices O'CONNOR, KENNEDY, and SOUTER. . . .

Make no mistake, the joint opinion of Justices O'CONNOR, KENNEDY, and SOUTER is an act of personal courage and constitutional principle. In contrast to previous decisions in which Justices O'CONNOR and KENNEDY postponed reconsideration of *Roe v. Wade,* the authors of the joint opinion today join Justice STEVENS and me in concluding that "the essential holding of *Roe* should be retained and once again reaffirmed." In brief, five Members of this Court today recognize that "the Constitution protects a woman's right to terminate her pregnancy in its early stages." . . .

. . . Our precedents and the joint opinion's principles require us to subject all non-de minimis abortion regulations to strict scrutiny. Under this standard, the Pennsylvania statute's provisions requiring content-based counseling, a 24-hour delay, informed parental consent, and re-porting of abortion-related information must be invalidated. . . .

If there is much reason to applaud the advances made by the joint opinion today, there is far more to fear from the CHIEF JUSTICE's opinion.

The CHIEF JUSTICE's criticism of *Roe* follows from his stunted conception of individual liberty. . . . He argues that the record in favor of a right to abortion is no stronger than the record in *Michael H. v. Gerald D.,* 491 U.S. 110 (1989), where the plurality found no fundamental right to visitation privileges by an adulterous father, or in *Bowers v. Hardwick,* 478 U.S. 186 (1986), where the Court found no fundamental right to engage in homosexual sodomy, or in a case involving the "firing of a gun . . . into another person's body." In the CHIEF JUSTICE's world, a woman considering whether to terminate a pregnancy is entitled to no more protection than adulterers, murderers, and so-called "sexual deviates." Given the CHIEF JUSTICE's exclusive reliance on tradition, people using contraceptives seem the next likely candidate for his list of outcasts. . . .

The CHIEF JUSTICE's narrow conception of individual liberty and *stare decisis* leads him to propose the same standard of review proposed by the plurality in *Webster*. "States may regulate abortion procedures in ways rationally related to a legitimate state interest. *Williamson v. Lee Optical Co.*, 348 U.S. 483 (1955); cf. *Stanley v. Illinois*, 405 U.S. 645 (1972)." . . .

But, we are reassured, there is always the protection of the democratic process. While there is much to be praised about our democracy, our country since its founding has recognized that there are certain fundamental liberties that are not to be left to the whims of an election. A woman's right to reproductive choice is one of those fundamental liberties. Accordingly, that liberty need not seek refuge at the ballot box.

In one sense, the Court's approach is worlds apart from that of the CHIEF JUSTICE and Justice SCALIA. And yet, in another sense, the distance between the two approaches is short—the distance is but a single vote.

I am 83 years old. I cannot remain on this Court forever, and when I do step down, the confirmation process for my successor well may focus on the issue before us today. That, I regret, may be exactly where the choice between the two worlds will be made.

Justice STEVENS, in an opinion omitted here concurred in part and dissented from Parts IV, V-B, and V-D of the joint opinion, voting to uphold the informed consent and reporting requirements, except for the provision for reporting on spousal notification, and voting to strike down as an undue burden the requirements for abortion counseling, a 24-hour waiting period, and spousal notification.

Chief Justice REHNQUIST, with whom Justice WHITE, Justice SCALIA, and Justice THOMAS join, concurring in the judgment in part and dissenting in part.

. . .

We think . . . that the Court was mistaken in *Roe* when it classified a woman's decision to terminate her pregnancy as a "fundamental right" that could be abridged only in a manner which withstood "strict scrutiny." . . .

The joint opinion of Justices O'CONNOR, KENNEDY, and SOUTER cannot bring itself to say that *Roe* was correct as an original matter, but the authors are of the view that "the immediate question is not the soundness of *Roe*'s resolution of the issue, but the precedential force that must be accorded to its holding." Instead of claiming that *Roe* was correct as a matter of original constitutional interpretation, the opinion therefore contains an elaborate discussion of *stare decisis*. This discussion of the principle of *stare decisis* appears to be almost entirely dicta, because the joint opinion does not apply that principle in dealing with *Roe*. *Roe* decided that a woman had a fundamental right to an abortion. The joint opinion rejects that view. *Roe* decided that abortion regulations were to be subjected to "strict scrutiny" and could be justified only in the light of "compelling state interests." The joint opinion rejects that view. *Roe* analyzed abortion regulation under a rigid trimester framework, a framework which has guided this Court's decisionmaking for 19 years. The joint opinion rejects that framework. . . .

In our view, authentic principles of *stare decisis* do not require that any portion of the reasoning in *Roe* be kept intact. . . .

The joint opinion discusses several *stare decisis* factors which, it asserts, point toward retaining a portion of *Roe*. Two of these factors are that the main "factual underpinning" of *Roe* has remained the same, and that its doctrinal foundation is no weaker now than it was in 1973. Of course, what might be called the basic facts which gave rise to *Roe* have remained the same—women become pregnant, there is a point somewhere, depending on medical technology, where a fetus becomes viable, and women give birth to children. But this is only to say that the same facts which gave rise to *Roe* will continue to give rise to similar cases. It is not a reason, in and of itself, why those cases must be decided in the same incorrect manner as was the first case to deal with the question. And surely there is no requirement, in considering whether to depart from stare decisis in a constitutional case, that a decision be more wrong now than it was at the time it was rendered. If that were true, the most outlandish constitutional decision could survive forever, based simply on the fact that it was no more outlandish later than it was when originally rendered. . . .

In the end, having failed to put forth any evidence to prove any true reliance, the joint opinion's argument is based solely on generalized assertions about the national psyche, on a belief that the people of this country have grown accustomed to the *Roe* decision over the last 19 years and have "ordered their thinking and living around" it. As an initial matter, one might inquire how the joint opinion can view the "central holding" of *Roe* as so deeply rooted in our constitutional culture, when it so casually uproots and disposes of that same decision's trimester framework. Furthermore, at various points in the past, the same could have been said about this Court's erroneous decisions that the Constitution allowed "separate but equal" treatment of minorities, or that "liberty" under the Due Process Clause protected "freedom of contract." The "separate but equal" doctrine lasted 58 years after *Plessy*, and *Lochner*'s protection of contractual freedom lasted 32 years. However, the simple fact that a generation or more had grown used to these major decisions did not prevent the Court from correcting its errors in those cases, nor should it prevent us from correctly interpreting the Constitution here.

Apparently realizing that conventional *stare decisis* principles do not support its position, the joint opinion advances a belief that retaining a portion of *Roe* is necessary to protect the "legitimacy" of this Court. . . . [T]he joint opinion goes on to state that when the Court "resolves the sort of intensely divisive controversy reflected in *Roe* and those rare, comparable cases," its decision is exempt from reconsideration under established principles of *stare decisis* in constitutional cases. This is so, the joint opinion contends, because in those "intensely divisive" cases the Court has "called the contending sides of a national controversy to end their national division by accepting a common mandate rooted in the Constitution," and must therefore take special care not to be perceived as "surrendering to political pressure" and continued opposition. This is a truly novel principle. . . . Under this principle, when the Court has ruled on a divisive issue, it is apparently prevented from overruling that decision for the sole reason that it was incorrect, unless opposition to the original decision has died away. . . .

The joint opinion agrees that the Court's stature would have been seriously damaged if in *Brown* and *West Coast Hotel* it had dug in its heels and refused to apply normal principles of *stare decisis* to the earlier decisions. But the opinion contends that the Court was entitled to overrule *Plessy* and *Lochner* in those cases, despite the existence of opposition to the original decisions, only because both the Nation and the Court had learned new lessons in the interim. This is at best a feebly supported, post hoc rationalization for those decisions. . . .

The sum of the joint opinion's labors in the name of *stare decisis* and "legitimacy" is this: *Roe v. Wade* stands as a sort of judicial Potemkin Village, which may be pointed out to passersby as a monument to the importance of adhering to precedent. But behind the facade, an entirely new method of analysis, without any roots in constitutional law, is imported to decide the constitutionality of state laws regulating abortion. Neither *stare decisis* nor "legitimacy" are truly served by such an effort.

For the reasons stated, we therefore would hold that each of the challenged provisions of the Pennsylvania statute is consistent with the Constitution.

Justice SCALIA, with whom the CHIEF JUSTICE, Justice WHITE, and Justice THOMAS join, concurring in the judgment in part and dissenting in part.

My views on this matter are unchanged from those I set forth in my separate opinions in *Webster v. Reproductive Health Services,* 492 U.S. 490 (1989) (SCALIA, J., concurring in part and concurring in judgment), and *Ohio v. Akron Center for Reproductive Health,* 497 U.S. 502 (1990) *(Akron II)* (SCALIA, J., concurring). The States may, if they wish, permit abortion-on-demand, but the Constitution does not require them to do so. The permissibility of abortion, and the limitations upon it, are to be resolved like most important questions in our democracy: by citizens trying to persuade one another and then voting. . . . A State's choice between two positions on which reasonable people can disagree is constitutional even when (as is often the case) it intrudes upon a "liberty" in the absolute sense. Laws against bigamy, for example—which entire societies of reasonable people disagree with—intrude upon men and women's liberty to marry and live with one another. But bigamy happens not to be a liberty specially "protected" by the Constitution.

That is, quite simply, the issue in this case. . . . The issue is whether [a woman's claim to a constitutional right to have an abortion] is liberty protected by the Constitution of the United States. I am sure it is not. I reach that conclusion not because of anything so exalted as my views concerning the "concept of existence, of meaning, of the universe, and of the mystery of human life." Rather, I reach it for the same reason I reach the conclusion that bigamy is not constitutionally protected—because of two simple facts: (1) the Constitution says absolutely nothing about it, and (2) the longstanding traditions of American society have permitted it to be legally proscribed. . . .

The Court's reliance upon *stare decisis* can best be described as contrived. It insists upon the necessity of adhering not to all of *Roe*, but only to what it calls the "central holding." It seems to me that *stare decisis* ought to be applied even to the doctrine of *stare decisis*, and I confess never to have heard of this new, keep-what-you-want-and-throw-away-the-rest version. . . .

I am certainly not in a good position to dispute that the Court has saved the "central holding" of *Roe*, since to do that effectively I would have to know what the Court has saved, which in turn would require me to understand (as I do not) what the "undue burden" test means. I must confess, however, that I have always thought, and I think a lot of other people have always thought, that the arbitrary trimester framework, which the Court today discards, was quite as central to *Roe* as the arbitrary viability test, which the Court today retains. It seems particularly ungrateful to carve the trimester framework out of the core of *Roe*, since its very rigidity (in sharp contrast to the utter indeterminability of the "undue burden" test) is probably the only reason the Court is able to say, in urging *stare decisis*, that *Roe* "has in no sense proven unworkable.' " I suppose the Court is entitled to call a "central holding" whatever it wants to call a "central holding"—which is, come to think of it, perhaps one of the difficulties with this modified version of *stare decisis*. I thought I might note, however, that the following portions of *Roe* have not been saved:

• Under *Roe*, requiring that a woman seeking an abortion be provided truthful information about abortion before giving informed written consent is unconstitutional, if the information is designed to influence her choice, *Thornburgh, Akron I*. Under the joint opinion's "undue burden" regime (as applied today, at least) such a requirement is constitutional.

• Under *Roe*, requiring that information be provided by a doctor, rather than by nonphysician counselors, is unconstitutional, *Akron I*. Under the "undue burden" regime (as applied today, at least) it is not. . . . Under *Roe*, requiring a 24-hour waiting period between the time the woman gives her informed consent and the time of the abortion is unconstitutional, *Akron I*. Under the "undue burden" regime (as applied today, at least) it is not.

• Under *Roe,* requiring detailed reports that include demographic data about each woman who seeks an abortion and various information about each abortion is unconstitutional, *Thornburgh.* Under the "undue burden" regime (as applied today, at least) it generally is not.

Roe fanned into life an issue that has inflamed our national politics in general, and has obscured with its smoke the selection of Justices to this Court in particular, ever since. And by keeping us in the abortion-umpiring business, it is the perpetuation of that disruption, rather than of any pax Roeana, that the Court's new majority decrees.

12

EQUAL PROTECTION OF THE LAWS

O NLY TWICE IN THE LAST HALF-CENTURY has the Supreme Court extended protection for economic interests under the Fourteenth Amendment's equal protection clause (see Vol. 2. Ch. 12). In 1989, the Rehnquist Court unanimously struck down a county's practice of assessing taxes on the basis of recent purchase prices, thereby giving long-term landowners much lower taxes. In that case, *Allegheny Pittsburgh Coal Co. v. County Commission*, 488 U.S. 336 (1989), Chief Justice Rehnquist found that the county's practice ran afoul of the Fourteenth Amendment's mandate for "rough equality in tax treatment of similarly situated property owners."

In 1992, along with several cases raising substantive economic interests under the due process clause (see page 91), the Rehnquist Court reviewed an equal protection challenge to California's constitutional amendment—otherwise known as Proposition 13—that limits property tax rates to 1 percent of assessed value. Proposition 13 was passed in 1978 and ignited a nationwide antitax movement. Under Proposition 13, properties bought before 1978 had their values rolled back to 1975 assessments and properties purchased after the adoption of the amendment were assessed on the basis of their selling price. The immediate impact was a halt to rapidly rising tax increases, but the long-term consequence has been a growing disparity in the taxes paid by long-term owners and recent purchasers. As a result, some homeowners pay as much as 17 times more taxes than their neighbors who bought homes before 1978. The owner of a $3.8 million, 8,000-square-foot mansion in

Beverly Hills, who owned the property before 1978, for example, pays about $3,200 in annual taxes, whereas a purchaser of that mansion now would pay about $38,000. At the same time, a recent buyer of a 1,000-square-foot bungalow that cost $370,000 pays $3,700 in taxes, or a little more than the owner of the mansion bought before 1978.

The constitutional attack on Proposition 13 in *Nordlinger v. Hahn*, 112 S.Ct. 2326 (1992), however, differed in important ways from that in *Allegheny Pittsburgh Coal Co.* In the latter case, the tax assessments were not "rationally related" to state laws and, moreover, were not mandated by a state constitutional amendment.

Writing for the Court in *Nordlinger*, Justice Blackmun upheld California's Proposition 13 and distinguished *Allegheny Pittsburgh.* In doing so, Blackmun observed that

[t]he appropriate standard of review is whether the difference in treatment between newer and older owners rationally furthers a legitimate state interest. In general, the Equal Protection Clause is satisfied so long as there is a plausible policy reason for the classification, the legislative facts on which the classification is apparently based rationally may have been considered to be true by the governmental decisionmaker, and the relationship of the classification to its goal is not so attenuated as to render the distinction arbitrary or irrational. This standard is especially deferential in the context of classifications made by complex tax laws. "In structuring internal taxation schemes the States have large leeway in making classifications and drawing lines which in their judgment produce reasonable systems of taxation." *Williams v. Vermont*, 472 U.S. 14 (1985). . . .

We have no difficulty in ascertaining at least two rational or reasonable considerations of difference or policy that justify denying petitioner the benefits of her neighbors' lower assessments. First, the State has a legitimate interest in local neighborhood preservation, continuity, and stability. *Euclid v. Ambler Realty Co.*, 272 U.S. 365 (1926). The State therefore legitimately can decide to structure its tax system to discourage rapid turnover in ownership of homes and businesses, for example, in order to inhibit displacement of lower income families by the forces of gentrification or of established, "mom-and-pop" businesses by newer chain operations. By permitting older owners to pay progressively less in taxes than new owners of comparable property, the Article XIIIA assessment scheme rationally furthers this interest.

Second, the State legitimately can conclude that a new owner at the time of acquiring his property does not have the same reliance interest warranting protection against higher taxes as does an existing owner.

Although agreeing with the majority's decision, in a concurring opinion Justice Thomas sided with dissenting Justice Stevens in criticizing the Court's attempt to distinguish *Allegheny Pittsburgh.* Thomas, though, would have overturned that prior decision because, as he put it, "*Allegheny Pittsburgh* represents a 'needlessly intrusive judicial infringement on the State's legislative powers,' " quoting *New Orleans v. Dukes*, 427 U.S. 297 (1976).

Only dissenting Justice Stevens deemed *Allegheny Pittsburgh* controlling and would have struck down California's Proposition 13 for arbitrarily discriminating against taxpayers. In his words:

In my opinion, it is irrational to treat similarly situated persons differently on the basis of the date they joined the class of property owners. Until today, I would have thought this proposition far from controversial. In *Zobel v. Williams,* 457 U.S. 55 (1982), we ruled that Alaska's program of distributing cash dividends on the basis of the recipient's years of residency in the State violated the Equal Protection Clause. . . .

Similarly, the Court invalidated on equal protection grounds New Mexico's policy of providing a permanent tax exemption for Vietnam veterans who had been state residents before May 8, 1976, but not to more recent arrivals. *Hooper v. Bernalillo County Assessor,* 472 U.S. 612 (1985). The Court expressly rejected the State's claim that it had a legitimate interest in providing special rewards to veterans who lived in the State before 1976 and concluded that "neither the Equal Protection Clause, nor this Court's precedents, permit the State to prefer established resident veterans over newcomers in the retroactive apportionment of an economic benefit."

As these decisions demonstrate, the selective provision of benefits based on the timing of one's membership in a class (whether that class be the class of residents or the class of property owners) is rarely a "legitimate state interest." Similarly situated neighbors have an equal right to share in the benefits of local government. It would obviously be unconstitutional to provide one with more or better fire or police protection than the other; it is just as plainly unconstitutional to require one to pay five times as much in property taxes as the other for the same government services. In my opinion, the severe inequalities created by Proposition 13 are arbitrary and unreasonable and do not rationally further a legitimate state interest.

In *Federal Communications Commission v. Beach Communications,* 113 S.Ct. 2096 (1993), the Rehnquist Court rejected an equal protection challenge to the Cable Communications Policy Act of 1984. In that legislation on cable communications, Congress drew a distinction between facilities that serve separately owned and managed buildings and those that serve one or more buildings under common ownership or management. Cable facilities in the latter category are exempt from regulation as long as they provide services without using public rights-of-way. The question presented was whether that distinction had a rational basis for the purposes of equal protection analysis. In upholding the act and writing for the Court, Justice Thomas reiterated that

[o]n rational-basis review, a classification in a statute such as the Cable Act comes to us bearing a strong presumption of validity, and those attacking the rationality of the legislative classification have the burden "to negative every conceivable basis which might support it." Moreover, because we never require a legislature to articulate its reasons for enacting a statute, it is entirely irrelevant for constitutional purposes whether the conceived reason for the challenged distinction actually motivated the legislature. . . . In other words, a legislative choice is not subject to courtroom fact-finding and may be used on rational speculation unsupported by evidence or empirical data.

Finally, the Rehnquist Court again reaffirmed an unwillingness to expand heightened scrutiny beyond the "rational basis" test in *Heller v. Doe*, 113 S.Ct. 2637 (1993) (see below). That case, however, also sharply split the justices over the application of the "rational basis" test. Writing for a bare majority, Justice Kennedy rejected an equal protection and due process challenge to Kentucky's laws distinguishing between mentally retarded and mentally ill individuals and providing different procedures for their involuntary commitment. In a dissent joined by Justices Blackmun, Stevens, and in part by O'Connor, Justice Souter in turn rejected the majority's analysis. Two brief, one-paragraph dissenting opinions were also filed by Justices Blackmun and O'Connor. On the one hand, Justice Blackum reaffirmed his view that cases involving mental retardation require heightened judicial scrutiny; he is now the only member on the Court to take that position. Justice O'Connor rejected that view, as did Justices Kennedy and Souter in their opinions. While O'Connor agreed with the three other dissenters that there was no rational basis for differential standards of proof in commitment proceedings for mentally ill and retarded persons, she sided with the majority on allowing guardians and family members to participate in commitment proceedings for retarded, but not for mentally ill, persons.

Heller v. Doe

113 S.Ct. 2637 (1993)

A class of involuntarily committed retarded persons challenged the constitutionality of Kentucky's statutes governing the civil commitment of retarded and mentally ill persons. Kentucky distinguishes and provides disparate treatment for those classes of persons in two important ways. At commitment proceedings for the retarded, the burden of proof is whether there is "clear and convincing evidence" that the person poses a danger to himself or others, whereas the "beyond a reasonable doubt" standard applies in proceedings for mentally ill persons. In addition, guardians and family members may participate in proceedings involving retarded, but not mentally ill, persons. Kentucky defended those distinctions on the ground that mental retardation, which is a developmental disability usually well documented in childhood, is easier to diagnose than mental illness, which may appear suddenly in adulthood. A higher burden of proof for the commitment of the latter thus ostensibly offsets the risk of erroneous determinations.

The Court's decision was five to four and six to three; the majority's opinion was announced by Justice Kennedy. Dissenting opinions were delivered by Justice Souter, who was joined by Justice Stevens and in part by Justice O'Connor, and by Justice Blackmun. In a separate opinion Justice O'Connor in part dissented and in part concurred.

Justice KENNEDY delivers the opinion of the Court.

We many times have said, and but weeks ago repeated, that rational-basis review in equal protection analysis "is not a license for courts to judge the wisdom, fairness, or logic of legislative choices." *FCC v. Beach Communications, Inc.,* [113 S.Ct. 2096] (1993). For these reasons, a classification neither involving fundamental rights nor proceeding along suspect lines is accorded a strong presumption of validity. Further, a legislature that creates these categories need not "actually articulate at any time the purpose or rationale supporting its classification." A State, moreover, has no obligation to produce evidence to sustain the rationality of a statutory classification. "[A] legislative choice is not subject to courtroom factfinding and may be based on rational speculation unsupported by evidence or empirical data." *Beach Communications.* A statute is presumed constitutional, and "the burden is on the one attacking the legislative arrangement to negate every conceivable basis which might support it," *Lehnhausen v. Lake Shore Auto Parts Co.,* 410 U.S. 356 (1973), whether or not the basis has a foundation in the record. Finally, courts are compelled under rational-basis review to accept a legislature's generalizations even when there is an imperfect fit between means and ends. A classification does not fail rational-basis review because it " 'is not made with mathematical nicety or because in practice it results in some inequality.' " *Dandridge v. Williams,* [397 U.S. 471 (1970)]. . . .

A statutory classification fails rational-basis review only when it " 'rests on grounds wholly irrelevant to the achievement of the State's objective.' " *Holt Civic Club v. Tuscaloosa,* 439 U.S. 60 (1978). Because ease of diagnosis [of mental retardation] is relevant . . . it is not "wholly irrelevant" to the achievement of Kentucky's objective, and thus the statutory difference in the applicable burden of proof survives rational-basis review. In any event, it is plausible for Kentucky to have found that, for purposes of determining the acceptable risk of error, diagnosis and dangerousness are the most critical factors in the commitment decision, so the appropriate burden of proof should be tied to them. There is a further, more far-reaching rationale justifying the different burdens of proof: The prevailing methods of treatment for the mentally retarded, as a general rule, are much less invasive than are those given the mentally ill. The mentally ill are subjected to medical and psychiatric treatment which may involve intrusive inquiries into the patient's innermost thoughts, and use of psychotropic drugs. By contrast, the mentally retarded in general are not subjected to these medical treatments. Rather, " '. . . mental retardation is . . . a learning disability and training impairment rather than an illness,' " *Youngblood v. Romeo,* 457 U.S. 307 (1982).

It is true that the loss of liberty following commitment for mental illness and mental retardation may be similar in many respects; but the different treatment to which a committed individual is subjected provides a rational basis for Kentucky to decide that a greater burden of proof is needed before a person may be committed for mental illness. . . .

There is a rational basis also for the other distinction challenged by respondents: that Kentucky allows close relatives and guardians to participate as parties in proceedings to commit the mentally retarded but not the mentally ill. By definition, mental retardation has its onset during a person's developmental period. . . . Based on these facts, Kentucky may have concluded that close relatives and guardians, both of whom likely have intimate knowledge of a mentally retarded person's abilities and experiences, have valuable insights which should be considered during the involuntary commitment process.

Mental illness, by contrast, may arise or manifest itself with suddenness only after minority, when the afflicted person's immediate family members have no knowledge of the medical condition and have long ceased to provide care and support. Further, determining the proper course of treatment may be far less dependent upon observations made in a household setting. Indeed, we have noted the severe difficulties inherent in psychiatric diagnosis conducted by experts in the field. In addition, adults previously of sound mental health who are diagnosed as mentally ill may have a need for privacy that justifies the State in confining a commitment proceeding to the smallest group compatible with due process. Based on these facts, Kentucky may have concluded that participation as parties by relatives and guardians of the mentally ill would not in most cases have been of sufficient help to the trier of fact to justify the additional burden and complications of granting party status. . . . As long as Kentucky "rationally advances a reasonable and identifiable governmental objective, we must disregard" the existence of alternative methods of furthering the objective "that we, as individuals, perhaps would have preferred."

Justice SOUTER, with whom Justice BLACKMUN and Justice STEVENS join, and with whom Justice O'CONNOR joins in part, dissenting.

To begin with, the Court declines to address Doe's argument that we should employ strict or heightened scrutiny in assessing the disparity of treatment challenged here. While I may disagree with the Court's basis for its conclusion that this argument is not "properly presented," I too would decline to address the contention that strict or heightened scrutiny applies. I conclude that the distinctions wrought by the Kentucky scheme cannot survive even that rational-basis scrutiny, requiring a rational relationship between the disparity of treatment and some legitimate governmental purpose, which we have previously applied to a classification on the basis of mental disability, see *Cleburne v. Cleburne Living Center, Inc.*, 473 U.S. 432 (1985) [in Vol. 2, Ch. 12], and therefore I need not reach the question of whether scrutiny more searching than *Cleburne*'s should be applied. *Cleburne* was the most recent instance in which we addressed a classification on the basis of mental disability, as we did by enquiring into record support for the State's proffered justifications, and examining the distinction in treatment in light of the purposes put forward to support it. While the Court cites *Cleburne* once, and does not purport to overrule it, neither does the Court apply it, and at the end of the day *Cleburne*'s status is left uncertain. I would follow *Cleburne* here. . . .

Without plausible justification, Kentucky is being allowed to draw a distinction that is difficult to see as resting on anything other than the stereotypical assumption that the retarded are "perpetual children," an assumption that has historically been taken to justify the disrespect and "grotesque mistreatment" to which the retarded have been subjected. As we said in *Cleburne*, the mentally retarded are not "all cut from the same pattern . . . they range from those whose disability is not immediately evident to those who must be constantly cared for." In recent times, at least when imposing the responsibilities of citizenship, our jurisprudence has seemed to reject the analogy between mentally retarded adults and nondisabled children. See, e.g., *Penry v. Lynaugh*, 492 U.S. 302 (1989) (controlling opinion of O'CONNOR, J.) (not "all mentally retarded people . . . —by virtue of their mental retardation alone, and apart from any individualized consideration of their personal responsibility—inevitably lack the cognitive, volitional, and moral capacity to act with the degree of culpability associated with the death penalty"). When the State of Kentucky sets up its respective schemes for institutionalization on the basis of mental illness and mental retardation, it too is obliged to reject that analogy, and to rest any difference in standards for involuntary commitment as between the ill and the retarded on some plausible reason.

Justice BLACKMUN dissented in a separate opinion, expressing his view that the Court should apply a heightened scrutiny test in cases involving the disparate treatment of mentally retarded persons.

Justice O'CONNOR concurred and dissented in part, agreeing with Justice SOUTER that Kentucky's differential standard of proof was irrational, but joining the majority in upholding the State's allowing guardians and immediate family members to participate as parties in commitment proceedings.

A. RACIAL DISCRIMINATION AND STATE ACTION

By a seven-to-two vote in *Powers v. Ohio*, 111 S.Ct. 1364 (1991), the Court held that criminal defendants may claim a violation of the Fourteenth Amendment's equal protection when objecting to a prosecutor's race-based exclusion of jurors through the use of peremptory challenges during jury selection (see page 206).

A majority of the Rehnquist Court went even further in *Edmonson v. Leesville Concrete Co.*, 111 S.Ct. 2077 (1991), when holding that parties in civil cases may not use peremptory challenges to exclude blacks from serving on juries. Writing for a six-member majority, Justice Kennedy found the "state action" to preclude such racial discrimination in civil cases under the Fourteenth Amendment and held that the Fifth Amendment's due process clause incorporated that holding and made it applicable to civil cases filed in federal courts as well. Kennedy reasoned that

> [w]ith a few exceptions, such as the provisions of the Thirteenth Amendment, constitutional guarantees of individual liberty and equal protection do not apply to the actions of private entities. This fundamental limitation on the scope of constitutional guarantees "preserves an area of individual freedom by limiting the reach of federal law" and "avoids imposing on the State, its agencies or officials, responsibility for conduct for which they cannot fairly be blamed." *Lugar v. Edmondson Oil Co.*, 457 U.S. 922 (1982). . . . We begin our discussion within the framework for state action analysis set forth in *Lugar*. There we considered the state action question in the context of a due process challenge to a State's procedure allowing private parties to obtain prejudgment attachments. We asked first whether the claimed constitutional deprivation resulted from the exercise of a right or privilege having its source in state authority; and second, whether the private party charged with the deprivation could be described in all fairness as a state actor.

> There can be no question that the first part of the *Lugar* inquiry is satisfied here. By their very nature, peremptory challenges have no significance outside a court of law. . . .

> Given that the statutory authorization for the challenges exercised in this case is clear, the remainder of our state action analysis centers around the second part of the *Lugar* test, whether a private litigant in all fairness must be deemed a government actor in the use of peremptory challenges. . . .

> In the ordinary context of civil litigation in which the government is not a party, an adversarial relation does not exist between the government and a private litigant. In the jury-selection process, the government and private litigants work for the same end. . . . [H]ere a private entity becomes a government actor for the limited purpose of using peremptories during jury selection. The selection of jurors represents a unique governmental function delegated to private litigants by the government and attributable to the government for purposes of invoking constitutional protections against discrimination by reason of race.

By contrast, Justice O'Connor, with whom Chief Justice Rehnquist and Justice Scalia joined, sharply disagreed with the Court's application of the state action doctrine to peremptory challenges in civil cases. As Justice O'Connor put it,

Not everything that happens in a courtroom is state action. A trial, particularly a civil trial, is by design largely a stage on which private parties may act; it is a forum through which they can resolve their disputes in a peaceful and ordered manner. The government erects the platform; it does not thereby become responsible for all that occurs upon it. As much as we would like to eliminate completely from the courtroom the specter of racial discrimination, the Constitution does not sweep that broadly.

While joining O'Connor's dissent, Justice Scalia wrote a separate dissent, lamenting what he viewed as the "consequences" of the majority's decision.

Subsequently, in *Georgia v. McCollum,* 112 S. Ct. 2348 (1992) (see page 206), the Court extended its ruling in *Edmondson* to bar the use of peremptory challenges in criminal cases to exclude potential jurors on the basis of their race. Once again, Justices O'Connor and Scalia dissented, while Chief Justice Rehnquist and Justice Thomas concurred even though they disagreed with the Court's ruling here and in *Edmondson.*

B. RACIAL DISCRIMINATION IN EDUCATION

Thirty-nine years after the watershed school desegregation ruling in *Brown v. Board of Education,* 347 U.S. 483 (1954) (see Vol. 2, Ch. 12), there remain about 500 school desegregation cases in lower federal courts around the country. Most involve either challenges by local school boards to court-ordered remedial plans for achieving and maintaining integrated public schools or challenges by blacks to changes in school board policies that they claim will perpetuate the vestiges of segregation. At issue are complex questions involving when and how school systems become fully integrated, or "unitary," and free from the vestiges of segregation. Lower courts, moreover, have been divided over how much proof school boards must show in demonstrating that present *de facto* racial isolation in school districts is unrelated to past *de jure* segregation, as well as what other conditions constitute vestiges of prior segregation. In addition, lower courts have been split on when judicial supervision of desegregation plans should end, and whether formally dual school systems that have attained unitary status may end desegregation policies, such as busing schoolchildren.

Despite conflicts and confusion in the lower federal courts over when desegregation remedies and judicial supervision should end, for more than a decade the Court provided little guidance. Indeed, the Court declined to review a major case dealing with the fundamentals of school desegregation since the late 1970s. But the Rehnquist Court signaled a willingness to tackle the vexing issues of judicial supervision of school districts' implementation of and compliance with *Brown*'s mandate in the 1990s. In the 1989 term, a bare majority of the Court upheld the authority of federal judges to order a school board to raise taxes in order to pay for a desegregation plan. Chief Justice Rehnquist and Justices O'Connor and Scalia, however, joined Justice Kennedy's sharp dissenting opinion in that case, *Missouri v. Jenkins,* 110 S.Ct. 1651 (1990) (see Vol. 2, Ch. 12).

The Rehnquist Court also carried over in its 1990 docket several school desegregation cases, including one appeal by the school board in Topeka, Kansas, which is an offspring of the protracted litigation stemming from the original 1954 ruling in *Brown.* Among the desegregation cases on its docket, the Court heard oral arguments in and decided only one case, *Board of Education of Oklahoma City Public Schools v. Dowell,* 111 S.Ct. 630 (1991). Without Justice Souter's participation, a bare majority held that school districts that were previously required by law to eliminate racial segregation could end the forced busing of students in favor of neighborhood schools, even though that entailed a return to a system of schools attended overwhelmingly by either black or white students. Writing for the majority, Chief Justice Rehnquist held that federal judges should end supervision of previously segregated public schools if court-ordered desegregation plans had eliminated "the vestiges of past discrimination."

In *Dowell,* Rehnquist's majority insisted that the Fourteenth Amendment does not apply to racially isolated schools that are no longer a product of state-imposed segregation. According to Rehnquist, school districts that once intentionally segregated may achieve unitary status, despite the fact that some schools remain overwhelming black or white, if (1) they have complied with judicial desegregation orders over a reasonable period of time, (2) they are not likely to return to their former ways, and (3) they have to the extent practicable eliminated "vestiges" of prior discrimination in the operation of their schools. In the chief justice's words:

[School desegregation] decrees . . . are not intended to operate in perpetuity. Local control over the education of children allows citizens to participate in decisionmaking, and allows innovation so that school programs can fit local needs. . . . Dissolving a desegregation decree after the local authorities have operated in compliance with it for a reasonable period of time properly recognizes that "necessary concern for the important values of local control of public school systems dictates that a federal court's regulatory control of such systems not extend beyond the time required to remedy the effects of past intentional discrimination." . . .

In considering whether the vestiges of *de jure* segregation had been eliminated as far as practicable, the District Court should look not only at student assignments, but "to every facet of school operations—faculty, staff, transportation, extracurricular activities and facilities." *Green.*

Dissenting Justice Marshall, joined by Justices Blackmun and Stevens, however, took a widely different view of *Brown*'s legacy and the "vestiges" of segregation in public schools. Notably, he would have held that the Oklahoma city school district had not achieved integration and that the persistence of racially identifiable schools necessarily established that the original constitutional violation had not been remedied. In his impassioned dissent, Justice Marshall observed that

[b]y focusing heavily on present and future compliance with the Equal Protection Clause, the majority's standard ignores how the stigmatic harm identified in *Brown I* can persist even after the State ceases actively to enforce segregation. It was not enough in *Green*, for example, for the school district to withdraw its own enforcement of segregation, leaving it up to individual children and their families to "choose" which school to attend. For it was clear under the circumstances that these choices would be shaped by and perpetuate the state-created message of racial inferiority associated with the school district's historical involvement in segregation. In sum, our school-desegregation jurisprudence establishes that the *effects* of past discrimination remain chargeable to the school district regardless of its lack of continued enforcement of segregation, and the remedial decree is required until those effects have been finally eliminated. . . . In a district with a history of state-sponsored school segregation, racial separation, in my view, *remains* inherently unequal.

Dowell, nonetheless, provided little guidance for lower courts and the hundreds of school districts seeking to regain complete autonomy and to escape judicial supervision. Both the majority and the dissenters reaffirmed the holding in *Green v. New Kent County School Board*, 391 U.S. 430 (1968), that lower courts should examine "every facet of school operations," including student assignments, faculty, staff, transportation, extracurricular activities, and facilities. But the Court left unclear the most important issues: whether and how school districts must show that presently racially isolated schools are not related to past intentional discrimination, and what other kinds of conditions may be considered "vestiges" of past *de jure* segregation.

Barely one month after *Dowell* the Rehnquist Court agreed to further address the continuing controversy over judicial supervision of remedial desegregation plans in agreeing to decide during its 1991 term *Freeman v. Pitts*, 112 S.Ct. 1430 (1992) (see page 265). Because Justice Thomas had not yet been confirmed by the time the Court heard oral arguments, he did not participate in the Court's decision. Although unanimous in their decision, the justices were not of one mind on how quickly or on what basis lower courts should halt their desegregation efforts. Justice Kennedy's opinion for the Court, which only Chief Justice Rehnquist and Justices White, Scalia, and Souter joined, represented a rough compromise on the closing of the *Brown* era. In reversing the appellate court's decision in *Freeman v. Pitts*, Kennedy held that lower courts may withdraw from supervising discrete categories of school operations, as identified in *Green*, once school districts show compliance with desegregation orders. Lower courts, moreover, need not wait for a period of years before doing so or await desegregation in all areas of a school system before they disengage. Kennedy's opinion, however, did not go far enough for Justice Scalia, who in a concurrence urged an immediate end to all judicial supervision of schools that no longer intentionally discriminate. At the same time, Kennedy's opinion appeared to go too far for Justices Blackmun, Stevens, O'Connor, and Souter. They countered in separate concurrences that lower courts should undertake a probing analysis before abandoning judicial supervision.

Dowell and *Freeman* thus chart a new course, not a dramatic reversal, pointing to a new period of litigation—a period not unlike that immediately after *Brown* but in which lower courts gradually move to relinquish, rather than assert, control over public schools.

Along with *Freeman v. Pitts*, the Court also decided *United States v. Fordice*, 112 S.Ct. 2727 (1992) (see page 269). Whereas *Dowell* and *Freeman* involved efforts to achieve integrated primary and secondary schools, *Fordice* provided the Court with an opportunity to revisit, after more than forty years, whether it is enough for college and universities to simply end past *de jure* racially discriminatory admissions policies, or whether they must do more to achieve racially integrated colleges and universities. Here, Justice White found that Mississippi's admission policies perpetuated the existence of racially isolated colleges and universities. In a separate concurring opinion, though, Justice Thomas expressed concern and support for the maintenance of historically all-black colleges. By contrast, in an opinion concurring in part and dissenting in part, Justice Scalia rejected the majority's reasoning and standards for lower courts reviewing desegregation challenges to institutions of higher education. Although symbolic in reaffirming the principles in *Brown v. Board of Education*, *Fordice*'s impact is considerably less than that of *Freeman*, because it provides guidance only for courts reviewing challenges to institutions of higher education in the fifteen states that once had *de jure* segregated schools, whereas courts supervising integration efforts in hundreds of cases involving primary and secondary schools will look to *Freeman* for guidance.

Freeman v. Pitts

112 S.Ct. 1430 (1992)

Despite the Supreme Court's watershed in *Brown v. Board of Education*, 347 U.S. 483 (1954), and its mandate for desegregation "with all deliberate speed," *Brown v. Board of Education*, 349 U.S. 294 (1955) (see Vol. 2, Ch. 12), the DeKalb County, Georgia, public school system (DCSS) made no effort to desegregate for more than a decade. In 1966–1967 the school board finally adopted a "freedom of choice" transfer plan that permitted blacks to go to formerly *de jure* white schools, but that had no impact on desegregating all-black schools. Then in *Green v. New Kent County School Board*, 391 U.S. 430 (1968), the Court struck down a similar "freedom of choice" plan in Virginia. The Court also directed lower courts to examine "every facet of school operations"—including student assignments, faculty, staff, transportation, extracurricular activities, and facilities—in achieving school desegregation.

Within two months of *Green*, Willie Pitts and other black parents and schoolchildren filed a class action against the DCSS to force it to abandon its freedom of choice plan. One year later a federal district court issued a consent order abolishing the freedom of choice plan, closing all formerly *de jure* black schools, and reassigning students to the remaining neighborhood schools. The court retained jurisdiction and continued to supervise the DCSS for more than a decade.

In 1986 Robert Freeman and other members of the DCSS filed a motion to lay the original litigation to rest and to obtain a declaration that "unitary status" according to factors identified in *Green* had been achieved. The district court concluded that the DCSS had achieved unitary status with respect to student assignments, transportation, facilities, and the extracurricular activities of the schools and required no further remedial efforts in these areas. But the court found continued "vestiges" of segregation in teacher and principal assignments, resource allocations, and the quality of education in different schools in the county. And the DCSS was ordered to continue to address these problems.

In appealing the district court's decisions, Pitts and other black parents countered that continuing racial imbalances in the DCSS were a vestige of past discrimination. In the more than thirty years since *Brown*, DeKalb County, along with the rest of the country, had changed. *De jure* segregation had ended but schools remained segregated. As the DeKalb County school district grew in population from less than 70,000 to over 450,000, the percentage of black students increased from a little more than 5 percent to 47 percent. Demographic changes and the migration of blacks and whites into suburbs resulted in racially identifiable schools. In 1986–1987, as Pitts's attorneys pointed out, 50 percent of the black students attended schools that were over 90 percent black, while almost 30 percent of the white students went to schools enrolling 90 percent whites. The persistence of racially identifiable schools, Pitts's lawyers argued, required continued efforts to integrate and judicial supervision of the DCSS's operations.

The Court of Appeals for the Eleventh Circuit reversed the district court, rejecting its "incremental" approach to determining unitary status and to ending its desegregation orders. According to the appellate court, the district court erred in considering *Green*'s factors as separate and independent categories. Achieving unitary status, it held, required the DCSS to maintain racial equality for at least three years in all six categories. The appellate court also ordered the DCSS to take radical measures to achieve integration, such as pairing and clustering schools, busing, and drastic gerrymandering of school zones. That decision was promptly appealed by Freeman and the DCSS to the Supreme Court, which granted review.

The Court's decision was unanimous; Justice Kennedy announced the opinion. Justices Scalia and Souter each concurred, as did Justice Blackmun, who was joined by Justices Stevens and O'Connor.

JUSTICE KENNEDY delivers the opinion of the Court.

. . .

Today, we make explicit the rationale that was central in [*Pasadena City Board of Education v.*] *Spangler* [427 U.S. 424 (1976)]. A federal court in a school desegregation case has the discretion to order an incremental or partial withdrawal of its supervision and control. This discretion derives both from the constitutional authority which justified its intervention in the first instance and its ultimate objectives in formulating the decree. The authority of the court is invoked at the outset to remedy particular constitutional violations. In construing the remedial authority of the district courts, we have been guided by the principles that "judicial powers may be exercised only on the basis of a constitutional violation," and that "the nature of the violation determines the scope of the remedy." *Swann* [*v. Charlotte-Mecklenburg Board of Education*, 402 U.S. 1 (1971)]. . . .

We hold that, in the course of supervising desegregation plans, federal courts have the authority to relinquish supervision and control of school districts in incremental stages, before full compliance has been achieved in every area of school operations. While retaining jurisdiction over the case, the court may determine that it will not order further remedies in areas where the school district is in compliance with the decree. That is to say, upon a finding that a school system subject to a court-supervised desegregation plan is in compliance in some but not all areas, the court in appropriate cases may return control to the school system in those areas where compliance has been achieved, limiting further judicial supervision to operations that are not yet in full compliance with the court decree. In particular, the district court may determine that it will not order further remedies in the area of student assignments where racial imbalance is not traceable, in a proximate way, to constitutional violations. . . .

The Court of Appeals' rejection of the District Court's order rests on related premises: first, that given noncompliance in some discrete categories, there can be no partial withdrawal of judicial control; and second, until there is full compliance, heroic measures must be taken to ensure racial balance in student assignments systemwide. Under our analysis and our precedents, neither premise is correct. . . .

That there was racial imbalance in student attendance zones was not tantamount to a showing that the school district was in noncompliance with the decree or with its duties under the law. Racial balance is not to be achieved for its own sake. It is to be pursued when racial imbalance has been caused by a constitutional violation. Once the racial imbalance due to the *de jure* violation has been remedied, the school district is under no duty to remedy imbalance that is caused by demographic factors. . . .

The findings of the District Court that the population changes which occurred in DeKalb County were not caused by the policies of the school district, but rather by independent factors, are consistent with the mobility that is a distinct characteristic of our society. . . . The District Court in this case heard evidence tending to show that racially stable neighborhoods are not likely to emerge because whites prefer a racial mix of 80% white and 20% black, while blacks prefer a 50%–50% mix.

Where resegregation is a product not of state action but of private choices, it does not have constitutional implications. It is beyond the authority and beyond the practical ability of the federal courts to try to counteract these kinds of continuous and massive demographic shifts. To attempt such results would require ongoing and never-ending supervision by the courts of school districts simply because they were once *de jure* segregated. Residential housing choices, and their attendant effects on the racial composition of schools, present an ever-changing pattern, one difficult to address through judicial remedies. . . .

To say, as did the Court of Appeals, that a school district must meet all six *Green* factors before the trial court can declare the system unitary and relinquish its control over school attendance zones, and to hold further that racial balancing by all necessary means is required in the interim, is simply to vindicate a legal phrase. The law is not so formalistic. A proper rule must be based on the necessity to find a feasible remedy that insures systemwide compliance with the court decree and that is directed to curing the effects of the specific violation. . . .

The requirement that the school district show its good faith commitment to the entirety of a desegregation plan so that parents, students and the public have assurance against further injuries or stigma also should be a subject for more specific findings. We stated in *Dowell* that the good faith compliance of the district with the court order over a reasonable period of time is a factor to be considered in deciding whether or not jurisdiction could be relinquished. . . .

The judgment is reversed and the case is remanded to the Court of Appeals.

JUSTICE SCALIA concurring.

At some time, we must acknowledge that it has become absurd to assume, without any further proof, that violations of the Constitution dating from the days when Lyndon Johnson was President, or earlier, continue to have an appreciable effect upon current operation of schools. We are close to that time. While we must continue to prohibit, without qualification, all racial discrimination in the operation of public schools, and to afford remedies that eliminate not only the discrimination but its identified consequences, we should consider laying aside the extraordinary, and increasingly counterfactual, presumption of *Green*. We must soon revert to the ordinary principles of our law, of our democratic heritage, and of our educational tradition: that plaintiffs alleging Equal Protection violations must prove intent and causation and not merely the existence of racial disparity; that public schooling, even in the South, should be controlled by locally elected authorities acting in conjunction with parents; and that it is "desirable" to permit pupils to attend "schools nearest their homes," *Swann*.

JUSTICE SOUTER concurred in a separate opinion.

JUSTICE BLACKMUN, with whom JUSTICE STEVENS and JUSTICE O'CONNOR join, concurring.

. . .

Whether a district court must maintain active supervision over student assignment, and order new remedial actions depends on two factors. As the Court discusses, the district court must order changes in student assignment if it "is necessary or practicable to achieve compliance in other facets of the school system." The district court also must order affirmative action in school attendance if the school district's conduct was a "contributing cause" of the racially identifiable schools. . . .

United States v. Fordice
112 S.Ct. 2727 (1992)

Mississippi's public university system began in 1848 with the establishment of the University of Mississippi, enrolling exclusively whites. In succeeding decades, the state erected additional single-race educational facilities. Two more black institutions were added in 1940 and 1950. Despite the Court's watershed rulings in *Brown I* and *Brown II* (see Vol. 2, Ch. 12), Mississippi's policy of *de jure* segregation continued. The first black student was not admitted to the University of Mississippi until 1962, when under a court order James Meredith was admitted to the University of Mississippi. More than two decades later, in 1985–1986, approximately 99 percent of the state's white college students were enrolled in historically all-white colleges, while 71 percent of the black students attended historically all-black schools.

This case stemmed from a 1975 lawsuit brought by black residents against Mississippi, and later joined by the federal government. They charged that the state perpetuated racially separate institutions of higher education through its admissions policies. When reviewing past desegregation cases, as in *Green v. New Kent County School Board*, 391 U.S. 430 (1968), involving elementary and secondary schools, the Supreme Court had rejected school boards' proposals that "freedom of choice" plans were enough. However, in *Bazemore v. Friday*, 478 U.S. 385 (1986), a bare majority of the Burger Court upheld a freedom of choice plan, when ruling that North Carolina State University had fulfilled its duty to desegregate its 4-H and Homemakers Clubs by simply offering open enrollment, despite the fact that the clubs remain, as a practical matter, racially segregated. Relying on *Bazemore*, a federal district court and the Court of Appeals for the Fifth Circuit held that the more exacting standard, set forth in *Green*, should not apply to institutions of higher education. Instead, the appellate court ruled that the *Bazemore* approach was more appropriate, because college enrollment is voluntary and because students are free to choose which institution they want to attend. The Department of Justice appealed that decision to the Supreme Court of the United States, which granted review.

The Court's decision was eight and one-half to one-half. Justices O'Connor and Thomas each concurred in the opinion, which was announced by Justice White. Justice Scalia delivered a separate opinion in part concurring and in part dissenting.

Justice WHITE delivers the opinion of the Court.

Our decisions establish that a State does not discharge its constitutional obligations until it eradicates policies and practices traceable to its prior *de jure* dual system that continue to foster segregation. Thus we have consistently asked whether existing racial identifiability is attributable to the State, and examined a wide range of factors to determine whether the State has perpetuated its formerly *de jure* segregation in any facet of its institutional system. . . .

We deal first with the current admissions policies of Mississippi's public universities. As the District Court found, the three flagship historically white universities in the system—University of Mississippi, Mississippi State University, and University of Southern Mississippi—enacted policies in 1963 requiring all entrants to achieve a minimum composite score of 15 on the American College Testing Program (ACT). The court described the "discriminatory taint" of this policy, an obvious reference to the fact that, at the time, the average ACT score for white students was

18 and the average score for blacks was 7. The District Court concluded, and the en banc Court of Appeals agreed, that present admissions standards derived from policies enacted in the 1970's to redress the problem of student unpreparedness. Obviously, this mid-passage justification for perpetuating a policy enacted originally to discriminate against black students does not make the present admissions standards any less constitutionally suspect.

The present admission standards are not only traceable to the *de jure* system and were originally adopted for a discriminatory purpose, but they also have present discriminatory effects. Every Mississippi resident under 21 seeking admission to the university system must take the ACT. Any applicant who scores at least 15 qualifies for automatic admission to any of the five historically white institutions except Mississippi University for Women, which requires a score of 18 for automatic admission unless the student has a 3.0 high school grade average. Those scoring less than 15 but at least 13 automatically qualify to enter Jackson State University, Alcorn State University, and Mississippi Valley State University. Without doubt, these requirements restrict the range of choices of entering students as to which institution they may attend in a way that perpetuates segregation. Those scoring 13 or 14, with some exceptions, are excluded from the five historically white universities and if they want a higher education must go to one of the historically black institutions or attend junior college with the hope of transferring to a historically white institution. Proportionately more blacks than whites face this choice: in 1985, 72 percent of Mississippi's white high school seniors achieved an ACT composite score of 15 or better, while less than 30 percent of black high school seniors earned that score. It is not surprising then that Mississippi's universities remain predominantly identifiable by race.

The segregative effect of this automatic entrance standard is especially striking in light of the differences in minimum automatic entrance scores among the regional universities in Mississippi's system. The minimum score for automatic admission to Mississippi University for Women (MUW) is 18; it is 13 for the historically black universities. Yet MUW is assigned the same institutional mission as two other regional universities, Alcorn State and Mississippi Valley—that of providing quality undergraduate education. The effects of the policy fall disproportionately on black students who might wish to attend MUW. . . .

We also find inadequately justified by the courts below or by the record before us the differential admissions requirements between universities with dissimilar programmatic missions. . . . [W]e think the 15 ACT test score for automatic admission to the comprehensive universities, as compared with a score of 13 for the regionals, requires further justification in terms of sound educational policy.

Another constitutionally problematic aspect of the State's use of the ACT test scores is its policy of denying automatic admission if an applicant fails to earn the minimum ACT score specified for the particular institution, without also resorting to the applicant's high school grades as an additional factor in predicting college performance. The United States produced evidence that the American College Testing Program (ACTP), the administering organization of the ACT, discourages use of ACT scores as the sole admissions criterion on the ground that it gives an incomplete "picture" of the student applicant's ability to perform adequately in college. . . . The record also indicated that the disparity between black and white students' high school grade averages was much narrower than the gap between their average ACT scores, thereby suggesting that an admissions formula which included grades would increase the number of black students eligible for automatic admission to all of Mississippi's public universities. . . .

A second aspect of the present system that necessitates further inquiry is the widespread duplication of programs. "Unnecessary" duplication refers, under the District Court's definition, "to those instances where two or more institutions offer the same nonessential or noncore program. Under this definition, all duplication at the bachelor's level of nonbasic liberal arts and sciences course work and all duplication at the master's level and above are considered to be unnecessary." The District Court found that 34.6 percent of the 29 undergraduate programs at historically black institutions are "unnecessarily duplicated" by the historically white universities, and that 90 percent of the graduate programs at the historically black institutions are unnecessarily duplicated at the historically white institutions. . . .

Because the former *de jure* segregated system of public universities in Mississippi impeded the free choice of prospective students, the State in dismantling that system must take the necessary steps to ensure that this choice now is truly free. The full range of policies and practices must be examined with this duty in mind. That an institution is predominantly white or black does not in itself make out a constitutional violation. But surely the State may not leave in place policies rooted in its prior officially segregated system that serve to maintain the racial identifiability of its universities if those policies can practicably be eliminated without eroding sound educational policies. . . .

Because the District Court and the Court of Appeals failed to consider the State's duties in their proper light, the cases must be remanded.

Justice O'CONNOR concurred in a separate opinion.

Justice THOMAS concurring.

. . .

[W]e do not foreclose the possibility that there exists sound "educational justification" for maintaining historically black colleges as such. Despite the shameful history of state-enforced segregation, these institutions have survived and flourished. Indeed, they have expanded as opportunities for blacks to enter historically white institutions have expanded. . . . Although

I agree that a State is not constitutionally required to maintain its historically black institutions as such, I do not understand our opinion to hold
that a State is forbidden from doing so. It would be ironic, to say the least,
if the institutions that sustained blacks during segregation were themselves destroyed in an effort to combat its vestiges.

Justice SCALIA concurring in the judgment in part and dissenting in part.

I reject . . . the effectively unsustainable burden the Court imposes on
Mississippi, and all States that formerly operated segregated universities,
to demonstrate compliance with *Brown I.* That requirement, which
resembles what we prescribed for primary and secondary schools in *Green
v. New Kent County School Board,* 391 U.S. 430 (1968), has no proper
application in the context of higher education, provides no genuine
guidance to States and lower courts, and is as likely to subvert as to
promote the interests of those citizens on whose behalf the present suit
was brought. . . .

In *Bazemore v. Friday,* we addressed a dispute parallel in all relevant
respects to this one. At issue there was state financing of 4-H and Home-
maker youth clubs by the North Carolina Agricultural Extension Service,
a division of North Carolina State University. . . . We confined *Green* to
primary and secondary public schools, where "schoolchildren must go to
school" and where "school boards customarily have the power to create
school attendance areas and otherwise designate the school that particular students may attend." . . .

Bazemore's standard for dismantling a dual system ought to control
here: discontinuation of discriminatory practices and adoption of a neutral admissions policy. To use *Green* nomenclature, modern racial imbalance remains a "vestige" of past segregative practices in Mississippi's
universities, in that the previously mandated racial identification contin-
ues to affect where students choose to enroll—just as it surely affected
which clubs students chose to join in *Bazemore.* We tolerated this vestigial
effect in *Bazemore,* squarely rejecting the view that the State was obliged
to correct "the racial segregation resulting from [its prior] practices."
And we declined to require the State, as the Court has today, to prove
that no holdover practices of the *de jure* system, e.g., program offerings in
the different clubs, played a role in the students' decisions of which clubs
to join. If that analysis was correct six years ago in *Bazemore,* and I think
it was, it must govern here as well. . . .

C. AFFIRMATIVE ACTION AND REVERSE
DISCRIMINATION

In an important 1993 ruling on standing, the Rehnquist Court made
it easier to challenge affirmative action and set aside programs for

women and blacks in *Northeastern Florida Chapter of the Associated General Contractors of America v. City of Jacksonville, Florida*, 113 S.Ct. 2297 (1993) (see page 18).

D. NONRACIAL CLASSIFICATIONS AND THE EQUAL PROTECTION OF THE LAWS

(1) Gender-based Discrimination

In the last three terms, the Rehnquist Court handed down two rulings on gender-based discrimination. Both involved questions of statutory interpretation, rather than the application of the Fourteenth Amendment's equal protection clause. In *International Union, American Workers, Aerospace, Agricultural Implement Workers of America, UAW v. Johnson Controls, Inc.*, 111 S.Ct. 1196 (1991), the Court held that the Civil Rights Act of 1964, as amended by the Pregnancy Discrimination Act of 1978 (PDA), precluded a "fetal protection" policy adopted by Johnson Controls, a Milwaukee-based manufacturer of automobile batteries. In a unanimous ruling in *Franklin v. Gwinnett County Public Schools*, 112 S.Ct. 1028 (1992), the Court also held that students in schools that receive federal funds may sue and win damages for sexual harassment and other forms of sex discrimination under Title IX of the Educational Amendments of 1972. These rulings are further discussed below in "The Development of Law: Recent Rulings on Gender Discrimination."

In its 1993–1994 term the Court will consider several cases pertaining to gender discrimination and sexual harassment, including *J.E.B. v. T.B.*, a Fourteenth Amendment challenge to the exclusion on the basis of gender of potential jurors in a paternity suit. At issue in *J.E.B.* is whether the Court should extend the ruling in *Batson v. Kentucky*, 476 U.S. 79 (1986) (see Vol. 2, Ch. 9), barring prosecutors from using peremptory challenges to eliminate jurors on the basis of their race, to also forbid them from striking potential jurors for reasons of gender. James E. Bowman argues that the *Batson* rule should apply and that he was denied equal protection in a paternity suit because prosecutors struck men from the jury panel. Over his objections, a jury composed of twelve women was empaneled; subsequently, the jury ruled against Bowman and he was ordered to pay $400 to $500 in monthly child support.

The Court agreed as well to review *Milligan-Jensen v. Michigan Technological University* (No. 92-1244), which raises the issue of whether employers can avoid liability under the Civil Rights Act of 1964 for discriminating against an employee if, in the course of litigation, unrelated evidence emerges that would have justified firing the employee in the first place. Patricia Milligan-Jensen successfully sued her former employer for sexual harassment and gender discrimination after she was dismissed from her position as a security guard. But an appellate court overturned the lower court's award of her back pay because she had failed to reveal on her job application that she had been convicted of driving while intoxicated, which would have justified termination of her employment, and hence Ms. Milligan-Jensen suffered no legal injury by being fired, even under discriminatory circumstances.

THE DEVELOPMENT OF LAW
Recent Rulings on Gender Discrimination

Case	Ruling
International Union, American Workers, Aerospace, Agricultural Implement Workers of America, UAW v. Johnson Controls, Inc. 111 S.Ct. 1196 (1991) Vote 9:0	While unanimously holding that the Civil Rights Act of 1964, as amended by the Pregnancy Discrimination Act of 1978, invalidated Johnson Controls's fetal protection policy barring fertile women from certain jobs in its automobile battery factory, the justices were divided on the extent to which companies are barred from such discriminatory treatment. Writing for the majority, Justice Blackmun held that federal laws prohibit such discrimination on the basis of gender and pregnancy, even for women who are actually pregnant.

In a concurring opinion joined by Chief Justice Rehnquist and Justice Kennedy, however, Justice White disagreed with the breadth of the majority's ruling and objected that on its view employers were precluded from excluding "even *pregnant* women from an environment highly toxic to their fetuses." Justice Scalia also concurred.

Case	Ruling
Franklin v. Gwinnett County Public Schools 112 S.Ct. 1028 (1992) Vote 9:0	Writing for the Court, Justice White held that students in schools that receive federal funds may sue and win damages for sexual harassment under Title IX of the Educational Amendments of 1972. Previously, *Cannon v. University of Chicago*, 441 U.S. 677 (1979), had held that Title IX implied a private cause of action, entitling individuals to bring lawsuits

under the statute. But until *Franklin*, the Court had not dealt with whether victims of sexual harassment may receive damages under Title IX. Chief Justice Rehnquist and Justices Scalia and Thomas joined the ruling, but in a concurring opinion questioned whether the Court should find implied causes of action when Congress has not expressly granted individuals the right to sue under federal legislation.

(3) Alienage and Age

Along with *Gregory v. Ashcroft,* 111 S.Ct. 2395 (1991) (see page 54), the Rehnquist Court handed down two other rulings on the application of federal laws barring age discrimination. Those rulings are summarized below in the table "Recent Rulings on Age Discrimination."

THE DEVELOPMENT OF LAW

Recent Rulings on Age Discrimination

Case	Ruling
Equal Employment Opportunity Commission v. Arabian American Oil 111 S.Ct. 1227 (1991) Vote 6:3	By a six-to-three vote the Rehnquist Court held that Title VII of the Civil Rights Act—which bans discrimination in the workplace based on race, gender, religion, and national origins—does *not* apply to companies doing business *outside* the United States. Justice Scalia concurred, while Justice Marshall, joined by Justices Stevens and Blackmun, dissented.
Gilmer v. Interstate/Johnson Lane Corp. 111 S.Ct. 1647 (1991) Vote 7:2	The Court held that the Age Discrimination in Employment Act of 1967 and the Federal Arbitration Act permit compulsory arbitration, as required under an employment agreement, of employee disputes over alleged dismissals involving age discrimination. Justices Stevens and Marshall dissented.
Astoria Federal Savings and Loan v. Solimino 111 S.Ct. 2166 (1991) Vote 9:0	In an opinion written by Justice Souter, the Court unanimously held that employees who accuse their employers of age discrimination under the Age Discrimination Act of 1967 may bring suits in federal courts, after state agencies have dismissed their complaints and without further appeals in state courts.

THE DEVELOPMENT OF LAW *(Continued)*

Case	Ruling
Gregory v. Ashcroft 111 S.Ct. 2395 (1991) Vote 6:3	Writing for the Court, Justice O'Connor applied the "rational basis" test to an equal protection challenge to Missouri's constitutional provision requiring state judges and other public officials to retire at age seventy. The state's law was deemed to have a rational basis given the undeniable effects of aging

and the limited utility in removing judges from office through impeachment and judicial elections. Justices White and Stevens concurred and dissented in part; Justices Blackmun and Marshall dissented.

INDEX OF CASES

Cases printed in boldface are excerpted on the page printed in boldface.